NARCISSISTIC PARE
INSECURE W

C000054628

A history of paren
1920s to present

Harry Hendrick

P

First published in Great Britain in 2016 by

Policy Press
University of Bristol
1-9 Old Park Hill
Bristol
BS2 8BB
UK
+44 (0)117 954 5940
pp-info@bristol.ac.uk
www.policypress.co.uk

North America office:
Policy Press
c/o The University of Chicago Press
1427 East 60th Street
Chicago, IL 60637, USA
t: +1 773 702 7700
f: +1 773-702-9756
sales@press.uchicago.edu
www.press.uchicago.edu

British Library Cataloguing in Publication Data
A catalogue record for this book is available from the British Library

Library of Congress Cataloging-in-Publication Data
A catalog record for this book has been requested

ISBN 978 1 4473 2256 6 paperback
ISBN 978 1 4473 2255 9 hardcover
ISBN 978 1 4473 2259 7 epub
ISBN 978 1 4473 2260 3 mobi

Cover design by Soapbox Design
Front cover image: Soapbox Design
Printed and bound in Great Britain by Clays Ltd, ST Ives Plc
Policy Press uses environmentally responsible print partners

But the effect of her being on those around her was incalculably diffusive: for the growing good of the world is partly dependent on unhistoric acts; and that things are not so ill with you and me as they might have been, is half owing to the number who lived faithfully a hidden life, and rest in unvisited tombs. (George Eliot, *Middlemarch*)

Contents

Contents

About the author

Since retiring from the University of Southern Denmark, Harry Hendrick has been an associate fellow at the History of Medicine Centre (2010–16), University of Warwick. He is the author of several books and numerous essays on the history of British childhood and youth, including *Images of Youth: Age, Class, and the Male Youth Problem, 1880–1920* (Clarendon Press, 1990), *Child Welfare: Historical Dimensions, Contemporary Debate* (Policy Press, 2003) and *Child Welfare and Social Policy: An Essential Reader* (Policy Press, 2005). He was one of the founding participants in what is now Childhood Studies – see his interview in C. Smith and S. Greene (eds) *Key Thinkers in Childhood Studies* (Policy Press, 2014).

Acknowledgements

I am pleased to record my thanks to the History of Medicine Centre at the University of Warwick for giving me an Associate Fellowship that allowed access to all the facilities of the library. I am especially grateful to the library's Document Supply staff who were always unfailingly helpful. I must also thank Isobel Bainton at Policy Press for accepting my garbled proposal and trusting that it would be turned into something readable, and Laura Greaves and Ruth Harrison for coping with my numerous corrections.

A number of colleagues and friends each read several draft chapters and offered many constructive criticisms and helpful comments: Hugh Cunningham, John Davis, Allison James, Paul Smith, John Stewart, John Welshman, and Mike Wyness. My thanks for their time and effort. I hope they feel it was worthwhile. I also wish to thank John Macnicol for his support over the years.

In many respects this book is a work of synthesis that draws on, and exploits, the work of those scholars whose writings have influenced my outlook and approach – though, of course, they are in no way responsible for the final outcome. While I have argued with some of their interpretations, I have benefited enormously from reading them. I have in mind in particular Karen Baistow, Zygmunt Bauman, Colin Crouch, Barbara Cruikshank, Anthony Elliott, Nancy Fraser, David Garland, Sue Gerhardt, Gail Gerson, Anthony Giddens, Neil Gilbert, David Harvey, Arlie Hochschild, Ann Hulbert, Eva Illouz, Alfie Kohn, George Lakoff, Christopher Lasch, David Marquand, Susan Neiman, Alice O'Connor, Jeremy Nuttall, Avner Offer, Nikolas Rose, Michael Sandel, Richard Sennett, John Stewart, Laurence Thomas, Mathew Thomson, Katie Wright, Jock Young, Elizabeth Young-Bruehal, and Eli Zaretsky.

Several of the ideas and arguments presented here were first aired in my previous books and essays. See, in particular: 'Optimism and Hope versus Anxiety and Narcissism: Some Thoughts on Children's Welfare Yesterday and Today', *History of Education*, 36, 6, November 2007, pp 747-768; 'Late Modernity's British Childhood: Social Investment and the Disciplinary State', in D. Buhler-Niederberger, J. Mierendorff and A. Lange (Hg) (2010) *Kindheit Zwiscen fursorglicem Zugriff und gesellscaftlicer Teilhabe*, Wiesbaden: VS Verlag. Springer Fachmedien Wiesbaden, pp 43-71; 'Age as a category of analysis in the history of childhood', in M. Luddy and J. Smith (eds) (2014) *Children, Childhood and Irish Society, 1500 to the Present*, Dublin: Four Courts Press, pp

389-413; 'Die sozialinvestive Kindeit', in M. Baader, F. Eber, W. Scroeg (Hg) (2014), *Kindeiten in der Moderne. Eine Gescicte der Sorge*, Frankfurt/New York: Campus Verlag, pp 456-91. I have also had the opportunity to raise many of the issues in papers delivered to seminars and conferences in Denmark, Germany, Ireland, Norway, and the USA, and in Britain at the universities of Edge Hill, Edinburgh, Kent (Medway), Plymouth, and Warwick.

I dedicate this book to the memory of Anne Hendrick, my mother, and Winifred McGuiness, my aunt; also to Josie and Eve, my daughters; Amelie and Josette, my granddaughters; and Vibeke, my wife.

Introduction

> Instead of a search for single origins, we have to conceive of processes so interconnected that they cannot be disentangled…it is the processes we must keep continually in mind. We must ask more often how things happened in order to find out why they happened…to pursue meaning, we need to deal with the individual subject, as well as social organization and to articulate the nature of their interrelationships, for both are crucial to understanding… how change occurs.[1]

In preparing to write his classic account of how liberals and conservatives think, where he defined as 'ideals' the conservative/liberal division between 'strictness' and 'nurturance', George Lakoff, the American cognitive linguist and political activist, recounts that he asked a friend how to identify the best indicator of liberal vs conservative political attitudes. His friend replied, 'If your baby cries at night, do you pick him up?'[2] We now live in an age when Gina Ford, 'Britain's number 1 best selling childcare author', and Jo Frost of *Supernanny* fame, among many others, can each garner a huge following for their advocacy of teaching babies to 'self soothe' through 'controlled crying'. Despite Lakoff's implication that liberals are more likely than conservatives to comfort their babies, the precepts of control, discipline, obedience and reward and punishment are subscribed to by child carers across the political spectrum, and are encouraged by parenting websites, the media, government pronouncements and health and welfare professionals.[3] But it was not always so; or, if it was, it was something of a guilty secret only quietly acknowledged. One has to go back to the inter-war period when behavioural 'habit' psychology, associated with the American psychologist J. B. Watson, and F. Truby King's rigid feeding schedules were popular to find a similar approach to infant and toddler care. Over the last 30 years or so, much of contemporary writing and commentary about 'parenting', particularly mothering,

1   J. W. Scott (1986) 'Gender: A Useful Category of Historical Analysis', *American Historical Review*, 91, 5, p 1067.

2   G. Lakoff (2002) *Moral Politics: How Liberals and Conservatives Think*, Chicago, IL: University of Chicago Press, p xv.

3   A. Kohn (2014) *The Myth of the Spoiled Child*, Boston, MA: Da Capo Press, Introduction.

has emphasised the stressful side of child rearing, the 'misery', and bemoaned what feminists refer to as 'intensive mothering' ('emotionally demanding, financially draining, labour consuming').[4] This book has no patience with these political claims, posing as sociological conclusions when in fact they are forms of 'advocacy research', that is, research designed to advance an ideological position.[5] Instead, it will ask how is it that 'tough love' parenting gurus have come to be so influential, and why is it that the government-sanctioned 'authoritative' mode of parenting puts so much emphasis on control and conditionality. Surely this tells us something about not only the politics of the socialisation of children, but also about ourselves – who we are, what we value, and what we aspire to be through our children or, more precisely, the *governing* of our children? Perhaps, in truth, what 'controlled crying' techniques, 'naughty steps' and 'reward charts' reveal is that we have come increasingly to see children as repositories for our own disgruntled and therapeutically tutored narcissistic emotions and attitudes, and that much of contemporary child rearing conceals a guilt-ridden malevolence, fearful and insecure, fuelled by an unacknowledged and deeply repressed 'childism' that is just as pernicious as sexism, racism, homophobia or any other disabling and discriminatory prejudice.[6]

The argument

This is a book about the changing culture of parenting from the 1920s to the present and, therefore, it is also concerned with the political and economic structures in which child rearing always exists. The book, however, is not a study of specific parenting policies and, while some aspects of parenting as 'lived reality' are considered, this is not my focus. Nor do I attempt to elaborate a programme for the future, although my preferences will be implicit throughout much of what follows. I would like my arguments to be taken as a commentary on selective themes and topics concerning changes in parent–child relations and in age relations more generally. The book is a call for us to pause and reflect on what we are doing and why we are acting as

---

[4]   S. Hays (1996) *The Cultural Contradictions of Motherhood*, London: Yale University Press, p 4. Somewhat bizarrely, these mothers are often accused of a kind of narcissism, presumably because their 'intensity' is seen to result from egotistical desire.

[5]   On feminism and the danger of 'advocacy research', see C. Hakim (1995) 'Five Feminist Myths about Women's Employment', *British Journal of Sociology*, 46, 3, p 449.

[6]   E. Young-Bruehl (2012) *Childism: Confronting Prejudice Against Children*, New Haven, CT: Yale University Press. For 'childism' see below, pp 19–20.

we are, and how we might act differently. Above all, I propose that the future is *not* inevitable. In speaking of the cultural, I refer to the variable mutuality of ideas and practices from which culture always reciprocally emerges. At the same time, I hope that I have avoided treating culture as autonomous phenomena, while keeping in mind that it is analytically distinguishable from society.[7]

The core of my argument is that building on the inter-war liberal child-rearing trend, from the late 1940s through to c. 1970s, the *ideology* of parenthood, together with important features of its *practice*, was politically and culturally informed by what were interlocking sets of social-democratic procedures and beliefs, emphasising collectivism, tolerance, optimism, charity, faith and a generosity of spirit regarding 'the future'. We can think of these values in terms of 'structures of feeling', or perhaps 'experience', described by Raymond Williams as referring to 'quality of life... a way of thinking and living.'[8] This is not to imply that these were fixed and universal features of the period, defined entirely by progressivism, but that they were standards that demanded respect and to which, broadly speaking, the popular ethos aspired, albeit in a muddled and often contradictory manner. In our post-1970s 'late modern' era, on the other hand, what Francis Fukuyama termed 'The Great Disruption', parental attitudes are much more inclined to regard children as a nuisance, a hindrance, a burden and as requiring a 'behaviourist' and cold-hearted discipline, a form of governing that is in part derived from neoliberal principles and in part from the not unrelated social liberationist and therapy culture of the post-1960s. It has been observed many times that the contemporary world is characterised not only by a socially and personally destabilising susceptibility to the charisma of greed, selfishness and fame, but also by anxiety, ambivalence, precarity, suspicion, impatience, pessimism and vindictiveness, all of which are uncomfortably embalmed within either a 'minimal' or a 'divided' self.[9] This self, I shall argue, has been interactively involved in three sets of childism: i) the child as an unharmonious presence, disruptive of cohesion, and the cause of apprehension and frustration; ii) the growth of a deeply felt parental desire to exercise a form of 'managerial' control over children,

7   S. Collini (1991) *Public Moralists: Political Thought and Intellectual Life in Britain*, Oxford: Clarendon Press, pp 62–3.

8   R. Williams (1965) *The Long Revolution*, London: Penguin/Chatto and Windus, pp 63–4; (1977) *Marxism and Literature*, Oxford: Oxford University Press, pp 128–36.

9   C. Lasch (1984) *The Minimal Self: Psychic Survival in Troubled Times*, New York: Norton; R. D. Laing (1965) *The Divided Self*, Harmondsworth: Penguin Books.

subjecting them to a kind of neoliberal contractual status; and iii) the display of an impatience with their little ways of being – described by the philosopher Onora O'Neill, in discussing adult obligations toward children, as denying them 'the genial play of life'.[10]

In thinking this way, I have in mind Jock Young's reference to 'the malaise of late modernity: a sense of insecurity, of insubstantiality, and of uncertainty, a whiff of chaos and a fear of falling'. The signs, he says, are everywhere:

> The obsession with rules, an insistence on clear uncompromising lines of demarcation between correct and incorrect behaviour, the decreased tolerance of deviance, a disproportionate response to rule-breaking, an easy resort to punitiveness and a point at which simple punishment begins to verge on the vindictive.[11]

I do not mean to exaggerate the gloom of modern life, for everywhere there are alternative ideals and practices exemplifying faith, empathy and altruism. Nonetheless, my claim is that in our era, for a variety of reasons, parenting has evolved to be increasingly 'narcissistic', a condition whereby, owing very much to pressures arising from collective social change, including the development of neoliberalism, knowledge of the self 'has become an end, instead of a means through which one knows the world'.[12] This is quite different from equating narcissism solely with a vulgar selfishness, since this militates against historical specificity. Human beings have always shown selfish and ethnocentric character traits, but they have not always been so mired in unhealthy subjectivity and imprisoned in the clamp of a global capitalism. Put another way, our despairing modern narrative is far more than merely a chorus of mythological decline; it is the product of the specific conditions and circumstances in which we find ourselves.

With regard to parent–child relations, one of the ways in which this narcissism displays itself is through a parenting approach that prioritises the urge to control children and which, despite its positive spin, relies ultimately on reward and punishment. Drawing on the 'new behaviourism' of American child development theory from the

---

[10] O. O'Neill (1992) 'Children's Rights and Children's Lives', in P. Alston, S. Parker and J. Seymour (eds) *Children, Rights and the Law*, Oxford: Clarendon Press, p 28.

[11] J. Young (2008) 'Vertigo and the Global Merton', *Theoretical Criminology*, 12, 4, pp 523–43.

[12] R. Sennnett (2002) *The Fall of Public Man*, London: Penguin Books, p 4.

late 1960s, the favoured parenting 'style' is known as the 'authoritative' to distinguish it from the 'authoritarian' and the 'permissive', both of which are deemed to be parentally deficient. Broadly speaking, authoritative parenting is promoted from within several conjoined moulds of what might be seen as 'rationalities' and 'technologies' used for fashioning different categories of governance.[13] First, since the late 1980s, the view that this particular style is the key to enhancing individual life chances and social cohesion has been expounded in virtually every official family policy document, and has underpinned agency practices in health, education, welfare and juvenile justice, while being taught in hundreds of government sponsored parent education (also known as 'support') programmes. Second, the ethos of the authoritative relationship is endlessly propagated in the media, mothers' magazines, and on parenting websites and chat-rooms and, although by no means universally accepted, has come to assume the status of a cultural norm. One of the most liberal and child-centred parenting psychotherapists has even claimed that 'the more emotionally aware people become, the more likely they are to become authoritative parents rather than Strict or Permissive ones'.[14] Third, the managerial strategies may also be 'learned' (a key behaviourist term) from child-rearing manuals advocating a variety of approaches, from 'tough love' to 'positive' parenting. A fourth cast has been the world-wide success of reality television parenting 'shows', most notoriously *Supernanny*, which spawned a mini-industry of accompanying books, DVDs, blogs, star charts and the infamous 'naughty step'. Clearly, parent education has an influential profile, one that is both financially lucrative for a substantial number of commercial suppliers, and cost effective for public authorities. This book will argue that the conglomerate of parenting programmes, characterised by therapeutic emotivism, constitutes a marketplace for child rearing which, vis-à-vis markets in general, has a 'corrosive tendency' to undermine moral standards since, as everything is for sale, it hesitates to pass judgement.[15] These programmes may be thought of as evoking a Giddens-like 'abstract

---

13   P. Miller and N. Rose (2008) *Governing the Present*, Cambridge: Polity, pp 15–16; rationalities are manners of thinking and 'ways of rendering reality knowable in such a way that [is] amenable to calculation and programming', while technologies are 'assemblages of persons, techniques, institutions, instruments for the conducting of conduct'.

14   S. Gerhardt (2010) *The Selfish Society*, London: Simon & Schuster, p 337.

15   M. J. Sandel (2013) *What Money Can't Buy: The Moral Limit of Markets*, London: Penguin, pp 9, 14.

system', one that 'empowers' parents with ostensibly new forms of knowledge and techniques, which the purveyors claim will enable them to counter personal and social problems of the kind found not just in raising children, but throughout their lives.[16]

Unsurprisingly, given the nature of contemporary political discourse, parent education expresses several neoliberal objectives. For instance, a critical feature of the taught courses is that the parent, usually the mother, must learn to discipline herself if she is to remedy her 'parenting deficit'. Through 'hard work' and learning 'new skills' she will become the self-directing, knowing and committed agent, responsible for her own person. Only as this kind of person will she ensure that her children develop approved social, educational and emotional behaviours, not least by acquiring the *habit* of obedience necessary for the smooth running of the consumer driven, wage-oriented, time-pressed and very often physically and emotionally exhausted household, in which precariously balanced social relations have become routine. In some ways, much of this is not entirely new in so far as the Spockian notion that responsible parenthood required the friendly but firm guidance of the 'ship's captain' was implicit in the 'progressive' parenting of the period, c.1920s–60s. But, as I shall urge, the *mood* (a prevailing emotional tone; a general attitude; a frame of mind) of adult–child relations, especially in the post–1945 social democratic years up to the 1970s, was both more culturally optimistic and forgiving of childish behaviour, and also less fearful and more open to egalitarian ideals and aspirations concerning age relations. To understand the development of what I define as neoliberal and narcissistic parenting, it is necessary to recognise the emotionality of such feelings for they do so much to inform parental attitudes.

The themes

Broadly speaking, the book has two principal and connected themes. First, the nature and rationale of the continuities and discontinuities that have signalled parenting since the 1920s, and how these have been influenced by, and exerted influence on, the broader markers of social change. Why did the liberal trend in child nurturing, which had been developing from strength to strength with social and political support, begin to decline from the 1970s onwards? Why is it that authoritative parenting as a concept and as practice has become so popular – why

---

[16] On 'abstract systems', see A. Giddens (1991) *Modernity and Self-Modernity: Self and Society in Late Modernity*, Cambridge: Polity.

the emphasis on authority, control, discipline, surveillance and anxiety? The answers, I suggest, can be found through an examination of the synergy between theories of child rearing and the varying social systems in which it always exists and is made real. The second theme refers to the multiple meanings and purposes of parenting in our modern times, focusing on the character of the age relations involved, and how they connect to the varieties of neoliberalism as embodied in what is thought of as culture. I am thinking here of the reconfigured political, economic and social structures with their new demands, uncertainties and opportunities as they have manifested themselves since the 1970s; the post-1960s politics of recognition and identity that first developed around feminism and gay and lesbian activism, and how this attained an institutional status lodged in political correctness; and the rise of the therapeutic society or, as it might be termed, the cultivation of (adult) suffering which, as a privileged voice, has tended to smother the subjectivity of children.

Regarding the first theme, there is a telling contrast between the increasingly liberal (though never libertarian) inter-war child-rearing style that reached something of an apotheosis during the 1960s, attached as it was to an expansive notion of social democracy, fused with a sense of national goodwill, and that of the post-1970s, which I characterise as a fearful, brittle, and childist-inclined parental narcissism. Despite the economic difficulties of the early post-war years and a certain amount of popular cynicism, nevertheless the period as a whole was enfolded in a temper – a distinctive emotional quality of experience – of social democratic optimism regarding the capabilities of individuals and the promise of a better world tomorrow. To a large extent this feeling grew out of the Keynesian settlement, notably the government commitment to the maintenance of full employment, and the legislation surrounding the foundation of the welfare state – and stretched forward through to the confidence and exuberance of the 1960s. All these developments, together with the critical factor of rising affluence, helped to set the tone for the permissive politics of the decade, during which time Britain became an enviable liberal society. This was a liberalism that 'rubbed off' on parent-craft, encouraging it to be empathetic and 'unconditional', while also encouraging the claims of 'children's rights' (vague and ill-defined though they were), particularly in the progressive sectors of primary education, and with reference to the understanding and treatment of juvenile delinquency. Since the 1970s, however, for a number of complex political, social and economic reasons, narcissism (always inconsistent and ambivalent) – as represented in displays of individualisation, and evincing a disturbing childism – has increasingly influenced parent–child relationships. Modern childrearing has become more technical than personal; nowadays the word emphasises the problematics of childcare rather than the pleasures.[17] Although the narcissism in question is not without the usual egotistical features, including shades of an unhealthy 'self love', it is less about self admiration as such; rather it emanates from a 'minimal self' that fears for its 'survival'.[18] In as much as this self, in searching for an 'authentic' personality, is both product and author of the peculiarities of individualised reflexivity, it experiences an irresolvable tension, which deleteriously affects the bond between parents and their children.[19]

For the second theme, my claim is that the subjective intimacies of parenting, hitherto barely recognised as having much of a presence in the grand theorising projects of sociology, are worthy of study for the insights they provide into the cultural evolution of personality/ character, and for what they reveal about the aforementioned workings of political rationalities and technologies through which they are prepared for personal and institutional use. These intimacies are also relevant to parenting as it connects with, and is influenced by, the attendant cultures of risk and uncertainty. The suggestion here is that aside from neoliberalism as a mode of governance, such features are lodged within three areas that dominate contemporary life: the prevalence of political disenchantment; alienation from institutional bases; and the 'emotional capitalism' that performs 'intimacy' through public displays of distress as an interpretation of the self – a self fixated with the idea of a protective and seemingly emancipatory 'identity' in order to succour its sense of minimalism.[20]

I shall show that formal parent education programmes, which promote the authoritative manner, are features of a politically designed project intended to remoralise parent–child relations in order to produce normalised, self-regulating, conformist worker-citizens in the long term and, in the short term, in addition to obedient children, skilled, confident and responsibilised parents. The task of these parents is to socialise their children to make them ready for school learning and labour market discipline, to habitualise them to the rigours of dual worker households, and to inculcate in them a respect for authority

---

[17]   R. Smith (2010) 'Total Parenting', *Educational Theory*, 60, 3, p 360.

[18]   Lasch (1984).

[19]   C. Howard (2007) *Contested Individualization: Debates about Contemporary Personhood*, Basingstoke: Palgrave Macmillan.

[20]   E. Illouz (2007) *Cold Intimacies: The Making of Emotional Capitalism*, Cambridge: Polity.

– rational routine and habit formation are being substituted for the hurly-burly of empathetic nurturing. The irony is that the Left, although worried about the voraciousness of global capitalism, remains fairly comfortable with the self-seeking individualism that embraces both the neoliberal enterprise ethic and the politics of identity. Its attachment to the latter skews its ability to counter the former. One of the requirements of this individualism (enraptured as it with the illusions of 'choice'), in an age of fragmented and diverse family forms (which it has encouraged), is the compliance of controlled, 'self caring' children whose imposed docility lessens their being as 'burdens' on parents, and who can be conveniently stored away in nurseries, leaving their mothers uncluttered to pursue gender equality in the labour market and their fathers free to chase career advancement relatively unhindered by childcare concerns. It was not without reason that New Labour's chic technocrats failed to grasp (or, more likely, chose to ignore) 'the moral limits of markets'.[21]

The broader context

Since notions of childhood are constitutive of social change, we need to see that in contrast to those of the 1920s–70s, current understandings of adult–child relations, including those of parents and their children, have become encoded in essentially conservative and pessimistic value systems, which are spawned in part through the politics of injustice that characterise the experience of children as a marginalised group. There are many interweaving reasons for this state of affairs, and cause and effect should not be oversimplified. It is helpful to consider the influence of two, and by no means always separate, post-1960s social convergences, which derive their impact from the conjunction of a multitude of personal, economic and global influences. The first and more specific convergence originated in popular unease at the perceived failure of the promise of the post-war settlement in relation to unemployment, poverty, housing and industrial conflict, which created a sense of bitterness and resentment. The second convergence revolves around the complex of what has been called 'the second crisis of modernity' which, as it developed under Thatcherism and beyond, dissolved the preceding stage of 'organised modernity'. By this I mean the often contradictory strands of the technologies of globalisation, suffused with individualisation, and the surfeit of ambivalences

---

[21] Sandel (2013); also his (2009) *Justice: What's The Right Thing To Do?*, London: Allen Lane, pp 75–102.

surrounding personal relationships.[22] Nor should we forget that these convergences preoccupy not only populations but also governments in their struggles to shape an amenable democracy to their own ends, but in such a way as to give expression to the popular will.[23]

In common with other commentators, and in accordance with risk theory, I suggest that despite the phenomenal growth of consumerism, greatly improved health and longevity, and an apparently unbridled will to freedom, aspects of our epoch have undermined confidence in the present and in our willingness to look forward in a positive manner. This has led to the emergence of a sickly and exaggerated introspection of the self characterised, often against our better impulses, by materialistic indulgence and a hedonistic privatism born of precarity. One important consequence of these tensions, notwithstanding a superficial commonality, has been to isolate the self (certainly what might be thought of as its spiritual affinities) to the detriment of the community and especially of children who, generally speaking, are powerless to counter the arbitrary authority of adults intent on pursuing 'life politics'.[24] I am thinking here not only of the disputed but nonetheless widely held views concerning the harmful consequences of divorce, cohabitation, the full-time wage labour of mothers of young children, the psychological pressures of the so-called 'work–life balance', and facets of negligence arising from the spread of 'MEism', but also of the more intimate structuring of child–adult relationships in terms of patience, self-sacrifice, listening, trust, sympathy and understanding.[25] In pursuing *our* therapeutic solace, little room has been left for the emotional lives of children as *beings* and a recognition that their minority status presents just demands for an equitable relational subjectivity between them and their parents. Children seem to have been reduced to deposits in adult-centric nostalgia, mined by an indeterminate and apprehensive vision of some incoherent longing on the part of adults.[26]

At the same time, however, this book is about more than the comings and goings of parent–child relationships, for in order to explain

---

[22] P. Wagner (2002) *A Sociology of Modernity: Liberty and Discipline*, London: Routledge.

[23] M. Freeden (1999) 'The ideology of New Labour', *The Political Quarterly*, 70, 1, pp 42–51; S. Driver and L. Martell (2002) *Blair's Britain*, Cambridge: Polity; C. Crouch (2011) *The Strange Non-Death of Neo-Liberalism*, Cambridge: Polity.

[24] For 'life politics', see Giddens (1991).

[25] S. Baron-Cohen (2012) *Zero Degrees of Sympathy: A New Theory of Human Cruelty and Kindness*, London: Penguin; A. Damasio (1995) *Descartes' Error*, New York: Penguin.

[26] Young-Bruehl (2012); Kohn (2015); P. Leach (1994) *Children First*, London: Penguin.

the changing nature and significance of 'parenting' (as with 'doing families', parenting is now something we *do* – 'a set of practices and activities'), it is necessary always to keep in mind the 'push and pull' of the broader context of social and economic change where parent–child relations constitute one of the most influential components of psycho-social subjectivity.[27] Too often sociological and historical accounts of the family and parenting are inclined to minimise the cultural *and* political significance of child rearing, treating it as an ancillary and passive category of social evolution and using it as a hook on which to hang either feminist claims concerning the alleged patriarchal nature of motherhood, or as homage to a sentimental notion of parental 'enduring love'. Identifying and examining the continuities and discontinuities that have signalled notions of parenting since the 1920s, will provide a better understanding of how adults have coped with the pressures and confusions, as well as the aspirations and visions, of social change.

My argument is that many of the coping strategies since the 1970s have involved the exploitation of children as forms of human capital in the continuously futile attempt to fulfil the grand designs of *our* 'life agenda', deemed to be so essential to 'saving the modern soul'.[28] The futility I speak of lies in the sense that as with *individualised* relationships, the modern individual suffers 'troublesome incarnations of ambivalence' and is always in pursuit of resolution but rarely finds long-term comfort.[29] According to Elizabeth Beck-Gernsheim, we are caught between two tendencies in individualisation. In one, with the collapse of 'traditional social relationships, bonds and belief systems', we are increasingly compelled to shape our own lives. In the other, what Talcott Parsons called the 'institutionalized individualism' of the world of work, welfare, law, education and the bureaucratic state, in producing their own regulations, we are required to learn to live with these new forms of social life as individuals.[30] The tragedy of our

---

27 On evolution of 'child-rearing' to 'parenting', see Smith (2010), pp 357–69; S. Rameakers and J. Suissa (2011) 'Parents as "Educators": Languages of Education, Pedagogy and "Parenting"', *Ethics and Education*, 6, 2, pp 197–212.

28 E. Illouz (2008) *Saving the Modern Soul: Therapy, Emotions, and the Culture of Self-Help*, Berkeley, CA: University of California Press; Giddens (1991); E. Beck-Gernsheim (2002) *Reinventing the Family: In Search of New lifestyles*, Cambridge: Polity; A. Elliott and C. Lambert (2006) *The New Individualism*, London: Routledge.

29 Z. Bauman (2003) *Liquid Love: On the Frailty of Human Bonds*, Cambridge: Polity, pp viii–ix.

30 E. Beck-Gernsheim (2002) *Reinventing the Family: In Search of New Lifestyles*, Cambridge: Polity, pp ix–x.

situation as it contributes, almost despairingly, to the cultivation of parental narcissism, is that 'the processes of individualisation generate *both* a claim to a life of one's own *and* a longing for ties, closeness and community'.[31] It is a discontent that haunts our imagination. In order to include children in 'the modern soul', this book proposes a 'moral clarity' guided by Kant's *categorical imperative*: 'However else I see you, I should see you as an end in yourself.'[32]

Within the folds of the book's two main strands, there is also a rippling concern to identify the reciprocity between neoliberalism and childist child rearing in order to illustrate something of what has happened to one of the Enlightenment's most resilient features, namely the idea of Progress (more precisely several different sets of progress) – with respect to virtue, moral advance and especially what used to be known as 'character'.[33] Although it may be unusual to consider such a major topic of political theory within the realm of parenting, character, which, in a rough and ready way, embodies virtue (at least it used to), is implicitly a principal interest of post-modern ethics. Thus, the character of parents towards their children, *and* that of our culture towards parenting, is relevant to the ever-pressing interest with how we are to live in an increasingly challenging globalised universe, and to the role we allot our moral sensibility – something this book portrays as a bulwark against the vicissitudes of unhealthy narcissism.[34]

Character is also seen as an important feature of modern citizenship, in particular as it connects to personality and the self. One view, sympathetically aired here, is that there has been a shift from a nineteenth-century emphasis on a subjectivity rooted in character which, in the spirit of classical humanism, I take to mean the will to discriminate between good and bad moral behaviour, to a (late) twentieth-century emphasis on personality, and that this paralleled a reinterpretation of citizenship into something more concerned with a modern reflexivity of the self, unencumbered by Victorian-style

---

[31] Beck-Gernsheim (2002), pp ix–x.

[32] S. Neiman (2008) *Moral Clarity: A Guide for Grown-Up Idealists*, London: Bodley Head, p 212.

[33] For the Enlightenment, see A. Pagden (2013) *The Enlightenment and Why It Still Matters*, Oxford: Oxford University Press.

[34] Z. Bauman (1993) *Postmodern Ethics*, Oxford: Blackwell.

angst.[35] It has been suggested that whereas building character used to involve the self in relation to 'conformity with a set of public virtues' (and the promotion of the best interests of society), the emphasis where personality is concerned involves 'a care of the self organized around the quest for a unique self' and that this 'marks a shift in the ethical requirements of effective citizenship'.[36] In brief, character informed a conception of citizenship that emphasised public duty, obligation and obedience. Personality heralds the calculated and freely chosen participation in a diversified public sphere in which obligations towards public institutions are dependent upon a cost–benefit calculus. This is the opposite from 'the Stoic virtue of self-command which enables us to control our passions when they distract us from what virtue requires'.[37] Hence, psychologically unhealthy 'care of the self' *necessarily* implies withdrawal into a never-never land of narcissism. Contemporary debates on character and citizenship, bearing in mind our fascination with personality, are inextricably bound up with a modish emotive attraction to the self as a reflexive project which, in facilitating our incorporation (intentionally or not) into neoliberal undertakings, aids the narcissistic impulse.

Clearly, rather than being a paean to the supposed opportunities and freedoms (for adults) that are said to prevail with the 'new individualism' and the 'transformation of intimacy', this study is more in the tradition of a cultural critique. At the same time, however, I believe that given the will on our part, and with the help of *reconstituted* 'therapies of freedom' – we might, and I am thinking here of the influence of the fraternal and forgiving aspects of the socialist tradition, with the proper reasoning, which includes the emotions (always part of the Enlightenment enterprise), be able to reclaim a universalist language of morality and idealism.[38] This is a language that in addition to focusing on community and equality embraces notions of 'good and evil,

---

[35] Illouz (2008); on character, see Collini (1991); on character and self, see C. Taylor (1989) *Sources of the Self: The Making of Modern Identity*, Cambridge: Cambridge University Press; R. Sennett (2004) *Respect. The formation of character in an age of inequality*, London: Penguin Books.

[36] M. White and A. Hunt (2000) 'Citizenship: Care of the Self, Character and Personality', *Citizenship Studies*, 4, 2, pp 93–116. Victorian ideas of character almost certainly involved a religious component – unlike personality. Perhaps our increasingly secular age has influenced the quest for the authentic self. I owe this thought to John Stewart.

[37] A. MacIntyre (1981) *After Virtue: A Study in Moral Theory*, London: Duckworth, p 218.

[38] N. Rose (1990) *Governing the Soul: The Shaping of the Private Self*, London: Routledge, pp 255–8.

heroism and nobility' and, therefore, helps us to reconnect with our better selves.[39] Such a course of action would reconfigure parenting as optimistically friendly and without reservation, rather than bleakly contractual and authoritative. It would also expand our moral vision to recognise and conquer childism and, therefore, include children equally as emotional and aspirational persons who, by virtue of their relative physical, emotional, legal and political powerlessness, require our self-sacrificial involvement in their lives as they *work* at growing up.[40] My qualified sympathies are with the parameters of modernity's Enlightenment, not those of its critics – political conservatives and propagandists of poststructuralist idioms, among others. I follow the spirit of Habermas's well known claim that the Enlightenment is 'unfinished', and to be corrected rather than rejected. Thus I proceed with his notion of 'the project of modernity' to imply the continued unfolding of its original forces. After all, our contemporary world, for all the postmodern hype, is an advanced form of the essence of nineteenth-century modernity, namely industrialism, capitalism and rationalism which, as numerous Victorians testified, was epitomised by the search for a self that is both morally and ethically at peace with more than just the sum of its own being.[41]

In what follows, I describe the processes through which the virtue of self-sacrifice has found itself cast out, paralleled as it has been by the demoralisation of our spirit through the loss of sentiment in preference to instrumentality.[42] No doubt, however, in rejecting the adult-centric perspective and casting aspersion on the popular view that parents always 'do their best' for their children, many readers will find this book to be controversial and provocative. I do not doubt the veracity of the parental intention because it is necessarily untrue; but for two reasons. First, the claim is psychologically and sociologically inadequate in explaining what is both relational and emotional behaviour, not least as it privileges parental standpoints, while normally minimising those of children. Second, because in its neoliberal guise, 'doing one's best' can be something of a Trojan Horse within which are concealed selfish, undemocratic and politically malign impulses. These critics will probably label my account heuristically inferior to their own

---

[39] Neiman (2008), pp 1–26; Bauman (1993).

[40] See A. Kohn (2005) *Unconditional Parenting: Moving from Rewards and Punishments to Love and Reason*, London: Atria Books.

[41] M. P. d'Entreves and S. Behabib (eds) (2007) *Habermas and the Unfinished Project of Modernity*, London: The MIT Press.

[42] R. Fevre (2000) *The Demoralisation of British Culture*, London: Continuum.

'small-scale empirical research' findings (which often conflict with the grand theories). They will say it derives from 'broad generalised statements' that have developed as 'explanations of social change and social relationships rather than specifically in relation to family life' and, therefore, despite having some empirical evidence to supplement their arguments, are not 'grounded theories' yielding inductive conclusions.[43] This tension has a long-standing history in the sociology of the family and I do not seek to resolve it. The warning that theoretical concepts 'not grounded in local contexts (can) more easily lend themselves to rhetorical purposes and can take on an ideological aspect' should be heeded – but the authors should also keep in mind the proverb: 'People who live in glass houses shouldn't throw stones.'[44] Notwithstanding this caution, my aim here is not so much to prove an argument; only to suggest its plausibility.

As a final introductory pointer, I emphasise that parenting *cannot* be attributed merely to 'structures' and 'laws'; propelled by 'forces' that are outside the realm of social actors; as if history itself had nothing to do with the human hand.[45] So, although the book constantly considers political, economic, legal and cultural structures as forces, none of this is meant to minimise the role of individual 'intentional action' in the responsibility of parents to treat their children with what the philosopher Laurence Thomas calls 'cherished uniqueness', underpinned by 'love' (which pips morality).[46] To do otherwise would be to suggest that the conscious choices of human beings are without influence, as if things are merely what they are. In arguing for a new socialist morality, nothing could be further from my view: we are responsible to the world as we have made it. It is up to us to keep the Barbarians from the gate.

---

[43] C. Smart (2007) *Personal Life*, Cambridge: Polity, pp 7–8; J. Brannen and A. Nilsen (2005) 'Individualization, Choice and Structure: A Discussion of Current Trends in Sociological Literature', *Sociological Review*, 53, 3, pp 412–28. For a different view, see D. Garland (2001) *The Culture of Control: Crime and Social Order in Contemporary Society*, Oxford: Oxford University Press, p vii.

[44] Brannen and Nilsen (2005), p 426.

[45] L. Boltanski and E. Chiapello (2005), *The New Spirit of Capitalism*, London: Verso, p x.

[46] L. Thomas (2006) *The Family and the Political Self*, New York: Cambridge University Press, p 19–48. As he says, a child may be treated morally but be unloved and, therefore, 'could not come to value itself properly', p 19.

Some methodological considerations

History, the present and ideology

There is always a tendency to mistake our present for a timeless normality and naturalness, forgetting why and how it came to be this way and, therefore, to risk losing a vital connection between it and our irrepressible affinity with the past. Hobsbawm's observation is apposite: 'Most human beings operate like historians: they only recognize the nature of their experience in retrospect.'[47] The 'history' presented here, however, is not entirely straightforward. On the one hand, some deference is paid to Foucault's sense of the present, meaning that there is less emphasis on narrative detail and more on identifying critical points of analysis. In his study of crime and social order in contemporary society, David Garland writes: 'The history I propose is motivated not by a historical concern to understand the past but by a critical concern to come to terms with the present…to trace the forces that gave birth to our present-day practices and to identify the historical and social conditions upon which they still depend.'[48] While I share this focus on tracing the forces from which our present has been fashioned, I do not endorse Garland's disinclination to know the past. Instead, I follow Christopher Lasch in seeing it as:

> a political and psychological treasury from which we draw the reserves (not necessarily in the form of 'lessons') that we need to cope with the future. Our culture's indifference to the past…furnishes the most telling proof of that culture's bankruptcy…the devaluation of the past has become one of the most important symptoms of the cultural crisis…a denial of the past, superficially progressive and optimistic, proves on closer analysis to embody the despair of a society that cannot face the future.[49]

This study subscribes to the value of that critically endowed 'treasury' as it seeks to lead the past to the present, not to learn lessons but to understand processes, objectives and influences and, perhaps what is most important, to show that the moral turpitude of our present

---

[47] E. Hobsbawm (1994) *Age of Extremes: The Short Twentieth Century, 1914–1991*, London: Michael Joseph, p 257.

[48] Garland (2001), p 2.

[49] C. Lasch (1979) *The Culture of Narcissism*, New York: Norton, pp xiii–xviii.

is not irrevocable; it can be changed through human endeavour – albeit that currently 'Western secular culture has no clear place for moral language.'[50] In this vein, I also endorse Foucault's inquiries in the sense that they 'always carried within them a critical, normative dimension, urging us to identify the dangers and harms implicit in the contemporary scheme of things, and to indicate how our present social arrangements might have been – and might still be – differently arranged'.[51]

This reference to *is* and *ought*, reminds us that the moment we begin to adjudicate between the two, we encounter ideology as goals and methods – often without realising it. And since parenting, although not an 'ism' ideology, is such an emotional subject, where notions of right and wrong are so prominent, we should recognise that much of what is presented as intuitively natural and normal is in fact profoundly *ideological* and, as such, 'shapes what and who we are, and who we believe we are, by virtue of the fact that we live in it and enact it'.[52] But grasping the beliefs, attitudes and values that give the concept its meaning is notoriously difficult. No wonder that ideology is always elusive and contested, not least when it is used disparagingly to suggest someone else's concept, rather than our own, as it points to a plurality of views, serving sectional interests. As used here, however, ideology (when openly recognised as such) is not necessarily a bad thing in that it implies ideas that are necessarily false or unrealistic. I think of it as meaning a more or less comprehensive vision involving abstract thought directed at underpinning social practice, since all political ideas 'are moulded by the social and historical circumstances in which they develop and by the political ambitions they serve' and, therefore, in this respect theory and practice are inseparable.[53] But, as I say, the vision of parenting is not coherent in the sense of being an 'ism' political system; rather, it expresses 'less explicit beliefs, assumptions and taken-for-granted conceptions', which legitimate apparently 'natural' and, therefore, 'inevitable' practices.[54] On the other hand, in its ideological form 'authoritative' parenting does share some of the characteristics of a political belief system in so far as it originates from

---

[50] Neiman (2008), p 5.

[51] Garland (2001), p 3.

[52] M. Freeden (2003) *Ideology: A Very Short Introduction*, Oxford: Oxford University Press, pp 1–2; N. Crossley (2005) *Key Concepts in Critical Social Theory*, London: Sage, p 153.

[53] A. Heywood (2007) *Political Ideologies: An Introduction*, Basingstoke: Palgrave Macmillan, p 3.

[54] Crossley (2005), p 148.

an 'action-orientated' duo of political ideas, namely behaviourism and neoliberalism and, in having the support of government and influential sections of psychological and educational science, is officially sanctioned with the intention of giving it a hegemonic status.[55] In this regard, ideology plays a key role in the processes of dissemination, legitimisation and re-invigoration, rationalising the practice as normal.[56] Gramsci famously noted that ideology aspires to be 'common sense', which is exactly what the mould of authoritative parenting seeks to achieve when, through a social-scientifically informed sleight of hand, its proponents transform what is fundamentally a particular political notion into a norm of cultural consensus.[57]

Childism, the sociology of childhood, and child-centred age relations

> [W]hen you are powerless, you don't just speak differently. A lot, you don't speak. Your speech is not just differently articulated, it is silenced. Eliminated, gone. You aren't just deprived of a language…you are deprived of a life out of which articulation might come.[58]

Broadly speaking, the methodological approach sustaining this book is that of what used to be called the new sociology of childhood which, for my purposes, has two connected research propositions. I say approach rather than theory in the hard social scientific sense of the word as the sociology of childhood has a relatively low level of grand theory.[59] Nevertheless, I intend that my methodology conforms to what even elementary theoretical frameworks can do, which is to 'systematize what is known, explain the *how* and *why* behind the *what*

---

55 Heywood (2007), p 5.

56 S. Hall, D. Massey and M. Rustin (2013) 'After Neoliberalism: Analysing the Present', *Soundings*, 53, Spring, p 17.

57 D. Harvey (2005) *A Brief History of Neoliberalism*, Oxford: Oxford University Press, pp 39–40.

58 Quoted in J. Evans (1995) *Feminist Theory Today: An Introduction to Second-wave Feminism*, London; Sage, p 104.

59 For examples of some theoretical work, see L. Alanen (1992) *Modern Childhood? Exploring the 'Child Question' in Sociology*, Research Report 50, University of Jyvaskyla; A. James, C. Jenks and A. Prout (1998) *Theorizing Childhood*, Cambridge: Polity; J. Qvortrup, W. A. Corsaro and M.-S. Honig (eds) (2009) *The Palgrave Handbook of Childhood Studies*; C. Jenks (1996) *Childhood*, London: Routledge, A. Prout (2005) *The Future of Childhood*, London: RoutledgeFalmer.

of…data, and change the existing order to solve problems'.[60] I begin with the concept of childism.[61] Put simply, the word means 'prejudice against children'. It is tempting to protest that we already have too many isms in our lexicon. Perhaps. But despite the word misopedia, 'hatred of children', originating in the eighteenth century, it had been erased from our vocabulary long before the twentieth century – unlike other Greek-derived group-hatred words: misanthropy, misandry and misogyny. Childism, however, does not necessarily refer to *hate*; rather it relates to words denoting prejudice (although hatred may be involved): racism, sexism, anti-Semitism and homophobia. But, unlike other forms of bigotry and discrimination, it has not been systematically explored. Childism seems to languish in a lonely tomb of irrelevance. We should acknowledge this fact, and ask why society prefers instead to focus on specific harms to children, such as 'abuse', 'neglect' and 'paedophilia', words that reveal the lack of a holistic descriptive category. It is also significant that by their nature these harms are positioned as being 'other' and, therefore, safely removed from 'us'. Until we have a term similar to, say, sexism, we shall not be able to understand the manifestations of prejudice against children. It was the concept of *sexism* that helped to make possible systematic analyses of women's oppression in a variety of circumstances, many of which had been 'unseen' until the word gained coinage. If we were to bring childism into our political dynamic, it would automatically give the concept a 'political resonance' and open our eyes to the discrimination experienced on a daily basis by children. Since it is difficult for children to be 'direct political actors', a recognition of childism would not necessarily ameliorate their condition. But it would make it more difficult for adults to ignore their 'oppression' in the sense that it would reveal children as a 'target group', that is, one 'whose members share characteristics and conditions that those prejudiced against them seize on and distort for their own purposes'. As it stands, childism is a malign force in human affairs, quietly and unobtrusively polluting our relations with those whom we have brought into the world.

Of the many categories of childism, here are a few examples from opinion pieces in the *Guardian* ('the world's leading liberal voice'):

---

[60] V. Bengston (2005) 'The Problem of Theory in Gerontology Today', in M. L. Jackson (ed) *The Cambridge Handbook of Ageing*, Cambridge: Cambridge University Press, p 3.

[61] The following description of childism draws on E. Young-Bruehl (2012) *Childism: Confronting Prejudice Against Children*, New Haven, CT: Yale University Press, pp 1–19. I sometimes refer to the 'adult-centric' perspective, by which I mean favouring adults without being prejudiced against children.

i) 'Why would anyone have children?' in which children are compared to poems: 'They're beautiful to their creators, but to others they're just silly and fucking annoying… Kids are even worse than poems, that's how bad kids are. You can't even fold them up, put them in your back pocket and sit on them';[62]

ii) 'Kids? I prefer animals…dogs and cats. Babies make me nauseous. I don't like the way they look, smell or sound…Puppies…are playful and adorable…There are no…redeeming features about babies. None';[63]

iii) Julie Bindel, columnist, lesbian activist, and founder of 'Justice for Women', commenting on the school holidays, writes that they 'have made it easier for the little monsters to follow me around' (into restaurants and museums); 'I have always been clear about children – some are fabulous once they grow into adults.'[64]

It is difficult to imagine any newspaper, let alone one with such liberal pretensions, publishing such vitriol were the subjects women, homosexuals, lesbians, ethnic groups or the disabled.[65] Similarly, at the time of the London riots, both the Labour MP David Lammy and the Mayor of London, Boris Johnson, called for the rules governing the parental right to 'smack' their children to be relaxed.[66] There was no outcry from the liberal media over this encouragement to violence against children, nor were they reprimanded by their respective parties. Clearly, 'political correctness' does not include children. Nowadays, 'hate crime' is illegal; 'age' crime, on the other hand, is unrecognised. Why is this? Nils Christie, the criminologist, has written, 'Acts are not, they *become*. So also with crime. Crime does not exist. Crime is created. Then follows a long process of giving meaning to these acts.'[67] At present, anyone can say anything about children.

---

[62] Tim Jonze (2012) *Guardian*, 8 April.

[63] Kate McKellen (2012) *Guardian*, 17 November.

[64] Julie Bindel (2006) *Guardian*, 1 July; and (2013), 5 May. For similar views in the American press, see Kohn (2014), pp 1–8.

[65] M. Freeman (2010) 'The Human Rights of Children', *Current Legal Problems*, 63, 1, p 1.

[66] Reported in *Daily Telegraph* (2012), 29/30 January.

[67] N. Christie (2000) *Crime Control as Industry: Towards Gulags, Western Style*, London: Routledge, p 22.

With childism in mind, this book is fundamentally informed by the child-centred perspective, situated in a *relational* context. Given the expropriation of linguistic meaning through the manipulation of language, perhaps best epitomised most recently in the rhetoric of New Labour, it is necessary to clarify 'child centred'. The term does not apply to those education, health and welfare policies and ways of thinking that prioritise social investment in children as a means to safeguard 'the future', secure social inclusion, raise academic standards in schools, prepare young people for the labour market and control their behaviour through ASBOs and techniques derived from behavioural psychology. Nor is it meant to be used in a derogatory manner as when feminists use it to demean what they call 'intensive' mothers. I cite the term to suggest an adult appreciation of the specificity of children's being, facilitating their participation as agentic-actors, engaging in a shared dialogue, and giving just recognition to their self-declared interests where possible.[68] This is not to always prioritise their interests over others, but to try to consider them, according to their *age*, in a social-democratic manner in which they receive what we may think of as 'the benefit of the doubt'.

My relational child-centred approach focuses on 'age/age relations' as the theoretical lens through which parent–child (and, more generally, adult–child) relations are examined.[69] Without pushing the comparison too far, age has a number of analytical affinities with gender, particularly in relation to what Joan Scott refers to as the 'social organisation' of 'difference', with all that this implies for power and authority and agency and participation, and in identifying and explaining how age 'hierarchies are constructed, legitimated, challenged and maintained'.[70] Some readers, though, while willing to accept a child-study paradigm in studies focusing specifically on 'child worlds', may find it difficult to take seriously a child-centred 'age' study that adopts a much broader perspective in examining the culture of modern parenting. But I think this focus is needed. While social science has privileged adult concerns, owing to children's lack of political authority little effort has been made

---

[68] Although I use standpoint in a 'weak' sense, I have taken my cue from D. Smith (2004) 'Women's Perspective as a Radical Critique of Sociology', in S. Harding (ed) *The Feminist Standpoint Theory Handbook*, London: Routledge.

[69] For a discussion, see H. Hendrick (2014) 'Age as a category of analysis in the history of childhood', in M. Luddy and J. M. Smith (eds) *Children, Childhood and Irish Society, 1500 to the Present*, Dublin: Four Courts Press, pp 389–413.

[70] J. W. Scott (1986) 'Gender: A Useful Category of Analysis', *American Historical Review*, 91, 5, pp 1053–75.

to incorporate them into analyses of late modernity, except for adult-focused inquiries into the so-called work–life balance, the dynamics of social exclusion/inclusion, left/feminist accounts of 'diverse' family forms and, more abstractly, the child's place in the 'normal chaos of love'.[71] The problem was succinctly recognised by Ann Oakley when she observed:

> The role of politics is highly relevant to an understanding of the parallels and differences between women studies and children's studies because it establishes a *crucial difference*. Women's studies grew directly out of the political movement for women's liberation; it emerged out of the politics of experience. But children's studies are not rooted in the same way in the movement of children to claim their own liberation…By and large it is adults who are making representations on behalf of children…Because of the power relations involved, it is likely to be men more than women who will defend children's rights.[72]

What follows seeks to integrate the child into our social analyses. It is not, however, a matter of simply substituting one preference (adult) for another (child). In order to understand the development of parental narcissism, and the roles played by the concept and practice of parental education/support in inculcating this cultural form, we need to grasp the intimacies of parenting as a social relationship involving layers of interdependence between parents and their children.

A working definition of 'narcissism'

The concept of narcissism, which is much debated in clinical and social scientific literature, has a number of prefixes and may refer to the social or cultural characteristics of a society, a concept of psychoanalysis, or a personality trait. In general there are two clearly defined categories: 'primary' (healthy) and 'secondary' (unhealthy) narcissism. Freud, saw 'primary' narcissism as a libidinal investment in the self in infancy, which is necessary for normal development of

---

[71] U. Beck and E Beck-Gersheim (1995) *The Normal Chaos of Love*, Cambridge: Polity.

[72] A. Oakley (1994) 'Women and Children First and Last: Parallels and Differences between Children's and Women's Studies', in B. Mayall (ed) *Children's Childhoods: Observed and Experienced*, London: The Falmer Press, p 20.

'healthy' self love.[73] Before children can invest their 'libidinal' energy in others, they experience an adaptive period of primary narcissism when they are ego-centric (this helps babies to survive) and unable to see the other's perspective. Healthy development means moving on from this primary state to investing libidinal energy in another person: from primary narcissism to 'object love'. The healthy narcissist dwells in self-esteem, feeling secure and confident; the antithesis being insecurity and inadequacy and the development of narcissism to protect the self against illness. Freud maintained that a healthy relationship required reciprocal love, without which feelings of self-regard are lowered. When a person's 'love object' does not return their love, or the love is frustrated in some way, they regress to 'secondary narcissism' – 'love rejected turns back to the self as hatred' – in order to gratify the self by way of a compensatory mechanism. The exact understanding of 'secondary' or 'pathological' narcissism is open to argument, but in terms of being sociologically applicable to contemporary culture, seven features have been identified: shame, 'magical thinking' (a form of illusion), arrogance, envy, entitlement, exploitation of others and poor boundaries that fail to appreciate the separateness of others.[74] My account tends to see narcissism as pertaining to a complex 'minimal self' concerned with 'survival', which is also readily apparent in what has been described as 'the glorification of egoism in Western culture and pop psychology'.[75] Since these features figure in the composite that is the individual person, it follows that they appear in our culture which, despite the social liberationist enthusiasm for individualisation, might itself also be justly described as 'minimal'.

This book argues that parental narcissism is characterised by a lack of faith in the future as both unknown and unknowable; it shudders before such uncertainty, completely unaware that desirable futures are necessarily derived from effort, imagination, patience and morally founded ideals that embrace the 'out there', the 'beyond' – the place where we meet the 'non-self'. Only then do we have the opportunity of attaining true recognition of our own person. As it is, this narcissism works with an already embedded adult-centric gaze that expresses an

---

[73] S. Freud ([1914]1991) *On Narcissism: An introduction*, in J. Sandler, P. Fongay, E. Spector Person (eds) *Freud's 'On Narcissism: An Introduction'*, London: Karnac Books.

[74] S. Hotchkiss (2003) *Why Is It Always About You?: The Seven Deadly Sins of Narcissism*, New York: Free Press; also W. K. Campbell and J. D. Miller (eds) (2007) *The Handbook of Narcissism and Narcissistic Personality Disorder*, Hoboken, NJ: John Wiley.

[75] Lasch (1984); M. R. Leary (2004) *The Curse of the Self: Self-Awareness, Egoism, and the Quality of Human Life*, Oxford: Oxford University Press, p vi.

unwillingness (perhaps an inability) to recognise the needs and wishes of children, not least that at different stages throughout their childhood they require convivial guidance, understanding and tolerance, rather than the managerial technologies of discipline. In place of empathy for children, parental narcissism privileges a confused, distorted, anxious and essentially self-regarding sense of self, particularly when through parent education it is emboldened by exposure to the deception of neoliberal 'empowerment'. The apparent benefit that comes with the mastery of child-rearing 'skills', promises self-esteem and self-confidence – the nirvana of contentment – portrayed as an essential prerequisite for mastery of one's children and, by implication, one's own life. Of course, in practice, this is a mirage promoted to escape the Freudian curse of the inescapable difficulties in being a *real* person.[76]

This form of narcissism is complex, multi-faceted and confusingly characterised in an ambivalent and contradictory manner, with beginnings and ends not always either clearly visible or immediately comprehensible. But such a self *is* substantially different from its social democratic counterpart. I suggest that it is marked by: i) a number of hedonistic vices, many of which involve the attachment to individualisation;[77] ii) personality weaknesses in confronting the inadequacies of late modernity; iii) an egoism intent on self-gratification through 'authenticity' ('a morally stunted process' Giddens calls it); and iv) the anxiety that characterises the minimal self together with the substitution of shame in place of guilt.[78] It is not a narcissism that emerged at a stroke, ready formed and fully emancipated. As a condition it has evolved historically and unevenly, partly from the ravages of economic neoliberalism and the distortion of moral politics, and partly from the post-1960s demand for cultural recognition in place of 'the good society', to its present fraught personification of globalised angst.[79]

Narcissism has served sociologists quite well. In having an affinity with personality and character it is a useful idea for the investigation of culture, which no doubt explains why it appears in so many modern studies of 'us'. Being interested in oneself is always hugely 'interesting'. But the fact is that we are torn between the 'brutal assertion of the

---

[76] Lasch (1984), pp 208–11; Giddens (1991), pp 43–4; A. Elliott (2001) *Concepts of the Self*, Cambridge: Polity, p 79.

[77] Beck and Beck-Gernsheim (1995), pp 1–10.

[78] Giddens (1991), pp 8–9, 68–9, 178.

[79] E. Zaretsky (2005) *Secrets of the Soul: A Social and Cultural History of Psychoanalysis*, New York: Vintage Books, pp 307–31.

self against the claims of others', and feeling uneasy about it.[80] With this in mind, it will be helpful to briefly consider selected comments taken from Christopher Lasch and Richard Sennett, two of the most influential of late modern cultural commentators, some of whose ideas inform this book. I have, however, little sympathy with Lasch's Freudian derived interpretation of narcissism as being the result of a failure to internalise (paternal–patriarchal) authority and, therefore, never having been able to develop a meaningful sense of identity.[81] And, contrary to Lasch, I believe that narcissism, as a concept, is sociologically valuable, irrespective of its psychoanalytical status. I treat it as a helpful sociological descriptor that is more than merely a synonym for "'asocial'" individualism.[82] I suggest that sociologically speaking, narcissism – following Erich Fromm – can indeed be thought of as a 'Metaphor of the Human Condition' without necessarily negating its clinical basis in aspects of self-hatred rather than self-admiration.[83] In taking Freud's idea of the self in conflict between 'unregenerate instincts and overbearing culture' and sharing his view that 'character' is the way in which we face the conflict between the two realities, this book portrays narcissism as a constant reminder of contemporary emptiness and our inability to find grace.[84]

Broadly speaking, I share Lasch's view that narcissistic character disorder derives from quite specific societal and cultural changes, including 'bureaucracy, the proliferation of images, therapeutic ideologies, the rationalization of the inner life, the cult of consumption…changes in family life and changing patterns of socialization'.[85] This disorder has produced a selfhood that is 'beleaguered', rather than 'narcissistic' in the egotistical sense. Lasch reminds us that it was the confusion 'of the self and the not-self', not 'egoism', that marked Narcissus: 'A minimal self or narcissistic self is…a self uncertain of its own outlines' – it's substance is more akin to 'identity' than to egoism.[86] Consequently:

> everyday life becomes an exercise in survival. People take
> one day at a time. They seldom look back, lest they succumb

---

80 Quoted in S. Gerhardt (2010), p 211.

81 Lasch (1979), pp 154–86.

82 Lasch (1979), pp 31–51. For a critique of Lasch, see Elliott (2001), pp 71–4, and Giddens (1991), pp 174–9.

83 Lasch (1979), pp 31, 27–30.

84 P. Rieff (1959) *Freud: The Mind of a Moralist*, Chicago, IL: University of Chicago Press, p 28.

85 Lasch (1979), p 32.

86 Lasch (1984), pp 16–19.

to a debilitating 'nostalgia'; and if they look ahead it is to see how they can insure themselves against the disasters almost everybody now expects. Under these conditions, selfhood becomes a kind of luxury, out of place in an age of impending austerity. Selfhood implies a personal history, friends, family, a sense of place. Under siege, the self contracts to a defensive core, armed against adversity. Emotional equilibrium demands a minimal self, not the imperial self of yesteryear.[87]

In other words, narcissism is about a lack of self-worth, and a search for meaningful intimacy that is forever frustrated by the very minimalism that demands it; it is about the self under siege, armed against adversity, which has displaced 'progress' with 'individual survival'.[88] At the same time, however, in its daily manifestations, narcissism as uncertainty is not entirely of free of either egotism as a preoccupation with the self, or as a feeling of superiority, both of which have been forces propelling a vacuous authenticity.

Much of Richard Sennett's work is concerned with the effects of global capitalism, typified by corporate powers, risk, and the constant innovation that undermines traditional norms and self-discipline and consequently hinders the development of a stable, confident self, producing instead fragmentation, dislocation and a retreat into 'privatism'.[89] This meets the requirements of late modernity's globalised capitalism: 'A pliant self, a collage of fragments unceasing in its becoming, ever open to new experience – these are just the psychological conditions suited to short-term work experience, flexible institutions, and constant risk-taking.'[90] When Sennett speaks of 'narcissistic character disorders', he refers to a self-preoccupation that prevents the individual from recognising the difference between the self and the external world. In such a world, where traditional authority has declined and a secular capitalistic urban culture has arisen resulting in an emphasis on 'sensation' and 'personality', which replaces the Enlightenment commitment to character:

---

[87] Lasch (1984), p 15.

[88] Z. Bauman (2007) *Liquid Times: Living in Age of Uncertainty*, Cambridge: Polity, p 103.

[89] For example, R. Sennett (2002); (1998) *The Corrosion of Character*, New York: Norton; (2006) *The Culture of the New Capitalism*, New Haven, CT: Yale University Press; (2004) *Respect: The Formation of Character in a World of Inequality*, London: Penguin Books.

[90] Sennett (1998), p 133.

impersonal experience seems meaninglessness and social complexity an unmanageable threat. By contrast, experience which seems to tell about the self, to help define it, develop it or change it, has become an overwhelming concern. In an intimate society, all social phenomena, no matter how impersonal in structure, are converted into matters of personality in order to have a meaning.[91]

Narcissism, says Sennett, is 'the protestant ethic of modern times'. In both narcissism and worldly asceticism, '"What am I feeling?" becomes an obsession...showing to others the checks and impulses of oneself feeling is a way of showing that one does have a worthy self.' In both, 'there is a projection of the self onto the world, rather than an engagement in worldly experience beyond one's control'.[92] Such a narcissistic self 'is an identity in which an individual's relation to others and the wider world is defined by attempting to control, order and master the flow of experience; such a self cannot easily tolerate ambivalence or complexity'.[93] This, I shall claim is what authoritative parenting instructs: be in control (have a contract); friendship is too risky.

---

[91] Sennett (2002), p 219.

[92] Sennett (2002), pp 333–4.

[93] Elliott (2001), p 150.

PART ONE

The origins of social democracy's family ideal: 1920s–1940s

Introduction

In some respects, this part of the book deals with a familiar series of developments and events covering, first, the shift in health and welfare discourse from children's bodies to their minds and, second, the move towards a psychoanalytic version of the amicable, peaceable and cooperative family. The main theme of the chapters is the 'reimagining' of age relations, most obviously in the inter-war period, hence the title of Chapter One; but also in Chapter Two in the debates about evacuation, problem families and homeless children. I argue that it was during the decades from the 1920s to the 1940s that adult–child age relations were literally re-imagined in an attempt to contribute to thinking through new ways of responding to a number of perceived 'crises' in western 'civilisation', in such a mode as to maintain, indeed, enhance, liberal values. This response involved trying to blend relationships not only within families, but also between different social groups, and those linking the state to a changing civil society. It seems clear that, notwithstanding some hesitancy, one of the distinctive features of this process was its optimism, a belief in human capabilities to do good, and a desire to relate individual relations to the broader social world.

As I say, what follows is not entirely unfamiliar in describing the coming of psychoanalytic thought and practice, the beginning of the rejection of behaviourism in child rearing, the influence of the child guidance movement, and the effect of a progressive pedagogy for younger children. What is emphasised here, however, is how these inter-war cultural trends were a foretaste of the post-1945 social-democratic liberalisation of parent–child relations (certainly among the middle class). In other words, social change in family life has a much longer and more complicated history than the popular documentation of wartime experiences might lead us to believe. It is important, however, to resist the blunt-edged Foucaultian characterisation of psychological 'science', as a means of social regulation.[1] Nor should we see the psychoanalytic shift in inter-war parenting in dour feminist terms as being about 'prescriptive notions of maternal adequacy'; this would be to privilege gender above other relevant and more important considerations.[2] Rather it was through the diversity of Freudianism (what W. H. Auden referred to as 'a whole climate of opinion'), and the popularisation of the psychoanalytic enterprise, that an increasing number of those involved in the different areas of psycho-medicine, education and welfare sought to help adults and children to develop their social selves in accordance with the making of a society that in the words of the influential American philosopher John Dewey was 'more worthy, lovely, and harmonious'.[3]

This was neither a naive goal, nor a concealed desire to serve a controlling state. Of course, the latter was never completely divorced from political concerns regarding social contentment and, therefore, social stability in a turbulent age, but it is a mistake to confuse the two as if there were no critical differences. Moreover, the psy-complex interventions, which continued throughout the war, embraced a worthy desire to solve a number of philosophical, sociological, political and psychological problems created by military conflicts on a scale hitherto unknown, as they affected all manner of personal relationships. Psychological knowledge was never *merely* an instrument of governance. The psychological imperative, as it developed during the inter-war years, and then between the years 1939 to 1945, was more than vulgar ideology. In specific situations, it was, like Law, 'an unqualified human good' with benefits for those affected by its procedures.[4] We should see the arc of the period as one of a re-imagining of all manner of child–adult relations of a kind quite different from what had gone before, not least because it drew on new developments in psychology, psychiatry and psychoanalysis, the result of which was the

---

1   N. Rose (1985) *The Psychological Complex: Psychology, Politics and Society in England, 1869–1939*, London: Routledge, Kegan and Paul.

2   C. Urwin and E. Sharland (1992) 'From Bodies to Minds in Childcare Literature: Advice to Parents in Inter-War Britain', in R. Cooter (ed) *In the Name of the Child: Health and Welfare, 1880–1940*, London: Routledge, pp 174–99.

3   G. Richards (2000) 'Britain on the Couch: The Popularization of Psychoanalysis in Britain 1918–1940', *Science in Context*, 13, 2, Summer, p 184; Dewey quoted in L. A. H. Smith (1985) *To Understand and to Help: The Life and Work of Susan Isaacs*, London: Associated University Press, p 222.

4   E. P. Thompson (1975) *Whigs and Hunters: The Origin of the Black Act*, London: Allen Lane, p 266.

liberalising of a pre-existing and rather repressive parenting culture. No less important, this new 'way of seeing' (and living) age relations was absorbed into the environment in which the psyche of the post-war social-democratic family was housed.[5] That this liberal humanism has encountered such bitter opposition in our late modern era would have left contemporaries aghast.

---

[5] J. Berger (1972) *Ways of Seeing*, London: BBC/penguin Books. This is helpful in reminding us that 'seeing' comes before words; it is through seeing that we establish our place in the world. I use this thought to suggest that the changing *mood* of child rearing was 'seen' before it was described – in the sense that we see it in our mind's eye and in this way come to know it. We are like the child 'who looks and recognizes before it can speak', p 7.

ONE

The re-imagining of adult–child relations between the wars

'The world has changed, and human nature is in a process of transition.' (Harold Nicolson)[6]

The paradox of the inter-war years: 'we danced all night' through what was a 'morbid age'

Uncertain and afraid
    As the clever hopes expire
    Of a low dishonest decade
    (W. H. Auden 'September 1, 1939')

A few years before Auden wrote his famous epitaph for the 1930s, Nigel Nicolson, the writer and politician, compared the mental geography of a couple marrying in the late Victorian period with that of the inter-war years. In the former, it was safe to assume that:

> whatever political or social changes might occur, the main structure of society...would remain the same...the continuance of a certain social and religious standard; the relations between the two sexes would remain comparatively uniform...such expressions as 'patriotism', 'imperialism', 'manliness', or 'loyalty' would retain their then existing values...They knew the formula which applied or contributed to these, for them, inevitable stages of development...They did not foresee that all social and religious sanctions would lose their former validity; that women would acquire greater independence of domestication...that the old affective terms would be exposed to questioning; that the whole stand of pleasure would change dynamically; that relativity would destroy all our certainties; and the unconscious blur all our thoughts...

---

6   H. Nicolson (1935) 'Introduction', in G. St Aubyn (ed) *The Family Book*, London: Barker.

or that…the parent would be faced with a complexity of disintegration in which the old formulas would appear as ineffective as willow wands in a typhoon.[7]

According to the eminent psychiatrist W. H. R. Rivers, the war had been 'a vast crucible in which all our preconceived views concerning human nature have been tested'. Under a 'Freudish' mantle, referring to 'all the terminology which the public, rightly or wrongly, identified as being psychoanalytic', it was thought that maybe personal and political violence, which seemed to be on the increase throughout Europe, was reflecting a universal human condition: perhaps the birth of an 'aggressive personality'.[8] This and other anxieties were fed by 'the General Strike and the airship, revolution and radium, Marxism, Modern Art, motor cars, movies, Marconi and Mussolini', all of which made it difficult to make sense of 'human nature'. In a world where 'reason' had shown its limitations, where it was being discredited by psychoanalysis, there was a desire to identify 'the underlying mechanisms of human sociality and harmony', to harness them in the face of social discontent so as to re-establish 'the fading frontiers between sanity and madness, normality and deviance'. If, as appeared, the 'Reality principle had broken down – nobody was sure anyway what reality *was*'.[9] And if Reality and Reason were in disarray, so, too, was the idea of certainty as the theory of relativity upset the Newtonian world view, becoming crudely popularised. Everything, it seemed, was unfixed.[10] Beatrice Ensor, a leading progressive educationalist, expressed a widely held view in prophesying that 'Applied to morals, this Law [Relativity] will revolutionise our ideas.'[11] The feeling among large sections of the intelligentsia and the political elite was that the western world was facing a 'crisis', referred to as 'the end of civilisation', as it struggled to save itself from a looming and apparently inevitable decline. Inevitable, it seemed, owing to the aftermath of the First World War's revolutions, the 'Great Crash' and perhaps the end of capitalism, struggles between democracy, communism and fascism, loss of faith in 'progress' and 'science', eugenic anxieties regarding the quality and size of the population, the conservative revolt against modernisation

---

[7] Nicolson (1935), in St Aubyn, pp 6–7.

[8] Richards (2000), pp 184–5.

[9] Richards (2000), quotations, pp 199–200.

[10] R. J. Selleck (1972) *English Primary Education and the Progressives*, London: Routledge and Kegan Paul, pp 115–19.

[11] Selleck (1972), quoted, p 116.

and the icons of modernity, the pervasive and demoralising fear of human aggression and the certainty of another war. The mood was evocatively affirmed by T. S. Eliot in *The Waste Land* (1922), when he described modernity as 'a heap of broken images, where the sun beats, and the dead tress give no shelter'.[12]

In an age of mass communication, the thesis of 'civilisation in danger' became immensely popular, in part because the world had not returned to 'normalcy' as expected after 1918 and, contrary to hopes that the war would end all wars, the 1920s and 1930s not only brought social unrest throughout Europe and economic depression, but also growing international political conflict that was correctly assumed would lead to further violence on a scale and of a nature hitherto unimaginable.[13] But the image of Europe in decline was not entirely new – after all, Nietzsche had declared that 'God is dead.' This was a judgement in sharp contrast to the nineteenth century optimism of Hegel and Marx, and one that presented man as 'a *fated* being'.[14] But the carnage of the First World War seemed to give credence to Nietzsche's pronouncement. However, not everyone agreed that civilisation was terminally impaired, and there were some small signs of optimism from the mid-1930s onwards. Nevertheless, the image of degeneration served as a measure of how contemporaries, with historical awareness, perceived the present; sometimes with an optimistic forbearance but often with pessimism exacerbated by the fact that there was no reassuring answer to the gloom-ridden adversity.[15] The inter-war crisis was fundamentally different from earlier upheavals because few people could escape the sense of unease, and were acutely conscious, as Nicolson's observation suggests, that they were living through an age of transition.

The old idea of the inter-war period as characterised mainly by poverty, hunger, mass unemployment, poor health and industrial strife has long given way to a more nuanced interpretation of the decades,

---

12 The British Psychological Society was only one of a number of august institutions expressing concern at the spread of 'irrational' violence throughout Europe. See its symposium, 'Is Aggression an Irreducible Factor?', *British Journal of Medical Psychology (1939/40)*, 18. For the 'crisis' theme, see *The Decline of the West* (Spengler, 1918); Freud's *The Future of An Illusion* (1927) and *Civilization and Its Discontents* (1930); *Can We Save Civilization?* (McCabe, 1932); *The Origins of Love and Hate* (Suttie, 1935); *Modern Man in Search of a Soul* (Jung, 1936); and *Personal Aggressiveness and War* (Durbin and Bowlby, 1939).

13 R. Overy (2009) *The Morbid Age: Britain between the Wars*, London: Penguin, p 2.

14 Quoted, Overy (2009), p 47.

15 Overy (2009), pp 19, 28.

one that recognises economic growth, falling prices, improvements in health and housing, the seeds of mass consumerism, the emergence of the leisure industry and, despite some attempts to foster home-grown fascism, the nine-day General Strike and the Jarrow Crusade of the unemployed, a relatively low level of social and political disruption. For large sections of the employed life was not too bad, and many undoubtedly 'danced all night'. For the unemployed and the long-term poor, however, life was indeed 'nasty, brutish and short', and whatever the scale of economic growth, it was certainly not an 'age of improvement' comparable to the mid-Victorian era. While the Victorians had believed in the idea of progress, the First World War dashed the sanguine reformism of the Edwardian years, and led 'to a prolonged mood of disillusionment' and a surfeit of brooding introspection.[16] The continuation of Liberalism, upon which 'Western civilisation' was deemed to rest, seemed to be at risk from the crisis in capitalism and from the emergence and growth in popularity throughout Europe of authoritarian ideologies and other forms of what were considered to be the 'irrational'. What if it were true, as Freud postulated, that 'men cannot live without civilisation, but they cannot live happily within it'?[17]

Inter-war science: children's bodies and minds and child rearing

Apart from the looming genius of Freud, a number of continental, American and British psychologists were revolutionising the field of child study. These figures included Jean Piaget, who was transforming if not creating modern 'child development' with his sophisticated 'ages and stages' model of childhood; Melanie Klein, who extended Freud's theory of infantile sexuality to encompass the 'phantasy' world of the young child, controversially portraying these toddlers as engulfed with phantasies of rage, violence, aggression and hatred; J. B. Watson, a staunch advocate of behavioural child rearing; and Arnold Gesell, the pioneer of 'developmental diagnosis'. In Britain, the psychiatrist H. Crichton Miller wrote an innovative guide outlining the role of psychology in helping parents to appreciate the 'Unconscious Motive' and the idea of 'Repression', both of which he claimed would help them to understand not only their children, but also more about themselves,

---

[16] M. Pugh (2008) *We Danced All Night: A Social History of Britain Between the Wars*, London: Vintage Books, p x.

[17] P. Gay (1988) *Freud: A Life for Our Time*, New York: Norton, p 548.

which was necessary in order to avoid child-rearing practices that led to nervous breakdown in later life.[18] One of two seminal figures was the educational psychologist Cyril Burt, best known for his work in the psychology of individual differences and mental testing, and for his writings on the treatment of juvenile delinquency.[19] The other personage was Susan Isaacs, generally agreed to have been the greatest influence on British education in the twentieth century, whose work focused on child development, education and child rearing, and who did so much to promote the ideas of Freud, Piaget, and Klein among educational psychologists and the wider reading public.[20]

Alongside the psychologists, one of the most widely read figures in infant care was F. Truby King, a New Zealand doctor whose behaviourally inclined *Feeding and Care of Baby*, which stressed the importance of training good habits and rigorous feeding by the clock, became increasingly popular after he visited a Mothercraft school in London in 1917 at a time of national concern over high infant mortality rates.[21] The school subsequently produced an even more popular and equally habit fixated manual, promoting 'an outline of the principles' taught by Truby King that remained in print with liberal amendments until the 1950s.[22] To a certain extent King's strictures and those of the manual reworked older nurturing practices, but for a time their claim to scientific soundness gave them both a new audience and a new legitimacy.

In thinking about the relationships between science, psychology and child raising, it is helpful to remember that the inter-war era was a period when a model of science based on 'systematic and rational investigation of the underlying causes and processes of health and disease' achieved dominance.[23] In its generality, the attraction of science proved helpful to different parenting moralities, including the strict Evangelical-type prescriptions of Truby King and Watson, and the liberal recommendations of psychoanalysis and child guidance, as espoused by Susan Isaacs. Soon, however, behaviourism was being

---

[18] H. Crichton Miller (1922) *The New Psychology and the Parent*, London: Jarrolds, pp 12, 19, 27, 31.

[19] L. S. Hearnshaw (1979) *Cyril Burt, Psychologist*, London: Hodder and Stoughton.

[20] Smith (1985); P. Graham (2009) *Susan Isaacs: A Life Freeing the Minds of Children*, London: Karnac Books.

[21] F. Truby King (1913, later edns to 1945) *Feeding and Care of Baby*, London.

[22] M. Lilliard (ed) (1924, 6th edn 1954) *The Mothercraft Manual*, London: Churchill.

[23] S. Sturdy and R. Cooter (1998) 'Scientific Management and the Transformation of Medicine in Britain, c. 1870–1950', *History of Science*, 36, 4, p 437.

challenged by the coming of the 'new psychology' (an English variant of Freudianism, which rejected the 'sex instinct'), the impact of the psychoanalytic method, and by the child guidance movement through its clinics, publications, and lectures, which contributed original and often definitive accounts of the emotional terrain of family life and child development.[24] In effect, the inter-war years saw the introduction of a therapeutically oriented child psychology as a way of thinking about children, whose references spread throughout medicine, law, education and social welfare. Although there was no single developmental path and certainly no unified theoretical approach, as a means of perceiving the emotional interiority of children (and of parents), the new psychology, with its construction of 'the psychological family', was a primary influence on the re-imaging children and, therefore, on child–adult relations.[25]

The family was regarded as a complex of psycho-dynamic relationships at the core of which, claimed psychotherapeutics, lay not behavioural habits but feelings and emotions involving love, guilt, jealousy, hate, dependency and a whole galaxy of fantasies.[26] For the Kleinians, 'phantasy' was critical; it encompassed the young child's universe.[27] For other strands of psychoanalytic thought, the 'real' environment of children was just as, if not more, important in affecting their behaviour and development.[28] When families were well functioning, all these components coalesced in harmony, or at least each family member was able to stabilise their respective tensions and organise them into a contented psyche. But the components could so easily go awry in children as evidenced in delinquency, maladjustment, and myriad forms of nervous and neurotic behaviour from enuresis to 'excessive' shyness.[29] These disturbances were symptoms of conflict-ridden family relationships, and if those involving children were to be avoided it was necessary to protect them from emotional injury which,

---

[24] Rose (1985), pp 182–90.

[25] Rose (1985) pp 176–96.

[26] J. Rickman (ed) (1936) *On the Bringing Up of Children by Five Psychoanalysts*, London: Paul, Trench and Trubner; S. Isaacs (1929) *The Nursery Years*, London: Routledge.

[27] M. Klein (1975 edn) *The Psycho-Analysis of Children*, London: Virago; T. J. Segal (1992) *Melanie Klein*, London: Sage.

[28] D. Riley (1983) *War in the Nursery: Theories of the Child and Mother*, London: Virago, pp 71–9.

[29] D. K. Henderson and R. D. Gillespie (1932 edn) *A Textbook of Psychiatry*, London: Oxford University Press, pp vii, 458–536.

if left unattended, could mar their maturation and lead to all sorts of mental difficulties in adulthood.

The place of origin for the psychologically harmonious parent–child relationship was determined by child-rearing principles and practices which, as all experts agreed, required professional and scientific guidance. In the late Victorian and Edwardian decades, despite the establishment of a Child Study movement, the corrective emphasis remained relatively fixed on obedience and discipline. By the end of the 1920s, however, psychoanalysis was instructing an ever growing audience in the importance of self-knowledge, the existence of a 'hidden self', and the reality of the unconscious mind. This audience appreciated that only when these 'discoveries' were acted on would 'more rational self-control and fuller personal development' become widespread.[30] But in human relations nothing was quite as it seemed. Thus, the psychologically informed claim from progressive opinion was that correction could best be accomplished by rearing mentally balanced and mature children through understanding the importance of their feelings and emotions, which should be absorbed into an accommodation with their parents' individuality. Otherwise, the social, economic, political and psychic consequences of child 'maladjustment', however it was defined, threatened to exacerbate various constituents of the crisis that extended well beyond the social cohesiveness of the family into the broader political arena. As a major inquiry into the mental health services concluded, given the abnormality of the times, there was a risk that minor maladjustment was 'liable to become serious mental disorder'.[31] There is no doubt that the proliferation of psychological texts, both academic and popular, and the increasing amount of research into different physical and mental features of children and childhood, together with the founding of child guidance clinics, was evidence of the eagerness of psychological practitioners to show that parent–child relations were vital to the health and emotional stability of children (and, therefore, of families), and that this concern was set within the context of contemporary anxieties. In responding to the view that civilisation was in crisis, the new psychology grasped

[30] E. Freeman Sharpe (1936) 'Planning for Stability', in J. Rickman (ed), pp 1–2; also her (1948) 'What the Father Means to the Child', *Problems of Child Development*, New Education Fellowship: London, pp 24–32.

[31] The Feversham Committee (1939) *The Voluntary Mental Health Services*, London: The Feversham Committee, p x.

its opportunity to reshape social relations, promoting itself as 'a science of social contentment'.[32]

Clearly, then, the space in which this 'psychological complex' was able to expound its vision for the human mind and its problems lay originally in the confusion, disillusionment and fear that followed the First World War. The new psychology, along with orthodox Freudians, emphasised the need to delineate what it was that constituted and motivated the soul. As part of this multi-faceted urge to come to terms with the forces of aggression, irrationalism, and cruelty which, it seemed to contemporaries, had been forged by war, the pre-existing interest in child development, organised through Child Study groups, was reinvigorated as psychological science.[33] In part this emerged from the Freudian view that we are merely 'stock characters in the perennial dramatisation of the family quarrel'.[34] But it was also because it was increasingly believed that knowledge of child nature was relevant to contemporary problems; in other words, it had a utilitarian value. The child, it appeared, was indeed father of the man. But children were not to be examined as isolated beings in the social firmament. What made the new psychology so significant was its alliance with 'the register of personal happiness, family relations, and social adjustment'.[35] It was this realignment that positioned the emotional condition of children and their relationships with adults as so central to national mental health and, therefore, to social wellbeing, and vice versa. Critically, however, in rejecting Watsonian behaviourism, psychoanalysts held that the sum of a human being was not an aggregate of behavioural *habits* acquired through socialisation. According to one of the first and most popular studies on the subject, the purpose of all education was to form the 'right sentiments and dispositions', and a 'liberal education' would ensure that the appropriate 'emotions are attached to the right objects, ideas and persons'. Once shaped, these sentiments and dispositions were then combined to make the '*Organized Self*', the quality of which constituted 'our *Character*'.[36] And this could only occur in the emotional landscape of the *normal* family where a

---

[32] Rose (1985), p 185.

[33] A. Wooldridge (1994) *Measuring the Mind: Education and Psychology in England, c. 1860–1990*, Cambridge: Cambridge University Press.

[34] P. Rieff (1959) *Freud: The Mind of a Moralist*, Chicago, IL: University of Chicago Press, pp 50–1.

[35] Rose (1985), p 184.

[36] J. A. Hadfield (1923) *Psychology and Morals: An Analysis of Character*, London: Methuen, p 23, emphasis original.

secure and responsive environment, providing for the development of appropriate relationships with things, persons and ideas, produced the stable, emotionally confident personality.

The worry for many observers was that a culture disturbed and undermined, as appeared to be the case in Britain, put the psychological integrity of the family and parent–child relations into question. In Eliot's 'modernity', where there were new 'strains and tensions and disruptive tendencies', which could make management of the 'difficult child' upsetting and disturbing, a situation developed whereby it seemed that increasing numbers of children became an 'enigma to their parents'.[37] In an attempt to conceptualise notions of 'maladjustment', as much as the child's apparently enigmatic character, psychotherapists advanced four reasons for their belief that nervous disorders originated in the environment of childhood. First, it was a time when the brain and mind were at their most impressionable, making them susceptible to parental suggestion. Second, children were 'unadapted to life' having not yet learnt to react to 'exigencies of fate'. Third, childhood was the time when we formed 'impressions of life': aggressive, stoical, easy going, diffident or snobbish. Fourth, it was during childhood that through self-consciousness, we learnt our attitude towards ourselves. This meant that although the single event may have life-long consequences, more important for normal child development was 'the general atmosphere of childhood', for this may give a child the 'wrong' attitude towards either life or itself.[38] The problem was that providing the proper 'atmosphere' was beset with difficulties. Nonetheless, by the early 1930s, among middle-class parents, and others, there was a noticeable turn away from behavioural influences towards a more empathetic mode of child rearing, sustained by an eclectic and revolutionary psychoanalytic perspective, which worked not on the character of parents, but on their personality – the difference being that a person may have admirable character traits, but lack imagination and have 'hardness of heart': 'It is personality that counts for the baby, the whole person emotionally.'[39]

---

[37] E. Miller (1930) 'The Difficult Child: A Medical, Psychological and Sociological Problem', *Mother and Child*, 1, 5, pp 162–7; J. Stewart (2013) *Child Guidance in Britain, 1918–1955*, London: Pickering & Chatto, p 1.

[38] Hadfield (1923), pp 17–19.

[39] Freeman Sharpe (1936), p 3.

Heroes of behaviourism: F. Truby King and J. B. Watson

There is some uncertainty as to the extent of behaviourist influence on child-rearing advice during the inter-war era. L. S. Hearnshaw claims that no British psychologist of standing was a behaviourist and quotes the contemporary professional view that behaviourism was 'silly' and that 'the fundamental subject matter of psychology is conscious experience, not conduct'.[40] It is true that in general behaviourism was not as popular in Britain as it was in the United States; it was certainly not 'triumphant'.[41] It seems reasonable to conclude, however, that a passive form of behaviourism was at work, one that implicitly acknowledged Watson and promoted his principles; and also that Truby King's widely dispersed advice on feeding and infant care exerted considerable influence, particularly at the level of everyday nursing and health visiting. So while in the upper echelons of academic psychology behaviourism's standing was undoubtedly low, at the mundane level of daily childcare in terms of stressing habit formation and moral strictness, the 'medical morality' of the hygienist movement of the inter-war years, with its authoritarian emphasis, successfully echoed many of the prescriptions of the older 'religious morality' of the eighteenth and nineteenth centuries as the 'morality of aseptic rationalism' superseded that of 'spiritual regeneration'.[42]

Thus *The Mothercraft Manual* was following a fairly well-worn path, although one now confirmed by hygienist 'science', in declaring:

> Self-control, obedience, the recognition of authority, and…respect for elders are all outcomes of the first year's training…The baby who is picked up or fed whenever he cries soon becomes a veritable tyrant…while…the infant who is fed regularly, put to sleep, and played with at definite times soon finds that appeals bring no response, and so learns that most useful of all lessons, self-control, and

---

[40] L. Hearnshaw (1964) *A Short History of British Psychology, 1848–1940*, London: Methuen, p 210. But Hearnshaw ignores the pervasive 'behaviourist' influence of F. Truby King. See also M. Thomson (2006) *Psychological Subjects: Identity, Culture, and Health in Twentieth Century Britain*, Oxford: Oxford University Press, p 136.

[41] C. Hardyment (1983) *Perfect Parents: Baby-care Advice Past and Present*, Oxford: Oxford University Press, p 165; also Urwin and Sharland (1992), p 181.

[42] J. Newson and E. Newson (1974) 'Cultural Aspects of Childrearing in the English-speaking World', in M. P. Richards (ed) *The Integration of a Child into a Social World*, Cambridge: Cambridge University Press, p 60.

the recognition of authority other than his own wishes...
To train an infant for the first year is comparatively easy,
but after that the child begins to resent authority and the
conscientious mother has to be prepared to fight and win
all along the line in matters small and great.[43]

Truby King was equally committed to the behaviourist belief in the
power of habit training:

the leading authorities of the day...all agree that the
first thing to establish in life is *regularity of habits*...[the
establishment of which] initiated by 'feeding and sleeping
by the clock', is the ultimate foundation of all-round
obedience. Granted good organic foundations, truth and
honour can be built into the edifice as it grows.[44]

The absence of regularity in babyhood, argued King, could lead
not only to hysteria, imbecility and epilepsy but also various forms
of degeneracy in adults. The well-regulated infant led on to the
healthy and morally upright adult citizen. Despite their behavioural
sympathies, however, neither the *Manual* nor Truby King ever reached
the unnerving sentiments of Watson's advice to parents:

The happy child? A child who never cries unless actually
stuck with a pin, illustratively speaking; who loses himself
in work and play; who quickly learns to overcome the small
difficulties in his environment without running to mother,
father, nurse or some other adult; who builds up a wealth
of habits that tides him over the dark and rainy days; who
puts on such habits of politeness and neatness and cleanliness
that adults are willing to be around him, at least part of the
day; a child who is willing to be around adults without
fighting incessantly for notice; who eats what is set before
him and 'asks no questions for conscience's sake'; who sleeps
and rests when put to bed...who puts away two-year-old
habits when the third year has to be faced; who passes into
adolescence so well-equipped that adolescence is just a
stretch of fertile years, and who finally enters manhood so

---

[43] Liddiard (1924), pp 160–1. By the 1954 edition, 'trained' had become 'rightly guided'.

[44] Newson and Newson (1974), quoted pp 60–1. Emphasis original.

bulwarked with stable work and emotional habits that no adversity can quite overwhelm him.[45]

Where Truby King had implicitly frowned upon tenderness, Watson explicitly warned parents against it. Being 'mawkish' and 'sentimental' could lead to all kinds of vices, including invalidism, the 'mother's boy syndrome' and hypochondria. It seems that Watson was designing 'the mechanical baby' suitable for what was widely seen as the prescribed virtues of American society: self-reliance and immunity to the stress and strain of a particular kind of modernity.[46] In some important respects, this approach easily gelled with that of the other major figure in American child psychology, also well known in Britain, the more liberally-minded Arnold Gessell with his developmental schema. The process of growing up, said Gessell, was 'a steady process of detachment, first from the apron strings, later from the home itself'.[47] This ideal, however, had embedded within it a critical behaviourist objective: the endorsement of self-sufficiency along with a trained adaptability to external demands.[48]

The emphasis on habit training and rigid routines of sleeping and eating involved a great deal of upset for young children. Historically, the crying child had been one of the nightmares of parents, particularly among the poor with their large families and overcrowded living conditions. Druggists had long made a good living out of the sale of opiates. In common with many childcare authors of the time, Truby King and Watson were adamant that parents should not 'give in' to a child's crying; 'no surrender' was the behaviourist slogan. In some quarters, in the past crying had been thought of as 'nature's voice'; in the 1920s, this was no longer so. It was accepted that there were occasions when crying indicated that something was wrong with the child in terms of what adults could understand and found acceptable. 'Naughtiness', however, was everywhere, and could easily be confirmed by the mother or nurse picking up the child to cease the tears. The solution was to leave the child to 'cry it out': 'The tiniest baby soon learns that you mean what you say.' Children should never be allowed to feel that they got their own way through 'tantrums' or similar displays

---

[45]   J. B. Watson (1928) *Psychological Care of the Infant and Child*, London: Allen and Unwin, pp 9–10.

[46]   D. Beekman (1979) *The Mechanical Baby*, London: Dobson.

[47]   A. Gesell (1925) *The Mental Growth of the Pre-School Child*, New York: Macmillan, p 381.

[48]   Urwin and Sharland (1992), p 183.

of loss of control.[49] While this attitude was not peculiar to behaviourist principles, they gave it the authority of medical science.

Susan Isaacs and the rejection of behaviourism

It is clear that within the context of a broadly based Freudian approach to therapeutic work with children, a collective opposition to behaviourism began to emerge, notably among psychoanalysts, psychiatrists, psychologists and psychiatric social workers in child guidance clinics. Together they challenged Watson's dogma by popularising 'the possibility that the will, the emotions, the passions were not simply fuel driving behaviour which was then controlled by conditioning; they were part and parcel of an individual psychology'. Children, they argued, 'could be in conflict with the environment in which they were growing up'.[50] The importance of this disclosure was that 'environment' became relevant not only in relation to post-war apprehension concerning aggression, violence and the demoralisation of what many observers saw as the Christian spirit, but also, in the light of the traumatic experiences of thousands of soldiers, to the perceived rise in mental instability as a consequence of being unable to tolerate stress and fear. Within behaviourism, the 'unconscious' and the world of 'phantasy' were unresolved, leaving the individual in a disturbed state. Yet it seemed to be indisputable that this disturbance – of children, parents and families – impinged on, indeed was a feature of, the inter-war crisis. The treatment of these neuroses was a pressing matter; even more urgent was the need to prevent them from arising in the first place.

By the mid-1930s, the new approach to childcare was evident in a number of parenting manuals. Mrs Frankenburg, for example, revised her views on 'undesirable habits', which were now seen as 'almost invariably the result of something wrong in the child's emotional life', and advised her readers to think in terms of the child's underlying anxieties, the confusions of coming to terms with the environment, and the need to work with the child's imagination and sense of itself, adding that 'Punishments for young children should be non-existent.'[51] A more significant public testament to the psychoanalytic perspective, however, was John Rickman's edited collection *On the Upbringing of*

---

[49] C. U. Frankenburg (1922) *Common Sense in the Nursery*, London: Cape; Anon (1934), *The Motherhood Book*, London: Amalgamated Press.

[50] Urwin and Sharland (1992), p 183.

[51] Frankenburg (1934 edn), Preface, pp 9–19, 154, 225.

Children by Five Psycho-Analysts (1936), published in response to 'an increasingly pressing demand' for a statement on child rearing from the psychoanalytical standpoint. As examples of the growing receptive mood toward psychoanalysis, Rickman recommended a number of books for the 'non-specialist reader' in order to 'throw light on the mind of the child'. In direct opposition to behaviourism, he argued that psychoanalysis had shown that 'the growth of the child's mind is a far more complicated process than was once supposed, and that much harm may be done to that growth if a method of upbringing is adopted which underestimates the complexities'. What seemed trivial to parents was often 'of vast importance to the child'. 'The really important factor in upbringing', said Rickman identifying the critical psychoanalytic precept 'is the *general attitude* of the parents, and the way in which the *ordinary details* of life are conducted' – what mattered in child rearing was 'lives lived, not things taught'. For Rickman, through the combination of Freudian science and Klein's work on child psychoanalysis, it was now possible to have 'an insight into the mind of the young child', which deepened understanding of 'that all-important bond – the relation between parent and child'.[52]

It was, however, Susan Isaacs who became the public face of opposition to behaviourism, and by the mid-1930s she was probably preferred reading to Watson.[53] Isaacs published several important books, including two popular texts for lay audiences, *The Nursery Years* (1929), and *The Children We Teach* (1932), founded an experimental school in Cambridge (Malting House), established the country's first Department of Child Development at London University, wrote an advice column in *The Nursery World* for seven years, gave evidence before the government Consultative Committee on Infant and Nursery Schools (1933), contributed to a variety of journals, directed *The Cambridge Evacuation Survey* (1941), and played a vital role in spreading the ideas of Piaget, Freud and Klein. By virtue of her scholarly and wide-ranging popular writing and lectures, and her many contacts, Isaacs became the most effective communicator of the Freudian/Kleinian understanding of young children, particularly the importance of their emotional development: fears, moods, anxieties, fantasies, loves, hates and aggression. Unlike Watson, Isaacs gave full measure to the negative themes of hate, jealousy, rivalry and anxiety in child development. In her academic work, in accordance with

---

[52] Rickman (ed) (1936), Preface, pp ix-xvi; also Mrs. Basil Hood (1935) 'Development of the Adolescent' in St. Aubyn (ed), p 486.

[53] Graham (2009), p 218.

Klein's theories, she usually tended to underplay influences derived from external and environmental factors, focusing instead on the unconscious; although in her advice column for mothers and nannies she was much more willing to admit the role of influences derived from home, parents and family.[54]

Although never denying the value of 'good habits', Isaacs set out to demolish the behaviourist approach. She wrote a critical review of Watson's book, hating his 'habit psychology' and 'cruel blunders with the rough handling of the mind', and was scornful of the exaggerated importance behaviourists attached to 'inculcating good habits and avoiding bad ones', just as she was critical of their focus on education as a means of 'conditioning' children's reflexes.[55] While she valued 'a firm background of regular routine and quiet control', she cautioned against parental inflexibility, recommending the need to leave room for 'minor variations as the child's own emotional needs fluctuate'.[56] Why, she asks, is it so difficult to inculcate the good habits re toilet-training? Why do children resist? With homage to Klein, she informs readers that recently 'We have learnt that all these bodily processes are of the utmost psychical significance, and carry with them profound unconscious fantasies, concerned with the child's relation to his mother and his mother's to him.' Aside from this, the child has to deal with 'a complex problem' even on the bodily side: 'He has to acquire a technical skill, the difficulty and complexity of which we constantly underestimate.'[57] If the child 'lives amongst clean people who are loving and understanding, as well as clean, the child will become clean and orderly like them'. In such an atmosphere, children learn that their fantasies about the harmful wastes are 'not based on reality'.[58] Regarding toilet 'training', she explains the difference between 'habit' and 'development':

> All these processes, the natural ripening of bodily skill and emotional balance, the tempering of fantasies by real experience, the acquisition of the creative arts, and identification with his parents, are going on together; and then presently they enable the child to achieve a normal orderly functioning of the primitive bodily processes with a

---

[54] Riley (1983), p. 79.

[55] Quotation in Graham (2009), p 210; also Isaacs (1936) 'Habit', in Rickman (ed), pp 123–4.

[56] Isaacs (1936) 'The Nursery as a community', in Rickman ed, pp 209–11.

[57] Isaacs (1936), 'Habit', p 141.

[58] Isaacs (1936), pp 153–4.

minimum of disturbance and difficulty. And this functioning gradually becomes more or less automatic. A habit is thus in the end achieved...not by early reflex conditioning, but as the outcome of a long and complex psychological development.[59]

One of the ways in which Isaacs helped to realign inter-war age relations was through her emphasis on recognising 'the particular emotional needs of each child':

> The child's inner psychic life has its own contribution to make to the complexity of his relation with his parents...we have not only to consider the behaviour of the parents... but what it means to the child himself, with all his limitations of feeling, of understanding and of experience...It is the way in which the particular qualities of the parents and of the real environment interact at every point with the child's own psychic processes that is the question before us...the fantasies of internalized objects [referring to the Kleinian view of the good and bad mother inside the child's head] are not at all easy for us to understand, since they are so remote from ordinary adult reality. But they are of the utmost importance for the child's emotional problems.[60]

When it came to 'tantrums', she was anxious to contextualise them 'in relation to internal objects', describing them as 'manifestations of acute anxiety'. By 'internal objects' is meant 'phantasised persecutors', inside the child's own mind and body; these are projected upon 'external thwarting persons'.[61] Thus, tantrums occur when children feel unable to control 'good' objects and their 'persecutors, internal and external, by the ordinary means of appealing or commanding words and actions'. The need of children to control the actual persons upon whom they depend 'for love and food, or whose actual aggression' they fear, is itself 'one of the motives for eating them up and incorporating them'. We incorporate 'not only to keep and to have what we desire, but also in order to control what we fear, by magical means.'[62] In this respect,

---

[59] Isaacs (1936), p 155.

[60] Isaacs (1936), pp 169–70, 175.

[61] Isaacs (1948) *Childhood and After: Some Essays and Clinical Studies*, London: Routledge and Kegan Paul, p 131.

[62] Isaacs (1948), p 142.

Isaacs was always alert to the adult-centric manner in which children were so often treated:

> If only we could give little children the same degree of consideration as we naturally extend to adults, we should be able to avoid many of our worst mistakes… if we avoid making the extraordinary assumptions that they are mere reflex machines and have no feelings or mental needs, we shall then be willing to take pains to understand what those feelings and needs are…whilst we are willing to take endless trouble to make a guest feel at home, to avoid hurting the feelings of a grown-up member of the family, or to extend the right expressions of sympathy to someone who has suffered a tragic loss, we are too often ready to let children endure all these things without the slightest understanding or help from us…[also] We talk about him in front of him, and sometimes even relate our own triumphs over him in a way which would lead us to be ostracised in adult society'.[63]

At the same time, while she advocated liberal and largely non-punitive child rearing, she was never a libertarian, preferring instead 'the better management of the instincts'.[64] Isaacs, like Freud, was a moralist and shared his view that 'civilization has been a vast effort at subduing the forces of nature'.[65] The struggle is very much about deriving 'lessons on the right conduct of life from the misery of living it'.[66] In Freud's theory of civilisation, life in society is 'an imposed compromise and hence…an insoluble predicament'. Whether, in common with Freud, she was ready to live with 'the most modest expectations for human betterment' is uncertain.[67] But she did intend to contribute to ameliorating the Freudian 'predicament'. And she understood, as did other psychoanalysts, that an 'autonomous life' no longer meant a Kantian 'control over the self', now it involved what has been described as looking 'in many directions simultaneously: toward personal life, the sphere of personal autonomy per se, as well as toward family, the

---

63 Isaacs (1936), pp 205–7; also 'The Trials of the Child', BBC talk, 1929, and 'A Child's Point of View', *The Nursery World*, 4 June 1930, both in Smith (1985).

64 Wooldridge (1994), p 131.

65 Gay (1988), pp 546, 547.

66 Rieff (1959), p ix.

67 Gay (1988), p 547.

community, religion and science'.[68] This is why it was so important that parents learn to 'understand and to help' their children's emotional lives and development (which also involved understanding themselves).[69] If the dialectic was not to explode catastrophically as Freud feared it might, and as it looked to many observers of inter-war Europe, then the re-writing of family emotions was essential.

For Isaacs, social solidarity depended on familial psychic unity since from a very early age a child is exposed to the tensions of jealous rivalry, love, longing and hate towards parents and brothers and sisters, and 'from these influences and conflicts are ultimately derived all the varied characteristics of later social life'. This was the 'central psychic situation' from which all social relations arose.[70] As a Freudian, she believed that in this family a degree of repression was unavoidable; it was 'essential to a balanced conscious life and adaptation to reality'. In Freudian terms, 'the sacrifice of the self is the beginning of personality'.[71] The 'primitive super ego' had to be kept in check. But note the positive nature of the language of restraint: 'What is required is the fostering of the child's belief in love and his sense of security in the real world. And this…is best fostered by a stable, ordered environment and the trust and consideration of the adults upon whom he leans.'[72] If the child is 'to attain security in the real world of social relations', the responsible adult, who acts as the disciplinary 'super ego', 'must exercise that function not for the purpose of prohibitions and punishments, but towards positive ends, opportunities and achievements'.[73] But the key consideration that characterised progressive middle-class parenting with respect to children's mental health and happiness was the answer to the question, 'What should we do?' Without knowledge, said Isaacs, by which she meant 'scientific' psychology, it was impossible to know how best to help them. 'Children all need our affection and sympathy; but they need also all our intelligence, and our patient and serious efforts to understand the ways of their mental growth.'[74] And she added the critical qualifier, of which she was a fervent advocate:

---

[68] E. Zaretsky (2005), *Secrets of the Soul*, New York: Vintage Books, pp 167–8.

[69] Smith (1985).

[70] S. Isaacs (1933) *Social Development of Children*, London: Routledge, p 298.

[71] Quoted in Wooldridge (1994), p 131.

[72] Isaacs (1933), pp 417, 424.

[73] Isaacs (1933), p 456; also Isaacs (1936), p 213, and *The New Era*, Sept–Oct, 1936, in Smith (1985), pp 291–8.

[74] Isaacs (1929), pp 2–3.

Obviously, we can only decide what we 'ought' to do and what we 'should' say when we understand what the children's behaviour means to them, and know the actual effect on them of what we do…What helps most…is the ability to enter into the child's own world with an informed sympathy, the general sense that his problems are problems of growth, and a patient and friendly interest in the ways of that growth'.[75]

This willingness to appreciate that children had their own perception of the world and that it could be a valid perception, was crucial to the liberal re-imagining of the parent–child relationship.

The child guidance movement

Understanding produces tolerance, and tolerance gives us the power to guide.[76]

The history of child guidance has been extensively and insightfully researched.[77] But there is room for a brief comment on its *cultural* contribution to liberal trends in inter-war age relations, particularly the way that it contributed to their changing tenor, not only by helping contemporaries to recognise and understand critical stages in child development, but also in addressing hitherto unacknowledged aspects of the moral economy of the family.[78] In so far as it grew out of the 'new psychology', child guidance, like much else in the post-1914 Freudian mapping of the human mind, was part of the response to the widely perceived illness that was said to characterise modernity which, however, as it began to be medicalised, was open to being cured.[79] There is little doubt that the intellectual atmosphere in which the movement operated was thrown into disarray as the social sciences and the physical world stumbled under the impact of the collapse of certainty, the apparent degeneration of reason, and

---

75 Isaacs (1929), pp 6–7; also her comments on 'obedience', pp 101–5.

76 E. Miller (ed) (1937) *The Growing Child and Its Problems*, London: Kegan, Paul, Trench and Trubner, p xii.

77 Rose (1985); J. Stewart (2013).

78 Rose (1985), pp 176–96.

79 Overy (2009), p 4; D. Armstrong (1995) 'The Rise of Surveillance Medicine', *Sociology of Health and Illness*, 17, 3, pp 393–404.

the crowning of relativity.[80] The task for child therapeutics, however, seemed to be fundamentally straightforward: given the prevalence of neurosis in modern life, there was an urgent need to counter it at source, namely in childhood, and the new psychology was particularly well suited to devise appropriate intervention strategies focusing on 'guidance'. Otherwise, if left untreated in alienating environments, childhood 'maladjustment'– the 'neuroses'– could affect familial social health, which in turn could have dire repercussions for the welfare of the wider community.[81] The child patients were treated within a therapeutic framework rather than through psychoanalysis as such, with referrals being mainly for minor emotional behavioural problems, usually having brought the children into conflict with adult authority.[82] Besides acting as remedial centres, through their personal contacts and institutional alliances, the clinics also facilitated a range of voluntary and governmental social and educational services embracing the nursery, the playground, the school, the courts and the home. While it is true that they hardly reached a wide audience, no more than a few thousand each year, it is a mistake to think only in terms of numbers reflecting the extent of the influence of the message of child guidance. Cultural change is rarely encompassed solely in numerical exuberance. It is more appropriate to see the clinics as representing a new institution that with reference to the therapies of the new psychology set out to identify, categorise, regulate and, above all, comprehend adult–child relations in order to guide and ultimately to influence them toward greater humanity for the betterment of what we would later think of as civil society.

The presence of child guidance was greatly enhanced by the establishment in 1927 of the Child Guidance Council (CGC) to 'advance the treatment of maladjusted, difficult, and delinquent children', later made more specific to include nervous conditions such as hysteria, anxiety, habit spasms, stammering, enuresis and difficulties

[80] Stewart (2013), pp 35–37; M. Thomson (2001) 'Psychology and the "Consciousness of Modernity" in Early Twentieth Century Britain', in M. Daunton and B. Berger (eds) *Meanings of Modernity: Britain from the Late Victorian Era to World War II*, Oxford: Berg, pp 97–144.

[81] W. Moodie (1929) 'Child Guidance', *Mental Welfare*, 10, 3, pp 98–103; G. A. Auden (1031) 'The Maladjusted Child', *British Journal of Educational Psychology*, 1, 3, pp 266–76.

[82] R. G. Gordon (1939) *A Survey of Child Psychiatry*, London: Oxford University Press, pp 266–7; H. Hendrick (2003) *Child Welfare. Historical dimensions, contemporary debate*, Bristol: Policy Press, p 105.

in eating and sleeping.[83] The Council promoted its work through professional journals, such as *Parents and Teachers*, popular magazines, especially *Mother and Child* (founded in 1930 and a crucial outlet for the therapeutic perspective) and *The New Era*, books in the *Home and School Library*, BBC radio talks, public lectures, conference presentations and numerous pamphlets. The CGC's strategy was to provide centres where children and their families could receive appropriate psychiatric attention, but more often they would simply be 'guided' in how to respond to the normal stresses and strains of family or school life.[84] Parents and teachers were advised to focus less on regulating children's habits and morals and more on understanding their feelings, wishes and anxieties.[85] As a result of such wide dissemination of psycho-analytic principles, at least among the informed middle class, the child was turned from the pre-Freudian habit-fixated figure of a mechanical mass to someone intensely more interesting and vulnerable in terms of nature and the ego, the id and the superego. One did not have to be a confirmed Freudian to know that what you did or did not do to your children was not without consequence for their social, emotional and moral development. To this extent, child guidance became a fixture in the inter-war debate on mental health, social welfare and the vicissitudes of 'character' at a time of collective introspection.

The clinics' psychoanalytic procedure was initially played down for fear of being linked to controversial Freudian theories of child sexuality. By the 1930s, however, this was less likely to be the case owing in part to the writings of Emanuel Miller, Director of the East London Clinic and, to a lesser degree, those of several Viennese analysts, including Alfred Adler, Hermione Hug-Hellmuth and Anna Freud.[86] While they were hardly major architects of English child guidance, in a diluted form their work, along with that of other Freudians and Jungians in child psychology, including the influential Margaret Lowenfeld, a pioneer of play therapy, filtered its way through the new psychology as a system of thought and as practice. Nonetheless, much of the treatment remained at the level of 'common sense' chats – no doubt psychoanalytically informed – with parents and children from the

---

[83] The Child Guidance Council (1928), London: Child Guidance Council; Hendrick (2003), p 101.

[84] Hendrick (2003), pp 106-107.

[85] Home and Schools Council (1935) *Advances in Understanding the Child*, London: Home and Schools Council.

[86] D. Thom (1992) 'Wishes, Anxieties, Play and Gestures: Child Guidance in Inter-War England', in R. Cooter (ed), pp 209–13.

psychiatrist, and home visits from the psychiatric social worker. The general approach was 'to use the simplest possible procedure which will attain the desired results…simple advice…special teaching', while attending to the strained relations within the family.[87]

What is less often emphasised is the role of child guidance in liberalising child rearing (although it is difficult to assess the extent of this influence): it rejected the idea that 'naughtiness' and 'original sin' could be remedied through discipline in favour of the newer scientific view that treatment for behavioural problems required familiarity with numerous causal threads that had to be disentangled and understood through recognising the psycho-dynamic quality of a child's life. Referring to children as 'incorrigible, nervy, highly strung or backward' merely described symptoms but explained nothing.[88] At the East London Clinic, for example, referral was rarely for 'emotional disturbances such as fear, anxiety, depression and excessive shyness', rather the most frequently mentioned complaints were for 'stealing, lying, unmanageability at home or at school, and educational backwardness'. On diagnosis the position was almost reversed: 'behavioural disorders as referred, 54 per cent – as diagnosed 41 per cent; nervous disorders as referred 4 per cent – as diagnosed 41 per cent', followed by habit disorders, speech defects, enuresis and sleeping and eating difficulties.[89] Underlying much of the diagnostic thrust of child guidance, and yet another feature of its influence, was the psychoanalytic theme that contributed so much to the understanding of childhood, namely that 'Learning to Drive is child's play, compared with – Learning to Live!…Learning to Live is harder – if courage fails fears, anxiety, shyness and failure takes its place.'[90] Thus it was no throwaway remark of the psychiatrist Bernard Hart when he advised that in order to guide effectively, 'we must begin with the conception of the child as a psycho-physical organism reacting to an environment composed of material, mental and social constituents'.[91]

The view among many psycho medics, educationalists, and welfare workers was that since the nature of the parent–child relationship was usually involved in the production of nervous and behavioural

---

[87] CGC Report, (1933), p 4, quoted in Hendrick (2003), p 106.

[88] Stewart (2013), p 85.

[89] Hendrick (2003), p 105.

[90] A flyer for the London Clinic, quoted in Stewart (2013), p 86; also E. Miller (1930) 'Early Treatment and Prevention', in his *Modern Psychotherapy*, London: Jonathan Cape, p 62.

[91] B. Hart (1931) *British Medical Journal*, 19 September, 'The Work of a Child Guidance Clinic', p 528.

disorders, parenting education was desirable if only to remind parents that they 'are not potters to mould clay, but gardeners to protect bulbs'. Douglas MacCalman, Secretary General of the CGC, wondered if it was a 'visionary dream…[that] a vast system of parent education could be organized?'[92] MacCalman looked to such an education to promote '[l]ove, thought, gentleness, serenity and a real desire to enter into the life of the child…and to see the child's point of view'. Such was 'the basis for an unhampered, sound and happy personality in the child, and for a quiet triumph over the early problems of babyhood'.[93] Not everyone, however, was so positive. William Moodie, Director of the London Clinic, was always keen (more so than many others in the new psychology) to emphasise that 'All social life depends on discipline.' But even he cautioned parents to exercise both 'authority and kindness'.[94] The objective behind this kind of parent education was to spread the message of the new psychology, namely that at a time of doubt as to the prospects of 'civilization and the ability of modern urban living to provide a good environment for mental health', its subjects were changing, rather than being merely a 'fixed, biological heritage in constant dialogue with environment'.[95] Psychology's ambitious undertaking was not merely to record human nature, but to change it.[96] In familiarising parents with the perceptions of the psychoanalytic 'turn', those involved – within and beyond the child guidance clinic – were determined to embed themselves culturally in the subjectivity of what those in the know called 'modernity'. And with the social and political aftermath of the mass slaughter in the trenches in mind, who could dispute the urgency of the task in hand.

The influence of progressive education

The relevance of 'progressive' education here is twofold. First, through spreading 'the faith', those educationalists committed to the progressive ideal, and with more than an eye on the new psychology, sought to introduce children (mainly of the middle class) to what they thought

---

92 Quoted in Stewart (2013), p 1.

93 D. R. MacCalman (1937) 'Address to Mothers: Familiar Problems of Child Upbringing', *Mother and Child*, 8, 3, pp 90–1, also quoted in Stewart (2013), p 89.

94 W. Moodie (1931) 'Some Problems of Childhood: Methods of Treatment', *Mother and Child*, 2, 7, pp 259–61.

95 G. Behlmer (1998) *Friends and Family: The English Home and its Guardians, 1850–1940*, Stanford: Stanford University Press, p 166.

96 Thomson (2006), p 61.

of as 'Higher Values', as opposed to those of the technocratic, scientific society in which they found themselves, and which horrified them in its lack of imagination, freedom and humanistic values.[97] Second, in proposing new ways of knowing children: seeing them, listening to them and, no less important, of being with them, progressives sought to reconstitute existing age relations, both inside and outside the classroom. There is little doubt that the progressive programme was radical – although there were numerous pathways to the progressive millennium, many of which were at odds with one another while straddling a spectrum from the mildly liberal to what often seemed crankish. The majority of participants, however, subscribed to the following beliefs: child psychology differed from that of adults; more attention should be paid to children's wishes and needs; children should be encouraged to explore their worlds and be given a large amount of free expression; and discipline should be minimal, usually without punishment, and always free of violence. What all this amounted to was a belief in the importance of self-realisation, in part attained through children practising self-government, despite it being a vague and confusing notion.

The origins of educational progressivism can be seen in both the Froebel movement (with its emphasis on learning by doing, the importance of play, and the use of objects rather than words in teaching practice for young children) and to a lesser extent Child Study groups (with their interest in mental and physical development), as they developed from the late nineteenth century. Perhaps also the new educational ideas were 'the last legacy' of the utopian impulse of the early twentieth century.[98] Among many educationalists there was certainly a mood of dissatisfaction with the existing system. In this vein, one of the first clarion calls for the renewal of human nature through education for self-realisation came from Edmond Holmes, a Theosophist and a government schools inspector, in his *What is and What Might Be* (1911). Describing elementary education, he wrote: 'Blind, passive, literal, unintelligent obedience is the basis on which the whole system of Western education has been reared.' The manifesto contributed to Edwardian debates concerning the role of education in human affairs at a time of considerable intellectual and political ferment, as did the opening of Homer Lane's radical and idiosyncratically Freudian influenced 'Little Commonwealth' for delinquent children in

---

[97] Graham, pp 104–5; R. Skidelsky (1969) *English Progressive Schools*, London, Penguin Books, p 245.

[98] Thomson (2006), p 118.

1913, and Maria Montessori's *The Montessori Method* (1912), although it presented 'freedom', 'individuality' and 'independence' in a less radical form than either Holmes or Lane. In this climate, the 'New Education' produced the progressives.[99]

It was, however, with the 1914–18 war, and the national introspective mood that accompanied its aftermath, that exploration of the meaning of 'education' provided the opportunity for the establishment of progressive schools. The post-war loss of confidence in Christian 'civilisation' encouraged a questioning of established norms and, in further undermining conventional liberal thought and its association with a linear account of Progress, the Freudian insurrection cast doubt not only on who the self was, but also on whether it was possible to ever to locate its source. In the enthusiasm for international organisations with the founding of the League of Nations, the New Education Fellowship (under the influence of Theosophy, the New Psychology, and strands of Freudianism), was established in 1921 with branches throughout Europe and the USA.[100] Less than a year earlier, the first issue of *Education for the New Era* appeared, setting the task of education as 'fostering the spirit of democratic brotherhood' in international and personal relations. This was the sustaining vision. The editor, the Theosophist Beatrice Ensor, an ex–Board of Education inspector, optimistically declared that 'Freedom, and Tolerance and Understanding have burst the doors so carefully locked upon them in the secret chambers of the souls of men, and are at present spreading abroad under the restlessness and destruction of these times.'[101]

Although many of the progressives saw themselves as Freudian, it is probably correct to say that the central theory of the New Education can be expressed in Jungian terms of 'Making the unconscious conscious', which involved 'removing the repressive forces…and…channelling… the libido, gently and with love, understanding and patience, into its authentic mode of expression', thus enabling individuals to realise their full potentialities.[102] Much of the faith in this self-realisation stemmed from the progressives' belief in the child's ability to self-educate. According to Mrs Ensor, 'all powers and capacities lie within the child, and…therefore, all education must be auto-education. The

---

[99] Selleck (1972), pp 3–31.

[100] W. Boyd and W. Rawson (1965) *The Story of the New Education*, London: Heinemann Educational; N. Whitbread (1972) *The Evolution of the Nursery-Infant School, 1800-1970*, London: Routledge and Kegan Paul, p 88.

[101] Ensor, quoted in Skidelsky (1969), p 141.

[102] Skidelsky (1969), pp 144–5.

function of the educator lies simply in the provision of external stimuli needed to start the process of auto-education along the avenues by which consciousness contacts environment.'[103] The substance of this approach, showing the influence of Susan Isaacs, was also accepted at official level in the Board of Education *Report on Infant and Nursery Schools* (1933), which stated: 'any realistic view of education must consider the infant school not as a place of instruction, but as an instructive environment in which the child, under the sympathetic care of his teacher, may cultivate his own garden'.[104] It is important to appreciate that the progressives were always concerned with much more than new techniques for learning or the scientific study of child development. Above all, they sought to contribute to the making of a new kind of world – a 'New Era' – whose citizens would have achieved a self-realised freedom of mind and spirit, and be internationalist and pacifist in outlook. Whether 'free expression' would produce such a citizen was never really explored. In truth, the progressives hoped that the children would evolve in the image of their ideals.

One of the core objections to progressive education was that it allowed the children too much freedom for their own good, jettisoned discipline in favour of licence, produced chaos in the classroom, encouraged selfishness and the development of individuals without self-control. Of course, terms such as discipline and freedom are problematic since their meaning is so subjective, and there were certainly conflicting views among the progressives. Montessori put her emphasis on 'active discipline' by which she meant self-discipline. Repressive discipline, she said, destroyed individuality.[105] Homer Lane, in his treatment of delinquent children, believed simply that 'a bad boy is an example of good qualities wrongly directed'. The 'cure' lay in being 'on the side' of the boys; in trusting their 'good' qualities and by allowing them 'self-regulation'.[106] A. S. Neill, taking his cue from Lane, was 'extreme' in this matter, as is clear from the contents of his prolific literary output.[107] Neill, who tended to think

---

[103] Quoted, Skidelsky (1969), p 148.

[104] Board of Education (1933) *Report on Infant and Nursery Schools*, London: Board of Education, p xviii.

[105] Whitbread (1972), p 5.

[106] Quoted in Skidelsky (1969), p 137; see also H. Lane (1928) *Talks to Parents and Teachers*, London: Allen and Unwin.

[107] For example, A. S. Neill (1932) *The Problem Parent*, London: Herbert Jenkins; (1937) *That Dreadful School*, London: Herbert Jenkins; and (1939) *The Problem Teacher*, London: Herbert Jenkins.

in terms of 'troubled' or delinquent children, saw externally imposed discipline as an extension of the coercion and moralising that had originally produced the delinquent condition. Against this and other progressive views, critics claimed that children should not have 'free speech' since they were psychologically incapable of managing their thoughts and emotions; others argued that 'free expression' was an illusion concealing the progressives' ideological objectives.[108] Percy Nunn, however, one of the most influential figures, claimed it as a fact that 'the records of psychoanalysis greatly strengthen the argument for making the autonomous development of the individual the central aim of education. They reveal…how disastrous it may sometimes be to force upon the growing character a form discordant with its principle of unity.'[109] And Freud certainly influenced several books on teaching.[110] Nonetheless, Susan Isaacs was also cautious about giving children 'too much' freedom. But according to one ex-teacher at the school she ran between 1924 and 1927, although there were some rules, Isaacs wished to show that these were not 'unalterable laws' and could be relaxed and changed; generally, 'discipline is very free. There is no punishment and little admonition.' Significantly, Isaacs, in common with not only British psychoanalysis, but also the progressive inter-war intellectual climate as it responded to the 'crises', was trying to discover what the balance should be between 'complete freedom' and 'complete control', and she always believed that 'control and authority needs to be both appropriate and loving…and exercised with understanding'.[111]

Progressive education was a cultural spur in the history of inter-war Britain. It can be likened to a tributary seeping into the flux of debates surrounding science and psychology, the critique of behaviourism, the aspirations of child guidance, and the host of vexed anxieties concerning western civilisation's neurotic insecurity. For many progressives, escaping from the consequences of uncertainty had to include the emancipation of the child through holistic education. The culture of the progressives, mixed bunch though they were, infused not only the specifics of educational theory and classroom practice, but also

---

[108] Cited in Thomson (2006), p 124.

[109] P. Nunn (1920) *Education: Its Data and First Principles*, London: Longmans Green and Co, p 55.

[110] N. MacMunn (1921) *The Child's Path to Freedom*, London: J. Curwen and Sons; H. C. Miller (1927) *The New Psychology and the Teacher*, London: Jarrolds; D. Revel (1928) *Cheiron's Cave: The School of the Future*, London: Heinemann.

[111] D. E. M. Gardner (1969) *Susan Isaacs*, London: Methuen, pp 58–64; Quotation in Smith (1985), p 297.

the mint in which adult–child relations were being re-imagined as part of the melee surrounding Freudianism's challenge to modernity. This is not to claim that the progressives played a significant role, but they were present doing their bit. In the culture where adults 'saw' and 'heard' children very imperfectly, the progressives questioned established procedural norms and proposed different, more liberal and more humane practices.

Freud, it hardly needs saying, was not a comforting sage. Perhaps it is strange, then, that so many of those who sought to advance progressive attitudes to child rearing and education should have been influenced, however little, by his theories – although many were only dimly aware of the tradition in which they worked. Others, however, knew full well what they were doing, albeit that they read him in their own way, and often in conflict with Jung. For many of the most influential voices in both child guidance and progressive nursery and infant education, the overall objective was to correct, through the application of reason, what appeared to occur in its absence – the upsurge of unreason and the irrational – in human affairs, which, as the chorus of despair at the time pronounced, had led to murderous aggression and a phalanx of personal neuroses. One of the paradoxes of Freudianism was its use of 'reason' to counter its declared despondency about the fortitude of reason to withstand the culture's predicament.[112] In all probability progressives of diverse persuasions took the idea of crisis as a warning of what might be, and not wholly as an indictment of what was.

The emphasis on psychoanalytic parenting as a way of 'helping' and 'understanding' children and parents (concepts that were so critical in the language of Isaacs, the child guidance movement, and throughout progressive education), was indicative of the belief among the psychological fraternity that it *was* possible to save human nature from total corruption, a necessary first step in preventing self-destruction. Thus many of them countered Freud's melancholic pessimism with the drizzle of a Jungian sense of hope. In this way they sought to establish a new relationship between discipline and freedom – the essence of a dialectic which, we should remember, had long preceded Freud as it rumbled through the Enlightenment, the industrial revolution, nineteenth-century Liberalism, and the revolution in the social sciences. And they were concerned not only for their relations with children and the emotional harmony of their families, but also on the grand scale with the threat of the annihilation of liberal values, which very nearly came to pass during 1939–45. It is this life-affirming ambition

---

[112] Richards (2000), p 188.

that is one of the principal differences between their expositions during the inter-war years of what parenting involved, and should involve, and what has come to be our own frail, yet posturing narcissism in its presence. On reflection, perhaps it was not such a 'low dishonest decade' after all.

Looking ahead

In what might be seen as in the fading wisps of the 'morbid age', a new kind of babycare manual arrived from the United States: C and M Aldrich's *Understand Your Baby* (1939) (US title *Babies are Human Beings*, 1938), which consciously looked toward what was seen to be a precarious wartime future. But it was also something of a clarion call for the recognition of children as *individual* persons and for their emancipation from parental ignorance of child development. The original title was significant in pointedly identifying babies as human beings, an identity that had been overlooked by the behaviourists. The British title, however, was important because, no doubt knowingly, it referenced the emphasis of the new psychology on the necessity of 'understanding' children if the psychodynamics of family emotions were to function smoothly, thereby, it was hoped, minimising present and future neuroses. In addition to sympathetically presenting the child's struggle with 'adaptive change' to the external environment, the Aldriches described the baby's way of doing things, explaining that 'babies are different' and how 'the baby responds to the world', while emphasising the need for 'warmth, cuddling, freedom of action and pleasant associations with food and sleep' rather than pushing these 'out of the way to make room for technique'.[113] In the USA, this was just the first of several manuals in what was to become the highly influential new liberal approach to child rearing – the 'fun morality' as it was later called. British readers would have found much of what the Aldriches wrote to be in a similar register to that of Susan Isaacs' advice column in *Nursery World*, as well as the recommendations of child guidance, and the many pronouncements of the progressive movement in education. In this respect, *Understand Your Baby* can serve as a bridge between the trend in inter-war child rearing towards more sensitive attitudes on the part of parents and, more generally, the wartime focus on the effects of evacuation, the origin of the image of 'the welfare child', and the projection of 'the child' as integral to the democratic family ideal.

---

[113] C. A and M. M. Aldrich (1939), *Understand Your Baby*, London: Black, p 120.

TWO

Wartime influences: from the evacuation to the Children Act 1948

There is not much doubt that the 'rediscovery' of the value of the family occurred during the Second World War. In many respects, this was both the culmination of numerous debates about the family dating from the late Victorian and Edwardian periods, and the beginning of a new social and political emphasis on its envisaged role as a core institution in the post-war welfare state, the centre-piece in what was to be an emancipatory social democracy.[1] At the end of the nineteenth century, social surveys had revealed the nature and extent of family poverty in response to which the Edwardian Liberal government began to create selective remedial services for particular needy groups – the sick, the unemployed, the elderly and children. With the onset of the inter-war slump and national austerity programmes, the condition of poor families became the subject of bitter controversy regarding levels of maintenance and standards of health and welfare.[2] As the evacuation experience was to show, despite the rising standard of living for the population as a whole, a large proportion, particularly the children of the poor, were malnourished and physically and mentally impaired. During the inter-war years, however, the family lost most of its prestige, as problems of old age, child neglect, delinquency, unemployment and mental instability were treated in a variety of institutions: the workhouse, the orphanage, the hospital, the reformatory and the prison, exemplifying the hygienist belief in preventing social contamination.[3] Moreover, although social science had identified the supportive nature of the family as a group, the *concept* of 'the family' in social theory lacked political influence. Only as a result of wartime disruption, especially the physical, social, and psychological upheaval caused by evacuation and the blitz was the strength of intra-familial relationships properly recognised and appreciated as being of communal

---

[1]   H. Hendrick (2003) *Child Welfare: Historical Dimensions, Contemporary Debate*, Bristol: The Policy Press, pp 19–86.

[2]   Hendrick (2003), pp 87–98.

[3]   J. Heywood (1978 edn) *Children in Care: The Development of the Service for the Deprived Child*, London: Routledge Kegan Paul, p 134.

and civic significance, and as institutionally necessary for good mental health. Thus by the end of the war few political interests doubted that the rebuilding of the family would be integral to the development of the post-war world.

Notwithstanding the familiarity of the material presented here, my hope is that it will be interpreted in such a way as to contribute to the dual purpose of this part of the book, namely in showing how and why age relations were developing through what were in effect processes of cultural change, and how these developments reflected new approaches to the family, what it was and what it should be. Inter-war social change, as we have seen, was significantly influenced by the emerging 'psychological complex', which did so much to promote new and more democratic forms of parenting based on psychoanalytic understandings of the mind of the child. This chapter shows the ways in which this development was further advanced during the war, primarily through the psychological and social research surrounding the evacuation schemes. But evacuation also brought with it revelations affecting both the concept of the family as an institution, and the social and economic conditions in which it lived, the latter giving birth to the idea of the 'problem family'. While this family posed difficulties for aspiring to what was thought of as the social-democratic ideal, it by no means undermined the goal since it was believed that it could be rehabilitated. Although children could be at risk, and the issue of child cruelty was raised, the general view was that this was not a priority. The more important concern by the end of the war was how to provide for children who for one reason or another were deprived of a 'normal home life' and, as the 1950s advanced, how to *prevent* children from coming into care in the first place. The chapter argues that the passing of legislation to supervise and humanise the care of these children helped to confirm not only the inter-war trend in the re-imagining of age relations, but also the importance of the 'ordinary good home'.

The evacuation

The government evacuation schemes initiated one of the most significant mass migrations of modern times. There were three waves of voluntary evacuation under official direction. During the first, beginning in September 1939, approximately 1.5 million people (826,959 unaccompanied schoolchildren, 523,670 mothers with pre-school children, and a further 7,000 children with disabilities) left dangerous urban areas for safe reception centres around Britain, where they were billeted on often reluctant hosts in return for a government allowance. Within a few months, some 900,000 evacuees had drifted home, including the majority of mothers with young children. The second wave came with the Blitz on London in the autumn of 1940 when some 1,250,000 adults and children were relocated, the majority returning home as the danger subsided. The third wave began with the flying bomb attacks in the summer of 1944 when 307,000 mothers and children left London and the south-east, and a further 552,000 mothers and children, together with old people and the homeless left under their own arrangements but with some government assistance. In addition, an estimated 2 million mainly middle-class children were privately evacuated, many of them moving abroad. Although London figures prominently in histories of evacuation, other major evacuating areas in England included Manchester, Liverpool, Newcastle, Birmingham, Salford, Leeds, Portsmouth, Southampton and Gateshead.[4] This, then, was an important experiment in social migration, albeit of a temporary nature, which understandably attracted widespread social scientific interest.

The reaction

The received post-war historical view of the effects of evacuation was that it helped to break down social class barriers and also those between town and country, thereby solidifying a sense of national unity, while also stimulating middle-class consciences into promoting social reform. From the 1980s, however, a revisionist interpretation of the Home Front began to appear, which concluded that 'the ideological consensus of wartime…was something of a myth' and that far from witnessing the emergence of a sympathetic attitude towards the poor, the older inter-war notion of 'the social problem group' gave way to that of the problem family.[5] That the anticipated beneficial effect of

---

4   J. Welshman (2010) *Churchill's Children: The Evacuee Experience in Wartime Britain*, Oxford: Oxford University Press.

5   R. Titmuss (1950) *Problems of Social Policy*, London: HMSO/Longmans Green; J. Macnicol (1986) 'The Evacuation of School Children', in H. L. Smith (ed) *War and Social Change: British Society During the Second World War*, Manchester: Manchester University Press, 3–31; J. Harris (1986) 'Political Ideas and the Debate on the Welfare State', in Smith (ed) (1986), pp 233–63; (1992) 'War and Social History: Britain and the Home Front during the Second World War', *Contemporary European History*, 1, 1, pp 17–35; J. Welshman (1998), 'Evacuation and Social Policy During the Second World War: Myth and Reality', *Twentieth Century British History*, 9, 1, pp 28–53.

the evacuation lived up to expectation for many thousands of billeted children is not in doubt, as their fond memories later testified. But it could hardly be said of the experiment as a whole. In addition to the scheme being badly thought out and often poorly organised by middle-class public school educated government ministers and civil servants who had no experience of children, mothering or working-class family life: 'Personality clashes, religious hatreds, differing habits of speech and behaviour, and old fashioned xenophobia all played a role' in casting evacuation as less than a qualified success.[6] The child evacuees, many from the slums, confronted a welter of hostility and prejudice.[7] Nonetheless, the claim that 'the unkempt, ill-clothed, undernourished and often incontinent children of bombed cities acted as messengers carrying the evidence of the deprivation of urban working-class life into rural hones' is not without substance.[8] True, it is clear from the protests of host families and surveys undertaken by middle-class investigators that the message was not always welcomed, but it was heard and eventually acted upon. Evacuation was important as an agent of social change in that it was a catalyst that helped to bring about welcome changes in social policies for children's well-being, while cohering demands for post-war reconstruction.

At the instigation of the National Federation of Women's Institutes (whose members had been shocked at the attitudes and behaviours they claimed to have found among the evacuees), the Women's Group on Public Welfare (WGPW) conducted a detailed investigation into the social condition of the urban poor, drawing on evacuation as 'the window through which town life was seen'.[9] It was clear from adverse host reactions to the children that the assurances of inter-war governments to have protected their health and welfare were largely unfounded, since so many of them arrived wearing poor quality clothing and shoes, and suffering from bad teeth, malnutrition and

---

[6]   M. L. Parsons (1998) *'I'll Take That One': Dispelling the Myths of Civilian Evacuation, 1939-45*, Peterborough: Beckett Karlson, pp 185–211.

[7]   T. Crosby (1986) *The Impact of Civilian Evacuation in the Second World War*, London: Croom Helm, pp 3, 5–10.

[8]   D. Fraser (1984) *The Evolution of the British Welfare State*, London: Macmillan, p 195; B. Wicks (1988) *No Time to Say Goodbye*, London: Bloomsbury, p xi. For contrary views, see the debate on 'the home front' in J. Welshman (1999), 'Evacuation, Hygiene, and Social Policy: The *Our Towns* Survey of 1943', *Historical Journal*, 42, 3, pp 781–807.

[9]   Women's Group on Public Welfare (WGPW) (1943) *Our Towns: A Close-Up*, London: Oxford University Press; Welshman (1999).

verminous bodies.[10] Investigators were appalled to discover among the evacuees what they claimed was their ignorance of basic table manners, any familiarity with flushing toilets and, most bitterly complained about, the apparent predilection for nocturnal bed-wetting (a major issue because it necessitated constant washing of bed linen). Many of these problems were attributed to behavioural weaknesses among wives and mothers, usually those found in the much maligned 'problem families'. Unlike the 'social problem group', however, which figured in social surveys in the 1930s, whose members were regarded as mentally and morally deficient, the problem family could be rehabilitated.[11] Among the characteristics of these families were 'wasteful spending' and the 'slum diet' (held to be responsible for much of child malnourishment); similarly skin disease and head lice were attributed to 'neglectful' parents who, the WGPW report urged, should be prosecuted and made subject to intensive education campaigns. In order to encourage cleanliness in relation to skin disease, physical training, swimming and games were recommended. In response to children's inadequate clothing and footwear, the report advised needlework classes for parents, boot and shoe making classes for older children, and instruction in tailoring, mending and knitting for boys. In many respects, the WGPW clearly thought along conservative lines in emphasising individual responsibility. But in acknowledging that evacuation had revealed a 'new angle' of town life, especially the light it threw upon the home conditions, the authors also distinguished between behavioural and environmental factors, such as the effects of overcrowding, unemployment and low wages, giving due consideration to each as a cause of poverty and domestic distress.[12] In its recommendations, while emphasising the importance of education in household management and parental discipline, the report called for improvements in housing, children's allowances, security of employment, and for reforms in health and welfare services. On publication, it's balanced and informed account made it an important focus for discussion on the rebuilding of the post-war family.

---

[10]   For details, see Hendrick (2003), pp 124–8.

[11]   J. Macnicol (1987) 'In Pursuit of the Underclass', *Journal of Social Policy*, 16, pp 293–318.

[12]   The report also criticised the inter-war official statistics for giving too optimistic a picture of social progress, and 'trade and industry' for failing to recognise their 'economic' and 'moral' duties to communities WGPW (1943), pp xi, xvi, xviii–xix.

The psycho-social impact of evacuation and returning home

One of the main values of evacuation from the psycho-medical perspective, following as it did the inter-war psychoanalytic characterisation of childhood, was that in undertaking such a huge geographical displacement of children, the schemes revealed the scale of hitherto hidden physical and mental ill health among the urban working-class child population.[13] No less significant, evacuation was also a proving ground for testing hypotheses about the strength of the child's ability to withstand trauma of various kinds, including the impact of the blitz, death and injury of loved ones, and separation from parents, family and friends through being abruptly moved to new families, new localities, and new schools. John Bowlby, Donald Winnicott and Susan Isaacs were among those who expressed their reservations about evacuation with respect to the likely emotional consequences of separation for young children.[14] Once the schemes were under way, numerous local, regional and national surveys were undertaken which, when combined with inter-war psychoanalytic research, represented the most intensive study of children's emotional wellbeing ever attempted in Britain, so much so that the children were 'seen' and 'heard' on a scale unknown in the past.[15] The overall and uncertain conclusion was that in terms of *serious* mental distress (breakdown, psychotic behaviour, violence) children's reactions generally appeared to be less damaging than had been anticipated. But, as post-war evacuee testimonies would show, it was necessary to distinguish between those children who clearly required child guidance treatment and those who *seemed* to be able to cope with their anxieties. The cause of the mental upset might be in experiencing enemy bombing raids, being sent away from home as an evacuee or, what turned out to be just as disturbing for many children (and their parents), returning home after months or years with a host family. Concerns referred to the scale of

---

[13] J. Stewart (2013) *Child Guidance in Britain, 1918–1955*, London: Pickering & Chatto, p 109.

[14] S. Van Dijken (1998) *John Bowlby: is Early Life. A Biographical Journey into the Roots of Attachment Theory*, London: Free Association Books, p 108.

[15] In addition to numerous local surveys and reports, the more well-known comprehensive reports included: S. Isaacs (ed) (1940) *The Cambridge Evacuation Survey: A Wartime Study in Social Welfare and Education*, London: Methuen; Barnett House (1947) *London Children in Wartime Oxford: A Survey if Social and Educational Results of Evacuation*, London: Oxford University Press; R. Padley and M. Cole (1940) *Evacuation Survey*, Report to the Fabian Society, London: Routledge; W. Boyd (ed) (1944) *Evacuation in Scotland: A Record of Events and Experiments*, Bickley, Kent: University of London Press.

less conspicuous trauma (and how to define and measure it), and its long-term consequences for children's emotional and psychological development. The fear was that within the seemingly stable home, there lurked a level of mental ill health, or at least emotional instability, that could be damaging for the individual child, the family and, not least, the evolution of social democracy.

A survey of the research literature on the effects of evacuation on children (nearly 200 studies), published in 1945 by the American psychologist Katherine Wolf, found almost no unanimity among researchers.[16] However, two studies by Anna Freud and her colleague Dorothy Burlingham, were especially influential in their consideration of nursery children's responses to bombing and destruction, tensions in foster families, being separated from their mothers (notably the manner of the separation), and the fate of parent–child relations thereafter.[17] Particular attention was given to the normal and abnormal 'outlets' whereby young children coped with their upset, including speech, play, 'phantasy', regression and general conduct.[18] One of the core claims made by Freud and Burlingham was that the behaviour of mothers in dangerous situations greatly influenced how their children reacted; another was that abrupt separation of children from mothers seemed to cause disturbing emotional distress with the children developing new fears and regressing developmentally. The mother, they concluded, was a crucial figure in the development of the young child's 'ability to love'.[19] Nonetheless, Wolf identified numerous methodological problems in the literature as a whole: no agreed methodology on statistics, lack of comparable material with children in peacetime, no tabulation of children's age, no dates given regarding at what stage during evacuation research was carried out, and no agreement on desirable qualitative levels. Moreover, no clear distinction was made between the 'formation of a neurosis…and the child's adaptation or maladjustment to his foster home'.[20] Where adaptation to the billet was the issue, there was virtually no agreement as to the effects of the

---

16 K. Wolf (1945), 'The Evacuation of Children in Wartime', *Psychoanalytic Study of the Child*, 1, pp 389–404.

17 D. Burlingham and A. Freud (1942) *Young Children in War-Time: A Year's Work in a Residential War Nursery*, London: Allen and Unwin, pp 41–62, 75ff; A. Freud and D. Burlingham (1944) *Infants Without Families: The Case For and Against Residential Nurseries*, London: Allen and Unwin.

18 Burlingham and Freud (1942), pp 62–75.

19 Freud and Burlingham (1944), pp 129–30.

20 Wolf (1945), pp 300–91.

psychological processes involved, except that adaptation itself *appeared* to be 'surprisingly high'. However, the main statistic in support of this conclusion came from just a single study claiming that only 46 out of 689 children were unable to adapt. When it came to the influence of the billet on the child's general behaviour, according to Wolf, the descriptions of behavioural change were on 'a superficial level'.[21] There was also no agreement as to whether evacuation *created* neuroses, in part because of the lack of relevant evidence on the incidence of child neuroses *prior* to the event.[22] Even so, Wolf thought it was safe to say that between 25 and 44 per cent of evacuated children suffered *neurotic* disorders, about one third of whom either acquired or suffered an aggravation of their condition owing to their experience. But identifying the individual responsible factors proved to be impossible, except that it seemed the child's age was of considerable influence. As regards other consequences, besides the lack of concentration among the school-age children, far more frequently mentioned was enuresis, 'the dominant symptom of the syndrome of evacuation neurosis'.[23] One study suggested a figure of 80 per cent of children 'immediately after evacuation' (however, in her Cambridge survey, Susan Isaacs found only 48 per cent of evacuees who attended the child guidance clinic to be enuretic). Cyril Burt, the doyen of British psychologists at the time, claimed that with evacuation there had been a 50 per cent increase of enuresis compared with the rate in peace time.[24] This seemed to be confirmed by the only other area of broad agreement found in the evacuation literature, which was that while the level of neurosis *formation* among evacuees was 'relatively low', their anxiety states were clearly apparent.

One of the most striking discoveries, noted by virtually all those who worked with the children, which was to be of the utmost influence on post-war socio-political thought in relation to child welfare services and the promotion of the social democratic family ideal, was that children's capacity to deal with evacuation (and also the effects of bombing) appeared to depend on their *prior* parental relationship, whether it was stable or one of conflict.[25] This seemed to confirm Bowlby's view, first stated in 1940 and reiterated many times in his subsequent work, and which was increasingly accepted throughout

---

[21] Wolf (1945), p 393.

[22] Wolf (1945), p 394.

[23] Wolf (1945), pp 395–96.

[24] Cited in Wolf (1945), p 395.

[25] Wolf (1945), p 396.

the social work and mental health professions, namely that '(E)very human being draws emotional sustenance and strength from those few people who constitute his home. Love and friendship are as vital to…the child, as bread and coal' – 'The child who feels happy and safe in his own home is the child who settles best in a foster-home. It is the child who has felt unhappy and insecure at home who finds it most difficult to leave it', although only a minority of children 'are seriously affected'.[26] Burlingham and Freud added their prestige to this view in noting that while everyone agreed 'that the lack of 'essential foods, vitamins, etc.,' in early childhood caused permanent bodily injury, it was not yet understood that 'the same was true for the mental development of the child', otherwise 'lasting psychological malformations will be the consequence…these essential elements are the need for personal attachment, for emotional stability, and for the permanency of educational influence'.[27]

Many observers noticed that linked to children's sense of security was their loyalty to parents, home and neighbourhood. In the letters older children wrote about their evacuation it was clear 'how dominant in their feelings is the love of home, of parents, of brothers and sisters, how intensely even the happily placed child may feel the loss of his own family'.[28] Above all else, children reported missing their parents. But, as a later survey grasped, 'they felt something more than a sentimental homesickness; rather they were aware of a strong natural affection holding the family together and a sense of "belonging" to a particular place and people'.[29] Susan Isaacs noted that the quick return home of many children 'emphasized still more deeply the crucial importance of family ties and the feelings of parents and children towards and about each other…The feeling of family unity and the intense resistance to its being broken up was apparent, too, in the reasons parents gave for not wishing to send their children away again'.[30] Once the bombing of the East End commenced, which necessitated renewed evacuation, Isaacs added in a footnote what many investigators, to their surprise, had recognised and which turned out to be significant for future policy, including attitudes toward the problem family:

---

[26] J. Bowlby (1940) 'Psychological Aspects', in Padley and Cole, pp 186, 188; (1951) *Maternal Care and Mental Health*, Geneva: WHO; also his (1953) *Child Care and the Growth of Love*, Harmondsworth: Penguin Books.

[27] Burlingham and Freud (1942), p 10.

[28] Isaacs (1940), p 7.

[29] Barnett House Study Group (1947), pp 107–9.

[30] Isaacs (1940), pp 7–8.

we have seen how this need to keep the family together and to cling to familiar home surroundings may override even the worst dangers. Among the simple and the poor, where there is no wealth, no pride of status or of possessions, love for the members of one's own family and joy in their bodily presence alone makes life worth living. So deeply rooted is this need that it has defied even the law of self-preservation, as well as urgent public appeals and the wishes of authority.[31]

The importance of preserving 'home and family' also became clear as reports from nurses and social workers in attendance at London Rest Centres for victims of the blitz saw how young children seemed to be better able to withstand the physical and emotional distress caused by the bombing, if it occurred while they were with their parents and siblings. This was later confirmed by Burlingham and Freud who argued that while the war was of comparatively little significance for young children so long as it was only a physical threat, it became 'enormously significant the moment it breaks up family life and uproots the first emotional attachments of the child within the family group'.[32]

Moreover, as Katherine Wolf appreciated, the child–parent relationships involved were not straightforward. She saw evacuation producing:

> a process in the child's mental apparatus that in turn adapts this apparatus to a separation from parents for an indefinite period. The child suspends his relationship to his parents for this given time. This creates a vagueness in his image of his home and probably produces a disturbance of his perceptive and imaginative processes in general…This arrangement seems to make adaptation…fairly successful and explains the low incidence of neurosis formation in children who did not show neurotic symptoms prior to evacuation.[33]

Wolf developed this analysis into a perceptive conclusion that encapsulates something of the sentiment that would come to be so influential in engendering the post-war social-democratic family. Children, she wrote, interpreted their role 'as a wartime guest very literally'. The child was:

---

[31] Isaacs (1940), p 9.

[32] Burlingham and Freud (1942), pp 29, 41.

[33] Wolf (1945), p 397.

only a guest, but a guest at a party, which was not of his choosing. Therefore he did not want to think too clearly of his losses. The child preferred to be a "War Time Guest" rather than a "Borrowed Child". In preserving his home somewhere in his mind, and in not allowing the new home to become a rival, the normal child from a normal home could adapt to the situation.[34]

Lest it be thought that this is an invitation to see children simply as resilient, protecting themselves from the tidings of the emotional storm, and that evacuation was of little or no consequence, it is now clear from thousands of adult testimonies that the experience was hardly ever without social and psychological consequences, and was never forgotten. Understanding the impact of evacuation on children has been compared to 'reading by a dark lamp', but if memoirists are to be believed, their experiences usually had a life-long impact on the psyche: either as 'scars that will never heal' or as 'memories...cherished[ed] to the end of their days'.[35] For many children, their situation created complex emotions that were raw and disturbing. One woman recalling her unhappy evacuation as a teenager, felt that 'the legacy has been a lifelong effort to cope with the feelings of isolation, loss of love and affection, a numbness, a deep searching for home and belonging'.[36]

By the end of 1945, Donald Winnicottt had made three radio broadcasts explaining in his own distinctive 'Freudian' language the emotional trials and tribulations of the returning child, which he hoped would lead to the spread of 'much-needed understanding of child care'. The first was addressed to the foster parents of the billeted child, the second to parents of the returning child, and the third explained what it meant for the child to be 'home again'.[37] Winnicott warned that there was a limit to the ability of both parents and children to keep alive their 'idea' of loved ones (when evacuation had lasted for

---

34 Wolf (1945), p 398.

35 Quotations in J. Summers (2011) *When the Children Came Home: Stories from Wartime Evacuees*, London: pp 246–306; also B. S. Johnson (1968) *The Evacuees*, London: Gollancz; Wicks (1988), pp 201, 71–105; R. Inglis (1989) *The Children's War: Evacuation 1939–1945*, London: Collins, pp 147–67.

36 Quoted in Summers (2011), p 246; also J. S. Rusby and F. Tasker (2009) 'Long-term Effects of the British Evacuation of Children During World War 2 on their Adult Mental Health', *Aging Mental Health*, 13, 3, pp 391–404.

37 D. W. Winnicott (1957) *The Child and the Outside World*, London: Tavistock, pp 83–97. Quotations in this paragraph therein.

years) and, therefore, returning children – older and taller – would not simply fit into place since the hole they made when they left may well have disappeared. On reunion, mother and child have to start all over again, sometimes in a situation where the child looks critically at 'home' (in comparison with the idealised view carried in the head). In effect the child had to rediscover his or her own home. In 'Home Again', Winnicott reminded his listeners and readers that children are noisy: schools, parks, back streets, he said, all now are filled with the sound of children coming and going and playing their games. Home is being re-established: playing out, coming in after a game for a meal, the evening bath, the bedtime story, the good-night kiss. Home coming can provide children with a 'new era of freedom of thought and imagination' but they need time 'to get to feel that what is real *is* real', Parents were urged to 'allow for a slow dawning of confidence' and he advises them that 'your life will be richer, but less your own'; but that they should be ready with 'an easy hug' to give their children 'the beginning of a new chance to come to terms with a hard world'.

Without the benefit of a psychological training, the host parents of two evacuees on returning them to their birth parents issued the following plea, which seems to capture what was best about the willingness people to care for and love those less fortunate than themselves and in so doing to provide them with a 'home': 'Here are your children...Mother and I have loved them with all our hearts. We ask you to keep alive their loyalty to us as we have kept alive their loyalty to you...may they never forget that they have two homes.'[38] But, of course, this left the children with the burden of reconciling their own feelings with those of their birth parents and their foster parents; they were also uncertain of 'place': where, exactly, they may have wondered, were the 'two homes' in their hearts? The significance of 'love' and 'home', however, was not lost on many of those health and welfare professionals involved in planning for reconstruction – these words, seemingly so straightforward, they recognised, had positive emotional value even in unlikely environments. Bowlby and Winnicott, leading advocates for the social-democratic family, always regarded love and home to be particularly significant in confirming not only the importance of the parent–child relationship for the mental wellbeing of families, but also as intangible and essential virtues for the vision of a democratic ideal without which, they felt, 'democracy' would be but a brittle facade, easy prey to corruption, disease, dismemberment and, in the cold war era, communism.

---

[38] Quoted in Summers (2011), pp 280.

Children, the family, and the idea of social democracy

Clearly, the evacuation experiment was a unique event in British history, a moment when the adult world looked directly at children – eyeball to eyeball, as it were: urban adults of all classes watched the evacuees (many from the slum areas of the big cities) walk through the streets, clutching gas masks, cases, bags and assorted packages, sometimes with a favourite cuddly toy attached (which was not always allowed), to catch trains and buses, often travelling hours with little refreshment or toilet facilities, to their strange and sometimes alien destinations. Provincial small town and rural Britain saw the children arrive tired, thirsty, hungry and also somewhat disorientated, where they were collected from church halls, school assembly rooms and assorted gathering points, by adoptive 'parents' (of all social classes), some of whom seemed to choose their children on the basis of what became the infamous cattle market phrase: 'I'll take that one.'[39] Many foster parents, perhaps the majority, did their best to treat the evacuees with consideration; they were hardly in a position to psychoanalyse their charges. On the other hand, very often children were left waiting about because locals refused to accept them, and had to trek around, led by the billeting officer who proceeded to browbeat reluctant hosts to accept a child or two. We have seen that once host families, billeting officers and volunteer helpers began telling their stories of the many children who arrived lacking suitable clothes and shoes, in a dirty and verminous condition, seemingly undisciplined and with an apparently overwhelming urge to wet the bed, those children became in effect emissaries to the national conscience from a cultural world that hitherto was known only to professional social explorers; otherwise it was either ignored or only half guessed at. Neville Chamberlain, the PM at the time, wrote to his wife: 'I never knew that such conditions existed, and I feel ashamed of having been so ignorant of my neighbours. For the rest of my life I mean to try to make amends by helping such people to live cleaner and healthier lives.' In this way, the child, particularly the evacuee, was cast as a central figure in the mythology of the Home Front.

It has also been shown that amid all the allegations of dirt and vermin, and ignorance of knives, forks and flushing lavatories, and vandalism, ingratitude and indiscipline, the fact that so many of the evacuees (children and mothers) sought a rapid return to their homes and their families, impressed observers who recognised the social value

---

[39] Wicks (1988), pp 52–67; Parsons (1998), p iv.

of such affective loyalty. We should not, however, sentimentalise this 'affection' as simply a desire of children and parents to be with one another, since the widespread hostility of host families, together with poor billeting conditions, more or less dictated that large numbers of evacuees – half of all those from London – would return home at the first opportunity.[40] All the same, the middle-class assumption of child 'neglect' and maternal fecklessness among the poor turned out to be more complex than first thought, in part because it was gradually appreciated that most (but not all) of the apparent neglect owed as much if not more to poverty and the physical and mental incapacity of already overburdened mothers to cope. The evacuation forced a new look at slum conditions: large families, overcrowding, bad housing, inadequate washing, cooking and heating facilities – made worse by meagre poor law allowances and often miserly local authority provision for the health and welfare of children and their mothers. These facts were not lost on the planners of post-war reconstruction policy.

For the making of democratic attitudes – in the sense of inculcating a dissatisfaction with the usual way of doing things – evacuation was a powerful lesson for the working class of the way in which their 'betters' treated the poor.[41] For every evacuee family directly affected there were others who heard the stories second- and third-hand as whole neighbourhoods digested the difference between the government's propaganda to maintain morale and the reality of their experiences or those of their relatives and friends in the host areas, weaving the knowledge into a tapestry of heightened consciousness of injustice and class prejudice.[42] Similarly, these experiences, especially the reluctance of so many of the middle class to accept their billeting responsibilities, also showed the left-leaning professionals involved in preparing plans for reconstruction that there was still a long way to go in fostering a 'national' democratic spirit – it might be in evidence among troops on the battlefield, but the home front was a more challenging environment. The idea that the camaraderie among soldiers would be easily transposed to civilian life was soon recognised to be unwarranted, not least because of the trauma many of them experienced on returning

---

[40] Crosby (1986), p 9.

[41] B. Holman (1995) *Evacuation: A Very British Revolution*, Oxford: Lion, p 147.

[42] Crosby (1986), pp 146–9.

home.[43] It was clear that the bringing to birth of a social democratic welfare state needed help – material, political and psychological. It would not occur naturally, but it was a viable vision.

The 'problem family' and social democracy

Broadly speaking, by 1945, against the background of two decades or more of insights provided by the new psychology, psychoanalysis and child guidance, together with its enhanced reputation for solidarity as shown during the evacuation, the working-class family was seen in a new and positive light as providing a means through which it would be possible to bind individuals to the ethos of a social democratic welfare state. The test case of this belief was the problem family about which there was a certain amount of cautious concern. The picture of the problem family as it emerged during the war was a development of Charles Booth's identification of the 'submerged tenth', redefined in the early 1930s as the 'social problem group', a term heavily laden with eugenic assumptions regarding mental deficiency and said to account for approximately 10 per cent of the population.[44] The WGPW *Our Towns* study (1943) famously claimed that the 'submerged tenth' still existed, within which were problem families who were 'always on the edge of pauperism and crime, riddled with mental and physical defects, and in and out of the courts for child neglect, a menace to the community of which the gravity is out of all proportion to their numbers'.[45] Despite the study also having a relatively progressive environmental perspective, and acknowledging that with public assistance such families could be rehabilitated, this assertion gave new fervour to the eugenicists and to a number of Medical Officers

---

[43] T. F. Main (1947) 'Clinical Problems of Repatriates', *Journal of Mental Science*, xciii, pp 354–63; R. English (1947) *The Pursuit of Purpose: An Essay on Social Morale*, London: Falcon Press; J Burke (2003) '"Going Home": The Personal Adjustment of British and American Servicemen After the War', in R. Bessel and D. Schumann (eds) *Life after Death: Approaches to a Cultural and Social History of Europe during the 1940s and 1950s*, Cambridge: Cambridge University Press, pp 149–60; B. Turner and T. Rennell (1996) *When Daddy Came Home: How Family Life Changed Forever in 1945*, London: Pimlico; J. Summers (2009) *Stranger in the House*, London: Pocket Books.

[44] Macnicol (1987), pp 293–318; (1999) 'From "Problem Family" to "Underclass", 1945–95', in R. Lowe and H. Fawcett (eds) *Welfare Policy in Britain: The Road from 1945*, London: Macmillan, pp 69–93; J. Welshman (2006) *Underclass: A History of the Excluded 1880–2000*, London: Hambledon/Continuum, pp 79–98.

[45] WGPW (1943), p xiii.

of Health (MOsH), who began to publish their own area surveys of families, thereby giving the concept some legitimacy in medical and social welfare circles.[46] While never any kind of centrepiece in plans for post-war reconstruction, the issue did feed into worries about the stability of social relations among the poor, particularly with reference to child neglect, which was a recurring topic. This can be seen in the WGPW's follow-up report on neglected children, which argued that the neglect was the result of 'the interplay of a great number of factors, psychological and economic', which become so overwhelming for mothers as to be unbearable. Among the many causes of neglect, besides poverty – size of family, mental deficiency and instability, alcoholism, 'apathy, irresponsibility, laziness', 'hopelessness', and marital disharmony – *ignorance* of childcare was seen as being of primary importance.[47] Reflecting the qualified optimism of the time, however, the report added that in many families 'these same adversities are overcome by courage and affection', and with regard to 'deliberate cruelty', the authors dismissed the causes as being 'yet little known', probably lying in 'subconscious motives'.[48] Echoing inter-war psychoanalytic teaching, the report warned that emotional neglect could have 'disastrous results' on the child's emotional and psychological development, and identified ideal childcare practice as: 'Training through gentle and wise discipline' coupled with 'a feeling of security given through natural affection and sympathy'. 'Happy relationships', it added, 'are the product of balanced personalities.'[49]

By the early 1950s, although no additional financial aid was being provided, the government was actively encouraging local authorities to intervene with families in distress through their Health committees, home helps, health visitors and mental health workers, the purpose being 'the maintenance of the family as a unit and the education and training of the mother in family care'.[50] The 'causes of unsatisfactory parenthood' were thought to be best dealt with through training in home craft, social casework, and an 'iterant home adviser service', rather than active teaching of so-called parenting skills. These naive views

---

[46]   J. Welshman (1996) 'In Search of the "Problem Family": Public Health and Social Work in England and Wales, 1940–70', *Social History of Medicine*, 9 (13), pp 447–65.

[47]   WGPW (1948) *The Neglected Child and his Family*, Oxford: Oxford University Press, pp 54–67.

[48]   WGPW (1948), p 71.

[49]   WGPW (1948), p 64.

[50]   Quoted in Welshman (1996), p 456; also D. V. Donnison (1954) *The Neglected Child and the Social Services*, Manchester: Manchester University Press.

may partly be explained by the rather primitive social theorising of the Ministry of Health, which saw the families as suffering from a disease with a clear aetiology that could be cured with regular housework.[51] On the other hand, while parenting advice on understanding the child and responding in an appropriately liberal manner was far more likely to be found in middle–class parenting magazines, some psychoanalytically informed guidance was being made available through statutory and voluntary services.[52]

From the mid–1940s onwards, however, these concerns regarding problem families affected social-democratic social theory in three respects. First, they revealed the tension among professionals, government officials, and no doubt much of the general public, between pronouncements on parenting responsibilities and the grim reality of life among sections of the poor. Second, they also highlighted the apparent contradiction between the negative rhetoric surrounding these families and one of the revelations of the evacuation schemes, namely that despite neglect their familial bonds were often intimate and solid. Given the importance being attributed to democratic family relationships, this could not be easily ignored. Third, as cultural forms, in claiming to identify degenerative lifestyles, the discussions implicitly promoted an idea of what 'the family' *should* be, while simultaneously identifying the economic, social and psychological stresses in conflict with the ideal. None of this was lost on those planning for post-war reconstruction, and it was particularly relevant for those on the Left who had in mind a socialist commonwealth with a citizenry to match.

Historical writing is always about judgement and it would be an error to exaggerate the importance of the unease. As mentioned, in one form or another, the problem family had been well known since the late-Victorian identification of the residuum. And while the concept had always greatly stirred eugenicists with their proposals for sterilisation of the 'unfit', it never became an obsession with the more influential reformers in government, the press and the professions. Throughout the 1940s and 1950s, undoubtedly it had its aficionados among MOsH and within social work circles, but they had little real influence on policy, at least not beyond recommending rehabilitation schemes.[53] And rehabilitation was the key idea to emerge from the debates, even among those, like the pacifist based Family Service Units, who were

---

[51] Welshman (1996), p 456; WGPW (1948), pp 64–6.

[52] Donnison (1954).

[53] Macnicol (1987), p 297; Welshman (2006).

most wedded to the problem perception.[54] This is not to say that it was not an issue, especially where children were involved, but it was only one among others of a more positive nature. The guiding view was that with care and attention, and greater provision of services, troublesome families, along with much else in social policy, could be successfully remade.

Nonetheless, there is one issue that deserves further consideration, namely child cruelty. It has been suggested that the 'strongest indication of the difficulties left by war, and of *a public anxiety about family life* that sits awkwardly alongside stereotypes of social stability, is the post-war debate over child *cruelty* in the home'.[55] It is true that there was some nervousness about the process of rebuilding the family, but reference to 'public anxiety' looks rather like sacrificing historical nuance to other preferences since there is little evidence of a politically significant debate about domestic child abuse. Certainly, some discussion occurred in social work circles over what was a complex matter owing to terminological confusion as to the difference between neglect and cruelty. With the establishment of Children's Departments under the Children Act 1948, and the expansion of social work, much of their remedial work with the problem families began to overlap with that of the NSPCC, which was anxious not to be made redundant and, therefore, made the most of its controversial prosecutions. By the mid-1950s, however, the Society had shifted its emphasis, probably under the influence of Children's Departments, to working to preserve the family.[56] Although cruelty attracted some attention from reformers, notably after the death of 13-year-old Denis O'Neil in early 1945 at the hands of his foster parents, the focus in children's social work was on neglect since as a hypothesis it was more easily integrated into the psycho-social analysis of families in need, particularly their allegedly inadequate housekeeping and childcare skills.

---

54   T. Stephens (1945) *Problem Families: An Experiment in Social Rehabilitation*, London: Pacifist Service Units/Gollancz; P. Starkey (2000) *Families and Social Workers: The Work of the Family Service Units, 1940–1985*, Liverpool: Liverpool University Press.

55   M. Thomson (2013) *Lost Freedom: The Landscape of the Child and the British Post-War Settlement*, Oxford: Oxford University Press, pp 68–9, emphasis added.

56   J. Packman (1975 edn) *The Child's Generation: Child Care Policy from Curtis to Houghton*, Oxford/London: Blackwell/Robertson, p 63. For some discussion of 'cruelty', see E. Chesser (1951) *Cruelty to Children*, London: Gollancz; A. Allen and A. Morton (1961) *This is Your Child: The Story of the National Society for the Prevention of Cruelty to Children*, London: Routledge; Donnison (1954), p 78.

'Cruelty', however, raised too many conceptual difficulties, besides those of how to provide 'child protection' other than through criminal prosecutions.[57] Far more prominent than any interest in domestic child abuse, was the sympathetic concern for the mother, since at the centre of each of the families 'there emerges one dominating feature – the capacity of the mother…It is her calibre that matters.'[58] These women were not wilfully 'cruel, reprehensible', rather they struggled with 'inadequate equipment, mental and material' and dealt with problems 'which would tax even those highly endowed'.[59] What these mothers suffered from, overwhelmingly, was 'lack of help' of the kind necessary to compensate for the multiple effects of poverty, character weaknesses, poor health and the absence of a knowledgeable understanding of child welfare. The critical issue (which pertained to the debate on rebuilding the family) was how to deal with neglect in order to *prevent* the break-up of the family, which was to be avoided wherever possible; as a government circular made clear: 'To keep the family together must be the first aim, and the separation of a child from its parents can only be justified when there is no possibility of securing adequate care of a child in its own home.'[60] This was the political circumstance in which the WGPW inquiry on 'neglected' children in families was undertaken as a semi-official supplement to the Report of the Curtis Committee (1946) on children deprived of a normal home. The inquiry was in response to the wish of the Committee for there to be a study into the prevention of deprivation in the *private* home, since its brief regarding 'public care' precluded such an investigation. According to the WGPW, although neglect was an 'urgent problem', it was confined to 'exceptional cases' and, we have seen, cruelty was (mistakenly) deemed to be rare, having apparently diminished in recent years.[61] Similarly, the main consideration for the Children's Departments was not cruelty, but how to extend the 1948 Act to allow for social workers to financially assist families in difficulties, neglectful or not, in order to prevent having to take their children into care.[62] In

---

[57] Packman (1975), pp 55–63; Allen and Morton (1961); Chesser (1951). See also correspondence in *The Times*, 12 July 1948; 6 July 1949; and Editorial, 12 Dec 1949.

[58] WPGW (1948), p 20.

[59] WPGW (1948), pp 22–3.

[60] Home Office Circular, quoted in Packman (1981 edn), p 73; also Hendrick (2003), pp 138–40.

[61] WGPW (1948), p 22. Bowlby (1953) also tended to disregard physical cruelty, putting the figure at between 3–5 per cent of children in care, pp 91–2.

[62] Donnison (1954), pp 3–4.

the confident post-war mood, it was felt that child neglect, where it existed, could be conquered through the agencies of the welfare state.

The Children Act 1948

The Children Act 1948, passed subsequent to the Curtis Committee report (1946), which established a national system of care and protection for disadvantaged children, reflected not only a more sensitive attitude towards those 'in care', critically the need to treat them as *individuals* rather than as an anonymous mass, but also a much more theorised perception of the family than had existed prewar.[63] The committee had been greatly influenced by the sum of research resulting from inter-war child guidance and work with evacuees, and particularly the evidence submitted by Isaacs, Winnicott, Bowlby and the psychiatric social worker Clare Britton. Members (including Sybil Clement Brown, a leading figure in psychiatric social work, and the child guidance psychologist Lucy Fildes) accepted the view of these witnesses that a loving, stable and secure domestic environment was a prerequisite for the healthy emotional and social development of all children. It was this belief that lay behind the committee's stress on Children's Officers (the appointment of which it recommended) providing a *personalised* (in the manner of a parent) service, seeing it as 'the solution of the problem referred to us'.[64] And with its potent imagery enfolded in the experiences of a murderous war, it served as a template for the promotion of the family, not as an abstract ideal, but as a reality that was commensurate with a commitment to the possibilities of the future.

Curtis had commented critically on the way in which children in many residential homes exhibited 'an almost pathological clamouring for attention and petting', whereas in better homes, 'where individual

---

[63] The main features of the Act included the establishment of local authority Children's Departments, each with its own university-educated Children's Officer and subordinate childcare officer, a *renewed* emphasis on fostering ('boarding out') in preference to residential homes, a greater emphasis on adoption where appropriate, and the partial responsibility of the Department for young offenders. In line with contemporary psychological thinking, the overriding aim was to restore children to their birth parents with the emphasis being on non-institutional care and 'keeping the family together'. At the time, there were an estimated 125,000 children 'deprived of a normal family life', 61,200 of whom were either war orphans or unclaimed evacuees, see Ministry of Health and Ministry of Education, *The Care of Children Committee, Report* (Curtis)p 27.

[64] *Curtis Report* (1946), para 441.

love and care had been given' their behaviour 'was quite different'.[65] The Children's Officer was meant to compensate for the absence of the parent and, therefore, was given 'parental functions'. She (it was correctly assumed that the majority of appointees would be women) would be 'the person to whom the child would look as guardian'.[66] Although she was to be degree educated, 'Her essential qualifications... would be on the personal side. She would be genial and friendly in manner and able to set both children and adults at their ease.'[67] The hope was that the Officer would know all the individual children in her care, and where this proved impossible groups of children should be allocated to her subordinates (in practice, this grossly underestimated the size of the workload). Something of the idealism is captured in a semi-fictionalised account of the working of the Act by John Stroud, one of the first Children's Officers, who wrote of the zeal with which they approached their work:

> There was a tremendous crusading atmosphere about the new service. Our impression at the University was that the country outside was dotted with castle-like institutions in which hundreds of children dressed in blue serge were drilled to the sound of whistles. We were going to tear down the mouldering bastions. We were going to replace or re-educate the squat and brutal custodians. I had a dream of myself letting up a blind so that sunshine flooded into a darkened room as I turned, with a frank and friendly smile, to the little upturned faces within.[68]

The Act was important in confirming the cultural turn that was under way in the care of children, which developed under the influence of the new psychology, child guidance and evacuation. It had three significant facets: a psychologically informed understanding of the phrase 'the child and the family'; a similar psycho-medical belief in the social and emotional value of 'a home life'; and the deployment of these perceptions in the evolving lexicon of the rhetoric surrounding the popular post-war objective of 'never again'.[69] These pervasive themes

---

[65] *Curtis Report* (1946), para 441.

[66] *Curtis Report* (1946), para 443.

[67] *Curtis Report* (1946), para 446.

[68] J. Stroud (1960) *The Shorn Lamb*, London: Longmans Green, p 8; also B. Holman (2001) *Champions for Children: The Lives of Modern Child Care Pioneers*, Bristol: Policy Press.

[69] P. Hennessey (1993) *Never Again: Britain 1945–1951*, London: Vintage.

sat alongside some degree of nervousness about the perceived low level of population reproduction, together with the need to counter wartime marital and family breakdown and the high rate of illegitimacy.[70] But while the Act had established an administrative structure and introduced a new sense of purpose in dealing with deprived children in taking them into care, it had little to say about, and allocated no funds for, what soon became a major concern, namely the problem of *prevention*: assisting the family to resolve its difficulties so as to make public care unnecessary.

As post–war social services grew to confront the increasingly sour and sombre mood regarding public welfare that developed throughout the 1960s (see Chapter Four), so the multiple difficulties involved in preventing social distress and in compensating for its effects became ever more problematic. The insights deriving from the research on evacuation and its aftermath, the optimism regarding the tenacity of intra-family relations, the belief that 'scientific' social policies could rehabilitate problem families, and the enthusiasm of the broad Left for a new kind of democracy embodying collectivist welfare, had appeared to promise a worthwhile future. The immediate concern was whether social democracy could be a force for Progress in a world that was still reeling from the scale of wartime death and destruction while facing the hardened ideological uncertainties of cold war politics and the use of the atomic bomb as morally legitimate. If socialists were thinking in terms of rebuilding the family in relation to mental and social advance, conservatives were more interested in family relations for reasons to do with the maintenance of tradition and social stability in a turbulent period. For the Left, the question was not just how to remain civilised, to escape the pre-war 'wasteland', but how to create a socialist citizenship; perhaps even the socialist commonwealth. This was the political model for the virtues of the much anticipated social-democratic family, whose inspired existence would be successfully challenged from the late 1960s by a very different set of ideals, embodying profound economic, social and political change, and representing a collective of interests that had little or no allegiance to anything other than itself. It was the beginning of new times.

---

[70] D. Riley (1983) *War in the Nursery: Theories of the Child and Mother*, London: Virago, pp 150–96; N. Rose (1990) *Governing the Soul: The Making of the Private Self*, London: Routledge, pp 151–77.

PART TWO

Characteristics of the 'Golden Age': 1940s–early 1970s

Introduction

We have seen that one of the principal objectives of post-war reconstruction was to deal with 'the grave and urgent problem of the renewal of our Family Life'.[1] At the heart of the rebuilding process, aside from fears of a declining population (which turned out to be unfounded), was the desire to improve on what was in some respects the troubled history of the family since the end of the First World War: the trauma of the loss of a generation in the trenches, followed by the physical and mental ravishes of the slump and the Great Depression and, as the evacuation revelations proved, the enduring presence of a substantial minority of families mired in poverty, bad housing and ill health. The spectre of the problem family tempered any complacency that families in general could be left to develop desired standards of behaviour without expert welfare guidance. The war brought death and destruction to millions of families, added to which were the psychological and emotional problems of evacuated children and of returning servicemen, often after years of absence. Moreover, as became apparent during planning for reconstruction, in important respects post-war society was certain to be much more psychologically demanding in terms of practising democratic welfare collectivism. And since few people doubted the institutional value of the family for the stability of social and political life, the growing awareness from the 1920s onwards of psychoanalytic pressures on personal subjectivity made the provision of appropriate post-war social, medical and welfare services a national priority. For those involved in providing these services, the parent–child relationship was seen as being fundamental to the nurture of emotionally mature individuals. In this regard, early efforts to rebuild the family embraced many of the inter-war trends that pointed the way to advances in the democratisation of its relationships, certainly

---

[1]   J. Marchant (ed) (1945) *Rebuilding Family Life in the Post-War World*, London: Oldams Press.

among the liberal middle class, accompanied by a new emphasis on the value of 'domesticity' and 'home' ('a name which is more dear… to people the world over than almost any other in their language'), and a similarly new appreciation of the family as a loving and secure environment.[2]

However, it became fashionable among post–1960s leftists, feminists and other social liberationists to debunk this family as 'oppressive', 'ideological', 'conservative', 'patriarchal' and 'idealised', as they listed its many imperfections. By far the most frequent criticism is that the 'ideal' is said to have depended on a gendered view of the home at the centre of which was the self-sacrificial and full-time mother; it is also claimed to have encouraged a smug privatism and social conservatism. Being of the so-called postmodern therapeutic age, these Jeremiahs find the idea of maternal self-sacrifice both offensive and unfathomable; they cannot conceive of parental (maternal) 'love' subsuming 'individualistic' morality.[3] The popularity of domesticity and committed mothering is attributed to the alleged cultural and political manipulation of the period, and the 'false consciousness' of the women who chose to be full-time housewives and mothers.[4] But we should be careful about allowing these interests to craft our historical perspective since their

---

[2] Quoted in Marchant (1945), p 5. It has been argued that post-war policy makers reshaped their vision of democracy, no longer emphasising 'human rationality, reason, and levelheaded choice', but how to produce citizens able to stand for civilisation and who could repress their 'natural' aggression, see M. Shapira (2013) *The War Inside: Psychoanalysis, Total War, and the Making of the Democratic Self in Postwar Britain*, Cambridge: Cambridge University Press, pp 18, 170. This book rejects the view that these policy makers turned their back on rationality and reason. Psychoanalysis certainly sought to create 'new types of democratic selves able to cooperate with one another', but this resolve had been proceeding throughout the 1930s (see Chapter One), and though its efforts were indeed enhanced by wartime experiences, as expressed in 'Bowlbyism', it remained steadfast in support of 'mental progress', rather than seeking to be a substitute for it. It is a complex interpretative issue, but in claiming that (British) psychoanalysis distanced itself from 'a humanist Enlightenment perspective', Shapira perhaps not only exaggerates the importance both of the influence of the war (better seen as a catalyst) and of psychoanalysis, but underestimates the cultural pull of the humanist outlook.

[3] L. Thomas (2006), *The Family and the Political Self*, New York: Cambridge University Press.

[4] For some 'classic' feminist expositions of this view, see B. Friedan (1963) *The Feminine Mystique*, New York: Norton; A. Oakley (1974) *Housewife*, London: Allen Lane; D. Riley (1983) *War in the Nursery, Theories of the Child and Mother*, London: Virago; E. Wilson (1980) *Only Halfway to Paradise: Women in Postwar Britain, 1945–68*, London: Tavistock Publications; M. Barrett and M. McIntosh (1982) *The Anti-Social Family*, London: Verso.

view is largely shaped by its failure to measure up to their claims for the politics of recognition; they refuse to acknowledge the aspirations and accomplishments of those who, in the aftermath of a genocidal world war, simply strove to make the world a better and safer place, and who looked on the home as a haven from which to start. This is not to portray the post-war Keynesian settlement as ideal, as unproblematically progressive in all respects, nor to deny the reality of the injury caused by contemporary racism, homophobia and sexism (and, of course, also childism). Nonetheless, we need to avoid being duped by the clever, knowing and patronising tone that is so prevalent in the writing of those who carp at the 'ideal' into believing that theirs is the truest analysis of its weaknesses, and who seek to position their construction of the past by way of a preface to a narcissistic agenda for late modernity.

There is something of an overlap between the themes of the two chapters (Three and Four) in this part of the book, since they both consider the family, the ideas of Bowlby and Winnicott, and the critiques of their work by feminists and others. The focus in each, however, is different. Chapter Three, in discussing 1940s/1950s left/liberal aspirations for social democracy, builds on the preceding account of wartime influences regarding evolving age relations and the making of a social-democratic vision of the family. I begin by examining the desire of many in the Labour Party to work towards framing the relationship between social democracy and the family in such a way that each would support the other, reinforcing its values and objectives. I argue that this was an important strand, albeit a muddled one, in left-wing thought at the time. The rest of the chapter examines the work and influence of paediatricians and psychoanalystists John Bowlby (a socialist) and D. W. Winnicott (a liberal) who, as we know, were seminal figures in understandings of post-war family dynamics, particularly concerning the mother–child bond, the importance of love as a value that is more than being in and of itself, and the place of 'home' in children's development. In place of the often ideologically tainted and stereotypical portraits from which these men have suffered, I try to offer a more nuanced and historically sensitive interpretation. If we are to understand the social character of family and parent–child relations as they developed into the 1960s, we need to place Bowlby and Winnicott in the context in which they made such significant contributions.

The five topics of Chapter Four cover a subject matter that is integral to the core component in my argument, namely the emergence by the end of the 1960s of an environment that gradually became more hostile to the social democratic family and to liberal progressive child rearing. The key themes centre on the concerted political attempts to undermine 'Bowlbyism' (and the influence of Winnicott) and the role of second wave feminism in that process.[5] In order to contextualise the 'dethroning' of Bowlby, and the early claims of feminism, the chapter also considers the emergence of new social problems in relation to the changing public perception of children, the aborted attempt to found a Children's Rights movement, which coalesced with the beginning of the end of 'progressive' state education, and the attitude of the New Left towards social democratic family ideals. My intention is that these two chapters will prepare readers for what I have termed 'parental narcissism in neoliberal times', which is examined in Part Four.

---

[5] Feminists continue to critique Bowlby and Winnicott, see M. Vicedo (2013) *The Nature and Nurture of Love: From Imprinting to Attachment in Cold War America*, Chicago, IL: Chicago University Press; and M. Shapira (2013).

THREE

Rebuilding the family: 1940s–1950s

'Subjectivity is neither a transcendent essence nor is it formed in a culturally neutral, ahistorical and social vacuum but is the product of specific cultural articulations and the material experiences of day-to-day existence.'[6]

'To make men and women better than they are' (Herbert Morrison)

With the Labour election victory in 1945, many socialists looked to improve human nature, even to create citizens for the anticipated Socialist Commonwealth that was said to be in the not too distant future – Michael Young, Director of the Labour Research Bureau, thought it would probably be 1960 before it arrived.[7] These socialist aspirations represent important themes here since parenting, in being as much a political as a socio-cultural enterprise, is inevitably bound up with their processes and outcomes. The interest in rebuilding family life after the war was by no means confined to those on the Left, for many liberals and conservatives also thought of it in terms of social democratic politics. For socialists, however, this meant Socialism as they hoped it was being made under the Labour government (1945–51). A key element in this Left thinking, sympathetically viewed by those liberals who had retained their faith in Progress throughout the inter-war crises, was that in different ways, people 'could be made better than they are': through Christian ethics, the giving and receiving of love, the habit of reason and, for those who consciously referenced psychoanalytic principles, also through non-authoritarian child rearing and schooling. For the intellectual Left–Liberal alliance, the idea of mental progress, liberal parenting, sound mental health and a comprehensive and universal welfare state were each linked to helping people to rally their potential which, it was assumed, would help to

---

6   J. Giles (1995) *Women, Identity and Private Lives in Britain, 1900–50*, Basingstoke: Palgrave Macmillan, p 2.

7   J. Nuttall (2006), *Psychological Socialism: The Labour Party and the Qualities of Mind and Character, 1931 to the Present*, Manchester: Manchester University Press, p 32.

sustain the principles and practice of social democracy during the cold war era of the 1950s. How widespread this view was is a matter of debate. Its significance, however, lay in the fact that it existed and that it could not be ignored; it was present as a reminder of what could and might be. In this sense, the cultural importance of Bowlby and Winnicott, and their followers, lay in their ability to link psychoanalytic ideas signifying humanistic imperatives of mothering to a social and political programme for the re-envisioning of democracy; under their guidance, the hitherto inexpressible became effable in a galaxy of tropes that unforgettably naturalised maternal 'attachment' as a basic human need.

These aspirations, however, needed to be grounded in an environment that would shelter and foster appropriate feelings in a democratically inclined and securely-based self. The wartime experiences of death, destruction, loss and grief left no doubt as to what that environment *should* be – famously expressed by Winnicott as 'ordinary good homes', a notion he turned into a powerful and multi-layered metaphor, a kind of national 'holding' environment.[8] The implication behind this insight was much more than simply an evocation of physical *place* (which politically referred to the urgent need post-war for houses, the places where families could be reunited after the enforced separation caused by war), it was 'place' *plus* security, cosiness, belonging, and empathy: the maternal breast at which an emotionally and physically blitzed people could find the sense of proportion and balance necessary to deal with the forthcoming dilemmas that collectivism would bring in reconciling *is* and *ought*.[9]

We are sometimes apt to forget that within the space of 31 years (1914–1945) the British people participated in two international wars that literally changed the world. The first of these wars introduced mass slaughter on an industrial scale, and the second witnessed a degree and kind of barbarism hitherto undreamt of.[10] We should pause and reflect on the scale of the violence and death and destruction, and harness our imagination to its mental consequences at a time when contemporaries

---

[8] D. W. Winnicott (1950) 'Some Thoughts on the Meaning of Democracy', *Human Relations* 3, pp 1744–86. Emphasis original.

[9] For a different view, regarding post-war 'idealisation' of family and maternity, see M. Thomson (2013), *Lost Freedom: The Landscape of the Child and the British Post-War Settlement*, Oxford: Oxford University Press, chapters 2 and 3.

[10] R. Bessel and D. Schumann (eds) (2003) *Life After Death: Approaches to a Cultural and Social History of Europe during the 1940s and 1950s*, Cambridge: Cambridge University Press, Introduction, pp 1–13.

were still coming to terms with the inter-war crises and the Freudian revolution of the mind. Evan Durbin, the Labour intellectual, soon to be a junior Minister in the Labour government, wrote of the 1930s:

> The world has changed, and changed out of all recognition, in the ten years since I and my friends spoke in small village halls…in favour of disarmament and the League of Nations…Living in this quiet island, still cut off from the trends of European feeling, it is difficult to believe in the cruelty and irrationality of the world around us. We are becoming hardened to its horrors.[11]

He then went on to describe the restoration of torture over a large area of Europe as 'a normal instrument of government', detailing the hideous practices in Russia and Germany, and recalling the thousands of civilians killed in Spain and China. 'Every device in the destructive hand of man…has been let loose upon the world to maim and murder men, women and children.' Of course, Durbin did not know that the coming war would turn out to be '*the* major, social and psychological turning point of our century', and that from the late 1930s to the late 1940s 'more people [would] be killed by their fellow human beings than ever before in the history of humankind'.[12] Understandably, this scale of violence imprinted itself upon the psyche of the second half of the twentieth century: 'The struggle to create a sense of stability and normality after such terrible events and experiences has been, in a deep psychological sense, a story of life after death – a search for an answer to the unarticulated and unanswerable question of how people can live a normal life after mass death'.[13]

Answers soon tumbled forth, and from the early 1940s to the late 1960s the powers and functions of government were not only extended but also redefined and remoulded. From the 1940s through to the late 1950s, the Labour Party looked to the establishment of a social democracy, tutored by socialism, in which individual moral

---

[11] E. Durbin (1940) *The Politics of Democratic Socialism*, London: G. Routledge and Sons, p 24.

[12] Bessel and Schumann (2003), p 1. Emphasis original.

[13] Bessel and Schumann (2003), p 4; N. Newcombe and J. C. Learner (1982) 'Britain Between the Wars: The Historical Context of John Bowlby's Theory of Attachment', *Psychiatry*, 45, pp 8–10.

improvement would occur, and character would be refashioned.[14] Not only socialists, however, but also many Liberals believed 'they were building a new kind of social and political order, rooted in a wholly new relationship between the citizen and the state'.[15] Such a project, set within the constraints of capitalism, had to contend not only with its own theoretical inadequacies, but also the difficulty in convincing voters as to the value of the sacrifice of certain personal freedoms in return for a collectivist security. The question facing reformers was how to transcend positive wartime experiences of comradeship into something more than the sum of their parts. How were they to be integrated into a communal psyche that eschewed aggression, authoritarianism, and the neurotic personality? The broad left attempted to achieve this goal throughout the period via the services of the welfare state, the promotion of the secure home and, centrally, the family, which was to be characterised by the companionate marriage, good enough mothering, and enlightened child rearing.

Of course, the Socialist Commonwealth never materialised. Instead, after winning a convincing general election victory in 1945, the ensuing economic crisis of 1947 left Labour struggling to hold onto some distant vision of a better world, and from 1951 it lost every general election until the Wilson government was formed in 1964. The Party had great difficulty in coming to terms with the morality of post-war consumerism, as well as the drift towards the permissive society and demands for sexual and gender equality. There is, however, more to this history than a story of failure, of so-called 'masculinist' party hacks sunk in their own prejudices and unable to understand and respond to the politics of the counter-culture. It is more instructive to see this period, sometimes described as the 'short life of British social democracy', as witnessing a struggle within Labour to craft a socialism fit for purpose, one that could accommodate a managed capitalism and collectivist welfare, while also fostering a citizenry sufficiently mature to understand the need for self-sacrifice and to act accordingly when called upon to do so.[16] But this proved to be controversial and

---

[14]   S. Fielding (1992) 'Labourism in the 1940s', *Twentieth Century British History*, 3, 2, pp 145, 148. See B. Jackson (2007) *Equality and the British Left: A Study in Progressive Political Thought, 1900–64*, Manchester: Manchester University Press, pp 151–227.

[15]   J. Harris (1986) 'Political Ideas and the Debate on the Welfare State', in H. A. L. Smith (ed) *War and Social Change*, Manchester: Manchester University Press, p 234.

[16]   J. Vernon (2010) 'The Local, the Imperial and the Global: Repositioning Twentieth Century Britain and the Brief Life of its Social Democracy', *Twentieth Century British History*, 21, pp 404–18.

difficult to sustain, not least because the Left never thoroughly analysed the ethics of relational sacrifice (for the 'other') when set against the understandable desire for the 'good life' that was being offered by the consumer revolution. The Party exaggerated the popular appetite for a new moral order, especially of socialism – the main demands were for jobs, housing, and social security.[17] But there *was* a widespread yearning for a new kind of Britain.[18] After having endured 'the people's war', 'Never again would there be mass unemployment, never again would there be meagre, or nil, health care for ordinary people, never again would there be slums.'[19] By the end of the 1950s, however, as British social democracy lurched into the 1960s, socialist morals and economics were more muddled than they had ever been. The normalisation of narcissism was still some years away, but second-wave feminism, sexual politics and the move towards individualist social liberation, together with the commercial promotion of 'style' and 'counter-culture', were within a hand's grasp. Britain was about to 'swing' – unfortunately (for the future of the Left), many in the Party thought the word referred to a piece of children's playground equipment.

To understand the manner in which Labour presented the politically potent and integrated image of home, family and child, it should be seen as aspiring to create the kind of citizenship that drew on the essential goodness of people – when directed by (socialist) reason. One of the purposes of socialism, said Herbert Morrison, soon to be Home Secretary, was 'to make men and women better than they are, and to promote "sweetness and light"'.[20] In this spirit, the 1950 general election manifesto insisted that 'Socialism is not bread alone… Economic security and freedom from the enslaving bonds of capitalism are not the final goals. They are the means to the greater end – the evolution of a people more kindly, intelligent, free, cooperative, enterprising and rich in culture.'[21] Michael Young, who helped draft

---

[17] Fielding (1992), p 152; J. Tomlinson (1991) 'The Labour Government and the Trade Unions', in N. Tiratsoo (ed) *The Atlee Years*, London: Pinter, pp 90–105; S. Fielding, P. Thompson and N. Tiratsoo (1995) *'England Arise': The Labour Party and Popular Politics in 1940s Britain*, Manchester: Manchester University Press, pp 19–45.

[18] Many conservatives shared the 'never again' mood – for example, Quintin Hogg, and later, the One Nation Group. My thanks to John Stewart for reminding me of this.

[19] Hennessy (1993), p 6.

[20] Quoted in S. Fielding (1995) '"To Make Men and Women Better Than They Are": Labour and the Building of Socialism', in J. Fyrth (ed) *Labour's Promised Land? Culture and Society in Labour Britain 1945–51*, London: Lawrence and Wishart, p 16.

[21] Quoted in Nuttall (2006), p 7.

the 1945 and 1950 election manifestos, felt that socialism was about 'human dignity' and 'communal solidarity'; and called for 'people's needs to be thought of psychologically as well as materially'.[22] The hope was that the Labour victory would produce a world, inhabited by 'a new race of people', who through the benign embrace of the state would fulfil their promise. If this aspiration were to be achieved, it was recognised that 'social life' – a constellation of inter-personal relationships – would have to be regulated and, therefore, it would be necessary to reorder all manner of group relations in the factory, the armed forces, the community and, of course, the family.[23] The liberal–left intelligentsia, much of which was psychoanalytically literate, understood that life in the Welfare State required citizens to subordinate themselves; there had to be a willing acceptance of the primacy of the group within a democratic framework. But more broadly, social democracy demanded a new kind of citizen to meet the challenges in confronting international communism, a revitalised capitalism, and the temptations of mass consumerism; citizens had to be brought to the point where they could regulate themselves.[24]

By the end of the war, if not before, sections of the Party were committed to the idea of mental progress as a prerequisite for achieving socialism.[25] 'Mental progress' has been associated with Stefan Collini's work on Victorian liberals and socialists who, aside from their implicit belief in economic and technological growth, also assumed intellectual and moral advance.[26] Here I follow Jeremy Nuttall who shares Collini's identification of this advance, and uses the term in relation to the idea 'of citizens both behaving more caringly and less selfishly towards others, and thinking more rationally and logically'.[27] There are evident facets of this conception in the Victorian idea of character, which involved rising above 'sensual, animal instincts and passions through the force of will'. This essentially liberal outlook was underwritten by 'a fundamental faith in the goodness and rationality of humankind

---

[22] M. Francis (1997) *Ideas and Policies under Labour, 1945–1951*, Manchester: Manchester University Press, chapter 2; Quotation in S. Brooke (1996) 'Evan Durbin: Reassessing a Labour "Revisionist"', *Twentieth Century British History*, 7, pp 40–1.

[23] For post-war 'group relations', see N. Rose (1990) *Governing the Soul: The Making of the Private Self*, London: Routledge, pp 40–52.

[24] Nuttall (2006), pp 29–67; Durbin (1940).

[25] Nuttall (2006), p 7.

[26] Nuttall (2006), pp 1, 9; S. Collini (1979) *Liberalism and Sociology: L. T. Hobhouse and Political Argument in England, 1880–1914*, Cambridge: Cambridge University Press, p 160.

[27] Nuttall (2006), p 1.

and the belief that individual moral improvement would lead to social progress'.[28] In deploying the idea of mental advance, Nuttall also draws on the political theorist David Marquand's terminology of 'moral reformers' who sought 'inner changes of value and belief' as opposed to those of a 'mechanical' persuasion who looked to 'outward changes of structure and law'.[29] According to Marquand, individualism can be passive and hedonist, or active and moralist; as can collectivism. 'Individual liberty can be valued...because it allows individuals to satisfy freely-chosen desires...Or...because it enables them to lead purposeful, self-reliant and strenuous lives, because it encourages them to take responsibility for their actions and...to develop their moral potential to the full.' By the same token, collective action and collective provision may be seen as instruments for maximising morally-neutral satisfaction, or as the underpinnings of personal and cultural growth, of engagement in the common life of the society and so of self-development and self-fulfilment.[30] In Marquand's view, from the mid-1940s to the mid-1950s, under the influence of the William Beveridge and Labour's Clement Atlee and Sir Stafford Cripps, a moralist–activist collectivism dominated. The period from the mid-1950s to the mid-1970s saw the emergence of passive–hedonist collectivism, informed by 'moral relativism', which created an ethical vacuum that left open the way for the New Right.[31] Of course, Labour's hierarchy was concerned with more than 'mental progress' as a feature of the psychology of socialism; normally it played a minor role with economic matters assuming greater significance. But it was *a* presence in the Party's language of moral ambition, even though by the early 1960s, mass consumerism, the often unthinking urge to sexual liberation, and the appeal of virtue relativism constrained the attempt to create 'caring, responsible and intelligent citizens'.[32]

One of the principal concerns of Labour's social democratic thought was how to reconcile what Evan Durbin referred to as 'cooperation and conflict', which on the grand scale concerned the causes of warfare, notably aggressive behaviour: 'The recent history of Europe' showed that 'There is no form of behaviour too ruthless, too brutal, too

---

[28] Quoted in Nuttall (2006), p 1.

[29] D. Marquand (1988) *The Unprincipled Society*, London: Jonathan Cape, p 20.

[30] D. Marquand (1996) 'Moralists and Hedonists', in D. Marquand and A. Seldon (eds) *The Ideas That Shaped Post-War Britain*, London: Fontana Press, pp 5–28.

[31] Nuttall (2006), p 10; Marquand (1996), pp 21–4.

[32] Nuttall (2006), pp 2, 8–9, 12–13.

cruel for adult men and women to use against each other.'[33] Almost certainly under the influence of his friendship with Bowlby, with whom he co-authored *Personal Aggressiveness and War* (1939), Durbin was convinced that through analytical psychology it was possible to understand 'the nature of the causes that determine the behaviour of individual human beings'; and from here, it was but a short step to throwing 'light upon the nature of society'.[34] The causes of 'simple' aggression, 'possessiveness, strangeness, frustration', he said, were common to all adults, children and other animals. 'But a repressive discipline drives simple aggression underground…and it appears in disguised forms', meaning 'displacement' (from a feared, hated or loved object to a secondary object) and 'projection' (a complex term simply understood as projecting 'our own characters upon others').[35] The critical point was that these mechanisms result 'in the typical form of adult aggressiveness – aggressive personal relations of all kinds – but above all in group aggression' where impulses are rationalised and hatred is justified.[36] Durbin believed that by itself neither intelligence nor education was sufficient for democracy, which 'is much more a result of character in a people than of law or learning. Its roots are emotional rather than intellectual. It is fundamentally a consequence of psychological health and the absence of neurosis', both of which are necessary for 'tolerance' and the 'willingness to bear responsibility'.[37] According to Durbin, psychoanalytic theory suggested 'tentatively' that the most likely method by which 'a reasonable temper in social relations could be produced' is through 'a free, or relatively free, emotional environment in early childhood'– freedom to express hatred and aggression, which will diminish aggression is later adult life.[38]

On the specific importance of child rearing, Durbin claimed that 'if children were actually brought up more freely they would be much happier, much more reasonable and much more sociable. It is obvious that social and international relations would greatly benefit if people were happier, more reasonable and more sociable.'[39] In their joint work,

---

[33] Durbin (1940), p 49; also Brooke (1996), pp 27–52.

[34] Durbin (1940), p 37.

[35] Durbin (1940), pp 57–62.

[36] Durbin (1940), p 60.

[37] Durbin (1940), pp 261–3.

[38] Durbin (1940), pp 263–6. Heredity and environment were also crucial, pp 267–9.

[39] Durbin (1940), pp 68–70; also E. Durbin and J. Bowlby (1939) *Personal Aggressiveness and War*, London: Routledge and Kegan Paul, p 41. However, as Nuttall (2006) says, the place of 'the family' was hardly developed in Labour theory, pp 51, 53.

Durbin and Bowlby had been even clearer as to their view on child rearing: 'Parents believe that children ought not to have what they want – that denial of impulse will make a good character. We hold that the opposite of this is the truth', and they continued:

> People greatly underestimate the rapidity and strength with which the social and affectionate impulses of the free child develop…the child, freed from frustration and unsympathetic discipline, will in fact become the very opposite of the popular picture of the 'spoiled child'. Instead of violent and ungovernable anger, inordinate selfishness, and vanity, the child that is not afraid to express its feelings is likely to exhibit affection, independence, sociability, and courage more rapidly and more naturally than a repressed child. Familial life is not a nightmare of disorder, or the false calm of strong discipline, but a moderately peaceful and very lively society of free, equal, and willing co-operation.[40]

This belief was central to their view that 'the kind of people who can support the responsibility, freedom, and toleration required by democracy are also likely to be peaceful. They are not peaceful because they are democratic. They are peaceful and democratic because they are the kind of people they are'.[41]

There is a debate as to the degree to which the Party remained ethical as opposed to becoming, by the late 1940s, focused on economic 'demand management' and utilitarianism in pursuit of economic efficiency.[42] But there is little doubt that Labour's ethical traditions continued to be *an* influential strand within its thinking. In 1949 Michael Young was one of those who called for a return to the Party's foundational ethics – 'dignity' and 'brotherhood' (meaning care of the 'other') – and a greater influence on 'human relations'. Young made three related recommendations. First, he reminded his readers of the psychoanalytical insight concerning the importance of early childhood for the development of personality, and called for more attention to

---

[40] Durbin and Bowlby (1939), pp 42–3. On the importance of avoiding the Nazi-style 'authoritarian personality' through liberal humanism, see R. Money-Kyle (1951) *Psychoanalysis and Politics: A Contribution to the Psychology of Politics and Morals*, London: Duckworth.

[41] Durbin and Bowlby (1939), p 49. On the making of citizens for democracy, see Shapira (2013), p 18, and my comment, note 2.

[42] Francis (1997), pp 34–64.

be given to children's emotional needs. Second, he suggested the establishment of a family advice service to help protect children from the adverse consequences of divorce in addition to an expansion of marriage guidance to help prevent divorce occurring. Third, he argued for the reform of teaching methods to be less authoritarian.[43]

As it emerged, the Party's view that the electorate had become more favourable to socialism than it had been during the inter wars, turned out to be exaggerated. Those who expressed the view that further education in social democracy was necessary in order to sustain a collectivist state were proved correct. This does not mean that nothing in human relationships changed, or that attitudes towards the state and the horizon of possibilities for individuals and families remained unaltered. But is it true that though the electorate supported Labour in establishing the welfare state, there was less wholehearted support for its ethical vision.[44] Putting the question this way, however, makes it an all or nothing affair, which distorts what happened not least by homogenising the Labour electorate and ignoring its different social constituencies. Leaving aside the political naivety of Labour in expecting widespread acceptance of its agenda for socialism, cultural change on the scale that such a vision would have required never comes in big boxes; usually it is packaged as bits and pieces, being shuffled around, and having an effect here and there while at other times being either resisted or misunderstood. Nor should we overlook the fact that the cultural revolution of the 'long sixties' (1958–1974) was about more than consumerism and narcissistic gratification. In some important respects it was also about hope and dignity and tolerance, albeit that many of these ideals (though not all) were soon overwhelmed by baser desires. Neither the Party's failures in the 1950s nor the 'conservatism' of the British electorate should be overplayed. When reading revisionist accounts of the short history of British social democracy, perhaps it would be wise to listen to the historian Peter Hennessy who says that when he looks through the historical documents:

> I still warm to the lack of defeatism on the part of ministers and civil servants, who thought and behaved, in those years, as though a better and fairer country could be constructed out of the wreckage of the early 1940s…They still strike me, and cause me to be a little moved by the nobility of it all.[45]

---

43 Francis (1997), pp 50–1, 55–6.

44 Fielding et al (1995), p 213.

45 Hennessey (1993), p 7.

John Bowlby and D. W. Winnicott: imperfect visionaries

[W]hat every human being loves and seeks to find again in life are the figures of his father and mother, in the forms of which they have been indelibly preserved in the depths of his mind. Every loss of love and goodness is a bitter re-experience of the inevitable frustration, loss and disillusionment he originally lived through in childhood.[46]

There can be no proper understanding of social democratic child-rearing culture without some knowledge of the work of John Bowlby, especially his *Child Care and the Growth of Love* (1953), one of the most humane documents of its time, and that of Donald Winnicott, famous for his enduring concepts of the 'ordinary devoted mother', the 'holding environment', the 'transitional object' and the idea that 'Home is where we start from'. Bowlby is best known for his seminal 'maternal deprivation' hypothesis, and as one of the founders of 'attachment theory' (attachment, separation and loss), which he developed into an overarching account relating to the influence of a child's first experiences on later development, and how the early relationship between mother (or mother substitute) and child was central to his or her healthy maturation. If the relationship was disrupted through abrupt and insensitive separation, this could result in the child experiencing 'separation anxiety', anger, grief and perhaps long-term disturbances.[47] Over the years, Bowlby came to look increasingly to ethology for scientific support for his attachment studies as he moved away from orthodox psychoanalysis with its Kleinian focus on the *internal* realm of the psyche, something that caused a serious rift between himself and the psychoanalytic community.[48] In helping to plot the social and political significance of parenting, Bowlby and Winnicott exerted considerable influence on popular understandings of family, home, mothering and child development, as well as, more generally, on the culture of child rearing within an evolving social democracy. Together, both men educated a generation on how important appropriate

---

[46] J. Riviere (1948) 'The Bereaved Wife', in *New Education Fellowship, Problems of Child Development*, London, 1948, p 23.

[47] J. Bowlby (1971, 1975, 1981) *Attachment and Loss* (3 vols), Harmondsworth: Penguin.

[48] F. C. P. van der Horst (2011) *John Bowlby – From Psychoanalysis to Ethology: Unravelling the Roots of Attachment Theory*, Chichester: Wiley-Blackwell; also S. Van Dijken (1998) *John Bowlby: His Early Life – A Biographical Journey into Attachment Theory*, London: Free Association Books.

mother–child relations were in providing children with the qualities that would further their psychic advance, helping them to grow into independent, mature and emotionally competent adults. In every age, in the sphere of personal intimacies of the sort that influence our characters and personalities, there are individuals who help to give that age its tone, who light up its imagination of the possible, and instruct its moral temper. Bowlby and Winnicott were such figures in mid-twentieth century Britain and, while their work has been disputed, reformulated and distorted, their insights, theories and ideals continue to be influential today. For more than half a century numerous critics have tried to undermine their core ideas, and while some have been dislodged, often though the ideological politics of feminism, and in collaboration with the economic imperatives of neoliberalism's need to bring women into the 'flexible' labour market, the attraction of their ethical appeal continues to resonate throughout debates about working mothers, nurseries, divorce, cohabitation and, as the sexual politics slogan puts it, 'families of choice'. The core image of Bowlby and Winnicott's iconography – the indisputability of the 'maternal', as the giving of love and security and as our place of origin, remains largely intact.

As part of the critique, many of Bowlby's ideas (and those of Winnicott) are often dismissively labelled 'Bowlbyism' which, with reference to the post-war settlement, refers less to his theories, than to 'the broader influence and popularization of some of his key assumptions, and the *ideological* and social and economic structures that encouraged this'.[49] The distinction, however, is politically suspect since its purpose seems to be to identify a supposedly illicit link between the popularisation of Bowlby's 'theories' (rather than 'assumptions') and an allegedly distorting 'ideological' (that is, patriarchal and liberal individualist) dogma, which used these the work of Bowlby for its own ends. Moreover, it tends to ignore the role of Winnicott whose focus on the 'ordinary devoted mother', certainly through his BBC radio talks, may be said to have contributed to Bowlbyism or, as it is thought of here, the developing drift of sensitivity and understanding in parent–child relations. The fact that Bowlbyism helped to make the family home 'into a site for living out the meaning of social democracy,

---

[49] Thomson (2013), p 79. Emphasis added. Feminists and leftists label 'Bowlbyism' as 'ideological', presumably as a health warning. Unfortunately, they fail to be as protective with regard to their own 'social constructions'. See, for example, Shapira (2013) in whose view Winnicott's radio talks contributed to a focus on '*conservative* family relationships', p 135. Emphasis added. For the standard feminist account of 'Bowlbyism', see Riley (1983).

extending the reach of the post-war settlement into civil society, and thereby acting as crucial glue in holding it together'[50] does not of itself lessen either its veracity or prove its cynical prostitution by a manipulative state. On the contrary, Bowlby, and those who shared his views, in connecting his professional work to his socialist understanding of democracy did not see any contradiction in so doing (nor did Winnicott through his liberal politics): what better purpose than to enlist notions of attachment and separation anxiety in the service of what they and many others hoped would be non-aggressive democracy, one of whose objectives was to maximise human goodwill.[51]

The truth is that the work of Bowlby and Winnicott represented 'the turn toward the mother' that occurred not only in psychoanalysis, but also in the broader spectrum of cultural heritage as when George Orwell described Britain as 'a family with the wrong members in control...A rather stuffy Victorian family...Still, it is a family'.[52] The critical shift within psychoanalysis, orchestrated by Melanie Klein, was from a focus on the Freudian Oedipus Complex and patriarchal authority to the Mother as the original authority figure – it put the Mother 'on the psychoanalytic map'.[53] It was no surprise, then, that the mother figure was pivotal to this family with her iconic place defined in Henry Moore's sculpture 'Madonna and Child', unveiled in 1943, in which the Blessed Virgin was conceived in the words of one of its sponsors as 'the one large, secure, solid background to life'.[54] Bowlby and Winnicott were members of the 'independent' school of British analysts who looked toward the community, the family and the growing sense of an increasingly emancipated self that needed an emotionally secure point of departure. The British school 'synthesized Freud's developmental stages with Klein's new emphasis on early infancy, but coloured these insights with an entirely different hue...

---

[50] Thomson (2013), p 82.

[51] Holmes (1993), pp 201–9; B. Mayhew (2006) 'Between Love and Aggression: The Politics of John Bowlby', History of the Human Sciences, 19, pp 19–35.

[52] Quoted in E. Zaretsky (1999) '"One Large Secure, Solid Background": Melanie Klein and the Origins of the British Welfare State', History and Psychoanalysis, 1, 2, p 148; also his (2005) Secrets of the Soul: A Social and Cultural History of Psychoanalysis, New York: Vintage Books, pp 193–216.

[53] Holmes (1993), p 3; also Zaretsky (1999), pp 141–5.

[54] Quoted in Zaretsky (2005), p 268.

[they] de-emphasized aggression and played up the mother–child link as the locus where personality forms'.[55]

The focus for Bowlby and Winnicott was the synergy of the secure bond between the 'good enough' mother–child relationship and the creation of social democratic citizens. In seeking this attachment, both men were spurred on by their wartime experiences in a psychoanalytic culture that had become increasingly political as it developed from the 1930s, seeking to understand the causes of violence, aggression and anxiety, and instructing government and the wider public in their findings in order to promote universal mental health. As the pacific objective of a post-war socialist democracy became increasingly strained in the cold war atmosphere of the 1950s, their focus remained on the rearing of emotionally healthy and mature individuals: an ideal of a kindly, thoughtful, tolerant and non-aggressive selfhood. Bowlby always emphasised the desirability of government agencies providing support for needy citizens to confirm a sense of social commitment to the collective good. Winnicott's liberalism, on the other hand, made him profoundly suspicious of the state and its services – in a letter to Beveridge he opposed the NHS as leading to the 'nationalisation of doctors' – bureaucracies were no good at thinking, that required individual human beings.[56] This probably explains why throughout his writings, he was always keen to emphasise that mothers' possessed important 'self-knowledge' about their babies and, therefore, rather than being pestered by state experts, should be given non-intrusive facilitative measures.

Before 'Bowlyism': Ian D. Suttie and the 'taboo on tenderness'

The anointment of the Mother, and the ensuing 'controversies' within British psychoanalysis, which broke into two main groups: the Kleinians and the Freudians, led by Anna Freud, are well known and need not be examined here. Bowlby and Winnicott, in their different ways, chose to situate themselves between the two paradigms on offer, emphasising the *real* relations of mother and child, as opposed to 'phantasy', according to Klein. These were presented as governing what Bowlby would come to term 'Attachment', involving the concepts of maternal deprivation, and loss, separation and anxiety; and for

---

[55]   G. Gerson (2004) 'Individuality, Deliberation and Welfare in Donald Winnicott', *History of the Human Sciences*, 18, 1, p 110; on the 'family setting', see N. Rose (1985) *The Psychological Complex*, London: Routledge, pp 176–96.

[56]   R. Rodman (2003), *Winnicott: Life and Work*, Cambridge: A Da Capo Press, p 8.

Winnicott they formed the context for 'the ordinary devoted mother', the 'holding environment', and the place of 'transitional objects'. In effect, Bowlby and Winnicott together initiated 'a sea change in the theory of mind', which no longer focused on a Freudian pursuit of 'sensuous gratification', but rather was 'structured by the quest for company and by the interaction with others that this quest prompts'.[57] This was to underline the basis of their entire life's work.

There was, however, another influential figure in this sea change, and a major influence on Bowlby, namely Ian Suttie, a Scottish analyst whose *The Origins of Love and Hate* (1935) established him as one of the most innovative and critical of the British post-Freudians.[58] According to the political theorist Gal Gerson, the ideas of Suttie, in opposition to Freudianism, constitute an ideology in that they denote 'a comprehensive outlook on culture and society that has both descriptive and evaluative aspects'.[59] Contra Freud's emphasis on the sexual instinct, Suttie emphasised the need for love and companionship as autonomous forces in human development, which were probably innately present in infants owing to their evolutionary adaptiveness; separation anxiety or loss, he thought, could produce hate, grief or psychosomatic ailments, depending on circumstances and, therefore, were important factors in personality development. A critical focus for Suttie was the infant–mother bond, which he saw as arising from the 'a need for company and as a discomfort in isolation'.[60] In his view, it was 'indisputable that a need for company, moral encouragement, attention, protectiveness, leadership...remains after all the sensory gratifications connected with the mother's body have become superfluous'. Bowlby, however, in common with others in the British school, saw it more in terms of the infant's need for *protection* against helplessness and dependence, which encouraged the child 'to seek love and security as such'.[61]

---

[57] G. Gerson (2009) 'Culture and Ideology in Ian Suttie's Theory of Mind', *History of Psychology*, 12, 1, p 19.

[58] Bowlby facilitated the reprinting of *Love and Hate* (1988),London: Free Association Books, for which he wrote an appreciative foreword crediting Suttie with the discovery of attachment and separation anxiety, p xvii. See Newcombe and Lerner (1982), pp 5–6; Gerson, 2009, p 19; Mayhew (2006); van der Horst (2011), p 15; G. S. Clarke (2006) *Personal Relations Theory*, London: Routledge. I have drawn on Gerson for the following summary, without always following her interpretation.

[59] Gerson (2009), p 20.

[60] I. Suttie (1963 edn) *The Origins of Love and Hate*, Harmondsworth, Penguin, p 31. Emphasis original.

[61] Newcombe and Lerner (1982), p 6; van der Horst (2011), p 17.

In practice, Suttie produced a humanist alternative to Freud's 'death instinct'. What the British school came to emphasise, with the help of Suttie's 'social vision', was that 'Humans seek company from the start, and the shape that this quest takes through the environment's responses patterns the mind.'[62] Natural selection, argued Suttie, had made humans, who were born defenceless, primarily sociable since only in this way can they procure their needs, which are initially provided by the mother who gradually distances the child from herself and through trust presents separation and the becoming of an individual self as part of her caring relationship. Close maternal care prepares the young child for entry into the wider, social world – through a system of 'substitutes' – 'we put the whole social environment in the place once occupied by the mother'.[63] The difference between Freud and Suttie is that the former sees a world in which conflict is inevitable; Suttie is much more optimistic. In substituting sociability (contact with others) for Freud's sexuality, Suttie envisions a more hopeful world, in which aggression is not innate; it is a product of circumstance. This belief causes him to adopt a remedial position towards society in order to make the environment benign.

Here, the biological mother is crucial to Suttie's world view. The greater influence of women as mothers in child rearing would lead to an enhancement of their status, as well as help to lift what he called 'the "taboo" on tenderness', most obviously manifested in behaviourism as a 'bias of anti-emotionalism', and also have a beneficial effect on the caring qualities of men.[64] The mother was fixed through biology, which decreed the 'further specialization of the female for the nurturance of the young'.[65] What Suttie sought to resurrect was the 'devotional idealistic love between mother and child'.[66] In some respects, Suttie's social vision – sociability, ability to avoid conflict, and a focus on the home and the mother – is essentially early twentieth century social reformism as it morphed into progressive opinion in the inter-war period.[67] As with features of 1940s socialist thought, Suttie draws on the Victorian ethic of altruism to shun selfishness in all its forms. Within the model, notions of fellowship and mutual care, as associated with the socialist R. H. Tawney and the Edwardian 'New Liberal'

---

[62] Gerson (2009), p 22.

[63] Suttie (1963 edn), p 31. Emphasis original.

[64] Suttie (1963 edn), p 86.

[65] Quoted in Gerson (2009), p 31.

[66] Mayhew (2006), p 23.

[67] Gerson (2009), p 33.

L. T. Hobhouse, promote 'Love, not material gratification...[as] the foundation of all social transaction. There can be no personal fulfilment without it.'[68] This 'basic benevolence' is traced back to mother–child relations and, therefore, to the family as the environment of 'disinterested love'. The essence of Suttie's position is that through the family, solidarity and sociability as virtues are integrated into the culture. By the early 1930s, it was clear to Suttie and numerous European liberal intellectuals that their vision of the social good was being challenged by rampant aggression. It is tempting to say that Suttie, along with Bowlby (and Winnicott), looked back to a pre-Oedipal world, one that was more stable, more unashamedly committed to Progress. But we should resist that temptation, and appreciate that the intention of Suttie (and of Bowlby and Winnicott), was not to indulge in nostalgia; rather it was to reconfigure the ethical strengths of late Victorian and Edwardian Christianity, science and progress in order to proceed to a practice of social democracy that was more altruistic, more socially emancipated, and more scientifically aware. As an objective, it was not without its flaws, but it was not regressive in substance.

Bowlby's mission 'to improve the community as a whole'

The politics of Bowlby, it has been observed, may be found between love and aggression.[69] When he was a dissatisfied naval cadet, before switching to medicine at Cambridge, and long before he rejected his father's conservative politics in favour of socialism, Bowlby wrote to his mother saying that he wanted a job that would 'improve the community'.[70] Unsurprisingly, it was in accord with his 'strong moral and social vision' that throughout his professional life Bowlby emphasised 'secure attachment' through what has been termed 'empathic, caring, compassionate, and cooperative social bonding' during infancy, which in turn facilitated 'resilience, self-confidence, emotional intelligence and spiritual–aesthetic appreciative dimensions fundamental to well-being that enhances appreciation of life'.[71] As Winnicott put it in one of his many insightful remarks, '*to be merely*

---

[68] Gerson (2009), p 34, referring to L. T. Hobhouse.

[69] Mayhew (2006), p 19; also Newcombe and Learner (1982), pp 1–11; van Dijken (1998), pp 103–28.

[70] Quoted in van Dijken (1998), p 46.

[71] Holmes (1993), p 200.

sane is not enough.[72] Bowlby relentlessly promoted the fundamental and timeless truth, as he saw it, namely that 'what is believed to be essential for mental health is that the infant and young child should experience a warm, intimate, and continuous relationship with his mother (or permanent mother substitute…) in which both find satisfaction and reward'.[73] Contrary to the myth, Bowlby never meant 'continuous' in the sense of a constant and unremitting presence. Rather, his emphasis was on continuity and consistency. He explained the circumstances in which children under the age of three years old could be left (for as long as ten days) with relatives and neighbours with whom the child was familiar – this was the key consideration: the child's familiarity with the substitute mother. His emphasis was on preparing the child for the separation and on the mother (or her substitute) appreciating and dealing sympathetically with the anxieties aroused in the child.[74] Bowlby saw the family (and the home – for both he and Winnicott these stood in relation to each other in providing emotional security, which was an essential prerequisite for the will to independence) as being the crucible for child rearing. Hence:

> The mothering of a child is not something which can be arranged by rota; it is a live human relationship which alters the characters of both partners…Such enjoyment and close identification of feeling is possible for either part only if the relationship is continuous…Just as the baby needs to feel that he belongs to his mother, the mother needs to feel that she belongs to her child, and it is only when she has the satisfaction of this feeling that it is easy for her to devote herself to him.[75]

And, with a nod toward his socialist commitment to self-sacrifice for the greater good, he added: 'In no other relationship do human beings place themselves so unreservedly and so continuously at the disposal of others.'[76] It is worth remembering that few people at the time (1940s/1950s), including the majority of pre-second-wave feminists

[72] Quotation in J. Issroff (with Christopher Reeves and Bruce Hampton) (2005) *Donald Winnicott and John Bowlby: Personal and Professional Perspectives*, London: Karnac Books, p .154. (Emphasis original).

[73] J. Bowlby (1953) *Child Care and the Growth of Love*, Harmondsworth: Pelican, p 11.

[74] Bowlby (1953), pp 16–17.

[75] Bowlby, (1953), p 75.

[76] Bowlby (1953), p 76.

and members of women's party political and voluntary organisations, doubted that the mother was the *best* parent to respond to her *young* child's needs, anxieties and wishes. In this respect, much of Bowlby's theorising was not surprising. Indeed, to some extent, he was merely reiterating the views of some illustrious forerunners who saw mother love as 'the cradle of all good sentiments'. For Freud: 'Love has its origins in attachment to the satisfied need for nourishment' and in this relationship 'lies the root of the mother's importance, unique, without parallel, established unalterably for a whole lifetime as the first and strongest love-object and as the prototype of all later love relations – for both sexes'.[77]

Since Bowlby's professional writing was deeply involved with his political beliefs, it is no surprise that after the war he was part of social psychiatry's engagement in 'adjusting the bonds of love' in such a way as to serve what he hoped would be a socialist social democracy.[78] Having become a non–Marxist socialist in 1927, and befriended Evan Durbin and Hugh Gaitskell (the latter a future leader of the Labour Party), Bowlby joined the New Fabian Research Bureau, from where he and Durbin argued for the importance of integrating 'rationalised love' into practical politics through the application of expert opinion in the organisation of government and its services.[79] This desire was clear in Bowlby's collaboration with Durbin in *Personal Aggressiveness and War* (1939) and in their shared 'domestic vision' (Durbin's *The Politics of Democratic Socialism* (1940) drew on Bowlby for its psychological section). No wonder, then, that Bowlby has been located within 'a technological conception of politics'. One example of this approach being his recommendation for the state to draw on the expertise of psychology and use 'trained professional social workers' to deal with billeting problems during the evacuation.[80] As to what part the social sciences might play in advancing a democratic socialism, this was highlighted in the Fabian conference organised by Durbin and G. D. H. Cole, 'Psychological and Sociological Problems of Modern

---

[77] Vicedo (2013), pp 21–22. Freud quote from *On Narcissism: An Introduction*, 1914, *Collected Works*, J. B. Strachey (ed), Vol 14, p 78.

[78] Rose (1990), pp 151–77; Holmes (1993), pp 201–9; H. Hendrick (2003) 'Children's Emotional Well-being and Mental Health on Early Post Second World War Britain: The Case of Unrestricted Hospital Visiting', in M. Gijswijt-Hofstra and H. Marland (eds) *Cultures of Child Health in Britain and the Netherlands in the Twentieth Century*, Amsterdam: Rodopi, pp 213–42; Mayhew (2006), p 19.

[79] Mayhew (2006), p 26; Rose (1990), p 163.

[80] Mayhew (2006), p 28.

Socialism' (1945), where Bowlby spoke on the theme of 'liberty and democracy'.[81] It is now too easily forgotten just how critical it was thought to be to secure popular 'willing cooperation' for the success of the welfare state, which is what Bowlby had in mind in calling attention to the fact that 'The necessity of humanity learning to live together peacefully and cooperatively has never been greater.' It was clear to many contemporary commentators, Bowlby included, that, on the one hand, the class-based controversies surrounding the behaviour of evacuees and the reluctance of many middle-class families to accept them into their homes, pointed to the absence of any firm degree of collective solidarity at a time of national crisis while, on the other, the loyalty of evacuees to their own families and neighbourhoods could be seen as evidence that these trumped those of the larger community. Loyalty to family was a social strength, but it was not without dangers for a broader collectivism. The risks, as was shown above, lay both in over-estimating the public's understanding of the likely sacrifices of individual liberties demanded by a welfare state, and the extent of its left-wing sympathies.[82]

This is why Bowlby warned that care would be required to overcome the psychological hurdles thrown up by persistent cooperative behaviour; it would require a balance of psychological and social forces 'not easily attained'. He cited the Tennessee Valley Authority scheme, with its remarkable degree of grass roots democracy, as a way to unleash 'undreamed of reserves of social energy'. Such willing cooperation required not only an agreed objective, it also demanded libidinalisation of group aims, which were best achieved if the individual's earliest libidinal relationship – with the mother – was undisturbed. The tolerant and loving family was seen by Bowlby (indeed, by British psychoanalysis) as crucial to political and social harmony, since it was in such families that 'all later personal relationships rest'. He always believed that 'social responsibility was an evolved psychological potentiality' made real through the mother–child relationship. Healthy and mature personal relationships, he said, were a political necessity in a Britain that needed to have 'an understanding and acceptance of the need for inevitable controls required for…full employment, a maximising of production…or a maximising of personal efficiency'. He concluded by advising his audience that 'The hope for the future lies in a far more profound understanding of the nature of emotional

---

[81]   Transcript Quoted in Hendrick (2003), pp 224–5. Later published as 'Psychology and Democracy', in *Political Quarterly*, 1946, 61–77.

[82]   Fielding et al (1995), pp 19–45.

forces involved and the development of scientific techniques for studying them.' All Bowlby's subsequent work – evidence before the Curtis Committee, his role as Director of the Parent's and Children's Department at the Tavistock, the authorship of the WHO Report on 'children who were homeless in their native country', his establishment in 1948 of a Separation Research Unit, and his subsequent research with James Robertson in the long-running campaign for unrestricted hospital visiting of children – was directed wholly or in part to realising this ambition.

It is true, however, that neither Bowlby nor Durbin gave much thought to the hard political problems involved in 'understanding... the institutions that comprise civilization...[and] how people's desires can be shaped by the type of society they live within'.[83] But it seems that Bowlby was much less interested in theorising the political process; instead, he wanted to engage what he thought of as science in changing institutional practice. We can see something of this approach, and its success, in the campaign for unrestricted hospital visiting for young children, which led to a new awareness of the young patient as a *person* (this status had already been achieved for children in care with the Children Act 1948), a recognition that was given official status by the 1959 Platt Report on the Welfare of Children in Hospital (which, incidentally, approvingly observed: 'parents are adopting a much more liberal and sensitive attitude than in the past').[84] The paediatrician Ronald MacKeith, speaking of James Robertson's famous film 'A Two-Year-Old Goes to Hospital' (1952), made as part of Bowlby's separation research programme, admitted that the film:

> opens our eyes to the quiet unhappiness that a young child in hospital may suffer much of the day...We do not want to see the grief and we see only a 'good' quiet child...We tend to dismiss all crying as unimportant...doctors, nurses and parents all do well to give a child, however small, credit for understanding – or feeling – what is said or felt.[85]

---

[83] Mayhew (2006), p 30.

[84] Hendrick (2003), pp 213–42; Shapira (2013), pp 214–29. The Platt Report should be seen as continuing the social-democratic concern for children's psychological welfare, alongside the Curtis Report (1946) and the WGPW study (1948). Shapira makes the rather odd comment that the recognition that young patients need their mothers with them was a 'constructed sensitivity', pp 198, 236. One wonders when 'sensitivity' is not 'constructed'?

[85] Quoted in Hendrick (2003), p 230.

Bowlby, can reasonably lay claim to have been instrumental in creating the environment in which this insight was possible.

The British School of Psychoanalysis appreciated that Freud and Jung had identified the critical paradox of modernity: Progress *and* Calamity.[86] The struggle between these two conclusions was perpetual, hence the need to protect the ideal of Progress through 'love', 'attachment' and the inevitable self-sacrifice these values called for personally and collectively at the level of family, friends, neighbourhoods and nations. For Bowlby, these virtues were essential for the realisation of socialist humanitarianism and for its sustenance. He seems here to have been more Jungian than Freudian in receiving the call of the former for a kind of 'spiritual renewal'.[87] Bowlby, as Jung recommended, accepted that the First World War had compelled recognition of 'the disappointment of the hopes and expectations of the ages'.[88] But, however ambiguous Jung (and Freud) may have been in their advice on the inter-war crisis, Bowlby, and those who shared his optimism about the human capacity to confront the psychosis represented by totalitarianism, racism and the mass slaughter of the Second World War, looked to love and its accoutrements to make a major contribution toward the post-war reconstruction of Britain. Once the war was over, as Bowlby saw, the demanding issue was whether Europe would be psychologically paralysed by its abject failures and crimes or would it be sufficiently mature through analysis (social, economic, political and personal) to heal itself. Bowlby recognised the scale of the impact on social thought and science that was wrought by Nazism, Fascism and later also Stalinism – these were the most brutal reminders of psychotic human aggression. But they could not be allowed to conquer the imagination of human potential in the realm of social democracy. This is what Bowlby grasped, helped perhaps through his close friendship with Durbin and his association with other Labour intellectuals (and which distinguished him from Winnicott for whom democracy rested far more solely in the bosom of the family). Hence this fuelled his concern with the non-Freudian notions of loss, separation and attachment. He wished to avoid what he thought of as *man's* destructive capacities. Old ideals of Liberal individualism alone were no longer sufficient. The willingness to embrace totalitarian forms of government, to engage in global war with the mass killing

---

[86]   R. Overy (2009) *The Morbid Age: Britain between the Wars*, London: Penguin, p 164.

[87]   C. Jung, 'The Spiritual Problem of Modern Man', English edn (1933) *Modern Man in Search of a Soul*, London; Kegan Paul, Trench, Trubner and Co.

[88]   C. Jung, quoted in Overy (2009), p 164.

of millions of civilians, and to produce atomic bombs was evidence of what could happen when human beings surrendered to what, in a different context, Hannah Arendt later famously called the 'banality of Evil'. In this respect, Bowlby's concern with 'child care and the growth of love' was his way of 'improving the community as a whole'.

D. W. Winnicott: 'the ordinary devoted mother' in the 'ordinary good home'

To the general public Donald Winnicott was best known for his talks on BBC radio, many of which were broadcast at a time during the 1940s and 1950s when there was considerable political and psychological interest in supporting families having to adapt, first, to the demands of war, and then to the challenge of the early post-war years. From a psychoanalytic perspective, the talks were intended to explain the role of parents in childrearing, particularly the vital importance of the mother to the development of the child's personality: the baby is a person from the start and it is through an intimate relationship with a 'devoted' and 'good enough' mother (who can be loved, hated and relied upon) that the baby develops into a healthy and mature adult individual.[89] Winnicott's influence was enhanced within the first year or so through the publication of five talks in a pamphlet with a title that expressed one of the themes of his life's work: 'Getting to Know Your Baby'. By 1949 he was even better known after his famous series, 'The Ordinary Devoted Mother and Her Baby' (the phrase 'ordinary devoted mother' having been given to him by his producer), and continued to be so throughout the 1950s and 1960s with his collection of essays and talks, *The Child the Family and the Outside World* (1964), selling 50,000 copies in its first three years and being reprinted four times before 1971.[90] Winnicott did not have a completely free hand in either choosing his topics or in the writing of his talks since his female producers were careful to edit and censor the material in ways they thought would further the goal of the BBC to 'educate' its listeners – subjecting them to 'indirect propaganda' – through conveying 'useful

---

[89] A. Karpf (2014) 'Constructing and Addressing the "Ordinary Devoted Mother"', *History Workshop*, 7, Autumn, p 84.

[90] See also his (1957) *The Child and the Outside World*, London: Tavistock. For Winnicott's life and work, with criticisms and rebuttals, see M. Jacobs (1995) *D. W. Winnicott*, London: Sage; also A. Phillips (1988) *Winnicott*, London: Fontana Press.

social messages', without disturbing or alarming them unduly.[91] Winnicott, however, claimed to abhor propaganda saying, 'I am trying to draw attention to the immense contribution to the individual and to society which the ordinary good mother with her husband in support makes at the beginning, and which she does simply *through being devoted to her infant*'; or, as he expressed it rather enigmatically in one of his talks, 'I cannot tell you exactly what to do, but I can talk about what it all means.' He always believed that parents did not need advice or instruction, but 'enlightenment about underlying causes'.[92] During the war the emphasis had been on doing one's bit, while in the post-war period it shifted to citizens' contribution to rebuilding the home and family through care of its members, especially children. Through his radio talks, his writings, and his numerous lectures to colleagues in medicine, social services and voluntary organisations, Winnicott played an important role in helping to implement this change of focus.

Winnicott's Liberalism

It has been said that one way of knowing Winnicott is through his affiliation to the Liberalism that originates with J. S. Mill and works its way through Edwardian New Liberalism to mid-twentieth century British social democracy.[93] Whether Winnicott's politics should or should not be associated with that liberal tradition is not particularly relevant here. Nonetheless, it is true that his contribution to the making of the social democratic family *was* liberal in sentiment, rather than what might be thought of as 1940s socialism. Liberal, that is, in the sense of being personal and individualist; although he always emphasised individuality as 'a social product'. He seems to have subscribed conditionally to the tradition of 'natural liberty', which emphasised the private rather than the public; where welfare was concerned, the duty of the state was to uphold private rights. This was in opposition to the view that the state (society) was an organism, involving public duties and rights.[94] In other words, Winnicott's remark that he saw babies only 'in relation to the mother's functioning' meant that for him

---

[91] Shapira (2013), pp 116–37; Karpf (2014), pp 82–106; also L. Caldwell and A. Joyce (2011) *Reading Winnicott*, London: Routledge.

[92] D. W. Winnicott (1964) *The Child, the Family, and the Outside World*, Harmondsworth: Penguin, pp 10, 16, 186. Emphasis original.

[93] G. Gerson (2005) 'Individuality, Deliberation and Welfare in Donald Winnicott', *History of Human Sciences*, 18, 1. For Winnicott and 'society', see Jacobs (1995).

[94] Harris (1986), pp 235–38.

people's individual identities depended on what has been termed 'their each having a sense of difference from others'; it depended 'on others' attention: 'Individual mind cannot be understood and analysed outside a social context.'[95] In this respect, the individual is a *product* of society. But there is a relationship *between* the individual and society since for Winnicott, 'the capacity to be alone' is always a consequence of being with someone: in infancy, the mother who provides a secure, 'holding' environment for the baby, from which the child derives confidence to move away and, therefore, to be separate is also to be involved.[96] Thus, 'Parental attention generates in the infant confidence in its own existence that is experienced – paradoxically – as independent of that of others. A stable home that is relatively free from anxieties is where individuality forms.'[97]

There are two critical features of this home. First, it is a holding environment, similar to the 'good enough mother' who provides for her infant in part by literally holding, bathing, feeding and caressing:[98]

> The mother is needed as someone who survives each day, and who can integrate the various feelings, sensations, excitements, angers, grief, etc. that go to make up an infant's life but which the infant cannot hold. The child is not yet a unit. The mother is holding the infant, the human being in the making…The early management of an infant is a matter beyond conscious thought and deliberate action. It is something that becomes possible only through *love*.[99]

What is important, however, is that the idea of holding is not confined to the mother and infant relationship, but extends to the mother and the family and beyond to the wider world.[100] Second, is Winnicott's description of the 'transitional object' (a blanket or toy the child carries

95   D. W. Winnicott (1965), *The Maturational Process*, London: Hogarth press, p 57; Gerson (2005), p 112; also C. F. Alford (2000) 'Levinas and Winnicott: Motherhood and Responsibility', *American Imago*, 57, 3, Fall, p 36.

96   Winnicott (1965), pp 29–36.

97   Gerson (2005), p 115.

98   Winnicott (1964), pp 86–7, 194.

99   Winnicott (1957) p 7. Emphasis original.

100 D. W. Winnicott (1986a) *Home is Where We Start From: Essays by an Analyst*, London: Pelican Books, pp 27–8; also Phillips (1988), pp 66.

around for security) as the child's 'first possession'.[101] Thus it embodies the theme of *connection* as it signals being simultaneously connected and separate: 'both me and not me, mother and not mother, all at the same time'.[102] The child has reached the stage where he or she feels sufficiently confident about the mother's care (which is internalised) that it is projected onto the object even when the mother is absent. It is a possession because it is recognised as such by others as an object, not as something internal to the child. Critically, the transitional object, as it emanates from confidence of ownership, bases itself on a willing trust in others.[103] In elaborating on concepts of trust, care, and also, indirectly, obligation, duty and self-sacrifice (of the mother for her child), Winnicott's liberalism appeared, for example, in stark contrast to horrors of the concentration camps (he had complained about British anti-Semitism), and as welcoming to post-war optimism and faith as practised by the ordinary devoted family.

For Winnicott, the household is situated in relation to the welfare state, which resembles a holding environment for its citizens. The citizens will be largely responsible for their own lives with certain discretionary powers being held by the state and its agencies. This is a liberalism that wishes to see the family free from state regulation, except in certain circumstances. The government must 'avoid interfering with the homes that can cope', although it should give assistance where necessary.[104] Society should facilitate the family, just as the family facilitates the child. This, of course, makes sense since Winnicott sees the family in 'the ordinary good home' as the font of democracy, hence the need for it to provide the secure environment, which produces the mature personality, and it – the 'ordinary good home' – can only to do this if free from arbitrary interference.[105] In linking Winnicott to Mill's liberalism, it has been claimed that he allows for the state to intervene – through law, medicine and social science – where individuals might

---

[101] D. W. Winnicott (1971) *Playing and Reality*, London: Tavistock, pp 1–2; Jacobs (1995), pp 53–4.

[102] Alford (2000), pp 236, 246; on transitional objects, Winnicott (1971), pp 1–25; Phillips (1988), pp 113–26.

[103] Gerson (2005), pp 117–18.Gerson explains this in relation to the political theory of Locke, Rousseau and Mill. My interest is with Winnicott's ideas concerning rights and possessions in relation to trust and healthy self-confidence used to inform notions of a consensual social citizenship.

[104] D. W. Winnicott (1986b), *The Family and Individual Development* (1965), London: Tavistock Publications, pp 114–20, 246.

[105] Winnicott (1986b), p 246.

be harmed by other family members as much as by the state itself.[106] What is being raised here, in part, is the liberal dilemma of under what circumstances does the state have the right to affect the personal behaviour (rights) of its citizens in order to protect the social good.[107]

The politics of post-war social democracy, however, aspects of which were under the influence of a socialist perspective, was re-contextualising the dilemma as the old liberal social services state of the Edwardian period was supplanted by the universal and comprehensive welfare state established by the Labour government. That Winnicott surrounded 'the autonomy of the home' with a range of social, medical and legal services for its assistance and, where necessary, also intrusion into the home and the curtailment of parental rights, was no more and no less liberal than was Bowlby's socialism in establishing a set of unshakeable connections between child development, mental health, the duties of government and the role of expertise.[108] But there *was* a difference of political belief between the two men. It has been correctly observed that because he was concerned with his patient's inner world, Winnicott was always less interested (than Bowlby) in the New Jerusalem – with 'future hope' – than with 'the inherent difficulties of life'.[109] For Winnicott the foundation of democracy lay with the family, in mothers and their infants (with fathers standing by as protectors), in their ordinary good homes, which served as the facilitating environment of democracy.[110]

Winnicott's contribution to social democratic parenting culture

Donald Winnicott was important in the making of a social democratic parenting culture because, always with mothers in mind, he identified

---

[106] Gerson (2005), p 123.

[107] Gerson claims that Winnicott's emphasis on 'participation and sociability' means that the 'positive liberty' of infants is bought by denying it to their mother: (2004) 'Winnicott, Participation and Gender', *Feminism and Psychology*, 114, 4, pp 561–62; also Shapira (2013), pp 131–2. For details, see below p 224, note 83. For a feminist defence of Winnicott, see J. Benjamin (1988) *The Bonds of Love*, New York: Panteon; and (1998) *Shadow of the Other*, London: Routledge; also Karpf (2014), p 100.

[108] Rose (1990), p 16.

[109] Quoted in S. Alexander (2012) 'Primary Maternal preoccupations: D. W. Winnicott and Social Democracy in Mid-Twentieth-Century Britain', in S. Alexander and B. Taylor (eds) *History and Psyche: Culture, Psychoanalysis and the Past*, London: Palgrave Macmillan, p 155.

[110] Winnicott (1986), pp 38, 58–9.

and explained the needs of young children in presenting society with its responsibility for the union of mother and child in a way that combined moral standpoint with nurture. Moreover, he consciously situated this responsibility in a historical moment that was eager to embrace belief and faith. Winnicott was always keen to stress the importance of 'understanding young children's human needs in a changing society', and to this end he advised his readers of the necessity to think 'all the time of the *developing* child', since the five-year-old is also '3 and 2 and also 1, and is also an infant being weaned or an infant just born, or even an infant in the womb'. It was a long way from birth to being five years old in terms of personality and emotional development, requiring 'the provision of certain conditions', which need only be 'good enough' since the child will increasingly be able to deal with failure and frustrations by 'advance preparation'. The conditions are not fixed in any way, but are in 'a state of qualitative and quantitative change' relative to the child's age and changing needs. The properly developed four-year-old child needs 'to have parents with whom to identify. At this important stage it is no good implanting morals and inculcating cultural patterns'. The key factor, aside from the home, which exists and continues to survive through the worst of times, 'is the parent, and the parent's behaviour, and the two parents' interrelationship as perceived by the child. It is this that the child takes in, or imitates or reacts against, and it is this also that the child uses in a hundred ways in the personal process of self-development.'[111]

All these conditions are necessary because 'the infant does not start off as a person able to identify with other people. There has to be a gradual building up of the self as a whole', just as there has had to be 'a gradual development of the capacity to feel that the world outside and also the world within are related things, but not the same as the self, the self that is individual and peculiar and never the same in two children'.[112] Babies need help and mothers need to know their babies if they are to help them; for example, 'to manage the awful transitions from sleeping or waking contentment to all-out greedy attack'; to overcome the fear of their own feelings; to face 'the raging lions and tigers' that dwell inside them. Only mothers can do this; only they could help the baby through his or her struggle with inner aggressiveness; only they can properly respond to babies' 'need to be known'.[113] Crucial to the role of the mother was her ability and willingness to

---

[111] Winnicott (1957), pp 3–13.

[112] Winnicott (1957), p 5.

[113] Winnicott (1964), pp 23, 21, 58.

provide the holding environment, which combines both attachment and separation in a single act so that the child may risk being alone; that is, 'risk being' – the freedom to fall into chaos – because one is held by another.[114] In one of his most illuminating contributions to parenting, Winnicott writes that this 'I AM moment is a raw moment; the new individual feels infinitely exposed. Only if someone has her arms around the infant at the time can the I AM moment be endured, or rather, perhaps, risked'.[115] Winnicott's overriding belief in 'The Mother's Contribution to Society' has been aptly summarised as follows: 'We owe mothers everything…mothers hold each of us in body and mind, so making our subjectivity possible. Without mothers to care for us, we should be insane.'[116] This might be seen as Winnicott observing things to be true, without offering a rational demonstrable proof of their existence. But perhaps this is *our* problem. What right do *we* have to demand rational proof? Perhaps 'Some experiences are so fundamental that they cannot be proven…proof is hardly the relevant category': one does not have to prove that 'people deserve to live, not die', or 'that life is worth living'. [117]

'Adjusting the bonds of love'

How true is it that in the early post-war period Bowlbyism led to the 'cocooning' of children in home and family and the curtailment of their 'freedom'? Mathew Thomson has argued that it 'pointed in two directions':

> it encouraged and justified a closing in of the landscape of the child: the most important thing…was the protection and love of home and family…[however] it also emphasized the importance of play, freedom, and social relations within that setting…As such, freedom was lost but also gained: lost in the sense that children were increasingly tied to the protection of the home and had less access to the outside world; gained in the sense that there was a new emphasis on freedom within the home and institution…However, it was

---

[114] Alford (2000), pp 247, 251.

[115] Winnicott, quoted in Alford, p 256; see also Jacobs, pp 36–7.

[116] Alford (2000), p 241.

[117] Alford (2000), p 242, with reference to Derrida's question to the philosopher Levinas asking 'How does he know all this?'

always difficult to satisfy expectations for both emotional security and freedom.[118]

Here a tension is set up between the two conditions, particularly as they came under pressure from changing economic and social circumstances, which undermined 'the locus of attachment', described as 'an idealized model of home and family'.[119] This thesis regarding 'lost freedom' is original in that it is a new accusation levelled at Bowlbyism. On the other hand, it is a little worn in repeating the ideological charge that 'the family' was *idealised*. In their rush to denigrate the child-centred home to which social democracy aspired, critics always confuse having an 'ideal' (as a noun embodying an 'idea') with 'idealize' (as a transitive verb meaning to represent in an ideal form). The significance of home and freedom is discussed in more detail below. For the moment, with reference to Bowlby and Winnicott, it seems unfair to suggest that their work encouraged a restriction on the freedom of children via the necessity for emotional security or that it constituted an 'idealization' of home and family, since both men were at pains to alert their readers to the vicissitudes of family life.[120] It is almost as if Bowlby's writings on aggression, the fragility of mental health, and the delicate politics of 'the group' in relation to fostering democracy, together with Winnicott's numerous essays on the ordinariness of emotional maturity, jostling along with his many references to human imperfectability, have been ignored in the urge to discover a 'lost freedom', which accommodates second-wave feminist and other social liberationist criticisms of Bowlbyism.[121]

Aside from the left/feminist critique of social-democratic child-rearing, the other main sceptical voice has been that of the Foucauldian scholar Nikolas Rose who, through the rubric of 'adjusting the bonds of love', concludes that '"the family" has come to operate as a social mechanism for producing and regulating the subjective capacities of future citizens and as the privileged pathway for the fulfilment of individual wishes and hopes'.[122] This seems to be saying that Bowlby and Winnicott were just two among many professionals in the psy complex – 'engineers of the soul' – who coaxed a generation into believing that it was creating its own subjectivity: the 'expert' as the

---

[118] Thomson (2013), p 79.

[119] Thomson 2013), p 79.

[120] For example, see Bowlby (1953) pp 82–93.

[121] Thomson (2013), pp 93–103.

[122] Rose (1990) p 151.

great illusionist! Rose's interpretation is at odds with the themes of this book in so far as he strives to create such a huge gulf between human agency and culture – as if the former is always inescapably contingent on the latter without any sense of its own volition. The view here is that the humane and potentially empowering declarations concerning the family, childcare, and parenting, as pronounced by Bowlby, Winnicott, Isaacs, Anna Freud, Klein, Suttie and numerous others, emerged from the range of social, economic, political and psychoanalytic analyses that characterised the inter-war and war years. These pronouncements were moulded to fit with the post-war mood of hopefulness about the use of scientific knowledge to provide a hands-on means of safeguarding children's emotional and, therefore, personality development, through what was in effect a form of parent education, the code words for which were 'helping' and 'understanding'. This is not to deny that there was also the instrumental belief (whose origins lay in many of those same inter-war analyses) among informed opinion that today's well-adjusted child, was tomorrow's emotionally stable democratic citizen.[123] But it would be short-sighted to see such cultural developments simply in terms of creating compliant citizens. If this were the case, then it would be true to say that the parent–child relationship had been recast primarily in terms of social investment in children as human capital (as *was* the case under New Labour). Something more was at stake, however, and it requires some explanation.

One reason why Bowlbyism made such progress was that it successfully helped contemporaries to envisage and articulate a humanistic desire, structured within the image of the social-democratic family, that could manifest itself in both private *and* public life. The flexibility of this ideal allowed it to meet the needs of a post-war society in an anxious and bereaved world, still uncertain how to reconcile the ambivalences of love and hate. In the search for reconciliation, Bowlbyism held sway in terms of Bowlby's well known declaration, as mentioned, that good mental health required babies and young children to experience a warm and continuous relationship that was satisfying and enjoyable for both mother and child.[124] The 'holding' arms of Moore's 'Madonna and Child' offered of the chance of success. The new psychology had morphed into a 'science of contentment', in which a new relation between subjectivity and the social order was formed within 'the matrix of the family', whereby emotions were harnessed

---

[123] Rose (1990), pp 151–77.
[124] Bowlby (1951), p 11.

into what by the 1950s was a welfare oriented social democracy.[125] In forwarding this sombre presentation, however, in the brooding colours of 'new technologies of *government*', which apparently lead us to 'govern our own souls', Rose instrumentalises feelings, sentiments and wishes, virtually reducing the work of psychoanalysis (and child guidance) to that of a ploy to 'draft the children as allies in their struggle to change social policies'. No doubt this was a feature of some of the agendas, but it was not the only one. Rose has it that through Bowlby 'Refined conceptions of the psychodynamics of childhood and the relations of mothering were to be linked in an expanded project for the regulation of the relations between mother and child, one that would be prophylactic and pedagogic as much as reactive and reformatory.'[126] In its bald state, this is true. But it ignores all the reciprocal comings and goings held in the matrix, as constituted by those 'conceptions' and 'relations'; in effect a labyrinth of responsive micro social intimacies. Thus it misses the interplay of personal loyalties they aroused, which were fully aware of those who would exploit their claim to integrity for duplicitous ends. Rose prefers to emphasise the '*regulation* of the relations' (emphasis added), which turns everything into an episode of governance. The hand of Foucault is too heavy here; it obscures the role of human agency (the combination of will and desire), which implements our urge to imagine or, dare one say it, to aspire to an ideal.

'Home is where we start from': the home as a 'holding environment'

> [F]or the first time in modern British history the working-class home, as well as the middle-class home, has become a place that is warm, comfortable and able to provide its own fireside environment − in fact a pleasure to live in.[127]

Home, in the most elemental sense, is both an idea and an image; but more than this, it is our beginning, the base from where we start to explore life: 'When father and mother are loving and united in the home, the child can reach out to an independent life of its own, and yet keep an intimate awareness of mutual affection and mutual need'.

---

[125] Rose (1990), p 156; also (1985) , pp 176–96.

[126] Rose (1990), p 163.

[127] Marks Abrams, 'The Home Centred Society', *The Listener*, 26 November, 1959, quoted in C. Langhamer (2005) 'Meanings of Home', in *Journal of Contemporary History*, April, pp 341–62.

The parents are 'unique and primary objects of love. All later loves…are built upon these first ones and in large part are substitutes for them.'[128] This is what Winnicott was getting at when he wrote:

> the home, which has as its basis the relationship between the parents, has a function to perform by existing and by surviving; the child's expressed hate, and the hate that appears in the disasters of dreams, can be tolerated by the child because of the fact that the home continues to function in spite of the worst and because of the best.[129]

As he says, the home is always with us – with both the good and bad memories and experiences: it is foundational to identity, and it never leaves us. The importance of home here is that it can be seen as the holding environment for social-democratic parenting; it provided ontological security, meaning 'confidence or trust that the natural and social worlds are as they appear to be, including the basic existential parameters of self and social identity'.[130] Under the impetus of the re-building of the family as part of the urge to social democracy, a concept embracing security and stability, 'home' achieved such an end for parents and children. It was, as we have seen, a 'holding environment' in three respects: first, the 'good enough mother' provides for the infant through her daily caring relationship; second, the image of 'holding' also facilitates relations between the mother and the family; and, third, through these to the outside world.[131] Thus the child 'is secure in the knowledge that there is someone to whom he is of value and who will strive…to provide for him until such time as he can fend for himself'.[132] It hardly needs saying that the home (conflated here with house, family, haven) is where basic social relations are in part

---

[128] S. Isaacs (1948) 'Fatherless Children', in *Problems of Child Development*, p 3.

[129] Winnicott (1957), p 4; see also his piece with Clare Britton (1948) on the home as the environment in which children learn to trust their parents and, therefore, themselves, 'The Problem of the Homeless Child', in *Problems of Child Development*, p 69.

[130] A. Gidddens (1984) *The Constitution of Society: outline of the theory of structuration*, Cambridge: Polity, p 376.

[131] Winnicott (1964) pp 86–7, 194, and (1986a), pp 27–8.

[132] Bowlby (1953), p 76.

formulated, lived out, and reproduced; it can reasonably be described as 'the crucible of our society'.[133]

The desire to rebuild home and family after the enormous disruption caused by the war is easily understood. More than 60,000 civilians were killed, and 80,000 were wounded in air raids, in addition to nearly 300,000 servicemen (including 4,000 women in the WAF) killed on active service and hundreds of thousands wounded and crippled. The devastation of the housing stock caused by the Blitz – 3.75 million houses destroyed – imposed a burden on social relations through overcrowding and lack of privacy, while the revelations of the evacuation schemes showed that thousands of houses were little more than slums unfit for human habitation.[134] No wonder, then, that housing and home should have preoccupied people's thoughts.[135] Post-war attitudes to home and family, however, were not entirely derived from wartime experiences. The rise in living standards for millions of people during the inter-war period affected their ideas about and expectations of home, family and leisure, just as women's magazines introduced their readership to new aspirations regarding domesticity and personal contentment. But it remains true that with the experiences of the war in mind, 'the one post-war trend that stands out above all the rest is the growing significance of the home'.[136]

Being beguiled by feminist myths

The post-war home has had a bad press from middle-class feminists and others who are keen to portray it as the locus of patriarchy and the exploitation of women, as inhibiting the communal life through unduly emphasising the individual household (privatism), as reproducing capitalist social relations, and as reflecting 'the tense domesticity and anxious conformity of the fifties' – a decade of 'right-

---

[133] For meanings of 'home', see R. Imrie (2006) *Accessible Housing: Quality, Disability and Design*, London: Routledge, pp 91–109; P. Saunders (1989) 'The Meaning of the "Home" in Contemporary English Culture', *Housing Studies*, 4, 3, p 178; S. Mallett (2004) 'Understanding Home: A Critical Review of the Literature, *Sociological Review*, 52, 1, pp 62–89.

[134] Quoted in Langhamer (2005), pp 341–62.

[135] Mass Observation *People's Homes* (1943), London: ASG Bulletin. Change No.4; *The Journey Home* (1944), London: ASG; Fielding et al (1995), p 37.

[136] J. Obelkevich (1994) 'Consumption', in J. Obelkevich and P. Catterall (eds) *Understanding British Society*, London: Routledge, p 144; Langhamer (2005), pp 341–62.

wing traditionalism and cultural stagnation'.[137] Feminists have claimed that 'women as mothers and nothing other than mothers was central to the vision of the 50s', a conservative period, symbolised 'through women, marriage and family'.[138] Pat Thane writes that 'Creating an attractive home', in the early post-war years, 'became an important *pastime* for many women and men...For many women, work in the home became, *sometimes at least*, pleasurable rather than the endless struggle.'[139] This kind of writing is in danger of denigrating millions of women in the name of feminism's identity politics. In reality, trying to make a nice home for a family was much more than a 'pastime', just as for many women keeping house *was* 'pleasurable' rather than being always an 'endless struggle', usually for those whose homes had benefited from the inter-war rising standard of living. This is not the place to fully unpack the condescension shown by so many feminists toward housewives and mothers, except to say that they insult the willing commitment of these women to expending physical and emotional time and effort on behalf of the family, just as they fail to understand the housewife who, in describing how the arrival of the automatic washing machine made the hand-wash redundant, remarked, 'Funny thing is, I love washing, it's my favourite job.'[140] Nor should it be overlooked that two thirds of women responding to social enquiries at the time saw their marriage as 'exceptionally happy' or 'very happy', with only 6 per cent being 'unhappy' or 'very unhappy'.[141] Near the end of the war, a WAAF expressed what seems to have been a popular wish: 'My plans are simple and ordinary. My aim is to return to... normality in an England at peace...I want to marry...I want children...I aspire to being a good cook and housewife, one who makes a house

---

[137] Wilson (1980), p 7; G. Crow (1989), 'The Post-War Development of the Modern Domestic Ideal', in G. Allan and G. Crow (eds) *Home and Family. Creating the Domestic Sphere*, Basingstoke: Palgrave Macmillan, p 20; Shapira (2013), p 115. For the difference between 'privacy', 'privatism', and 'private property ownership', which casts doubt on the charge that 'a home of one's own' encouraged privatism, see P. Saunders and P. Williams (1988) 'The Constitution of the Home: Towards a Research Agenda', *Housing Studies*, 81, pp 81–93, and Saunders (1989), pp 183–86.

[138] Quoted in W. Webster (1998) *Imaging Home: Gender, 'Race', and National Identity, 1945–1964*, London: University College London Press, p x.

[139] P. Thane (2003) 'Family Life and "Normality" in Postwar Britain', in Bessel and Scumann (eds) p 202.

[140] Quoted in E. Roberts (1995) *Women and Families: An Oral History, 1940–1970*, Oxford: Blackwell, p 30.

[141] E. Chesser (1957) *Love and Marriage*, London: Pan Books, pp 397–406.

and a home.'[142] A similar sentiment was expressed by Margaret Powell, who had begun life as a domestic servant before becoming a writer. On leaving service to get married, she recalled:

> I didn't want to go out to work. The time never hung on my hands at all…I was a feminist and stuck up for the rights of women…I asserted an independence as regards running the home…before I felt that home life wasn't enough…I had collected a family of three children, so that any aspirations I had had to go by the board for the time being. Looking after three children is a fulltime job to me at any rate, because I was a mother in the full sense of the word, I think.[143]

Not all feminists have been dismissive and prejudiced in their accounts of home, housewifery, mothering and domesticity. Several have argued that 'it is possible to paint a positive picture of housewifery', citing the importance of housework and its accompanying skills in giving women 'high status in the family and community'.[144] Sarah Ruddick challenges the usual negative portrayal of motherhood, saying that 'Many mothers, whatever their other work, feel part of a community of others whose warmth and support is hard to match in other relationships.'[145] Joanna Bourke has criticised feminists for undervaluing women's roles and negating their rational choice in choosing to become full-time housewives; and Judy Giles reminds us that 'home may be understood as both constricting and fulfilling', and that for 'millions of women…domesticity is a primary concern and an actively created

---

[142] Quoted in I. Zweiniger-Bargielowska (2000) *Austerity in Britain: Rationing, Controls, and Consumption, 1939–1955*, Oxford: Oxford University Press, p 105; also H. A. L. Smith (1986) 'The Effects of War on the Status of Women', in H. A. L. Smith (ed) *War and Social Change*, Manchester: Manchester University Press, pp 217–18.

[143] Quoted in Webster (1998), pp 154–55.

[144] Zweiniger-Bargielowaska (2000), pp 103–4. 'Black' feminists have been much less critical of 'the family' in that they see it as a supportive institution in resisting colonialism and racism. See Webster (1998), p 188, note 7.

[145] S. Ruddick (1990) *Maternal Thinking: Towards a Politics of Peace*, London: The Women's Press.

space'.[146] In answer to the question put to female panellists by Mass Observation in late 1942, 'What does "Home" mean to you?', one woman replied: 'You never realize what home means to you until you have founded one yourself and created a family of your own. To us it means all, security, happiness, comradeship.'[147]

A common feminist response to this sort of understanding of what marriage and domesticity involved has been to argue for a 'false consciousness' imposed through patriarchy as a structural relationship, as when Ann Oakley dismissed women's favourable disposition as 'a rationalization of inferior status'.[148] Other responses have been to claim that women were being deceived by the propaganda thrust of the post-war 'companionate marriage', the benefits of which were 'all on the husband's side', while stay-at-home wives who criticised their wage-earning 'sisters' were really 'sublimating' their own 'frustration'.[149] In answer to the view that many women wanted to give up war work and return to the home, Denise Riley replies, on the one hand, that women's wishes could not be revealed 'by stripping away a patina of historical postscripts and rewritings' and, on the other, by posing the idea that 'Women *really* did want to work, they did want nurseries; if we read the responses to these flat questionnaires *correctly*, we can *surely* decipher these wishes.'[150] It is hard to argue against this kind unreason. So often the gender perspective fails to understand that in home as lived experience, there is always a tension, which often 'begets its own negation', not least where the public/private dichotomy is concerned, which in turn disturbs the image of the so-called 'isolated' wife and mother.[151] Feminists also tend to project the view that the choice was

---

[146] J. Bourke (1993) *Husbandry to Housewifery: Women, Economic Change, and Housework in Ireland, 1890–1914*, Oxford: Clarendon Press, chapter 3; (1994) *Working-class Cultures in Britain 1890–1940: Gender, Class and Ethnicity*, London: Routledge, pp 167–97; Giles (1995), pp 2, 44; and (1993), 'A Home of One's Own: Women and Domesticity in England, 1918–1950', *Women's International Forum*, 16, pp 239–53.

[147] Langhamer (2005), p 344.

[148] Oakley (1974), p 233.

[149] C. Smart (1984) *The Ties That Bind*, London: Routledge and Kegan Paul, pp 28–32; J. Finch and P. Summerfield (1991) 'Social Reconstruction and Companionate Marriage', in D. Clark (ed) *Marriage, Domestic Life and Social Change*, London: Routledge, p 31; D. Smith Wilson (2006) 'A New Look at the Affluent Worker: The Good Working Mother in Post-War Britain', *Twentieth Century British History*, 17, pp 206–29; for a different view, see Langhamer, 2005, p 356–7.

[150] Riley (1983), pp 188-96. Emphasis added.

[151] For discussion, see Mallett (2004), pp 74–7.

either domesticity *or* the life of the 'free' wage-earning woman. But this is a crude contrast that fails to acknowledge the diversity of female attitudes towards domesticity and its relationship to the public sphere.[152]

The importance of 'ordinary good homes'

If we value historical veracity, we need to disregard the ideological view that by nature the post-war home was a stifling, manipulative, conservative and oppressive institution, intent on reproducing patriarchy and capitalism, and appreciate its complexity and its mass popularity. The fact is that as it was being re-built, the home was seen as a potent force in the making of social democratic parenting. But there was more to the ambitions of British psycho-medicine than simply proselytising a democratic form of parent education: in collaboration with the Left (in its many varieties), it was also about trying to create a different kind of universal human being, suitable not only for a non-aggressive yet robust democracy, but for a more advanced civil society. And we should be clear that this does not mean that progressive childcare was not seen as a moral good in itself (certainly by the likes of Bowlby and Winnicott and the many others who shared their moral politics), for it was a feature of mental progress. Failure to recognise this would be to misunderstand not only 'the turn to the Mother' but also that part of the psychoanalytic tradition from the inter-war years as it fused with strands of 'humanist psychology', which developed during the late 1940s and 1950s. It was as a moral good that child care, as advocated by Bowlby and Winnicott, was seen as indispensable to the creation of a new world order and, together with 'the Mother', the home was the place to start from.

With home in mind, it is worth saying a little more about the claim that as a result of Bowlbyism, there occurred 'a closing in of the landscape of the child'. The fact is that Bowlby and Winnicott, and the health and social services they influenced, rarely lost sight of the streets beyond the home. Melanie Klein may have been focused on internal phantasy but Bowlby and Winnicott were not. Winnicott in particular was conscious of the power and importance of the outside world, as he showed in his writings on evacuation and the importance of public play. What was the holding environment about if not preparing children for, and sending them out into, 'the wider realm' – it is 'mainly important and satisfactory if it grows for each individual *out of* the street

---

[152] Zweiniger-Bargielowska (2000), p 106; also Giles (1995), p 19.

outside the front door, or the yard at the back'.[153] As regards Bowlby, we have only to look to his socialist aspiration for social democracy, the essence of which was his concern with group dynamics and the ability of individuals to get along with each other in the collectivist welfare state. Bowlby joined with Winnicott in the view that the mother–child dyad was the starting point for the journey from a shared 'ME' to the independent 'I': what else, if not an expanding landscape for the child.

Moreover, Bowlbyism always appreciated the value of play as a means of understanding and coming to terms with 'environment', meaning home and the beyond and, therefore, learning about sociability.[154] Through play children learned not only how to explore their physical and mental surroundings, and to increase their knowledge and skill, but to express their 'own ideas and feelings with regard to … personal relationships'; play was 'also the safety value whereby experiences that are overwhelming…can be relived in a more bearable form'.[155] In other words, as the social worker Clare Britton (Winnicott's wife) explained, play enabled children to achieve harmony between themselves and the environment; it was the means whereby they came 'to terms with reality', which is 'extremely complicated'.[156] No one who grew up in the late 1940s and 1950s can fail to forget the numerous excursions for 'play' away from home: to the sand dunes for a day by the sea with soggy sand-filled tomato sandwiches and warm lemonade, a tram ride to the end of the line with slightly fresher sandwiches to eat at the terminus, war games on the bomb sites coupled with 'do or dare' into the cavernous bomb shelters, fishing in the local canal, hide and seek through the dark back entries that marked out working-class neighbourhoods, and the perilous journey to and from school involving diplomatic negotiations in order to cross the territorial borders patrolled by gangs of nine-year-old boys – all of which was safely contextualised by having come from, and knowing that one would return to, home.

In terms of its politics in the broadest sense, Bowlbyism was expressly concerned with citizenship, a critical task at the time given the world's recent history and its new uncertainties; it understood implicitly that if citizenship were to be real, that is, able to live organically in a collectivist state, then it had to be the product of a psychologically integrated personality in which the internal and the external were at

---

[153] Winnicott (1964), pp 179–239, emphasis added; 1957, p 94.

[154] See M. Lowenfeld's (1935) *Play in Childhood*, London: Gollancz.

[155] H. Bristol (1948) 'Play and Mental Health', *Problems of Child Development*, p 33.

[156] C. Britton (1945) 'Children Who Cannot Play', *New Education Fellowship Monograph*, 3, November, pp 12–27.

peace with each other. Bowlbyism did not so much 'retreat' as the collective imagination that held together the various constituents of the social-democratic family was emotionally and culturally undermined in being confronted by historical forces that transformed social and economic life over the last three decades or so of the twentieth century. Chapters four and six discuss some of the forces that have characterised late modernity, inspiring political realignments and adverse policy initiatives, not least those in response to the perceived weaknesses of the social democratic state.[157] For the moment, we may list second-wave feminism, a voracious demand for the instant gratification of desire, including credit-based mass consumerism, a motley collection of claimants on the inadequacies of welfare provision, and the rejection of the Labour Party by the New Left in favour of continental philosophers and the politics of identity. None of these groups had much regard for the 'other' – apart from when it involved the narcissism of Lacan's mirror image – and, therefore, they had little or no will 'to make men and women better than they are'.

---

[157] David Garland (2001) *The Culture of Control: Crime and Social Order in Contemporary Society,* Oxford: Oxford University Press, p 75 and chapter 4.

FOUR

The 'long sixties': 1958–1974

'Modernity is not one discourse, but the site of intersection of several, which do not sit easily together.'[1]

The 'long sixties' was much more than a permissive moment; rather it was a historic period of social and cultural change that brought about the 'end of Victorianism'.[2] The optimism of the late 1950s, when the British people, it was said, 'had never had it so good', was very different from the 'false optimism' of the early 1970s as the country approached the moment in 1976 when the Labour politician Anthony Crosland announced 'The party is over', meaning the end of the post-war 'Golden Age'.[3] During the years circa 1958–1974, through a series of statutes, Britain became a more humane, civilised and tolerant society, the most liberal in Europe – if not the world. In areas such as capital punishment, abortion, divorce, homosexuality, theatre and literary censorship, contraception, and equal pay, progressive legislation made Britain an easier place in which to live.[4] In 1959, the future Home Secretary Roy Jenkins, along with Crosland, one of the architects of the permissive society, exhorted prospective voters: 'Let us be on the side of those who want people to be free to live their own lives, to make their own mistakes, and to decide, in an adult way and provided they do not infringe the rights of others, the code by which they wish to live.'[5] This recommendation was not quite as open-ended as it seemed and there was clearly an element of 'moral engineering'

---

[1] A. O'Shea (1996) 'English Subjects of Modernity', in A. O'Shea and M. Nava (eds) *Modern Times: Reflections on a Century of Modernity*, London: Routledge, p 19.

[2] A. Marwick (2003), *British Society since 1945*, London: Penguin Books, pp 113–23; A. Marwick (1998) *The Sixties*, Oxford: Oxford University Press, pp 679–700. D. Sandbrook (2007) *White Heat: A History of Britain in the Swinging Sixties*, London: Penguin Books, pp 326–66.

[3] Marwick (2003), pp 141–7; E. J. Hobsbawm (1994) *Age of Extremes*, London: Michael Joseph, p 403.

[4] A. Crosland (1956) *The Future of Socialism*, London: Cape, p 355.

[5] R. Jenkins (1959) *The Labour Case*, London: Penguin Books.

involved. But at the time it was a worthy ambition pointing toward a more enlightened conception of social democracy.

This is not to say that there was universal approval for the reforms, as numerous surveys revealed the often huge gulf between popular and liberal opinion.[6] In evaluating these years, the record of reform has to be set against the political indulgences, the immaturities, the greed, the violence and the way in which hedonistic desire was confused with vision, which also characterised the long sixties. By the late 1950s, with the coming of affluence and consumerism, modernity seemed to have less to do with rationality and restraint, than with 'immediacy, impact and sensation' – character, perhaps partly reflecting growing secularism, began to give way to 'personality'.[7] Within a decade it was clear that underlying the making of the sixties was a new kind of capitalism, rapacious, 'cool', and seemingly so friendly, which quickly identified new outlets, produced new products, employed a new labour force, evolved a new way of selling goods and, ever so slyly, packaged itself as lifestyle. In effect, this was the time when capitalism undertook the mass marketing of 'identity' as democratic and emancipatory, cleverly associating itself with counter-cultural references as a personal right. The diverse implications of these changes for people's lives, however, make it an especially difficult era in which to discuss the ideals and practices of social democracy in the private and public spheres, and none more so than in that of child rearing. Such is the context in which the main theme of this chapter is set: why was it that social-democratic parenting culture, which had been full of promise in the 1950s and the 1960s, and had effected important liberal changes in parenting, lost so much of its leverage by the mid-1970s?

Before looking in detail at some of the critical influences on patterns of child rearing, it will be helpful to briefly describe a few of the overarching causes of change. The spectre of the problem family continued to encroach on a number of child welfare policy issues, such as juvenile delinquency and child neglect and cruelty, particularly as these families were enveloped in the broader socio-political debate initiated in the 1960s by the reluctantly acknowledged 'rediscovery' of poverty, which undermined the claims of the welfare state to have abolished economic distress and with it social inequality. In this respect, child rearing, and gradually also the family as an institution, became embroiled in numerous criticisms of the post-war settlement, and the

---

6   Sandbrook (2007), pp 338–42.

7   M. Francis (1999) 'The Labour Party: Modernisation and the Politics of Restraint', in B. Conekin, F. Mort and C. Waters (eds) *Moments of Modernity*, London: Rivers Oram, p 168.

conflicting proposals from right and left to restructure it. But more than this, the increasingly shrill critique of the complainants helped to discredit the underlying social-democratic principles of the settlement, as well as the emotional rhetoric – a not to be underestimated 'way of seeing'– that was such an important feature of its edifice. A specific and long-running difficulty, further undermining social-democratic ideals, and made worse by deepening poverty, was how to prevent children from being taken into local authority care. The failure of the 1948 Children Act to provide proper financial resources for *prevention* proved to be an intractable problem, leading to further confusion about the distinction between deprivation and depravation. The negative public, and increasingly middle-class, reaction to the rising rate of juvenile delinquency and youth revolt also threatened both the conceptual cohesion of welfarism and the practical ability of the social services to withstand political criticism. Moreover, the debates on delinquency not only highlighted the ambiguity of the traditional justice/welfare model of the juvenile court system at a time when it was under pressure, but also revealed the uncertainties as to the social–philosophical foundations underpinning relationships between parents, the family and the state.

The integrity of the social-democratic family as a cultural form in mood and practice was further compromised by two profoundly political arguments in education. First, the hostile response, across the political spectrum, to the radicalising of age relations involved in the short-lived Children's Rights Movement which, within the context of the cultural revolution, attempted to revolutionise schooling and question the purpose of education. Second, the far more extensive and significant debate on (socialist) 'egalitarianism' versus (conservative) 'merit': was the objective to create a meritocracy, or a society of equals? This proved to be a seminal struggle with far reaching consequences into the 1980s and beyond between the left-wing of the Labour Party and conservative opinion generally (including Labour voters). The debates had a negative effect on the developing family ideal in that they implicitly questioned the desirability of liberalising child-rearing practices and the promotion of democratic child–adult relations in general. In common with many others, these issues contributed to the growing public scepticism towards the humanist claims of social democracy.

Parent–child relations and the changing perception of children

The 'rediscovery of poverty'

In order to understand the importance of poverty in the politics of 1960s Britain, and the role it played in bringing the short life of British social democracy to an end, the full impact of its 'rediscovery' has to be kept in mind. It may be hard now to grasp how it could ever have been thought that poverty either had been or could be abolished by the welfare state, but for a time that did appear to be the case. The effect of its rediscovery spread beyond the recognition of social distress; it touched the core of what the post-war settlement was supposed to have been about, namely the remoulding of a nexus of social and political roles linking citizens to the state that promised them 'never again'.[8] The social-democratic family, along with the belief in liberal–left civic virtue, was a casualty of what was widely seen as the breaking of that promise. There is no doubt that the realisation that poverty had not been eradicated, 'represented a fundamental shift' in the way in which Britain conceived itself.[9] No less important for the history of age relations, it also signalled a significant shift in the perception of *young* children who, mainly through compensatory educational programmes (in GB and the USA), came to be seen less as belonging in the family and increasingly as resource material in social investment programmes.[10]

During the 1950s the popular view was that poverty was well on the way to being abolished through growing affluence and the implementation of welfare services, and that gross inequality would soon be a thing of the past. Not only did the welfare state seem to offer 'a permanent solution to the problem of social justice', but according to the American sociologist Daniel Bell, under the influence of modernisation, western societies were witnessing 'the end of ideology'. Yet from around the same time, accounts of the standard of living began

---

[8]   J. Harris (1996) '"Contract" and "Citizenship"', in D. Marquand and A. Seldon (eds) *The Ideas that Shaped Post War Britain*, London: Fontana Press, pp 122–38.

[9]   K. Banting (1979) *Poverty, Politics and Policy: Britain in the 1960s*, London: Macmillan, p 1; also L. Platt (2005) *Discovering Child Poverty: The Creation of a Policy Agenda from 1800 to the Present*, Bristol: The Policy Press, pp 89–114.

[10]   This began to occur through the recommendations and follow up of the Plowden Report, *Children and their Primary School*, 1967, on which see H. Silver and P. Silver (1991) *An Educational War On Poverty: American and British Policy-making, 1960–1980*, Cambridge: Cambridge University Press.

to appear suggesting that poverty had not been eliminated.[11] Richard Titmuss, Professor of Social Administration at the LSE, together with his protégés Brian Abel-Smith and Peter Townsend, fractured the complacent view that the welfare state had solved or nearly solved the problem of want. Through their concept of *relative* poverty, Abel-Smith and Townsend showed that the proportion of those in poverty had risen from 7 per cent in 1953–4 to 14.2 per cent in 1960 (from 4 million to 7.5 million people, including 2.25 million children).[12] Evidence began to mount proving beyond reasonable doubt that despite comprehensive welfare provision, millions of people still found themselves below or near the poverty line as determined by benefit levels.[13] It was also beginning to look as if Beveridge's principles, especially those underlying the social security system, on which so much of the welfare state was based, would be abandoned as they could no longer withstand the constant flow of criticism from conservatives and from left-wing professionals, academics, and a number of voluntary and local organisations, including the influential Child Poverty Action Group (CPAG).[14] This was a tremendous blow to the Labour Party.[15] In an important sense, the threat of the rediscovery to the goals of social democracy was foreseen by Peter Townsend:

> The Labour government is compromising too readily with entrenched interest, is avoiding the need to confront racial and social prejudice with moral authority, is failing to introduce institutional change and is forgetting that in this growingly more complicated world it must, like Alice, run even faster to stay in the same place and to preserve, still less extend, existing human rights.[16]

---

[11] Silver and Silver (1991), pp 147–57.

[12] B. Abel-Smith and P. Townsend (1965) The Poor and the Poorest, *Occasional papers on Social Administration*, No 17, London: Bell, pp 57–8. On the relativity of poverty, see Platt (2005), pp 106–8; also K. Coates and R. Silburn (1970) *Poverty: The Forgotten Englishman*, London: Penguin.

[13] R. Lowe (1993) *The Welfare State in Britain since 1945*, Basingstoke: Macmillan, pp 135–41.

[14] Lowe (1993), pp 141–50.

[15] Banting (1979), pp 74–99.

[16] P.Townsend (1967) *Poverty, socialism, and Labour in Power*, London: Fabian Society, pp 31–2.

So it was that the first serious question mark was cast over the likelihood that the post-war settlement would advance the cause of Progress – it had seemed as if it would be so easy. In many respects, however, poverty continued to be sidelined in the media glare that glamourised the sixties, and 'swinging London'. But the doubts concerning the efficacy of the settlement would not go away. For all those who cared to look, it was a reminder, however unfairly placed, that to be effective, Winniciott's 'holding environment' required the basic materials of life.

The spectre of juvenile delinquency

Although the problem of juvenile delinquency was a critical feature of the political culture of the 1960s and early 1970s, it remained conceptually nebulous. During the course of the 1950s, early optimism regarding child welfare receded through the ambiguities surrounding the distinction made between *deprivation* and *depravation*, which had last been raised in inter-war debates on the juvenile justice system, and now began to gather purchase again. Although there was some concern about levels of child neglect (deprivation), it seemed, despite the unreliability of criminal statistics, that the juvenile delinquency rate *was* rising. Having been expected to decline in post-war society, by 1961 the proportion of indictable offenders under 17 was 107 per cent more than in 1938, in 1963 it was 125 per cent more, and by 1965 it had risen to 133 per cent.[17] Liberal criminologists and social workers were quizzed as to the meaning of, and relation between, deprivation/depravation, as critics asked who was being protected from whom, and who most needed protection. These were the issues that the Ingleby Committee (appointed by the Home Office in 1956) set out to investigate.[18] The subsequent Report, which emphasised children in trouble, led to the Children and Young Persons Act 1963 that, as part of its focus on preventing delinquency, gave local authorities powers to counter child neglect in order to keep more children in

---

[17] H. Hendrick (1994) *Child Welfare: England 1872–1989*, London: Routledge, p 229.

[18] *Report of the Committee on Children and Young Persons* (hereafter the Ingleby Report, 1960), London: HMSO.

their own homes.[19] In doing so, however, it explicitly re-established the link between deprivation and depravation, saying that it was not sufficient to protect children from 'neglect' – 'something more positive was required' if they were to get 'the best upbringing possible'.[20] Since children who were *deprived* of this upbringing risked becoming delinquent (*depraved*), parents were to be assisted in their child rearing: 'it was the duty of the community to provide through its social and welfare services the advice and support' parents and children needed.[21]

According to *The Times*, the guiding principle of the Criminal Justice Act 1948, was that 'there must be no despair of humanity'.[22] By the late 1960s such a sentiment sounded a little naive as the welfare consensus, around which the liberal–progressive principles of childcare had been established, was beginning to dissolve. As one sociologist wrote, 'when the highly specific conditions changed, so the faith of the counsellors entered a period of convulsion. In particular the forgotten questions of power, social structure and social class posed themselves.'[23] While the level of youthful criminality was disheartening, more than a statistical rise in convictions was involved. The real anxiety arose from a sense of cultural change, not only among conservatives, but also from a growing feeling of unease that permeated the consciousness of the liberal middle class. From the 1950s, there was growing public concern about the attitude and behaviour of working-class youth which, it was said, threatened the 'British way of life'. Nowhere was this fear more clearly displayed than at Conservative party conferences, always a barometer of popular prejudice by no means confined to party members. In 1958, conference was roused by claims regarding 'this sudden increase in crime and brutality which is so foreign to our nature and our country', and the 'make-believe gangsters strolling about the streets as if they are monarchs of all'. There was no doubt as to what

---

19 Ingleby continued the 'welfare model' approach in British juvenile justice policy, and reiterated the belief that forms of moral and physical neglect were the antecedents of criminal delinquency. See Labour Party report: *Crime: A Challenge to US All* (1964), and White Papers: *The Child, the Family and the Young Offender* (1965) and *Children in Trouble* (1968). For Ingleby, see Hendrick (1994), pp 225–7; also J. Packman (1975) *The Child's Generation: Child Care from Curtis to Houghton*, Oxford and London: Blackwell/Robertson, pp 114–22.

20 Quoted in Hendrick (1994), p 224.

21 Ingleby Report (1960), pp 5–6

22 Quoted in V. Bailey (1987) *Delinquency and Citizenship: Reclaiming the Young Offender, 1918–1948*, Oxford: Clarendon Press, pp 302–3.

23 G. Pearson (1975) *The Deviant Imagination*, London: Macmillan, p 132.

was causing this calamitous situation: the 'lack of parental control, interest and support', the 'sex, savagery, blood and thunder' in films and on television, and the 'smooth, smug and sloppy sentimentalists who contribute very largely to the wave of crime'; no wonder young people were 'no longer frightened of the police, they sneer at them'. The BMA expressed its concern more soberly: 'The society in which today's adolescents find themselves is one of bewildering change…the whole face of society has changed in the last twenty years…a decrease in moral safeguards, and the advent of the welfare state has provided a national cushion against responsibility and adversity.'[24]

The voices of what during Thatcher's government would become popular punitiveness, however, though gaining confidence, were not yet in the ascendant. The last throw of the Fabian social-democratic dice came with the passing of the Children and Young Persons Act 1969, which believed in casework for deprived families, regarded delinquency and neglect as a symptom of deprivation, and was committed to de-institutionalisation.[25] The thrust of the Act was to decriminalise as much as possible of the system for both the 10–14 and 14–17 age groups, leaving the social care of the 'delinquents' to be undertaken by the new local authority 'family service' departments.[26] The Act has been judged to be 'the high point of therapeutic familialism as a strategy for government through the family'.[27] In the heated political atmosphere of the period, however, the promise of the welfare state was becoming harder to maintain, not least because the social, economic and educational arguments of the emerging New Right were gaining in intellectual and political credibility.

Nonetheless, the long sixties did not witness the complete demise of either the ideal of social-democracy or of the desire to continue promoting a liberal-parenting culture. Social-democratic thinking on juvenile delinquency, for example, looked to try to involve parents more directly in 'treatment' schemes, encouraging them to assume

---

[24] Quotations in G. Pearson (1983) *Hooligan: A History of Respectable Fears*, London: Macmillan, pp 12–13, 16.

[25] N. Frost and M. Stein (1989) *The Politics of Child Welfare*, London: Harvester Wheatsheaf, p 81. The Act was only partially implemented as Labour lost the 1971 general election.

[26] Hendrick (1994), pp 231–5.

[27] N. Rose (1990) *Governing the Soul: The Making of the Private Self*, London: Routledge, p 175.

more responsibility for their children's behaviour.[28] Unfortunately, Labour Party opinion on juvenile delinquency lacked any theory of causation; instead the reforms focused on the proposal for a family service, which would replace the Children's Departments.[29] For many Labour reformers the objective in organising social welfare around a concept of family need was to uphold what were described as 'human' values and social skills and to counter the hedonism and acquisitiveness of the decade. In this respect, reformers drew on the pre-war thought of Christian socialist intellectuals, such as R. H. Tawney, which stressed 'the values of co-operation, mutual service, self-respect, and respect for others'.[30] What was little realised at the time, was that this sentiment was being overtaken by the intellectual vibrancy of the New Right, and also by a series of developments – economic, political and cultural – which the social-democratic Left found difficult, if not impossible, to understand.[31]

From Children's Departments to the personal social services

Unsurprisingly, the 'ordinary devoted mother' in the 'ordinary devoted home' could hardly be more closely associated with the goals and objectives of local authority provision for children in care and those likely to come into care. Here, if anywhere, the principles of social-democratic parenting would surely guide professional behaviour and practice. And yet, by the mid-1950s the optimism of the 1948 Children Act seemed misplaced. Even at the time, the fact that the Act focused on children 'deprived of a normal home life', that is, those 'in care', meant that those who were neglected or cruelly treated in their own homes were left without full legislative protection. There were two fundamental difficulties in developing the preventive approach. First, there were the professional rivalries between the health and education departments and Children's Officers and childcare officers, in addition to disagreements as to how to raise the standing of social work as a profession, and how it should be organised. The critical issue, however,

---

28 Quoted in J. Clarke (1980) 'Social Democratic Delinquents and Fabian Families', in National Deviancy Conference (ed) *Permissiveness and Control: The Fate of the Sixties Legislation*, London: Macmillan, p 86.

29 Clarke (1980), p 88.

30 Clarke (1980), p 89.

31 J. Nuttall (2006) *Psychological Socialism: The Labour Party and the Qualities of Mind and Character*, Manchester: Manchester University Press; L. Black (2003) *The Political Culture of the Left in Britain 1951–1964*, Basingstoke: Palgrave.

in which childcare got caught up, was the structure of what was known in social work circles as the 'personal social services'.[32] The second difficulty seemed to be equally irresolvable: how to obtain the necessary monetary support for all the programmes envisaged.

By the early 1950s, the increasing number of children coming into care was putting a financial strain on resources. At the same time, however, efforts were being made to encourage children's departments to enquire into the conditions of children thought to be suffering domestic neglect, which led to a greater emphasis being given to the processes involved in prevention.[33] In 1960 the Ingleby Report recommended that local authorities be given a 'general duty' to prevent and forestall child neglect in their own homes, although no mention was made as to either additional resources or the allocation of legal responsibilities between government departments and Ministries. As one expert remarked, the Committee had stumbled into the 'jungle' of personal social services – 'a jungle haunted by primitive prejudices and infested with professional and political pressure groups of the most ferocious kind'.[34] In effect, Ingleby was prioritising the prevention of juvenile delinquency and, reflecting the Fabian socialist view, saw neglect (which could lead to 'depravation') in terms of the 'maladjustment of personal relationships' within the family and, therefore, deemed it imperative that 'social and welfare services' should provide families in trouble with 'advice and support' so that children received the best possible rearing.[35] In other words, prevention was moving up the social services agenda negatively by virtue of seeing children as *threats*. On the plus side, however, the recommendation that the task be given to children's departments led to the protection of children in care being *extended* to those in the domestic home. On the other hand, the politics surrounding Ingleby (for example, power struggles between the childcare service and MOsH) pointed to the difficulties in embracing 'a wide spectrum of families' in the arms of the social–democratic state.[36] Despite these difficulties, following the preventive provisions of the Children and Young Persons Act 1963, by

---

[32] *Report (1968) of the Committee on Local Authority and Allied Personal Social Services* (hereafter Seebohm), London: HMSO, pp 52–89; J. Cooper (1983) *The Creation of the British Personal Social Services, 1962–1974*, London: Heinemann Education.

[33] Packman (1975), pp 54, 62.

[34] Quoted in Packman (1975), p 64; see Ingleby Report (1960), chapter 2.

[35] Ingleby Report (1960), chapter 1.

[36] Packman (1975), p 65.

1970, while 42,000 children were admitted into care, 220,000 were helped in their own homes.[37]

Around the time that juvenile delinquency was becoming a critical political topic, the nature of social work itself was also being discussed, partly in relation to the size and character of the caseloads arising from the 'rediscovery' of poverty. As preventive work developed throughout the 1960s, social workers found themselves more intimately involved in a range of family relationships and situations, often requiring collaboration with colleagues in other departments. Consequently, not only were calls made for greater inter-departmental coordination in order to develop a more comprehensive approach to preventive strategies, particularly in relation to the link between depravation and deprivation, but a theory of welfare was encouraged to accommodate the comprehensive needs of working-class families.[38] The 1968 Report of the Seebohm Committee established to inquire into the messy matter of social provision had as its goal the creation of an effective family service to be established through 'Social Services Departments', which were to be generic in nature and community based, and in so doing bring to an end the independent childcare service.[39] Although the childcare lobby had called for gradualism, it failed to persuade the Committee, and so children lost their dedicated spokespersons to an assortment of more powerful and more influential interests who argued that 'preventive thinking' had become 'too family and child-centred'.[40] The Seebohm Report was implemented by the Local Authority Social Services Act 1970, which saw the creation of the Fifth Social Service, after education, health, social security and public housing (between 1971 and 1976 the number of social workers rose from 10,346 to 21,182). Broadly speaking, the new service reflected the commitment of the liberal left to state intervention and the efficacy of the expert.[41] By the mid-1970s, however, the promise of the new departments was fading into memory as the limitations of their assumptions became apparent and the social and economic contexts in which they operated

---

[37] Packman (1975), pp 69–71; Hendrick (1994), pp 227–9.

[38] Packman (1975), pp 155–6; Lowe (1993), pp 261–79; Cooper (1983), pp 54–68.

[39] Seebohm, pp 11–12; Packman (1975), pp 156–71; E. Younghusband (1978) *Social Work in Britain: 1950–1975*, London: Allen and Unwin, pp 239–49.

[40] Quoted in Packman (1975), p 161.

[41] M. Langan (1993) 'The Rise and Fall of Social Work', in J. Clarke (1993) *A Crisis in Care? Challenges to Social Work*, London: Sage, p 47.

underwent change.[42] The scandal surrounding the death of Maria Colwell, murdered by her stepfather in 1973, while in council care, exacerbated the pessimism that had begun to affect social workers as many turned to a new, more client-based approach and a minority, under New Leftist influence, entered what was termed their 'radical hour' with an enthusiasm for participatory decision-making.[43] Within a few years the advent of the first Thatcher administration began and rapidly gained ideological confidence, further exposing the political and cultural weaknesses of the post-war consensus.

Dethroning Bowlby?

Historians should never accept a source at face value. When we consider the politically motivated criticisms of the social-democratic family ideal, and those directed at Bowlby (and Bowlbyism) in particular, it is worth knowing the identity of the critics and something of their motivations, as well as the circumstances in which their critiques were produced. This is an especially difficult undertaking with respect to Bowlby. It hardly needs saying that his work has been central to what remains a controversial, often vitriolic, and mainly feminist inspired debate concerning the social politics of mothering, the family and gender relations, in which he has been repeatedly misrepresented and caricatured. And while it is the case that as a prolific author, with an evolving thesis (attachment theory), and writing for many different audiences, at times he could be oblique and confusing, we should appreciate that he worked within a historical context that was marked by numerous political and professional disputes, which affected the way in which his ideas were produced and received. This led him to have a number of critics within the psychoanalytic community, as well as in medicine and psychiatry, and his later adoption of an ethological outlook further strained relations. In other words, in looking at what happened to Bowlby's ideas, the politics of science has to be kept in mind, as much as that of feminism and other social liberationist critiques.

It has been suggested that the 'most scathing criticism' of Bowlby came from the American anthropologist Margaret Mead and the British

---

[42] N. Parton (2014) *The Politics of Child Protection*, London: Palgrave Macmillan, p 19; Lowe (1993), pp 268–9.

[43] J. Clarke (1993) *A Crisis in Care? Challenges to Social Work*, London: Sage; M. Langan and P. Lee (eds) (1989) *Radical Social Work Today*, London: Unwin Hyman; R. Bailey and M. Brake (1975) *Radical Social Work*, London: Edward Arnold.

social scientist Barbara Wootton, writing in a WHO reassessment of the theory of maternal deprivation.[44] Mead and Wootton were two of the leading public intellectuals of their day and though they were hardly conventional second-wave feminists, neither had any time for stay-at-home mothers. Mead, the more internationally prominent of the two, 'a celebrity in her twenties', with strong views on a range of issues, was considered to be one of the most influential women in America, regularly offering advice on a variety of topics to an audience of millions.[45] In her 30s, she became a mother and immediately secured a nurse for the child and thereafter for the next 15 years or so, when she was not away doing field work or working for the government in Washington, lived in New York in the home of the charitable foundation director Lawrence Frank and his family. Mead shared the downstairs with her husband, daughter, the daughter's nurse and her daughter and, during the war years, two English evacuees; upstairs the Franks lived with their five children. Frank's wife, Mary, was 'the maternal center of the household'. When asked if she was jealous that Mary had displaced her, Mead replied 'that jealousy was culturally produced, an emotion she did not feel'.[46] One of her biographers, Hilary Lapsley, dryly observes that 'The American version of wifehood and motherhood had never been congenial to Margaret.' The fact is that Mead, who personified the political ambitions of American anthropology as it competed for influence among other social sciences, was the embodiment of female careerism. Betty Friedan recalled that when Mead and her husband (Geoffrey Bateson, also a famous

---

[44] M. Thomson (2013) *Lost Freedom: The Landscape of the Child and the British Post-War Settlement*, Oxford: Oxford University Press, p 94; also A. Oakley (2011) *A Critical Woman: Barbara Wootton, Social Science and Public Policy in the Twentieth Century*, London: Bloomsbury, pp 221–7; J. Stewart (2013) *Child Guidance in Britain, 1918–1955*, London: Pickering & Chatto, p 183; S. Yudkin and A. Holme (1969) *Working Mothers and Their Children: A Study for the Council of Children's Welfare*, London: Sphere, pp 95, 101, 137–9; H. Gavron (1968) *The Captive Wife*, London: Penguin, pp 129-34. For the critiques of Bowlby, see M. Mead 'A Cultural Anthropologist's Approach to Maternal Deprivation', and B. Wootton 'A Social Scientist's Approach to Maternal Deprivation', both in WHO (1962), *Deprivation of Maternal Care: A Reassessment of its Effects*, Geneva, pp 45-62 and 63-73 respectively. However, aside from being referenced by Yudkin and Holme, and Gavron, the broader influence of the *Reassessment* is by no means clear.

[45] P. Mandler (2009) 'Margaret Mead amongst the Natives of Great Britain', *Past and Present*, 204, pp 149–72.

[46] Quoted in H. Lapsley (1999) *Margaret Mead and Ruth Benedict: The Kinship of Women*, Amherst, MA: University of Massachusetts Press, p 287.

anthropologist) visited her college, they were referred to as 'God the Mother and Jesus Christ'.[47] Lapsley sums up Mead at 40 as 'a woman who appeared to be in command of her destiny, unhesitatingly shaping the circumstances of her life with a loyalty to her own needs unusual for a woman of her time'.[48]

Exactly how the WHO came to commission a 'reassessment' of Bowlby's original study is unclear.[49] Mead and Bowlby knew each other from the WHO sponsored Study Group on the Psychological Development of the Child, which met during the 1950s, and they were no doubt aware of each other's views. As an anthropologist, Mead shared with the neo-Freudians the desire to combine Freud's insights into the human psyche with cultural relativism 'by emphasising the role of social cultural forces rather than universal "drives" in the individual's achievement of mental integration', and objected strongly to what she saw as the sidelining of anthropology, for example, by psychoanalysts, noting the 'provincialism of studies based only upon modern societies'.[50] She was keen for anthropology to displace psychiatry, medicine, economics, sociology and psychology as a means of addressing social and political concerns, and to this end promoted a 'culture–personality' group, while pushing for comparative studies to provide 'corrections to simplistic formulations', which, she claimed, ignored the lessons of 'whole cultures'.[51] The essence of her criticism of Bowlby was that his views constituted the 'reification into a set of universals of a set of ethnocentric observations on our own society'.[52] Elsewhere, however, she was less guarded, giving vent to her ideological objections in referring to the problem of mother–child separation as 'a new and subtle form of antifeminism in which men – under the guise of exalting the importance of maternity – are tying women more tightly to their children than has been thought necessary since the invention of bottle feeding and baby carriages'.[53]

Barbara Wootton was a major presence in British social science from the 1950s to the 1970s. She was a progressive and influential

---

[47] Quoted in Lapsley (1999), p 287.

[48] Quoted in Lapsley (1999), p 288.

[49] WHO (1962), pp 7–8.

[50] Mandler (2009), p 152.

[51] Mandler (2013) *Return from the Natives: How Margaret Mead Won the Second World War and Lost the Cold War*, New Haven, CT: Yale University Press; Mead (1962), pp 45–7.

[52] Mead (1962), p 58.

[53] M. Mead (1954) 'Some Theoretical Considerations on the Problem of Mother–Child Separation', *American Journal of Orthopsychiatry*, 24, 3, p 477.

voice in a variety of causes (many concerning children's welfare in the justice system), a prominent figure in the House of Lords, and an influential member of a several committees and organisations. Wootton embraced a number of issues about which she seems to have thought that everyone else was wrong and she was right. As several reviewers noted, her influential book on social science and social pathology was 'deeply coloured by her personal viewpoint', while one remarked that 'Although the purpose of the book is not destructive, the author is not able to conceal her talents in this direction.'[54] With regard to Bowlby's theory of maternal deprivation, Wootton grouped her objections around his failure to investigate how many maternally deprived children did *not* become anti-social; what she termed a slovenly approach to the use of statistics; the confusion between 'separation' and 'deprivation'; the failure to consider the role of economic factors, as opposed to relationship issues, in causing mental and emotional anguish; the failure to use proper controls in case studies; and the substitution of dogmatic opinions in place of scientific evidence.[55]

The criticisms of Bowlby, and those who shared his views, should be seen in the broader context of Wootton's fierce attack on three contemporary social scientific trends: i) the methodologies and growing influence of medicalisation (psychiatry) on the 'treatment' of anti-social and criminal behaviour, as well as in areas such as child guidance – she objected to medicine as science taking the place of traditional morality; ii) the alleged intellectual and theoretical pretentiousness of social workers, particularly those with psychiatric qualifications – harbingers of medicalisation; and iii) the moral, medical and legal confusions of criminology, at the time a subject with uncertain foundations and struggling for academic recognition.[56] Wootton's penetrating but selective critique was hugely controversial, certainly among social workers at the LSE (the principal training institution). It is hard to appreciate nowadays the acerbity of the disputes on these matters, which often criss-crossed political allegiances. Bowlby, as a

---

54 Quotations in Oakley (2011), pp 227, 226.

55 B. Wootton (1959) *Social Science and Social Pathology*, London: Allen and Unwin, pp 136–56; and her essay in WHO (1962), pp 63–73. Mary Ainsworth, Bowlby's colleague, wrote a detailed rebuttal to all the criticisms in the reassessment: WHO (1962), pp 97–165.

56 Wootton was much taken with 'anti-psychiatry', and the theories of Thomas Szasz, perhaps failing to see the conservative undercurrents: Oakley (2011), p 224. On these, see P. Sedgwick (1982) *Psycho Politics*, New York: Harper and Row. For a useful discussion of anti psychiatry, see M. Thomson (2006) *Psychological Subjects: Identity, Culture and Health in Twentieth-Century Britain*, Oxford: Oxford University Press, Chapter 8.

medical man, psychiatrist, psychoanalyst, social–democratic socialist, advocate of child guidance, supporter of local authority intervention in childcare, pioneer of attachment theory and author of numerous articles and studies used in the training of social workers, was exposed to a number of different assaults from vested interests, few of which had the welfare of children as their first priority.[57]

One of the best known critical accounts of Bowlbyism in the 1960s was Yudkin and Holme's study of working mothers and their children. On the one hand, these authors argued that Bowlby was misunderstood, particularly in relation to his phrase 'continuous relationship' between mother and child, which had been taken too literally; on the other hand, however, they held him responsible for the prevailing negative attitude toward working mothers with young children, which they described as a 'prejudice'.[58] They cited Mead in support of their view

---

[57] Another study, which is said to have undermined Bowlbyism, was that of the psychiatrist Hilda Lewis whose account of 500 children at a reception centre for placing children in care claimed that there was no relationship between the separation of children from their families and the *long-term* effects on their behaviour. H. Lewis (1954) *Deprived Children: The Mersham Experiment: A Social and Clinical Study*, Oxford: Oxford University Press. But this hardly caused waves (Bowlby sent a short response to the *Lancet*). In his review of maternal deprivation, Rutter gave it just a brief footnote. M. Rutter (1972, 2nd ed. 1981) *Maternal Deprivation Reassessed*, London: Penguin Books, p 103. It is worth noting that Lewis was the wife of Aubrey Lewis, then the doyen of English psychiatry at the Maudsley Hospital. Bowlby had been Lewis's student in the mid-1930s where he had found him to be very critical of psychoanalysis – 'we agreed to differ' – although he always saw it as a potentially important medical approach. Quotation, in S. van Dijken (1998) *John Bowlby. His Early Life. A biographical journey into the roots of attachment theory*, London: Free Assocation Books, p 69; for Lewis and psychoanalysis, see M. Shepherd (1986) 'A Representative Psychiatrist: The Career, Contributions and Legacies of Sir Aubrey Lewis', *Psychological Medicine* (supplement 10), pp 11–12. Other figures to emerge from the Maudsley under Lewis' tutelage, who were critical of Bowlby (and Winnicott), the child guidance ethic, and psychoanalysis included the hugely influential behaviourist H. J. Eysenck, his pupils A. D. B Clarke and A. M. Clarke, experts on 'mental subnormality', and the educational psychologist Jack Tizard, campaigner for nursery education, who dismissed child guidance as 'wrongly conceived', quoted in A. Wooldridge (1994) *Measuring the Mind: Education and Psychology in England, c. 1860–1990*, Cambridge: Cambridge University Press, p 317; for Eysenck's influence, see M. Derksen (2001) 'Science at the clinic: Clinical psychology at the Maudsley' in G. C. Bunn, A. D. Lovie and G. D. Richards (eds) *Psychology in Britain: Historical Essays and Personal Reflections*, Leicester: BPS Books, pp 267–9; also Thomson (2006), pp 258-61.

[58] Yudkin and Holme (1969), pp 88, 96.

that 'a close relationship with one person is more a cultural than a biological matter', and that this close relationship 'is by no means always present in other cultures and at other times'. But they admitted that whatever Mead claimed, in practice it was usually the mother who was the main carer.[59] This helped to explain the fact that although some six million married women worked, two and a half million of whom had children under 16, only 750,000 had children under five; how many of these were three and under (which was the critical age for Bowlby and Winnicott) was not known.[60] Despite their criticisms of Bowlby, Yudkin and Holme did *not* recommend full-time employment for mothers of the under-threes.[61] Perhaps they were influenced by a Report from the Centre for Human Development at London University, which concluded that children left from infancy all day in a 'substitute environment' were likely to have a less close relationship with their mothers than 'both would wish', and cast further doubt on whether the under-threes could be adequately cared for by the limited staff in nurseries.[62] All in all, Yudkin and Holme conceded that regarding the effects of mothers' employment on children the evidence either way was inconclusive – there were so many unanswered questions raised by so many variables.[63]

There were no such doubts expressed by the psychiatrist Michael Rutter in his *Maternal Deprivation Reassessed* (1972), the most scholarly critique of Bowlby's influence. Either through good luck or planning on the part himself and the publishers, Penguin, the book appeared just as the Women's Liberation Movement (WLM) was emerging from the student politics of 1968, under the guidance of the Women's National Co-Ordination Committee, 1970, with its four demands: equal pay, free contraception, abortion on demand, and free 24-hour nurseries. The core issue for feminists was the cluster of grievances around the home, marriage, the family, childcare and the working mother, and at the heart of this cluster was Bowlby's thesis on maternal deprivation. This was the context in which Rutter's reassessment appeared. As the Editorial Foreword to *Maternal Deprivation Reassessed* observes, however, with regard to the differences between Bowlby and Rutter, despite the latter being a 'hard-headed experimentalist...it is remarkable that their

---

[59] Yudkin and Holme (1969), p 137.

[60] Yudkin and Holme (1969), p 30.

[61] Yudkin and Holme (1969), pp 96, 187–9.

[62] Included in Yudkin and Holme (1969), pp 135–67, p 133.

[63] Yudkin and Holme (1969), p 110–11.

conclusions have so much in common'.[64] In later years, Rutter gave the impression that there were few if any fundamental differences between Bowlby and himself, and that Bowlby, 'an honest man', accepted his revisions.[65] But there *were* differences and in the increasingly polemical climate that marked the early 1970s, differences mattered. Along with others, Rutter called for more attention to be given to the variables 'indiscriminately' combined within 'maternal deprivation' and he sought to explore the possibility that 'different psychological mechanisms may account for different types of outcome'. Moreover, not only did the effects of different types of 'maternal deprivation' need to be considered, but so, too, did disorders of the brain and hereditary factors. He was also keen to highlight the problematic nature of the term 'maternal deprivation' since the deleterious influences were *not* specifically related to the mother and were *not* due to deprivation. Using the dictionary definition of deprivation as meaning 'loss' or 'dispossession', Rutter claimed that the damage came not from 'loss' but from 'lack' or 'distortion' of care, adding, like a true experimentalist, that there was more to child-rearing than the 'mystical importance' placed 'on the mother' and 'love'.[66] Rutter doubted whether children were 'innately monotropic', just as he questioned 'the whole notion of bonding' in relation to separation, arguing that separation may or may not be harmful, but it is the relationship itself that required examination.[67] One of the most important developments in maternal deprivation research, he said, was the nature of the individual differences in children's responses to deprivation, with more attention being given to the mother–infant relationship prior to separation as an influence on the response to separation. In his conclusion, Rutter claimed that the term 'maternal deprivation' should be abandoned since 'the experiences included under the term...are too heterogeneous and the effects too varied for it to continue to have any usefulness'.[68] Although the anti-Bowlby climate during the long sixties should not be exaggerated, Rutter's critique was influential, not only because of his professional prestige, but because it appeared just when second-wave feminist 'knowledge' was beginning to be formulated as part of the reculturalisation of British society: feminist social science (especially

---

[64] M. Rutter (1981 ed) *Maternal Deprivation Reassessed*, Harmondsworth, Penguin, p 7.

[65] Rutter, Interview by Normand Carrey (2010) in *Journal of the Canadian Academy of Child and Adolescent Psyciatry*, 19, 3, pp 212–17.

[66] Rutter (1981 ed), p 125.

[67] Rutter (1981 ed), pp 126.

[68] Rutter (1981 ed), p 130.

sociology and psychology), feminist literary studies, feminist political science, feminist philosophy and so on. In this environment, at this time, Rutter was a useful chap to have onside.

Second-wave feminism: the 'captive wife'

The sixties are so well known, so etched in our modern folklore, that it is tempting to unfold these years in facile generalisations of cultural change, of the kind that preoccupy the 'lifestyle' pages of contemporary broadsheets. It was certainly the case, however, that the old political language of class was replaced with gender, just as 'class traitors' became sexists and misogynists. In place of derivatives from Liberalism's long debate with the Enlightenment, a new form of fundamentalism emerged in the sense of requiring 'strict adherence to a set of basic principles', 'a refusal to find common ground', a committed (dogmatic) attachment to what are treated as 'irreducible truths' – all to promote women's 'emancipation', meaning freedom from patriarchy, the traditional heterosexual nuclear family, and the burdens of mothering and motherhood.[69] In pursuit of their ends, feminists have always been alert to the value of making their voices heard across a range of social scientific outlets, through which they have repeated a litany of claims and allegations, usually underscored through cultural relativist mantras, one of the favourite being that motherhood may be a biological state, but there is nothing 'natural' about it as an institution – it is a 'social construction'.[70] Repetition is an old political device used to frame a discourse in such a way as to disable opponents through restricting the inclusion of themes and topics other than those favouring one's own perspective.[71] Perhaps unsurprisingly, then, the long sixties, in so far as it witnessed the birth of an politically trenchant feminism, which replaced the older Fabian-type variety, saw the beginning of the process whereby many of the post-war ideals of liberal parenting within the social-democratic family, were dislodged. By no means was

---

[69] J. Nagata (2001) 'Beyond Theology: Toward an Anthropology of "Fundamentalism"', *American Anthropologist*, 3, 2, June, pp 481–98. In part, this has arisen from the jettisoning of socialist politics and assumptions. I owe this latter point to Paul Smith.

[70] Feminists are fond of using it as a derogatory term: S. Hays (1996) *The Cultural Contradictions of Motherhood*, New Haven, CT: Yale University Press, p 13.

[71] G. Lakoff (2004) *Don't Think of An Elephant! Know Your Values and Frame the Debate*, Vermont: Chelsea Green Publishing; also his (2002) *Moral Politics: How Liberals and Conservatives Think*, Chicago, IL: University of Chicago Press.

feminism wholly responsible for the 'retreat' of Bowlbyism, but it was a significant force.[72]

From the 1950s through to the mid-1960s, a number of studies appeared, several written by Fabian feminists, examining from a sociological perspective the changing nature of the family, marriage, motherhood and women's employment.[73] By the late 1960s/early 1970s, however, the younger generation of feminists – products of the expansion in post-war higher education, notably the new universities in the 1960s, overwhelmingly middle class, and among the first to be exposed to 'postmodern' theorising, began to question the concept of the family and to demand full equality between the sexes in all realms of public and private life, and in so doing centred female identity as the substance of cultural politics. At the heart of the WLM were local 'consciousness raising' groups, propelled by the slogan 'the personal is political', manifesting themselves in a number of specific campaigns: abortion, free nursery care, greater access to wage labour, equal pay, domestic violence, and so on. This 'second-wave' feminism found expression through a number of authors whose works, some of which proceeded from Simone de Beauvoir's *The Second Sex* (1953), have since becomes feminist classics.[74] These were among the original contributions to the making of a specifically feminist social knowledge, a project that successfully combined academic writing with political activism.[75] Although influenced by the American women's movement, which exuded a particular virulence, British feminism tended to be less so.[76] No British feminist infamously compared the family to 'a comfortable concentration camp', or characterised motherhood as

---

[72] For the notion of a 'retreat', see Thomson (2013), pp 93–105.

[73] E. Slater and M. Woodside (1951) *Patterns of Marriage*, London: Cassell; G. Gorer (1955) *Exploring English Character*, London: The Cresset Press; M. Young and P. Willmott (1957) *Family and Kinship in East London*, London: Routledge and Kegan Paul; A. Myrdal and V. Klein ([1956]1962) *Women's Two Roles: Home and Work*, London: Routledge and Kegan Paul; E. Bott (1957) *Family and Social Network*, London: Tavistock Publications; V. Klein (1965) *Britain's Married Women Workers*, London: Routledge and Kegan Paul; R. Fletcher (1962) *The Family and Marriage in Britain*, Harmondsworth: Penguin Books; P. Jephcott (1962) *Married Women Working*, London: Allen and Unwin; F. Zweig (1962) *The Worker in an Affluent Society: Family Life and Industry*, London: Heinemann.

[74] For example, Betty Friedan, Kate Millett, Shulamith Firestone, Germaine Greer, Juliet Mitchell, Sheila Rowbotham and Ann Oakley.

[75] P. Abbott and C. Wallace (1997) *An Introduction to Sociology: Feminist Perspectives*, London: Routledge, pp 227–42.

[76] Marwick (1998), pp 679–700.

'a condition of terminal psychological and social decay, total self-abnegation and physical deterioration'.[77] All the same, the home-grown movement was not entirely lacking in barbs of unpleasantness.

In what sense did the WLM affect social-democratic trends in family life, in particular parenting culture? It has been suggested that by the 1960s 'the mounting disquiet over Bowlbyism' could be traced in the *Guardian/Observer* women's pages.[78] It is true that the women's editor Mary Stott used the women's section to propagandise the supposed iniquities of Bowlbyism, and the paper's letters page led to the founding of two middle-class organisations: the Housebound Wives' Register (HWR) (1961) and the Pre-School Playgroups Association (PPA) (1961). But whether this reflected a 'mounting disquiet' is debatable. It was rather the case that these organisations revealed the natural desire on the part of housewives for company and recreation, but of the kind that could be *combined* with their roles of wife and mother. The *Guardian/Observer*, however, was determined to present material from contemporary social research in such a way as to encourage a feminist consciousness.[79] This gave it an important role in moulding the specific frustrations of young, educated middle-class women into a broadly based critique of the companionate marriage, the ethic of domesticity, and motherhood.[80] But the *Guardian* identikit of the frustrated, isolated, bored mother 'tied' to, and 'imprisoned' in, the home was an ideological oversimplification of the way in which the majority of mothers saw their lives. Moreover, for all the talk of facilitating choice for women, one of the less commented on traits of feminism were the guilty feelings it induced in those who chose to be full-time wives and mothers.[81] What the WLM was starting to do, by way of constructing its critique and fine-tuning its political tactics, was to take many of the normal frustrations of marriage,

---

[77] B. Friedan (1963) *The Feminine Mystique*, New York: Norton, pp 282–309. Firestone, quoted in Friedan, p 49.

[78] Thomson (2013), pp 96–7.

[79] At least two of its occasional columnists were determined to promote feminism: Katherine Whitehorn (1963) *Observer*, 17 February and Lois Mitchinson (1963) *Guardian*, 16 January. For the campaigning role of the paper's 'Mainly for Women' section under Stott, see D. Chambers, L. Steiner and C. Leming (2004) *Women and Journalism*, London: Routledge, pp 37–41.

[80] On these frustrations, see A. Davis (2012), *Modern Motherhood: Women and Family in England, 1945–1970*, Manchester: Manchester University Press, pp 146–53.

[81] Davis (2012), p 151; J. M. Pahl and R. Pahl (1971) *Managers and their Wives*, London: Allen Lane, p 139.

family life, child rearing, housework and domesticity and fuse them with commonplace subjective insecurities and widely experienced economic and occupational constraints, in order to assault the ideal of the social-democratic family. In effect, the unavoidable conflicts and ambivalences that are inherent in any human relationship were being morphed into an economic, social, political and psychological matrix of the 'oppression' of women as housewives and mothers.

Something of this social development can be seen in Hannah Gavron's *The Captive Wife* (1966), one of the key British feminist texts of the decade. Gavron acknowledged that income and housing were the main indices of the quality of family life, especially where there were young children. In her sample of 96 London women (divided between working and middle class), while the middle class lived in relatively spacious accommodation, 20 per cent of the working class lived in private and council blocks of flats, and 71 per cent in rooms with three to four families to each Victorian terrace house. Space was at a premium, particularly for young children's play. Bad housing was just one factor reducing domestic harmony. Others included the growing volume of traffic that made it unsafe for children to be in the street, and the isolation of many young mothers owing to the demise of the traditional stable populations of London boroughs. The majority of marriages, she admitted, were 'happy', although many working-class women felt that they had married too young, and there was some disquiet that the idea of marriage had been 'over valued' with expectations being too high.[82] But by a slender majority, wives felt their marriages to be more egalitarian than those of their parents. As was commonly understood, the stresses and strains on women in marriage usually began with the coming of babies, especially the first birth, which unsurprisingly could induce feelings of anxiety and insecurity.

In accordance with her title's emphasis on 'captivity', suggesting the imprisoned wife and mother, Gavron was keen to answer her own question: 'How tied down were they?' Among the middle class, 40 per cent of mothers felt that they should be with their young children all the time; 52 per cent thought that 'a small amount of separation did their children no harm'. Only 8 per cent of the sample felt that their presence was unimportant for children. With a nod towards her ideological preference, Gavron summarised: 'most [middle-class] mothers felt psychologically *tied* to their young children, and

---

[82] For contrasts and similarities, see E. Roberts (1955) *Women and Families: An Oral History, 1940–1970*, Oxford: Blackwell; Davis (2012); A. Haggett (2012) *Desperate Housewives, Neuroses and the Domestic Environment, 1945–1970*, London: Pickering & Chatto.

felt themselves compelled to stay at home whatever their personal preferences'. However, 'only a small minority seemed really isolated in the same way as were the majority of working-class mothers'.[83] But this was not surprising since much of the working-class isolation was that of mothers living in high rise blocks. On the other hand, citing the Newson's study of infant care in Nottingham in support, Gavron notes that the middle-class mother, unlike her working-class counterpart, does not wish to subsume herself in the family and expects 'to be an independent person in her own right' and to this extent finds young children frustrating.[84] The working-class mothers seemed to have had more of a struggle to 'keep their heads above water'.[85] One finding, perhaps indicative of a newish trend, was that as in the middle class, the degree to which working-class fathers participated in child rearing was 'quite striking'. As to whether working-class mothers were 'tied down', 79 per cent of them said that they felt that they should be with their children all the time. Clearly anxious to find a way of negating this positive response to childcare, Gavron wondered whether this was due to 'genuine feelings' or the realisation that there were few alternatives.[86] These mothers, however, did find it hard making provision for their children to play safely and relatively quietly (owing to a fear of upsetting neighbours), since the streets were increasingly out of bounds, especially for flat dwellers.[87] In general, it seems that working-class mothers had less opportunity than middle-class mothers to leave their children for a while with relatives or friends, although why this should be so given their fairly extensive social contacts with family is unclear.[88] Where paid employment was concerned, the majority of middle-class mothers stopped work after the birth of their first baby.

---

[83] H. Gavron (1968) *The Captive Wife*, London: Penguin Books, pp 78–9.

[84] Gavron (1968), pp 78–9; J. Newson and E. Newson (1963) *Patterns of Infant Care in an Urban Community*, Harmondsworth: Penguin. For a nuanced account of family and child-rearing social change during the period, emphasising the 'having fun as a family' mode (and the ambivalent feelings it aroused) and the greater involvement of fathers, see also J. Newson and E. Newson (1968) *Four Years Old in an Urban Community*, London: George Allen and Unwin. For the 1970s, see their (1976) *Seven Years Old in the Home Environment*, London: George Allen and Unwin.

[85] Gavron (1968), p 82.

[86] Gavron (1968), p 88.

[87] Gavron (1968), pp 88–9; also J. Mogey (1956) *Family and Neighbourhood: Two Studies in Oxford*, Oxford: Oxford University Press; J. Maizels (1961) *Two to five in high flats*, London: The Housing Centre.

[88] Gavron (1968), pp 95–105.

While nearly half thought it was wrong to leave their babies, 37 per cent continued working, usually part time, and 30 per cent would have done some work had proper childcare facilities been available.[89] Among working-class mothers, 54 per cent thought it wrong to leave their children; 11 per cent had no desire to work again; and 29 per cent said that their husbands opposed their return to work (in the middle class, the figure was 11 per cent).[90]

A rather different perspective on women's attitudes during this period has been given by Ali Haggett in her oral history of middle-class housewives' neurosis, the domestic environment, and child-rearing attitudes during 1945–70.[91] Haggett suggests that these women 'believed that they were undertaking a worthwhile role and often found great satisfaction in it'.[92] When they did experience mental stress, this was often caused more by marital difficulties than childcare. But even when they found it hard to find intimacy and companionship within marriage, they were 'still able to gain joy and satisfaction from their role as mothers and homemakers', seeing 'themselves as part of a team effort', and placing the care and nurture of their children 'as their priority in life'.[93] She tellingly observes that the idea that mothering and homemaking are *necessarily* pathogenic, underplays 'the ways in which personal relationships, both past and present, might influence the onset of psychiatric and psychosomatic symptoms'.[94] While some mothers with small children lost confidence and felt frustrated, others sought ways to exercise their imagination and resourcefulness through participating in Pre-School Playgroups, baby-sitting circles, Church activities, the Women's Institute, and so on.[95] As Angela Davis found in her study of motherhood in Oxfordshire, the type of community a mother lived in profoundly influenced her maternal and wifely experiences.[96] Moreover, while boredom and isolation certainly could

---

[89] Gavron (1968), pp 114–15.

[90] Gavron (1968), pp 120–1.

[91] A. Haggett (2007) 'Housewives, Neuroses, and the Domestic Environment in Britain, 1945–70', in M. Jackson (ed) *Health and the Modern Home*, London: Routledge, pp 84–110, and her (2012). See also Davis (2012) which, although gender specific, implicitly questions some feminist stereotypes.

[92] Haggett (2007), p 84.

[93] Haggett (2007), pp 85, 89, 93.

[94] Haggett (2007), p 88.

[95] Haggett (2007), p 92.

[96] Davis (2012), pp 35–40, 48–9. This was emphasised by the Newsons (1968), pp 27–47 (see note 84, reference to the Newsons).

be contributory factors to depression and negative mothering, other causes included marital difficulties, divorce and home–work tensions.

During the 1960s, feminism undoubtedly began to focus on what Gavron chose to call the 'conflict and ambivalence' governing the role of women in a changing society. These changes included not only the political consequences of post-war reconstruction, but also those deriving from the spread of mass consumerism, higher education for girls, the advance of sexual permissiveness, urban redevelopment and a new sense of self in relation to parents, marriage and gender. Older understandings of what constituted the feminine psyche were clearly being questioned. The WLM was subverting conventional attitudes to marriage, the family and the community just at the moment when social-democratic ideals were beginning to lose confidence in themselves. In this space, feminists found a place for the desire to be 'ME', and so the 'us' of class consciousness (always a fractious togetherness) receded before the personal 'I'.[97] The radical feminist Elizabeth Wilson has freely admitted of her training as a psychiatric social worker, 'my work was to help women to be better mothers – not an aim I had much sympathy with…What I'd wanted from psychoanalysis was to understand myself, not police other women.'[98]

Much of Gavron's account, however, far from documenting women's domestic 'oppression', could also be read as confirming the degree to which social-democratic aspirations prevailed at the time, particularly the idea of the companionate marriage and child-centred maternal care, to which the new feminism felt it had to make a determined challenge.[99] During the early post-war decades, numerous studies noted the increasing opportunity for married women to enter the labour market, as well as the declining size of family, the greater emphasis placed upon companionate marriage styles, and a new kind of masculinity with husbands and fathers becoming more family and child centred.[100] The feminist tactic, however, was to 'correct' the sociological status of these surveys by deploying a 'gendered

[97] On the transition, see Hobsbawm (1994), pp 305–6.

[98] Quoted in W. Webster (1998) *Imagining Home: Gender, 'Race' and National Identity, 1945–1964*, London: UCL Press, p 117.

[99] Again, these aspirations are evident in the findings of the Newsons. See above, notes 84 and 96.

[100] S. Brooke (2001) 'Gender and Working-Class Identity in Britain during the 1950s', *Journal of Social History*, 34 (Summer), pp 773–95; L. King (2012) 'Hidden Fathers? The Significance of Fatherhood in Mid-twentieth Century Britain', *Contemporary British History*, 26, 11, pp 25–46.

perspective'.[101] According to Elizabeth Wilson, prior to feminism, the role of sociology 'was to give a reassuring view of "ordinary life", reaffirming a core of British normality beneath the alarming surface appearances of crime, vice, and disintegration…Both the questions asked and the methodology used ensured that no really disturbing features of women's lives would be brought to light.'[102]

From the publication of Juliet Mitchell's pioneering essay 'The Longest Revolution', the optimistic sociological portrayal of the developing social-democratic family was categorically rejected in favour of a feminist sociological knowledge. Mitchell started by ridiculing Peter Townsend's classic humanist sentiment: 'The chief means of fulfilment in life is to be a member of, and reproduce, a family.'[103] This, she wrote, was nothing more than a 'conservative belief' held by someone considering himself to be 'progressive'. Thus began what became an identifying trait of feminist writing: the attribution of conservative values to those who disagreed with any of its fundamentalist precepts. For Mitchell, the family, 'a cultural creation… Like woman herself', was the 'lynchpin' of women's oppression since it confined her to 'reproduction'.[104] Similarly, Ann Oakley, displaying an equally childist attitude, lamented 'a child-oriented society', and advised women that they had 'no inherent natures' and, therefore, 'It is on their conditioning that destruction needs to be inflicted.'[105] Elsewhere she proclaimed that '(The) primary loss of women in becoming mothers…is a loss of identity'.[106] 'The housewife role', she recommended, 'must be abolished. The family must be abolished. Gender roles must be abolished', and continued to elaborate on the

---

[101] A. Davis (2009) 'A Critical Perspective on British Social Surveys and Community Studies and their Accounts of Married Life, c. 1945–1970', in *Cultural and Social History*, 6, pp 47–64.

[102] E. Wilson (1980) *Half-Way to Paradise*, London: Tavistock, pp 68–9. Ann Oakley is credited with pioneering a feminist sociology of housework and motherhood. See her *Housewife* (1974a), London: Penguin, and *The Sociology of Housework* (1974b), Oxford: Blackwell. See also (2005) *The Ann Oakley Reader*, Bristol: Policy Press.

[103] Quoted in J. Mitchell (1966) 'The Longest Revolution', in *New Left Review*, 40, December, p 12.

[104] Mitchell (1966), pp 11, 20.

[105] Oakley (1974a), pp 203 (186–221). For childism, see also her (1981) *Subject Women*, New York: Pantheon Books, pp 222–3.

[106] Oakley (1974a), p 221, also (2005), p 180. A common image in feminist writing is the child as a thief, responsible for the 'loss'.

'myths' of motherhood.[107] Perhaps no voice was more hyperbolic than that of Germaine Greer who flamboyantly inserted housewifery into the oppressive and cloying closet of 'misery', along with 'Loathing and Disgust', 'Abuse', 'Resentment' and 'Rebellion', declaring: 'a housewife's work has no results; it simply has to be done again', before adding that 'Bringing up children is not a real occupation because children come up just the same – brought up or not.'[108] The stylised absurdity of these and similar statements was successfully used by feminists to conjure up a bleak universe of women's oppression, presenting it as virtually the singular experience of womanhood.

Children's rights and the beginning of the end of 'progressive' education

We do not hear much about it nowadays, but there was another corrosive development that served to weaken the will to social-democratic parenting, namely the political reactions to the existence from the late 1960s through to the mid-1970s of a Children's Rights Movement. Broadly speaking, the movement (though 'movement' exaggerates its coherence), founded by socialists and anarchists, set out to humanise pupil–teacher relations in state schools through abolition of corporal punishment, encouraging free expression, and introducing a child-centred curriculum. The chances of success were always slim since as an organisation it had neither the funds nor the political skills necessary to establish itself, and from the beginning it faced uncompromising political resistance from the government, local education authorities, teachers' unions and the media.[109] Moreover, it never resolved the tension between pursuing radical reforms and arguing for de-schooling. But for several years the claim that children should have rights, and their promotion as an oppressed group, limped along the fringe of popular culture. As an idea, it found expression in a number of publications, including magazines such as *Children's Rights* and *Liberation Education*, a pioneering collection of essays *Children's Rights*, and through the introduction to a British audience of the works of leading radicals in American education: Ivan Illich, John Holt, Everett Reimer and Paul Goodman. In addition, there were the collected writings of anarchists and socialists, notably the children's

---

[107] Oakley (1974a), pp 222, see also pp 186–221.

[108] G. Greer (1970) *The Female Eunuch*, London: Paladin, p 278.

[109] J. Shotton (1993) *No Master High or Low: Libertarian Education and Schooling in Britain, 1890–1990*, Bristol: Libertarian Education.

author, Leila Berg, Colin Ward's edited volume, *Vandalism*, and Chris Searle's *Stepney Words*, based on his classroom teaching of literature as 'critical literacy', which caused outrage and led to his dismissal.[110] The politics of children's liberation was also formally supported by the National Council for Civil Liberties (NCCL) through its booklet *The Rights of Children and Young Persons* (1967), and *History Workshop*, a group of New Left historians, hosted a popular 'Children's Liberation' conference in 1971.

From the institutional perspective, it looked as if inter-war progressive education would continue to expand under the influence of the government-commissioned Plowden Report (1967), which recognised the value of, and explicitly encouraged, the liberal- progressive trend, albeit that in practice it was limited to about 10 per cent of state primary schools.[111] Despite a great deal of hue and cry about indiscipline and the decline of behavioural standards from the political Right, secondary education (comprehensives, secondary moderns and grammar schools) remained stubbornly resistant to liberalisation. Michael Duane's attempt to democratise *Risinghill*, the comprehensive where he was Headmaster, ended with sensational headlines and the school's closure by the local authority.[112] Many of the criticisms of British education made by the radicals, however, were also evident in some of the academic work at the time, and among the Labour intelligentsia – if not the government.[113] It seemed that perhaps children might be helped to break out of their confinement as welfare subjects, and gain a measure of political respect as citizens. This was not to be. By the early 1970s, the magazine *Children's Rights* was descending into leftist/anarchist fantasy politics through publishing a 'Children's Angry Brigade Communique No

---

[110] Paul Adams (ed) (1971) *Children's Rights*, London: Panther Books; L. Berg (1972) *Look at Kids*, London; C. Ward (ed) (1974), *Vandalism*, London; C. Searle (ed) (1971), *Stepney Words*, London: Centerprise Publications. For an instructive overview, see Thomson (2013), pp 200-205.

[111] *Report of the Central Advisory Council for Education (England) Children and Their Primary Schools* (the Plowden Report) (1967) vol 1, pp 101–2; B. Simon (1991) *Education and the Social Order, 1940–1990*, London: Lawrence and Wishart, pp 380–82.

[112] L. Berg (1968) *Risinghill: Death of a Comprehensive School*, Harmondsworth: Penguin Books.

[113] J. W. B. Douglas (1964) *The Home and the School*, London: MacGibbon and Kee; B. Bernstein (1971) *Class, Codes and Control*, London: Routledge and Kegan Paul; A. H. Halsey, ed (1972) *Educational Priority, EPA Problems and Policies*, vol 1; M. F. D. Young, (ed) (1971) *Knowledge and Control*, London; Collier-Macmillan. See Wooldridge (1994), pp 320–4.

1', which encouraged children to take direct action.[114] It was a sign of serious conflict within 'the movement' and the absence of a more politically savvy outlook among its cadre.

The response of the establishment to this radical moment is enlightening, both in terms of understanding the pressures on the liberal tendencies around the social–democratic family, and also as an example of how certain features of the permissiveness of the sixties were rejected by both Conservative and Labour governments. But we should be aware that such moments often have a history and that the reaction may be as much to that history as to the moment itself. The history in question is complex and involves the interrelated themes of 'opportunity, equality and social class' that were embodied in the aforementioned political struggle between a meritocratic conception of education (the IQ and 11+ examination), with its respect for the values of order, hierarchy and authority (privileging grammar schools), and one that favoured egalitarianism (and, so it was alleged, implicitly prioritised working-class culture).[115] The first significant step in the response was the publication of the *Black Papers on Education* (five during 1969–77). The focus of the critique had several targets: egalitarianism and environmentalism, the newly established and left–wing 'sociology of education', the theory and practice of permissiveness, children's rights, anti–authoritarianism, and a lot more.[116] The *Black Papers'* authors particularly wanted to see an end to the expansion of comprehensive schools and to re-establish the practice of academic selection as a means of reasserting the principle of merit. They were also anxious to curtail the so-called 'radicalisation' of the primary school sector. But in truth their main objection was to what they correctly

---

[114] Thomson (2013), pp 200–5.

[115] Wooldridge (1994), pp 294–339. For 'opportunity, equality and social class', see Silver and Silver (1991), pp 158–86; also Simon (1991), p 318; and for an influential critique of 'traditional educational theories and practices', see Young (ed) (1971).

[116] B. Cox and A. E. Dyson (eds) (1969) *Black Paper 1: 'Fight for Education'*, London: The Critical Quarterly Society; (1969) *Black Paper 2: 'The Crisis in Education'*, London: The Critical Quarterly Society; (1970) *Black Paper 3: 'Goodbye Mr Short'*, London: The Critical Quarterly Society; also C. B. Cox and R. Boyson (eds) (1975) *Black Paper 4: 'The Fight for Education'*, London: Dent; (1977) *Black Paper 5: 'Black Paper 1977'*, London: Temple Smith. For a response, see D. Rubinstein and C. Stoneman (eds) (1970) *Education for Democracy*, Harmondsworth: Penguin; see also F. Musgrove (1987) 'The Black Paper Movement', in R. Lowe (ed) (1987) *The Changing Primary School*, London: Falmer; Simon (1991), pp 396–401.

saw as an attempt by the Left to redefine the meaning and purpose of education in a social democracy.

As conservatives, this intellectual coterie gave voice to widespread concerns about the nature of contemporary social change, of which the evolution of age relations in education was but one manifestation. In turbulent times, however, the ways in which adults regard and treat children can often be a marker of the unsettling of tradition. The notion of children's rights and bids to humanise teaching were regarded as politically motivated attempts to spread not only the culture of egalitarianism, but also the destabilising features of its associated libertarianism, notably the 'decline' in standards of moral conduct, which seemed to conservatives to be epitomised by the student disruption of universities as it reached its international height in 1968.[117] Viewed from the emerging New Right perspective, what was in process was the initiation of a debate on the condition of Britain with regard to its changing cultural identity and its attitudes to power and authority. The *Black Papers* successfully sought to establish a new analytic context within which future discussion would occur, thereby allowing it to more or less set the terms on a range of matters well beyond the confines of education.

In his account of the conservative critique, Adrian Wooldridge perfectly captures the characteristics of the left-wing radicals when he says that they demanded 'self-expression and personal involvement' and sought to 'dismantle...the whole apparatus of order, gradation and personal distinction'. Moreover, they rejected the idea of 'categories and boundaries' since these threatened to 'divide individuals and to restrict the expression of feeling and the fulfilment of desires'. As Wooldridge observes, the favourite authors of the egalitarians (at least among the New Left, though not of Labour Party stalwarts and older social democrats) – Foucault, Laing, Marcuse, Illich and Norman O. Brown – 'specialised in the subversion of received categories' and sympathised 'with those, such as criminals, lunatics or homosexuals' who were the victims of official classification and institutionalisation.[118] Wooldridge also aptly summarises the contents of the *Black Papers*' portrayal of 'educational decline and social decay' as: 'tension in the home' as a result of the liberalising influence of Dr Spock; 'anarchy in the infant and junior schools' with permissive teachers preferring 'hedonism to work discipline and self-discovery to instruction'; a

---

[117] C. Cockburn and R. Blackburn (1969) *Student Power*, Harmondsworth: Penguin; Wooldridge (1994), pp 300–6.

[118] Wooldridge (1994), p 338.

general decline in teaching and behaviour in senior schools; and widespread student unrest in universities.[119]

The critique had two fundamental and wide-ranging features which, though often clumsily articulated, were always deeply felt and politically potent. One (shared by some on the old Labour left), was a rejection of the psychoanalytic culture that informed the post-war settlement, not only the influence of Bowlby, Winnicott and their followers, but also the psychotherapeutic perspective of social workers, environmental town planners, the 'new criminologists', and even the Fabian-inspired tradition of social administration and public service.[120] The other, as Wooldridge notes, was a long-standing, though often muffled, discontent with left-wing ideas concerning the use of education to bring about equality, and to undermine so-called traditional values of order, deference and stability. Conservatives wrote about educational standards, 'but their real fear (like that of Mathew Arnold) was anarchy'.[121] Unsurprisingly, then, the *Black Papers* came to be seen as representing the views of those who were anxious about the direction they felt British society was taking in what was clearly the beginnings of a very different economic, political and social order from that for which Keynes and Beveridge had legislated. Among those interests who were worried and unsettled by aspects of permissiveness was the new middle class, insecure but ambitious products of the re-ordering of post-war capitalism, particularly the restructuring of the labour market, and also a more prosperous working class, no longer automatically supporting Labour, who in the face of a faltering welfare state looked to education to advance their children's social mobility.[122] None of these anxieties were answered by the Labour government, which was gradually losing its credence among young people and the many sections of the Left, especially over its support for US policy in Vietnam. For these interests, the 1960s may be seen as 'The Decade of Disillusion'.[123] But what

[119] Wooldridge (1994), p 385, drawing on 'Education: The Backlash Starts', *Observer*, 23 March 1969, p 10.

[120] M. Thomson (2006) *Psychological Subjects*, Oxford: Oxford University Press, p 254; Thomson (2013), pp 205–14.

[121] On education and equality, see Simon (1991), chapters 6–11. Quotation in Musgrove (1987), p 111, see also pp 115–21.

[122] On the economic, industrial and educational developments, see E. J. Hobsbawm (1999) *Industry and Empire from 1950 to the Present Day*, Harmondsworth: Penguin, pp 298–316, and (1994), pp 287–319.

[123] D. McKie and C. Cook (1972) *The Decade of Disillusion: British Politics in the Sixties*, Basingstoke: Macmillan.

also helped to weaken the social-democratic ethos, apart from the unprincipled pragmatism of the Labour Party, together with mounting national economic difficulties, were the diverse programmes of the New Left and its allies; not children's rights advocates or the minority of radical teachers, since they had no influence, but rather those activists in the academy, the media, teachers' unions, local government and social work who chose to espouse continental social and political theories in pursuit of a variety of agendas dictated by gender, sexuality and the revolutionary delusions of sectarian politics.

Some left-wing attitudes toward 'the family'

What, then, of the position of the Labour Party and the Left and their engagement with the social-democratic family? This is not the place to comprehensively consider the political culture of Labour during the long sixties. But it is important to briefly note where the Party stood in relation to the assault on the social-democratic ideals with which so many of its members had been and continued to be actively involved. It seems fairly clear now that at all levels Labour failed to seize an opportunity to revitalise itself in recognition of social change and chose instead to be by turn hostile, subservient, and commonsensical in the face of the social, economic, cultural and political trends and events that characterised the period. The New Leftists, associated with the *New Left Review (NLR)* and 'revolutionary' papers such as *Black Dwarf*, tended to split into doctrinaire groups, some of whom were enamoured by the likes of Fanon, Laing, Althusser and Foucault, by 'discourses' on 'sexualities' (the emerging gay/lesbian movement), and by the prospect of harmonising the discordant features of Marxism, feminism and Freudianism into a political programme that suited their own despairing outlook – 'despairing' because for all their revolutionary ardour, there was a lack of faith in little else besides their own momentum that by the mid-1970s was proved to be disastrously false. It would be unfair to say that this was true of the Left as a whole, although there were relatively few dissenting voices with regard to protecting the loving and increasingly child-centred family.

Ronald Fletcher, the liberal sociologist most associated with defending and popularising the family and marriage, was forced to argue against conservative and religious moralists, feminists, and prominent New Leftists (such as Robin Blackburn of the *NLR*), who wrote in terms of the family being a 'domestic mystification' buttressing bourgeois society and serving the forces of production.[124] The old conservative criticism, Fletcher remarked, had referred to the decay of the family, now it was charged with being restrictive and suffocating, and an upholder of the status quo.[125] He cited the work of psychiatrists R. D. Laing and David Cooper, both of whom, to the delight of the social liberationists, indicted 'the family' for causing and exacerbating psychological distress.[126] In being attacked from both the right and the left, however, there is no doubt that in the cultural, economic and political melee that was developing from the late 1960s, the energy of the social-democratic family – along with 'Bowlbyism' and the liberalising drift in parent–child relations – began to be sapped. Fletcher found himself to be a lonely and besieged voice.

Where Labour was concerned, bearing mind that it had done so much to foster the psychologically informed 'companionate' family of the post-war settlement, the response was more complex, not least in its disapproving attitude toward many of the pleasures of 'domesticity': kitchen gadgets, washing machines, television, gardening and even 'tidiness'.[127] The Party found it hard to come to terms with the new affluence (and the 'Americanisation' of British culture) beginning in the 1950s, and during the years it was out of office between 1951 and 1964 it floundered in an era of rapid social change, and continued to have difficulties during Prime Minister Harold Wilson's New Technological Age up to losing the 1970 general election. Yet, as is well known, it had also presided over a raft of progressive legislation that set the scene for so much of what we think of permissive Britain. Those who gave some kind of (qualified) welcome to affluence were the Labour 'revisionists' and sections of the New Left (although usually in their very different ways), and they all proved better able to adapt to modernity than old labour; although revisionists had little specific to say about the role of the family in the affluent society.[128] Richard Crossman's (non-revisionist) plea, made in 1960, to the Party to refuse 'in any way to come to terms with the affluent society', which fitted with its 1950s' emphasis on morality and ethics, was certainly wrong-headed in its utter failure to acknowledge that economic and social change

---

[124] Quoted in R. Fletcher (1973 edn) *The Family in Britain*, Harmondworth: Penguin, p 26; see also R. Blackburn (1969) 'A Brief Guide to Bourgeois Ideology' in Cockburn and Blackburn.

[125] Fletcher (1973 edn), pp 24–6; also pp 257–63.

[126] For a Left critique of Laing et al., see Sedgwick (1982).

[127] Black (2003), pp 27–30.

[128] Black (2003), p 2; Nuttall (2006), p 74.

called for a new political analysis.[129] Labour was left unable to discuss with the electorate the nature of a socialist-inspired moral stance that could accommodate affluence, consumerism and style, and gender, as well as personal issues.[130] This failure (along with others that were not always under Labour control), which was hardly repaired under the Labour governments of 1964–70, facilitated not only the advance of the New Right in the mid-1970s, but also exposed the Left spectrum to the baneful influence of the neoliberal narcissism that characterised the social liberationist agenda.

Labour's 'moral-activist' phase, during which many of its members, in pursuit of mental progress, sought to 'make men and women better than they are', needs to be considered in relation to the dimming of the ideal by the end of the 1960s, and with it the inclination to promote the social-democratic child-rearing. In discussing 'moral activism', to reiterate the schema of David Marquand,[131] we saw that he suggests that in place of 'collectivism' and 'individualism', we should think of a 'more subtle distinction between two conceptions of the Self, of the good life and of human possibilities and purposes'. On one side of the divide, there are those individuals who 'pursue their own preferences without interference from others' (satisfaction and passivity), and then there are those 'for whom the Self is a growing and developing moral entity, and the good life is one in which individuals learn to adopt higher preferences in place of lower ones' ('effort, engagement and activity'). Marquand termed these conceptions 'hedonist' and 'moralist', crossed with 'passive' and 'active', and used them to construct a rough and ready chronology for describing post-war Labour governments: from the mid-1940s to mid-1950s dominated by a moralist-activist collectivism; from the mid-1950s to the mid-1970s, the emphasis was on passive-hedonist collectivism, informed by moral relativism.[132] What is particularly relevant for the themes of this book is that the ensuing 'moral vacuum' left Keynesian social democracy vulnerable to the incipient neoliberal morality of the New Right. More specifically, throughout the 1960s and into the 1970s, by virtue of the hedonism, the passivity and the growing moral relativism, the family, parenting and child centredness (never having had the highest priority) were increasingly left to fend for themselves against the mainly negative

---

[129] Quoted in Black (2003), p 2, see also pp 12–40.

[130] Black (2003), p 84.

[131] For earlier reference to Marquand, see p 95.

[132] D Marquand (1996) 'Moralists and Hedonists' in Marquand and Seldon (eds), pp 5–28; Nuttall (2006), pp 10–12, 68–125.

features of the encroaching and politically ecumenical politics of recognition, buttressed by the 'culture of complaint'.[133]

The New Left offered no help here for it had its own 'revolutionary' critique, fused with those of feminism and gay and lesbian campaigns. Looking back from the 1980s, this trend was belatedly recognised by Peter Willmott, one of the 'older' socialists: '[T]he generally confident spirit of the post-war years had begun to crumble, particularly among intellectuals and idealistic students. The new mood was more radical, often Marxist, and community studies was criticised for treating problems in a fragmented way, while distracting attention from more fundamental structural issues.'[134] He could also have mentioned the increasingly popular conservative critique of community studies (for being too left-wing), environmentalism and the idea of equality.[135] This aside, with the founding of the New Universities in the 1960s, 28 sociology departments were established which, with their young staff, proved to be a congenial home for the Marxist-left and feminists who from the mid-1970s were ensuring that along with postmodern social theory, gendered 'structural issues' came to figure prominently in the syllabus. In so doing, this shift in emphasis, reflecting different interests of a new generation, aided conservatives in developing their assault on the fundamentals of the post-war settlement.

In 1968 Perry Anderson, a major New Left theoretician, wrote of the social-democratic tradition in British sociology whose 'record of listless mediocrity and wizened provincialism is unrelieved'. The ethical-socialist A. H. Halsey observed that 'Anderson's prejudice prevents him from appreciating the radicalism of these post-war British sociologists.' Halsey, in referring to the sociologists – 'provincial radicals' he called them – went on to identify what was perhaps the fundamental difference between social-democratic socialists and the rest:

> They were confident that the democratic institutions invented by the Victorian and Edwardian working class, the Unions, the Co-Operative Societies and the Labour Party were the foundations of a New Jerusalem, a free and socialist Britain. If their Party and the Atlee government lagged behind, their idealistic impatience called for renewed radical

---

[133] For the politics of recognition, see pp 301–304; R. Hughes (1999) *Culture of Complaint: The Fraying of America*, Oxford: Oxford University Press.

[134] P. Willmott (1985) 'The Institute of Community Studies', in M. Bulmer (ed) *Essays on the History of British Sociological Research*, Cambridge: Cambridge University Press, chapter 8.

[135] Wooldridge (1994), pp 294–318.

persuasion. It did not require a total therapy of revolution and massacre of people by their own countrymen. Resolve, pressure, argument, and firm insistence of democratic action would be repeatedly necessary over a long haul. But democracy and decency need never be abandoned.[136]

One has only to peruse the *NLR* (or any feminist/'revolutionary' publication) at the time to see how far away these sentiments were from those of the radical vanguard.

---

[136] A. H. Halsey (1985), 'Provincials and Professionals: The British Post-War Sociologists' in Bulmer (ed), pp 151–64.

PART THREE

Influences and examples from the USA

Introduction

In 1960, after eight years of Dwight Eisenhower's Republican presidency, there was a resurgence of liberalism with the election of John F. Kennedy. In less than a decade that resurgence was shattered by the 'civil war' of the 1960s – political assassination, urban riots, civil rights campaigns, student revolution, and the anti-Vietnam war movement – leaving in its trail the failure of the 'Great Society' programme of social reform and the war against poverty, the fragmentation of the New Left, and the rightward drift of many liberal intellectuals. Perhaps more tellingly was the disintegration of the Democratic Party's traditional coalition of the white working-class, African Americans, and other ethnic groups. The coalition collapsed amid fractious and often violent recrimination, manifested in the resentment of the middle- and working-class at having to pay for reform programmes for the poor, continuing urban and racial unrest, and political divisions among the Democrats themselves.[1] But some lasting progress was made during the 1960s: civil rights, women's liberation, sexual freedoms and a number of personal liberties all witnessed significant advances. By the time Nixon left office in 1974, however, American society was no more equitable than it had been at the start of the Great Society initiative, the fracturing of cities continued apace, an urban 'underclass', composed mainly of ethnic minorities, emerged amid a culture of violence and despair, and consumer capitalism, entering its 'post-industrial' phase, began to shed blue-collar jobs.[2] All this is well known.

Less familiar is the coming of the 'new behaviourism' in health, education and social welfare, and the promotion of the psychologically

---

[1]   D. Steigerwald (1995) *The Sixties and the End of Modern America*, London: St Martin's Press; M. Isserman and M. Kazin (2000) *America Divided: The Civil War of the 1960s*, Oxford: Oxford University Press; M. J. Heale (2001) *The Sixties in America: History, Politics and Protest*, Edinburgh: Edinburgh University Press.

[2]   Steigerwald (1995), p 2; Heale (2001), pp 2–3.

defined 'authoritative parenting style' (in opposition to the 'authoritarian' and the 'permissive'), both of which crossed the Atlantic to become increasingly influential in Britain. Since the advent of the behaviourist tendency and the authoritative style are central to the arguments of this book regarding the move from social-democratic parenting to parental narcissism, in order to understand the nature of their appeal in Britain (which is considered in Chapters Seven and Eight) this chapter describes their origins and the reasons for their acceptance in the United States.[3] On the one hand, the chapter focuses on the interrelationships between the objectives of the new behaviourism, the collapse of liberalism and the reaction against 'the crisis of authority' and, on the other, the search for an alternative to the alleged failure of 'permissive' child rearing – particularly in relation to the retractions of Benjamin Spock who over the years qualified his earlier liberal attitudes as he argued that parents had become too permissive and it was time to redress the balance.[4] This means first familiarising ourselves with the rudiments of the turn to 'the child of democracy' in the 1940s and the onset of liberal parenting, known as the 'fun morality'. Second, it is necessary to appreciate the significance of the contextual trauma of 'America Divided', and its implications for liberalism.[5] Third, we also need to recognise the degree to which social science was looked to, originally for inspiration, guidance, and knowledge, and by the end of the 1960s for solace in the face of fear, confusion and failure: 'the idea that scientific knowledge holds the key to solving social problems has long been an article of faith in American liberalism'; similarly, with the fostering of American psychology's 'will to empower'.[6] The chapter concludes with the claim that 'authoritative

---

[3] On 'policy transfer' from the United States to Britain, see D. P. Dolowitz with R. Hulme, M. Ellis and F. O'Neill (2000) *Policy Transfer and British Social Policy: Learning from the USA?*, Buckingham: Open University Press; A. Deacon (2000) 'Learning from the US? The Influence of American Ideas Upon "New Labour" Thinking on Welfare Reform', *Policy and Politics*, 28, 1, pp 5–18.

[4] B. Spock (1946, rev edns 1957, 1968, 1976, 1985, 1998), *Common Sense Book of Baby and Child Care*, New York: Duell Sloan.

[5] M. Mead and M. Wolfenstein (1955) *Childhood in Contemporary Cultures*, Chicago, IL: University of Chicago Press, pp 169–73; Isserman and Kazin (2000).

[6] A. O'Connor (2001) *Poverty Knowledge: Social Science, Social Policy and the Poor in 20th Century U.S. History*, Princeton, NJ: Princeton University Press, p 3; B. Cruikshank (1994) 'The Will to Empower: Technologies of Citizenship and the War on Poverty', *Socialist Review*, 23, 4, pp 29–55, and (1999) *The Will to Empower: Democratic Citizens and Other Subjects*, London: Cornell University Press.

parenting', itself a product of scientific knowledge, originated mainly as a component in the scheme to save liberal individualism in the face of the post-1968 conservative revival – though it soon evolved into a tool of the neoconservative movement. In so doing, it sent an important cultural message regarding how liberals saw the American family in what was clearly a new era.[7] In some senses, as subsequent chapters will show, this was to be replicated in Britain in that with the demise of the post-war settlement and the rise of, first, the New Right followed by New Labour and, second, the coming of neoliberalism and globalised corporate capitalism, ruling elites determined to construct a new kind of 'social contract' between the state and citizen, in which a reformulated parent–child relationship was to be a critical feature.

---

[7] On some of the contradictions of the liberal/feminist approach to child rearing, see R. J. Plant (2010) *Mom: The Transformation of Motherhood in Modern America*, Chicago, IL: University of Chicago Press; also D. Weinstein (2013) *The Pathological Family: Postwar America and the Rise of Family Therapy*, New York: Cornell University Press.

FIVE

Social science and American liberalism

Parenting democracy's children

The 1940s: creating the democratic culture in an 'age of anxiety'

American scholars tend to see the 1960s as the decade when the country's moral values began to shift significantly. With regard to liberal child-rearing, however, even before the 1950s, there were indications of what turned out to be important cultural changes. Despite the popular critique of Momism, which portrayed mothers as overbearing and suffocating to the extent that they were responsible for 'emasculating the nation', encouraging the spread of homosexuality, and rearing a generation of sons whose neuropsychiatric condition made them unfit for military service, from the late 1930s, until the advent of the new behaviourists in the 1960s, parenting advice became far more child empathetic than it had been for most of the inter-war period when the punitive and habit obsessed behavioural psychology of J. B. Watson tended to hold sway.[8] It is important to keep in mind, however, that Watson was never unopposed as the 1930s increasingly reflected broadly Freudian interests concerning the development of the child's personality, as well as Arnold Gessell's influential theory of developmental maturation.[9] Furthermore, the United States was far from immune to the tremors of the European 'crisis of civilization', not least the rise of Fascism and Nazism, which produced a wave of Jewish refugees who brought with them an acute awareness of the dangers for democracy of the cultivation of 'the authoritarian personality', a

---

[8]   J. B. Watson (1928) *Psychological Care of the Infant and Child*, London: Allen and Unwin. For Momism, see P. Wylie (1942) *Generation of Vipers*, New York: Farrar and Rhinehart; Plant (2010), pp 19–54, 86–117; E. Herman (1995) *The Romance of American Psychology: Political Culture in the Age of Experts, 1940–1970*, Berkeley, CA: University of California Press, pp 276–84.

[9]   For example, A. Gessell (1930) *The Guidance of Mental Growth in Infant and Child*, New York: Macmillan. For discussion, see A. Hulbert (2003) *Raising America: Experts, Parents and a Century of Advice about Children*, New York: Vintage Books.

concept that exerted considerable influence on social scientists.[10] This was almost certainly in the mind of those attending the White House Conference on Children in a Democracy (1940) which, in promoting the theme of children as citizens, raised some fundamental questions about the nature of the parent–child relationship at a moment of such historical uncertainty.[11]

One of the most talked-about baby books of the decade, Charles and Mary Aldrich, *Babies are Human Beings* (1938) (English edition, *Understand Your Baby*, published in 1939, with 20 reprints up to 1949), gave parents 'the promise of the "secure" child in a "world of change"' and encouraged mothers to enjoy their babies, albeit 'in an intelligent way'.[12] Although the Aldriches used Freudian/Kleinian images, describing the infant and toddler as 'this entirely self-centred barbarian' in conflict with his or her environment, they constantly reminded readers of the 'baby's dilemma': to preserve 'I', while also 'growing up'. To this end, they focused on 'the baby's way' of eating, sleeping and eliminating, and were quick to advise parents to help the child make the necessary accommodation in accordance with 'the reality of development', noting that parents often confused the effects of their 'training' regimes with the fact that the child had merely gotten older and grown up a little more.[13] One of their principal recommendations, contrary to behaviourism, was to fondle babies; the human need for cuddles being particularly noticeable in young babies. Where the emphasis in the Aldriches was on babies as human beings, once the war was underway it morphed to keeping them safe for democracy, and on demonstrating democratic principles to children through home management and child rearing.

---

[10]   C. Lasch (1977) *The Culture of Narcissism: American Life in an Age of Diminishing Expectations*, New York: W. W. Norton, pp 85–96.

[11]   T. Richardson (1989) *The Mental Hygiene Movement and Social Policy in the United States and Canada*, New York: SUNY Press, pp 152–54; Hulbert (2003), pp 172–3.

[12]   C. A. Aldrich and M. Aldrich (1938) *Babies are Human Beings*, New York: Macmillan, English edn (1939) *Understand Your Baby*, London: Black; also D. Beekman (1979) *The Mechanical Baby*, London: Dobson.

[13]   Aldrich (1939); also M. Ribble (1943 – eleven reprints over the next ten years) *Rights of Infants*, Oxford: Oxford University Press.

The urge to democracy preoccupied a number of authors.[14] For C. Madeleine Dixon, the crux of the matter was that 'we Americans... want unity, but we want individuals'. Consequently, it was vital to keep in mind that 'While we are making a world safe for democracy we must preserve in children readiness for democracy – these are the people in whose hands the new world order will be moulded.'[15] For Dorothy Baruch, the problem was that the fight for democracy demanded some reigning in of individual liberties, 'As a result, our children see in the world about them no very true picture of democratic living', and yet it was important that children 'should *like* what constitutes democracy. They should have a warm, familiar, expansive feeling about democracy and sure knowledge of the principles upon which it rests...if they are to live democratically, they should know what constitutes democracy ... democracy must not be something you-speak-of-but-do-not-live-by'. The essential ingredient for democracy was '*Free participation*... not the forced participation of the Nazis...People in a democracy must *want* to participate. Children growing up in a democracy must learn that participation can be satisfying and good.'[16] Similarly, child developmentalists Gesell and Ilg presented the cultivation of the individual child as necessary for a democratic culture, transmitted through the family.[17] Working within the prevailing liberal social science paradigm, they portrayed the family not as a miniature state, but as a 'biological and cultural group' through which 'old traditions' were transmitted and 'new social values' were created:

> A totalitarian 'Kultur' subordinates the family completely
> to the state, fosters autocratic parent–child relationships,
> favors despotic discipline, and relaxes the tradition of

---

[14] Besides Spock, among the better known are C. Madeleine Dixon (1942), *Keep Them Human*, New York: John Day Company; Dorothy Baruch (1942) *You, Your Children and War*, New York: Appleton; Louise Cripps Glemser (1943), *Your First Baby*, New York: A.S. Barnes and Co.; Dorothy V. Whipple (1944) *Our American Babies*, New York: Barrows; Arnold Gesell and Frances L. Ilg (1943) *Infant and Child in the Culture of Today*, London: Hamish Hamilton; Edith Buxbaum (1949) *Your Child Makes Sense: A Guidebook for Parents* (English edn with Foreword by Anna Freud, 1951), London: Allen and Unwin. For the teaching of 'democracy' during the cold war era, see J. Cohen-Cole (2014) *The Open Mind: Cold War Politics and the Sciences of Human Nature*, Chicago, IL: University of Chicago Press, pp 13–34.

[15] Dixon (1942), pp 11, 16.

[16] Quoted in Beekman (1979), p 173. Emphasis original.

[17] Gesell and Ilg (1943), pp 9–14.

> monogamy…A democratic culture…affirms the dignity
> of the individual. It exists in the status of the family as a
> social group, favors reciprocity in parent–child relationships,
> and encourages humane discipline of the child through
> guidance and understanding…Liberty is the life principle
> of democracy, in the home as well as in the community…
> The concept of democracy…has far reaching consequences
> in the rearing of children.[18]

This democratic inclination towards liberal child-raising helps to explain why these books had much less to say about discipline than their predecessors, and recommendations, usually derived from Gesell and Ilg, were always from the child's perspective. Mothers were urged to remember that 'whatever the shape of the world to come, by giving the best to your baby…you will have equipped him with the inestimable blessings of good health, kindliness and courage…That will be the greatest contribution you could possibly make to the new, peaceful society of our dreams.'[19] What is evident here is the continuing rejection of a mechanistic behaviourism as a way of describing and understanding human behaviour, and the introduction to parents of the neo–Freudian approach to bringing up children.[20]

Dr Spock's 'unstable world'

Popular opinion sees Benjamin Spock as the father of permissiveness; this is not altogether true. Although Spock was a liberal Freudian in many respects, he is best characterised as 'a conservative radical', who between the 1940s and the 1970s expounded three different approaches in his *Common Sense Book*: the 1946 'liberal'; the 1957 'cold war' disciplinarian; and, in 1968, his rejection of child-centredness, when he urged parents to rear their children to serve others rather

---

[18] Gesell and Ilg (1943), pp 9–10.

[19] Cripps Glemser (1943) quoted in Beekman (1979), p 176.

[20] This was a feature of the 'culture-and-personality school of social science, which rejected biological causation in favour of culturally determined diverse patterns of behaviour': J. Meyerwitz (2010) '"How Common Culture Shapes Separate Lives": Sexuality, Race, and Mid-Twentieth-Century Social Constructionist Thought', *Journal of American History*, 96, 4, pp 1057–84.

than, as he alleged, themselves.[21] This is not to minimise the degree to which the 1946 edition was important, not just in advising against corporal punishment but in strongly recommending informed and flexible parenting attitudes, particularly with respect to discipline, peer group relations and, much less emphatically, treating children as good persons.[22] In thinking about the concept of 'children of democracy' and of the place of Spock in the making of a conducive nurturing environment, it is helpful to see him as a member of an inter-war intellectual circle that included some of the major figures in American social science at a time when it was attempting to comprehend and programme not only 'aggression', but also the development of (American) 'character' in the culture of a precarious age.[23] Spock's manual reflects many of his (and their) preoccupations; it is 'a document of cultural disintegration', reflecting the unease that Spock felt about his world, which was characterised by the Great Depression, the threat of totalitarianism, the experience of war and, perhaps above all, Freud's *Civilisation and Its Discontent*. At the centre of this crisis ridden world was 'an unstable infant and child – fearful, frustrated, insecure and potentially destructive'.[24] In response Spock sought to create 'a society that was more cooperative, more consensus-oriented, more group-conscious, and a society that was more knowable, more consistent, and

---

[21]   L. Z. Bloom (1972) *Doctor Spock: Biography of a Conservative Radical*, Indianapolis, IN: Bobbs-Merrill; Spock (1968 edn), p xvi. By 1968, when conservative critics were holding him responsible for the lack of respect for 'authority' shown by the student activists, Spock was anxious to disassociate himself from permissiveness, even though he knew that it was his anti-war stance that lay behind the criticisms (Spock, 1994). From his 1957 edition (pp 1–2) onwards he was moving toward the position of later cultural critics in warning of the influence of the growing therapeutic culture on what he saw as young people's self-centredness (1968 edn, p xvi), but which he attributed in part to 'permissive' child rearing. These paragraphs broadly follow William Graebner (1980) 'The Unstable World of Benjamin Spock: Social Engineering in a Democratic Culture, 1917–1950', *Journal of American History*, 67, 3, pp 612–29; see also M. Sulman (1973) 'The Humanization of the American Child: Benjamin Spock as a Popularizer of Psychoanalytic Thought, *Journal of the History of the Behavioral Sciences*, 9, 3 (July), pp 258–65; M. Zuckerman (1975) 'Dr. Spock: The Confidence Man' in C. Rosenberg (ed) *The Family in History*, Philadelphia, PA: University of Pennsylvania Press, pp 179–207.

[22]   A. Petigny (2009) *The Permissive Society: America 1941–1965*, New York: Cambridge University Press, pp 37–41.

[23]   Graebner (1980), pp 614–15; Herman (1995), p 36; Hulbert (2003), pp 246–84; Sulman (1973), pp 258–65.

[24]   Graebner (1980), p 613.

more comforting'. He wrote to achieve discipline rather than licence and, therefore, his 'democratic' model of child rearing called for 'the family as a small group, the parent as a group leader, and the child as an occasional participant in a group decision-making process'. That this model should have been designated as permissive is ironic since its content belied 'the word's laissez-faire connotation', an affiliation that he would definitely have disowned.[25] Spock's permissiveness arises not so much from a respect for the child; its purpose, in a 'too competitive, too modern' society, was to guard against what he saw as children's innate instability, their potential for tyranny, and their incipient demagoguery, and to provide a child-rearing method that fostered their security in order to protect society from chaos.[26]

We should not, however, exaggerate the difference between Spock and other experts, none of whom choose libertarianism in preference to liberalism. In practice, by the 1950s, the dilemma they all faced as liberal social scientists in the cold war era, with the threat of atomic warfare looming, was how to distinguish between authoritarianism and the need for authority (of parent and state) while simultaneously fostering necessary individualism – a classic liberal dilemma: Spock's advice to parents was to 'Stay in control as a friendly leader.'[27] The intention was that 'permissiveness' should be part of a new democratic authority structure, which was being tailored for education, industrial relations, care of the aged, and other institutional settings – all were to allow increased participation. Always, however, 'those who offered such freedom expected to achieve through it a heightened sense of obedience to constituted authority'.[28] Of course, once this jurisdiction began to be challenged by feminism, the New Left, the youth culture, and urban rioters, the permissive illusion became transparent. In response, both conservative revivalists and elements of liberal opinion, who were shocked by the narcissism of the counter-culture, turned to behavioural social science, particularly the new behaviourists, to establish what may be seen as a post-liberal disciplinary culture.[29]

---

[25] Graebner (1980), p 613.

[26] Graebner (1980), pp 613, 616.

[27] Graebner (1980), pp 619–20, 622.

[28] Graebner (1980), p 629.

[29] On counter-cultural narcissism, see E. Zaretsky (2005) *Secrets of the Soul: A Social and Cultural History of Psychoanalysis*, New York: Vintage, pp 307–31.

The 1950s

In the meantime, despite the continuing critique of Momism, during the 1950s the American family, bolstered by psychology's 'liberalising impulse' to believe that everything was knowable and every problem remediable, though never free of underlying identity crises of one sort or another, entered something of a heyday in popular culture, expressing the optimism of a soaring economy and an increasing sense of national self-confidence.[30] The traditional nuclear family found its nest through the baby boom beginning in the early 1940s, and with the age of affluence and the growth of suburbia. During this period, not only did family size increase, but divorce rates declined and a record number of Americans married, pursuing the wholly desirable 'companionate' ideal. Christine Beasley, reflecting the influence of Spock and his circle, and the programme of the Mid-Century White House Conference on Children and Youth (1950), with its emphasis on developing 'the healthy personality', caught the optimistic mood in her description of domestic democracy, which preached 'individual fulfilment through group participation', with chapter headings such as 'The Family and Democracy', 'Group Morale and Family Fun', 'The Family Council', 'The Nature of Love' – all with 'a warning' that 'democracy is not easy'.[31] On the horizon, however, though hardly recognised until much later, the cultural emphasis on motherhood and domesticity was increasingly in conflict with feminist politics and the therapeutic privileging of self-realisation.[32]

---

[30] Petigny (2009), pp 15–22; S. Mintz and S. Kellogg (1988) *Domestic Revolutions: a social history of American life*, New York: Free Press; E. Tyler May (2008) *Homeward Bound: American Families in the Cold War Era*, New York: Basic Books; Hulbert (2003); M. Halliwell (2013) *Therapeutic Revolutions: Medicine, Psychiatry and American Culture, 1945–1970*, New Brunswick, N.J: Rutgers University Press.

[31] C. Beasley (1954) *Democracy in the Home*, New York: Association Press, pp 213–26; for the Mid-Century Conference, see Hulbert (2003). Beasley was almost certainly also influenced by Erik Erikson's influential paper to the Conference on the 'Eight Ages of Man', a theory of the development of the life-cycle of the ego, published as *Childhood and Society* (1950). On Erikson's caution re the making of 'personality', see Hulbert (2003), pp 195–200.

[32] Plant (2010), pp 116–17. Not for the last time, it was liberals who were most critical of American motherhood, whereas social conservatives defended it: R. Feldstein (2000) *Motherhood in Black and White: Race and Sex in American Liberalism, 1930–1965*, Ithaca NY: Cornell University Press. On how Momism's 'mother blaming' was reconciled with 'glorified motherhood and suburban domesticity' of the 1950s, see Plant (2010), p 88.

Many of the emotional and social difficulties that pervaded American society at this time have been attributed to the nuclear, child-centred family which, according to some historians, embodied the worst of what they like to call the conservative decade. The companionable and child-centred home has been described as making an 'exaggerated' effort 'to salvage intimacy in a bureaucratic, impersonal world'.[33] This condescending view underestimates the significance of the psychological and political trend toward greater parental empathy in child rearing, albeit that it was largely found among middle-class mothers.[34] It did not occur to critics, even after the majority of their own Utopias proved to be neither durable nor truly progressive, that this 'family' might have been a rational attempt to recover from the Depression and the war, to imaginatively counter not only the perceived threat of totalitarianism and the atomic bomb, but also to conscientiously work through the ideas and recommendations of the latest social scientific research for the benefit of its members, while simultaneously displaying a democratic sensitivity to the lives of its children. There is a certain irony in the fact that the dissipation of post-war optimism in child rearing, aided and abetted by constant sniping from the gallery of assorted leftist curmudgeons, coincided with the loss of faith by liberals in their own ideals and the rise of a therapeutic culture, which many of them came to look on with askance.

However, this is not to say that all was well in Eisenhower's America, with its many social and political flaws. But the idea that 'permissiveness' sprang into being in the 1960s ignores the emergence of the 'permissive turn' that began in the mid-1940s. It also overlooks the aforementioned cultural optimism that arose in the 1950s under the influence of rising expectations, the expansion of higher education, a

---

[33] Steigerwald (1995), p 252. On family therapy, see Weinstein (2013).

[34] Petigny (2009), pp 42–3. For the related issue of child-rearing patterns and the making of personality, see R. R. Sears, E. E. Macoby and H. Levin (1957) *Patterns of Child Rearing*, Evanston, IL: Row-Peterson. For Kurt Lewin's experiments on 'democratic' and 'authoritarian' leadership styles, see A. J. Marrow (1969), *The Practical Theorist*, New York: Basic Books. For authoritarian homes breeding 'prejudiced' people, see T. Adorno, E. Frankel-Brunswik, D. Levinson, and N. Stanford (1950) *The Authoritarian Personality*, New York: Harper Bros. At the time, the study of child-rearing patterns was important for its contribution to the behavioural sciences' project to pursue 'the integrative study of culture and personality' in searching for the American 'national character' – a character that would withstand not only the stresses of the cold war but from the late 1950s also help in the 'war against poverty' and in coming to terms with the tensions in 1960s' America: O'Connor (2001), pp 102–7; also Meyerwitz (2010).

new faith in the promise of science, including the 'democratisation' of psychology, and the erosion of Calvinism in favour of secularisation.[35] Nonetheless, few of those who welcomed the 'liberal reawakening', and the election of John F. Kennedy as President in 1960, foresaw the degree to which the decade would witness a civil war in the cities that contributed so much to the conservative revival, and the decline of liberal child rearing. In order to understand this transition, we need to recognise the significance of the failure of President Johnson's Great Society programme, for this, too, was responsible for the loss of faith in liberalism and the rise of authoritatively parenting, attractively wrapped as it was in the rhetoric of empowerment.

The 'Great Society': the 'war on poverty', and the 'will to empower'

I intend to establish working groups to prepare a series of conferences and meetings on the cities, on natural beauty, on the quality of education, and on other emerging challenges. From these studies, we will begin to set our course toward the Great Society. (President Johnson's speech at the University of Michigan, 22 May 1964)

The Great Society

Once Johnson was inaugurated in 1964 after Kennedy's assassination, he continued the precedent set by the former President's 'New Frontier' administration in establishing 'task forces' composed of academics and other experts to begin to craft new legislation covering agriculture, anti-recession policy, civil rights, education, the economy, health, income maintenance, the environment, transportation, urban problems and natural resources. At the same time, he began his Great Society programme by ensuring that the Kennedy initiated Civil Rights Act, the most significant measure for equal rights for black Americans since the Reconstruction era, was passed into law. Other measures, designed to stimulate the economy, such as Kennedy's proposed tax cuts, were also enacted. Johnson's ambition, was to out-liberal Kennedy by introducing a new and more audacious reform programme designed to reclaim 'another America', whose populace was ensnared within

---

[35] See Petigny (2009).

'a web of disabilities', making poverty a matter of 'culture'.[36] To this end, Johnson greatly enlarged the scope of the existing anti-poverty programme, so that it became *his* 'War on Poverty'. But the 'war' was not about giving 'doles' to the poor, and certainly not to the urban black poor. One feature of the plan sought to create jobs through the tax cuts, which were intended to encourage consumer spending, production and investment. Essentially, however, the strategy to reduce poverty – as encompassed in the Economic Opportunities Act 1964, which was aimed primarily at the white and rural poor – rather than being about job creation, involved government-sponsored schemes to help the poor to help themselves through job training and educational advancement.[37] There was no attempt either to redistribute income or redesign the economy, both of which was beyond the will and the ability of the Democratic Party with its conflicting demographic and political allegiances.[38] Instead, in describing the educational features of the War on Poverty, Johnson reportedly emphasised that 'people are going to *learn* their way out of poverty'.[39]

But Johnson faced four insurmountable problems, which in the end destroyed his Programme and with it 1960s liberalism: the Vietnam war that increasingly demanded his attention and divided America; the backlash against civil rights, especially once African-American urban areas began to riot in Northern cities; the hugely unfulfilled expectations raised by the rhetoric of the Great Society, particularly in relation to jobs and housing, that led to political anger and the fragmentation of alliances; and the demands of the increasingly factionalised New Left, which exacerbated tensions and schisms within the Democratic Party. The weakness of the Great Society ideal was that it sought to accomplish too much in too brief a period with too little attention to detail, not least to the effects of its programmes

---

[36] M. Harrington (1962) *The Other America: Poverty in the United States*, New York: Penguin Books, p 156.

[37] For the programmes, see P. Marris and M. Rein (1982, 2nd edn) *Dilemmas of Reform*, Chicago: University of Chicago Press.

[38] Isserman and Kazin (2000), pp 109–10; A. Matusow (1984) *The Unravelling of America: A History of Liberalism in the 1960s*, New York: Harper and Row, pp 217–71; J. T. Patterson (1994) *America's Struggle Against Poverty, 1900–1990*, New Haven, CT: Harvard University Press.

[39] On significance of early childhood education, see M. A. Vinovskis (2005) *The Birth of Head Start*, Chicago, IL: University of Chicago Press. Quotation in H. Silver and P. Silver (1991) *An Educational War on Poverty: American and British Policy-Making, 1969–1980*, Cambridge: Cambridge University Press, p 39.

locally and nationally on a number of different political, racial and class constituencies. By implication, the schemes promised quick remedial action, which was unrealistic given how deeply embedded were the social problems concerning poverty, ill health, racism and urban disintegration. The public policy analyst Daniel Patrick Moynihan, who was involved with the launch of the war on poverty programme, later confessed that it had been 'oversold and underfinanced to the point where its failure was almost a matter of design'.[40] Moreover, in pursuit of the reforms, Johnson omitted to give due consideration to the white working poor and to middle America and, therefore, lost their allegiance. Consequently, by the time Richard Nixon entered the White House in 1968 to spread further the conservative message that the poor were trapped in a 'cycle of dependency', the decline of liberalism was well under way.

The 'will to empower'

One of the most intractable problems faced by those administering the Programme lay in trying to persuade the poor to act on what social scientists, administrators, and politicians saw as their 'own behalf'. So it was that the idea of empowerment emerged out of the 1960s as a strategy with near universal appeal, uniting a number of different groups, campaigns, policies and objectives.[41] Since this is a concept we shall encounter in considering the new behaviourism, it is worth briefly noting its relevance to the war on poverty and the research industry in which it figured prominently.[42] Although not often used conceptually in the 1960s, empowerment was associated with reform movements and with the New Left's interest in self-government and autonomy.[43] But what was rarely recognised was its ambiguous nature in relation to 'powerlessness' – they were treated as separate notions, not as interdependent in the sense that to be self-governing is to be

---

[40] Quoted in Isserman and Kazion (2000), p 192.

[41] Cruikshank (1994), p 29. On 'empowerment as professional practice', see K. Baistow (1998) *Behavioural Psychology as a Social Project: From Social Engineering to te Cultivation of Competence*, University of London, Goldsmith's College, Ph.D thesis, pp 181–200. Note also the earlier post-war precedent in 'humanistic psychology', especially the influence of Carl Rogers, founder of 'client-centred' therapy. Cited in Petigny (2009), p 20.

[42] O'Connor (2001), pp 213–41.

[43] Cruikshank (1994), p 30.

subject to the power of oneself.[44] Where government is concerned, Foucault observes that what 'defines a relationship of power is that it is a mode of action which does not act directly and immediately on others. Instead, it acts upon their actions, on existing actions or on those which may arise in the present or in the future'. Thus the subjejctivity of individuals is linked to their subjection.[45] Empowerment, then, is not necessarily a democratic goal.

The problematic nature of the concept is apparent once it is realised that the underlying assumption of those involved in combating poverty was that it was caused by the *powerlessness* of the poor, not by either the decisions of those in power or the related economic and political structures. In line with psychological theories of motivation and competence – 'locus of control', 'learned helplessness' and 'self-efficacy' – the view was that 'Poverty is a condition of need, helplessness and hopelessness'; in other words, it was not an objective fact (not that these facts were denied) but a subjective experience of incapacity.[46] Only by reducing this sense of powerlessness could progress be made to help the poor to help themselves through education and social learning. Thus government activity was focused on attempting to bring the poor into a participatory role in the programmes.[47] But, in confronting what seemed to be the unwillingness of the poor to become activated in their own interests, reformers had to face the limit of democratic government which, if it were to be successful, required that the poor *willingly* participate.[48]

Since government is always dependent upon knowledge if it is to govern, it was necessary that the poor be known as a group; only then could they be made the subjects of reform. It was Michael Harrington, through his thesis that 'poverty is culture', who provided the inroad into identifying and locating the poor. The poor, he wrote, numbering some 40 million people, 'are invisible', living in their own 'culture' – 'they are a different kind of people. They think and feel

---

[44] Cruikshank (1994), p 31.

[45] Quoted in Cruikshank (1994), pp 32–3.

[46] Quoted in Cruikshank (1994), p 36; on the theories, see K. Baistow (2001) 'Behavioural Approaches and the Cultivation of Competence', in G. C. Bunn, A. D. Lovie and G. D. Richards (eds) *Psychology in Britain: Historical Essays and Personal Reflections*, London: BPS Books, pp 311–14.

[47] Marris and Rein (1967).

[48] Cruikshank (1994), p 30.

differently', and this was passed down from generation to generation.[49] Despite Harrington's socialist intentions, the idea of a 'culture of poverty' had unfortunate consequences since important distinctions were lost as 'the disparate and diverse groups of people' – divided by gender, region, race and class – 'came to occupy the category of "the poor" [and] were transformed into a calculable, knowable grouping' that could be used by government.[50] In the search for a way of empowering the poor, Harrington had called for a 'vast social movement'. He hoped to link up middle-class activists with 'the daily concerns of working people and the poor'. As it was, the latter were never empowered, and 'the new liberalism remained a movement of, by, and for the educated middle class', the political consequences of which were to be profound.[51] In putting such an emphasis on demography and behaviour, the reform programme was fatally weakened by being without a realistic sense of how to either unite what was always a fractious and fragmented 'community' or enliven its varied constituents with the means to affect economic change.[52] Moreover, despite poverty research being in a much better position at the end of the Johnson era than when he came to office, the accomplishments obstructed room for political change – mainly by focusing on matters of individual pathology – through the pretence of 'the analytic ethos of neutrality', which eventually in the 1980s and 1990s led to the undermining of the US welfare state.[53]

---

[49] This view was derived from the anthropologist Oscar Lewis who coined the term 'culture of poverty', O. Lewis (1959) *Five Families: Mexican case studies in the culture of poverty*, New York: Basic Books. On this see O'Connor (2001).

[50] Cruikshank (1994), pp 40–1.

[51] Harrington (1962); Isserman and Kazin (2000), p 125.

[52] O'Connor (2001), pp 122, 150–1.

[53] O'Connor (2001), pp 194–5.

The 'new behaviourism'[54]

> [F]reedom is not conceived negatively as the absence
> of influences or simply the lack of external constraints.
> Rather, it is defined positively in terms of the skills at one's
> command and the exercise of self-influence upon which
> choice of action depends.[55]

Where parenting is concerned, just as the behavioural sciences were
actively involved in the war on poverty, so they were in seeking to
establish a liberal version of the traditional disciplinary family after
the allegedly anarchic 'flower power' years of the 1960s had, so it was
claimed, descended into destructive permissiveness. In committing
themselves to newly framed disciplinary regimes for children, liberals
hoped not only to assuage the complaints of feminists regarding the
so-called 'burden' of permissive child rearing on mothers, but also
to offer a cultural counter to conservatives. As a first step, it seemed
that the empowerment of parents with effective disciplinary skills was
a good place at which to begin, not least because, following earlier
trends in the post-war democratisation of psychology, from the mid-
1960s behaviourists exhibited 'a self-avowed interest in the prediction
and control of behaviour'.[56] In pursuit of this ambition, there was
a concerted effort made to 'give away' psychology, partly with the
behavioural issues raised by the war on poverty in mind, but also the
growing interest in therapeutic comforts, which was intended to bring

---

54 Behavioural psychology is the formulation of the persons 'primarily in terms of (their)
   behaviour rather than in terms of mentalistic constructs like "personality"'. The
   behavioural approach, which uses 'learning theory', 'maintains that the performance of
   behaviour is dependent upon antecedent and consequent conditions (reinforcement)
   that either strengthen or weaken that "response", that is, make it more or less likely
   to be repeated...The term "stimulus" is used to refer to the antecedent condition and
   the term "reinforcement"... to describe and explain the role of those consequences of
   a "response" which serve to strengthen or weaken it...reinforcement may be positive,
   negative or...aversive...Strategies designed to change behaviour by eliminating
   "unwanted" or "undesirable" responses frequently depend upon aversive techniques to
   make the behaviour as unattractive as possible to the "learner".' A particular strategy is
   the 'constructional approach' which claims to build on existing 'behavioural "strengths" by
   the exclusive use of positive reinforcement' (Baistow, 2001, pp 327–8).

55 A. Bandura (1974), 'Behavior Theory and the Models of Man', *American Psychologist*, 29, p
   865.

56 Baistow (1998), p 56. This section draws heavily on Baistow (1998; 2001).

about a vast extension of the jurisdiction of behavioural psychology. The immediate desire was to create 'the autonomous, self-managing behavioural subject' who, it was hoped, would help to solve the major social problems that divided America without recourse to significant economic or political reform.[57] The emergence and popularity of behavioural approaches, in terms of the 'giving away' process, however, was something of a paradox since after years of bad publicity regarding its authoritarian, anti–democratic and punitive practices, by the late 1960s behaviourism was said to be in decline. And yet from around the same time, the behavioural approach (carefully disassociated from the excesses of behaviourism), including the growth of 'humane' behaviour modification programmes, designed by clinical psychologists for the 'cultivation of competence' among a variety of 'targets', including parents, became more widespread than ever.[58]

Changing concepts and the 'giving away' of psychology

From the 1960s behavioural psychology underwent a number of conceptual, strategic and technical shifts, resulting in the emergence of a 'socially sensitive' profile befitting the commonplace description of America as a 'psychological society' with reference to personality and culture. This was the sub-text of the presidential address of George Miller to the American Psychological Association (APA): 'Psychology as a means of promoting human welfare', and of Albert Bandura's address a few years later, 'Behaviour theory and the models of man'.[59] With the ongoing turmoil of 1960s' America in mind, Miller proclaimed that there were a number of human problems 'whose solutions will require us to change our behaviour and our institutions', which called for a 'psychological revolution'.[60] A key theme of his

---

[57] Baistow (2001), p 311. For the behavioural sciences 'revolution', see O'Connor (2001), pp 102–7; D. F. Featherman and M. A. Vinovskis eds (2001) *Social Science and Policy Making. A Search for Relevance in the Twentieth Century*. Ann Arbor, MI: University of Michigan Press; for the enlargement of psychology's jurisdiction, see Herman (1995), pp 239–75; Petigny (2009), pp 15–52; J. H. Capshew (1999) *Psychologists on the March: Science, Practice, and Professional Identity in America, 1929–1969*, Cambridge: Cambridge University Press.

[58] Baistow (2001), pp 309–11. On the 'cognitive therapy' revolution that overtook the old behaviourism, see J. Cohen-Cole (2014).

[59] Miller (1969), 'Psychology as a Means of Promoting Human Welfare', *American Psychologist*, 24, pp 1063–75; Bandura (1974), pp 859–69.

[60] Miller (1969), p 1063.

speech was that psychology, in its 'revolutionary potential', should be 'given away' to 'everyone' for only in this way would ordinary people learn to be effective and, therefore, to change how they viewed themselves and their capacities.[61] Here he was rejecting the old image of behaviourism as being primarily concerned with controlling individual behaviour in preference to promoting a variant of self-esteem – a long-running theme in American psychology – as a feature of psychology's 'humanistic tide' with psychologists, the majority of whom were outside the academy, seeing themselves as a 'third force' between psychoanalysis and traditional behaviourism.[62] Miller sought to make psychology relevant to the problems of everyday life, with the psychologist acting not as a scientist, but as a citizen.

Psychology was to be more than a 'technological fix', it heralded what Miller called a 'new conception of man' with implications for all the subjectivities of human life, and would be used by 'everyman, every day' in a variety of situations.[63] By 'everyman', Miller meant everyone from 'a supervisor having trouble with his men' to 'a ghetto mother who is not giving her children sufficient intellectual challenge'.[64] The claim was that as people came to feel more confident and effective, so they would become more efficacious. Conscious of the project's ambition, Albert Bandura, a major figure in the behaviourist programme, was also keen to downplay the reputation of behaviourism for coercive treatments in behaviour modification programmes in prisons and other institutions, including those for autistic and 'difficult' children, and he stressed that 'reinforcement techniques' would be for 'human betterment' and not for 'social control'.[65] Individual freedom was to be expanded by 'cultivating competencies' and by 'eliminating dysfunctional self-restraints'.[66] By the 1970s, behavioural psychology was being promoted as a means whereby in a humanistic manner it could effectively enhance people's 'self-directing potentialities'.[67]

A further significant development in assuaging fears of authoritarian behaviourism, was the introduction of the 'constructional approach'

---

[61] Miller (1969), p 1071; on the 'giving away', see Capshew (1999), pp 241–58.

[62] Miller (1969), p 1069; also Herman (1995), pp 193, 264–9.

[63] Baistow (1998), pp 64–5; Miller (1969), p 1066–7.

[64] Miller (1969), p 1073.

[65] Bandura (1974), p 863. For Bandura's critical role in bringing together behavioural and cognitive approaches through his work on 'self-efficacy', see his (1977) *Social Learning Theory*, London: Prentice Hall, pp 191–215.

[66] Bandura (1974), p 865.

[67] Baistow (1998), p 67; on behaviourism and 'solving the American dilemma', pp 81–90.

intended for solving social problems which, in popularising 'behaviour therapy', emphasised respect for human rights and the role of 'positive reinforcement' rather than aversive techniques.[68] The value of this approach was that it rejected a 'pathological orientation' in preference for the cultivation of competence. At the same time, however, on both sides of the Atlantic during the 1970s, there was an increasing focus on 'behaviour modification as pure technique' (although never without its critics).[69] Advocates claimed that there was no need to understand why the 'technique' worked, sufficient that it did so; no need to teach theory to the non-professionals (including nurses and parents) – to do so would hinder the spread of behavioural approaches and opportunities for para/non-professionals to practise. The emphasis on technique also implied that the behavioural problems were themselves technical rather than pathological and, therefore, in one sense, the problems in the well community were 'normalised'.[70] However, as Karen Baistow shows, despite the de-psychiatrisation of problems, they were still identified as requiring professional services. Consequently, 'the simultaneous normalisation of the problematic and problematisation of the normal', which formed the basis for a form of behaviour modification, meant that ordinary, everyday behaviour became open to the jurisdiction of psychologists, as well as health, welfare, and education practitioners.[71] By way of gaining access to this 'everyday behaviour', in their seminal text, *Behavior Modification in the Natural Environment*, Tharp and Wetzel advocated a change from the traditional dyadic model of doctor–patient/psychologist–client method of treatment to a triadic model of consultant–mediator–target, using professionals as supervisors and consultants rather than therapists – 'the helping enterprise must be despecialized'. The consultant role 'as "contingency managers" was to rearrange environmental rewards and punishments' in relation to specific behaviours. However, 'it was parents, spouses, siblings, friends, employers or others in the "target's" natural environment who carried out the new reinforcement contingencies' – they became the mediators between the psychologist and the 'target', to whom psychology

---

[68] I. Goldiamond (1974) 'Toward a Constructional Approach to Social Problems: Ethical and Constitutional Issues Raised by Applied Behaviour Analysis', *Behaviorism*, 2, pp 1–84; Baistow (2001), pp 314–16.

[69] Baistow (1998), pp 70–74; (2001), pp 316–18.

[70] On the shift from the pathological to the normal, see R. G. Tharp and R. J. Wetzel (1969) *Behaviour Modification in the Natural Environment*, New York: Academic Press.

[71] Baistow (2001), p 318.

was to be given away.[72] Furthermore, at a time when there were an insufficient number of professionals to deal with the demands of mental health in all its forms, coupled with the low status of psychologists and psychiatrists, the matter of the cost of treatments was gaining in importance, especially with the onset of conservative economic policies. Consequently, the giving away of behavioural psychology to non-professionals to deliver 'practicable technologies' promised to be an attractive means of reducing costs.

The 'autonomous, self-managing behavioural subject'

> We believe the personal sense of powerlessness felt by low-income people is a major cause of their isolation and apathy...To encourage education and social learning...it is necessary to decrease the sense of powerlessness.[73]

Bearing in mind the 'liberalising impulse' of post-war psychology, it is not surprising that from the 1960s, when membership of the APA was increasing from under 3,000 in 1940 to over 30,000 by 1970, the political failure to discipline 'counter-cultural' youth, quell the urban/racial riots, and motivate the poor made psychological explanation more appealing, just as the Great Society initiative, with its 'mass treatment programmes', provided a major arena in which behavioural psychology could develop and expand its remit.[74] The principal development, from the late 1950s, was a refocusing of the approach away from the punitive behaviour modification of others to helping people to be the authors of their own 'responsible' behaviour, leading to the emergence of the self-regulating behavioural subject; by implication one that was empowered.[75] The emphasis in the approach was on moving away from an institutionalised base and out into the community – where psychology could be democratised – to look for opportunities to implement new strategies among a diverse population. Critically important was the role played by psychology in the new focus on 'self-determinism' rather than 'environmental determinism'. This idea of 'reciprocal determinism', a version of 'social learning theory', involved seeing the individual as active rather than passive – as 'interactional and transactional' – as affecting just as much as being

---

[72] Tharp and Wetzel (1969), pp 1–3, also 44–60.

[73] George Brager, Director of Mobilisation for Youth, quoted in Cruikshank (1994), p 37.

[74] Herman (1995), pp 208–13.

[75] Baistow (2001), p 311.

affected by the environment.[76] In emphasising 'reciprocal determinism' in social learning theory, Bandura redesigned the role of human agency, which now focused on mutuality and the transactional in the shaping of the relationship between individuals and their environment, and also on how individual self-beliefs connected to behaviour.[77] The core problem was that people 'often do not behave optimally' and, therefore, it was up to psychology to help them through inculcating a 'self-efficacy mechanism', resulting in 'self-directing capacities', to develop the means to control their own lives.[78] This was intended to lead to two distinct outcomes: *control* of the self in relation to imposed restrictions of whatever kind; and the *management* of the self in order to pursue self-determined goals.[79] Unlike pre-1960s radical behaviourism, which dismissed 'mentalism', the humanistic social learning approach believed that individual and social changes were 'best achieved through the promotion of capacities rather than by the elimination of deficits' and by the adoption of explanatory models focusing on 'competency' rather than 'defect'.[80]

A critical insight was that individual behaviour had much to do with the degree to which people felt able to influence the outcome of situations, and this in turn was connected to the concept of the 'locus of control'. The 'internal' locus referred to people who believed that their own actions could affect an outcome, whereas those with an

---

[76] Bandura integrated cognitive learning theory and behavioural learning theory to arrive at four determinants for learning: observation (environmental); retention (cognitive); reproduction (cognitive); and motivation (both). 'Social learning' theory postulates that people learn within a social context – from 'observing', 'imitating' or 'modelling' others. The focus is on 'rewards' and 'reinforcements' or punishments that we receive for our behaviours. A key feature of Bandura's approach was to counter the personal sense of powerlessness among low-income groups through emphasising self-determinism. People needed help in learning to behave 'optimally', and this could be given through inculcating 'perceived self-efficacy', a 'central mechanism in human agency', A. Bandura (1982) 'Self-efficacy Mechanism in Human Agency', *American Psychologist*, 37, p 122.

[77] On the reintroduction of the person into behavioural psychology through the 'cognitive revolution' of the 1960s, see S. Marks (2012) 'Cognitive Behaviour Therapies in Britain: The Historical Context and Present Position', in W. Dryden (ed) *Cognitive Behaviour Therapies*, London: Sage; also Baistow (1998), p 77.

[78] Bandura (1982), pp 122–47.

[79] Baistow (2001), p 312.

[80] Bandura (1974), pp 859–69.

'external' focus felt incapable of affecting outcomes.[81] A similar theory referred to the not dissimilar idea of 'learned helplessness' whereby the past actions of people determine whether or not they act decisively to achieve their goal in the future. A third construct was Bandura's theory of 'perceived self-efficacy', namely the faith of individuals in their own ability to implement change in their lives. Bandura saw inefficacy as being the result of a sense of futility stemming from a belief that no matter what we do, it will not have the desired effect.[82] Critics, however, suggested that the emphasis on the 'self-contained individual' merely confirmed the 'cultural ideal' found in North America. The locus of control approach, for example, made the individual's perception of powerlessness appear to be a sign of failure to make adaptation to reality, thereby ignoring structural inequality. This resulted in a 'blaming the victim' conclusion.[83] The outcome was a continuing emphasis on narcissistic self-realisation, rather than political, social and economic change.

Notwithstanding such criticism, both the rhetoric of the 'giving away' process and the ambition to create self-determined, optimally behaving individuals successfully transformed mental health approaches, while also 'normalising' children's 'problem' behaviour (reducing it to a matter of technique), and making it amenable to forms of behaviour modification. It is important to see, however, that while behavioural psychology was busily changing its discourses, outside the university and the conference hall of the APA another kind of revolution was quietly occurring that was to have repercussions in Britain, namely the emergence of *clinical* behavioural psychology bringing with it behaviour therapy and behaviour modification programmes.[84] By the late 1970s, these programmes were apparently having success not only in the fields of psychiatry and clinical psychology but also in the amelioration of difficulties in rehabilitation, and in solving education and social and community problems: 'no other approach or set of techniques has achieved such widespread applicability'.[85] Thus, for all the talk about the humanising effects of the new behaviourism, and the making of efficacious human beings, clinical behavioural psychology had not

---

[81] J. B. Rotter (1966) 'Generalised Expectancies for Internal Versus External Control of Reinforcement', *Psychological Monographs*, 80, pp 1–28.

[82] Bandura (1982), pp 122–47.

[83] Baistow (1998), pp 20–21, 81–90; also Cruikshank (1994), pp 29–50.

[84] Baistow (1998), p 67.

[85] Quoted in Baistow (1998), p 67.

abandoned its desire to 'condition' what it saw as 'good behaviour', very often ignoring civil liberty issues.[86]

Behaviourists and behaviour modification in the 'natural environment'

During the 1970s, despite behaviourism's intellectual decline within the academy, and the rise of the 'humanistic movement' in the cognitive sciences, ironically, behavioural theory and practice was diversified and extended, not least in the fields of mental health and family life where old problems of child rearing were being recast through new behavioural conceptualisations and reformulations and made amenable to behavioural solutions.[87] The fundamental view was that 'There are no separate principles for abnormal behavior and for the normal': 'the laws of learning, like the rains, fall upon us all'.[88] This led to a three-fold focus: the 'natural environment' (home and school), the 'behaviouralisation' of the parent–child relationship and the creation of the concept of parent training, and the emergence of paraprofessionals and parents as the 'new behaviourists'.[89] By 'behaviouralisation' was meant the introduction of the behavioural approach, using social learning theory, into parent-child relations in order to problematise 'issues' in a new way while simultaneously offering new solutions to the reformulated 'problems'. Indeed, Tharp and Wetzel influentially advanced behaviour modification as 'appropriate to almost any setting', claiming that the 'natural environment' was best suited for intervention because the 'reinforcers' were present and it was there that the contingencies of their behaviour normally occurred. Moreover, they saw early intervention in the child's environment as essential since future mental and anti-social disorders were predictable in early childhood and, therefore, 'trained' parents were a prerequisite of prevention.[90]

By the early 1970s, there was an increasing number of studies looking into training parents in the application of behavioural principles to the behaviour of their children.[91] A consequence of

---

[86] Herman (1995), p 122.

[87] Baistow (1998), pp 92–115. For the famous debate between Carl Rogers and B. F. Skinner on humanism vs behaviourism, see Capshew (1999), pp 226, 229, 235–9.

[88] Tharp and Wetzel (1969), p 5. Hence the invention of the concept of 'learning difficulty'.

[89] Baistow (1998), p 93.

[90] Tharp and Wetzel (1969), p 3; S. O'Dell (1974) 'Training Parents in Behaviour Modification: A Review', *Psychological Bulletin*, 81, 7, pp 418–33.

[91] Baistow (1998), pp 99–101.

this new interest in the everyday practices of child rearing was the redefining of 'parent' from *'being'* to *'doing parenting'*, which was seen to require a set of particular *skills* (based on 'know-how' rather than 'knowledge') that had to be learnt.[92] This meant that in addition to the child's behaviour being problematised, 'untrained' parental behaviour was also seen as problematic – the child's behaviour could only be modified through a behaviourally modified – empowered – parent. A significant dimension of this process was that neither the children's 'problem' behaviour nor the behaviour of the parent were attributed to any psychoanalytic causation, nor to intra-family psychodynamics, but rather to 'maladaptive adjustment', which was deemed to be *the* serious matter: 'These problems need to be confronted and effectively resolved since neglect or mismanagement can lead to more serious difficulties.'[93] Unsurprisingly, then, the solution lay in not in the application of any kind of psychoanalytic approach, but through the work of the behaviourally 'adapted' parent. Unlike the psychodynamic approach, knowledge about the person mattered much less than the behavioural rules of experimental psychology.[94] In fact, a 'virtue' of behavioural training was that it did not require therapeutic skills, only the ability of the parent to work under direction.[95]

Parents as new behaviourists, having emerged through being taught 'technique', were a valuable resource since they could also be used in the training of other parents and, therefore, besides maximising person power, they were a continuous and cost effective supply of labour.[96] During the 1980s the availability of parents and the associated behaviour modification programmes to which they subscribed proved helpful in dealing with a range of social problems that continued to beset post-1960s' American society. Parents as figures in need of 'adjustment', and as agents in adjusting their children's 'maladjustment', became integral to the whole process of the so-called democratising of psychology as it attempted to reconcile the individual with the social. In considering

---

92 Baistow (1998), p 101. Emphasis original.

93 C. Schaefer and H. L. Millman (1982) *How to Help Children with Common Problems*, New York: Van Nostrand.

94 Capshew (1999), p 236.

95 S. Bijou (1984) 'Parent Training: Actualising the Critical Condition of Early Childhood Development', in R. Dangel and R. Polster (eds) *Parent Training: Foundations of Research and Practice*, New York: Guildford Press, chapter 1.

96 W. Yule (1975) 'Teaching Psychological Principles to Non-psychologists', *Journal of the Association of Educational Psychology*, 10, 3, p 6; R. F. Dangel and R. A. Polster (eds) (1984) *Parent Training: Foundations of Research and Practice*, New York: Guildford Press.

the meaning behind the giving away of psychology and the shift to a so-called humanistic behaviourism, it is necessary to recognise the historicity of 'American psychology's enduring moral project...."To know our fellow man to do them good'" in the quest for "'Self-Realization" or "Actualization'" – a project with 'immoral aims'.[97] Or, as the psychiatrist Robert J. Linton has written, it was all about a search to account for selfhood 'as a flexible and dynamic response to the environment'.[98] After all, 'in the modern world change appeared to be the only constant of personality'.[99] It was to be on ongoing search, described by Tom Wolfe in his seminal essay on 'The Me decade' as the 'Third great awakening' (the previous ones having been religious) which, where parent–child relationships were involved, was characterised by a shift in models of parenting from the 'permissive' to a less optimistic and more narcissistic mode.

Saving liberal individualism: Diana Baumrind and the invention of 'authoritative' parenting

> We are becoming cannibalized...We didn't sass the policeman when he told us to move. Now in school they call teachers 'motherfuckers'.[100]

What is authoritative parenting?

One of the most influential contemporary approaches to contemporary parenting, which accorded with the new behaviourism, originated in the work of developmental psychologist Diana Baumrind through her typology of parenting styles, defined as 'authoritarian', 'authoritative', and 'permissive', each formulated through two measurements: parental responsiveness ('warmth') vs unresponsiveness, and parental

---

[97] G. Richards (1995) '"To Know our Fellow Men to do Them Good": American Psychology's Continuing Moral Project', *History of the Human Sciences*, 8, 3, pp 15–16.

[98] Quoted, Capshew (1999), p 264.

[99] Capshew (1999), p 264.

[100] A working-class Italian American, quoted in Isserman and Kazin (2000), p 201.

demandingness (control) vs undemandingness.[101] In her preference for the authoritative style, Baumrind synthesised two opposing psychological traditions: pre-war behaviourism, associated with regimented, punitive and authoritarian child rearing, characterised by 'high control' ('Too hard' and low on 'warmth'), and the post-war 'vulgar' Freudian aversion to excessive parental control ('high warmth' but 'too soft'), which was said to characterise 'permissive' child rearing during the 1940s–1960s. The former approach emphasised individual behaviour in social and familial environments, the latter focused on the needs of individual children. Authoritative parents were apparently high on *both* 'control' and 'warmth'. The empasis, however, was on 'firm control' being at the heart of the authoritative model.[102] Significantly, Baumrind, citing Spock's introduction to his 1957 edition, opposes 'unconditional love', claiming that it does not require the child to 'become good, or competent, or disciplined', and she is emphatic that 'the rule of reciprocity, of paying for value received, is a law of life that

---

[101] D. Baumrind (1966) 'Effects of Authoritative Parental Control on Child Behaviour', *Child Development*, 37, pp 887–907; and her (1972) 'Some Thoughts about Childrearing', in Urie Bronfenbrennner (ed) *Influences on Human Development*, Hinsdale, IL: Dryden Press; (1996) 'The Discipline Controversy Revisited', *Family Relations*, 45, pp 405–14; (1991) 'The Influence of Parenting Style on Adolescent Competence and Substance Use', *The Journal of Early Adolescence*, 11, 1, pp 56–95; (2012) 'Differentiating Between Confrontive and Coercive Kinds of Parental Power-Assertive Disciplinary Practices', *Human Development*, 55, pp 35–51. A fourth ideal type 'rejecting–neglecting' was added by E. E. Macoby and J. A. Martin (1983) 'Socialization in the Context of the Family', in P. H. Mussen (ed) *Handbook of Child Psychology*, Vol 4, New York: Wiley.

[102] For a critical discussion of the concept of control, see W. W. Grolnick (2003) *The Psychology of Parental Control: How Well-meant Parenting Backfires*, Mahwah, NJ: Lawrence Erlbaum Associates, pp 1–10; S. Greenspan (2006) 'Rethinking "Harmonious Parenting" Using a Three-Factor Discipline Model', *Child Care in Practice*, 12, 1, January, pp 5-12; C. Lewis (1981) 'The Effects of Parental Control: A Reinterpretation of Findings', *Psychological Bulletin*, 90, 3, pp 547–63; A. Kohn (2005) *Unconditional Parenting*, London: Atria, pp 60–5.

applies to us all'.[103] She also approves of corporal punishment (within the context of 'warmth'), dismisses criticisms of punishment as 'utopian' since 'structure' in families requires 'contingent reinforcement', and describes non-enforcing parents as 'indecisive'.[104]

The theoretical basis of the typology clearly relies upon what has been termed a 'two-factor' model of discipline: 'control' and 'warmth', which enlists as measuring tools the concepts of parental 'demandingness' and 'responsiveness'.[105] Demandingness, says Baumrind, refers to 'the claims parents make on their children to become integrated into the family whole, by their maturity demands, supervision, disciplinary efforts and willingness to confront the child who disobeys'; while responsiveness refers to 'the extent to which parents intentionally foster individuality, self-reputation, and self-assertion by being attuned, supportive, and acquiescent to children's special needs and demands'.[106] There is no sympathy here for the family as a 'cultural workshop' which, within the bounds of democratic reciprocity, 'affirms the dignity of the individual person'.[107] In using the model of 'control' and 'warmth' – a 'quasi-Hegelian dialectic' – Baumrind sought to reconcile what had hitherto been thought incompatible, namely the psychoanalytic and the behaviourist approaches, claiming that her 'style' would give young children both behavioural direction and Freudian acceptance (she was particularly critical of psychoanalysis for giving too much attention to independence and separation and too little to interdependence).[108] Much of Baumrind's influence lay in the ecumenical nature of her appeal: the overall objective of 'positive childrearing goals' embodied in authoritative parenting is 'to foster moral character and optimal

---

[103] Baumrind (1972), pp 276–8. For Baumrind's economic model of 'paying for value', see Kohn (2005), p 234, note 14; also his discussion in (2014) *The Myth of the Spoilt Child*, Boston, MA: Da Capo Press. Given Baumrind's Marxist-socialist background, and the context of 1960s 'client-based' therapeutic culture, it seems that her attitude to the socialisation of children with reference to 'reciprocity' and 'interdependence' was very much dictated by the Leftist (including feminist) hostility to liberal humanism as expressed in her rejection of 'unconditionality' and liberal individualism, leading her to favour a 'social-context position' (interdependence) for child rearing (Baumrind, 1991, p 60). See H. Vande Kempe (2000) 'Baumrind, D. B.', *Parenthood in America*, Santa Barbara, CA: ABC-CLIO, pp 80–84.

[104] Baumrind (1996), pp 405–14.

[105] Greenspan (2006), p 5.

[106] Baumrind (1991), pp 61–2.

[107] Gesell and Ilg (1943), p 10.

[108] Greenspan (2006), p 6; Baumrind (1972), p 281.

competence. Character is what it takes to will the good, and competence is what it takes to do good well.'[109] There was no place here for the view that while authoritative parenting might promote 'external' obedience, it retarded the internalisation of adult values, or for the inclusion of 'tolerance' as a third factor, making for a more 'integrative' model, or for 'considerateness' in a parent–child relationship seen as 'an art, a combination of perceptiveness and imaginativeness'.[110] For parents of a certain persuasion, including feminists tired of 1950s momism, and educators looking to heal the scars of America's civil war, the authoritative style promised a satisfying third way. In that it referred to a loss of faith in progress, it was also a response to the tumult surrounding not only the crisis of the Democratic party, but of liberalism itself in the age of the 'new utopianism' as expressed through the culture of narcissism.[111]

Baumrind and her historical context

In many respects Baumrind's work was part of the critical and often contradictory reaction among conservatives, liberals, socialist-Marxists, and feminists (bearing in mind the many contemporary idiosyncratic alliances) to a number of socio-political trends within the behavioural sciences, and to that kaleidoscope of social ferment that was America from circa 1940s through to the end of the 1960s. Baumrind shared the article of faith of American liberalism, namely that scientific knowledge was indispensable to the solution of social problems.[112] She also shared the view of the APA that psychology should be prominent in offering solutions to the problems of human welfare and, as a new behaviourist, that people could be behaviourally modified into social responsibility. Baumrind was a member of a community of scholars who found themselves dealing not only with long-standing issues of the American 'character' and the 'making of personality', but with all the political and cultural issues thrown up by the Great Society programmes and the less than successful outcomes of so many of them, including those involving deficit parent–child relations, especially among the poor, as well as with what many observers perceived to be the damaging consequences of the lurch into a soggy version of Rogerian therapeutics. In 'inventing' her typology, Baumrind addressed a research tradition that included

---

[109] Baumrind (1966), p 406.

[110] C. Lewis (1981), pp 547–63; Greenspan (2006), pp 8–10; Gesell and Ilg (1942), p 10.

[111] Zaretsky (2005), 307–31.

[112] O'Connor (2001), p 3; Cohen-Cole (2014); Herman (1995).

experiments in group leadership styles: democratic, authoritarian, and laissez-faire; ongoing projects on the effectiveness of 'social learning' theories, particularly with reference to aggression and frustration; and the anthropologically orientated study of child-rearing patterns among 400 families.[113] Baumrind, then, did not appear from nowhere, and she shared her discipline's enthusiasm to bring order, self-confidence, and a renewed sense of purpose to Liberal America.

By the late 1960s, for their different reasons, an assortment of political interests across the political spectrum was intent on destroying what it saw as the failed liberal state. Allowing for the inherent economic, social, gender, racial and political complexities in what proved to be a toxic atmosphere, permissive child rearing was increasingly linked with a range of deficits. These arose, so it was claimed, from parents being too accepting of children's impulses, desires and actions, inflicting too little punishment, making too few demands on their time, behaviour or family responsibilities, allowing them to regulate their own activities and imposing few standards for behaviour or achievement.[114] We can easily see that these deficits tuned in to the interests of several different and often opposing constituencies: those of a range of conservative attitudes in politics, the Church and the professions; the long-standing critique of 'Momism'; the search for the American 'national character'; and the feminist assault on 'housewife mothers' who were described as 'dependent, passive, childlike; they have given up their adult frame to live at the lower human level of food and things'.[115]

Baumrind's easy to grasp parenting schema, drawing as it did on a number of earlier studies, provided an appealing alternative to authoritarianism and permissiveness. The authoritative style chimed with those liberals who felt that the politics of the 1960s had failed America: the Great Society, the urban riots, the anti-war movement and, particularly, the educational war on poverty. A new and tougher strategy was required for the rebuilding of liberalism. But the typology was also attractive at the practical level to those involved in the administration of the early intervention parenting programmes for young children, especially Head Start, designed to simultaneously

---

[113] A. J. Marrow (1969), pp 123–38; J. Dollard, L. W. Doob, N. E. Miller, D. H. Mower and R. R. Sears (1967) *Frustration and Aggression*, New Haven, CT: Harvard University Press; R. R. Sears et al (1957).

[114] K. Asmussen (2011) *The Evidence-Based Parenting Practitioners Handbook*, London: Routledge, p 84.

[115] B. Friedan (1963) *The Feminine Mystique*, New York: Norton, pp 282-309; see above, pp 148–9. For discussion of mother blaming and Friedan, see Plant (2010), pp 146–77.

responsibilise mothers and prepare their children for school discipline and successful goal orientation, both of which were deemed to be essential if the poor were to '*learn* their way out of poverty'. An essential feature of the early intervention was helping parents to establish 'firm habits of good behaviour', which would allow for a 'relaxed control' during adolescence.[116] Where children were involved, this was a clear rejection of the mood of Rogers' 'unconditional positive regard' in client-based therapy, and of 'unconditional love' which, according to Bandura, 'would make children directionless, impossible and completely unpredictable'.[117] The behavioural approach was also attractive to those liberals who, perhaps to their surprise, found a limit to the liberalism that they felt was responsible for what seemed like the chaos they saw around them. Authoritative parenting offered to produce children who would embody the ideal of American citizenship, which was always spoken of in vague generalities as exhibiting reasoned conformity with group standards without loss of individual autonomy or self-assertiveness.[118] In 1991, in reiterating her message at the dawn of an era that witnessed the intensification of neoliberalism, and President Clinton's notorious promise 'to end welfare as we know it', Baumrind, buoyed up through her loyalty to a left/feminist view of interdependence (the philosophical 'ethic of care'), described the anxious liberal parent, eager for the 'success' of their children, and wrestling with social tensions filtered through a neo-conservative ordained self:

> They (the parents) monitor and impart clear standards for their children's conduct. They are assertive, but not intrusive and restrictive. Their disciplinary methods are supportive, rather than punitive. They want their children to be assertive as well as socially responsible, self-regulated as well as cooperative.[119]

Of course, no one thought of asking children what they wanted to be.

---

[116] Baumrind (1996), p 408.

[117] C. Rogers (1951) *Client-Centred Therapy*, Boston, MA: Houghton Mifflin; and (1961) *On Becoming a Person,* Boston, MA: Houghton Mifflin; A. Bandura (1969) *Principles of Behaviour Modification*, New York: Holt, Rinehart and Wintson, p 79. For 'unconditional love' in child rearing, see Kohn (2005).

[118] Baumrind (1966), p 905.

[119] Baumrind (1991), p 62.

In some senses the rhetoric of social science in the 1950s was more apposite by the end of the 1960s as the United States moved from one turbulent decade into the uncertainty of the next. Erik Erikson had warned that socialisation needed to provide a child 'with a conscience which will guide him without crushing him and which is firm and flexible enough to fit the vicissitudes of his historical era', and Margaret Mead had advised that American children were coming to maturity in 'the most rapidly changing culture of which we have any record in the world'.[120] For Baumrind, and those who shared her essentially childist perspective, the perceived failures of the 1960s to solve the enormous economic, social, cultural and political problems were more than sufficient evidence that 'permissive' – normally white, middle-class, and politically liberal – socialisation, which had characterised child rearing since the early 1940s, was itself part of the problem. Principally, it had failed to provide society with citizens who practised cooperation, perseverance, responsibility, tolerance, respect and coherence: virtues – so several Great Society investigative commissions claimed – that were apparently unknown to the poor, the young and large sections of the 'black' communities. That many parents in these constituencies were barely acquainted with liberal child raising escaped comment.

Many leftists, as well as conservatives, agreed with the cultural critic Philip Reiff (with just cause) that there had been 'a triumph of the therapeutic' in place of religion in daily life, a profound cultural change that had lessened the sense of individual moral culpability.[121] But more than this, it was also said that permissiveness in its various forms had contributed to the 'learned helplessness' that made solving the problems of poverty and inequality seem increasingly unlikely. How, then, asked disenchanted social scientists, could psychology be 'given away' to the undisciplined, the illiterate, the incapacitated, and the dysfunctional? The answer lay in the reconceptualised behaviourism that sought to make these people ready for empowerment through educational programmes, as administered by trained personnel in natural environments. Where parent–child relations were concerned, the new behaviourism, drawing on social learning theory, found the authoritative approach a willing ally in empowering parents, turning them into Baumrind's responsible, self-regulated and cooperative subjects who would be effective in socialising their children for a revitalised America.

---

[120] Quoted in Hulbert (2003), pp 206–7.

[121] P. Rieff (1966) *The Triumph of the Therapeutic: Uses of Faith after Freud*, Chicago, IL: University of Chicago Press.

In the United States the unsettling personal experiences during the 1960s of the professional middle class led it to lose its faith in the progressive ideals associated with welfarism, especially where the urban poor (black and white), the criminal and the young were involved. This loss of faith was exacerbated by the dawning of neoliberalism that gathered pace under Reagan, and which capitalised on popular discontent (middle class and respectable working class) with 'benefit cheats' (the poor) , the counter-culture, 'big government', militant trades unionism, the 'break-up' of the family, and so on. This discontent facilitated the introduction of reactionary policies in the sense that they were antipathetic to the social revolution and the social democracy that had characterised the post-war decades. It is important to note, however, that it was not so much their economic policies that made conservatives appear attractive, rather it was their ability to offer a clearly defined and easy to understand alternative to the confusion and some would say chaos of the preceding decades. It was an alternative that appealed to people's fears and prejudices as much as their hopes and ambitions. In place of liberal ambivalence and ambiguity, and the constant assessment of counter claims, the new neo-conservatism offered certainty, rigour, tradition and discipline.[122] This new culture was to work in a number of arenas, one of which was 'parenting' – here the embittered middle class and political conservatives found common ground. Something similar, as we shall see, was to occur in Britain.

---

[122] D. Garland (2001) *The Culture of Control: Crime and Social Order in Contemporary Society*, Oxford: Oxford University Press, pp 96–102, 148–50.

PART FOUR

Parental narcissism in neoliberal times: 1970s to the present

Introduction

By the early 1970s the support of both the professional middle and respectable working classes for progressive liberalism, which had been such a prominent and critical feature of the post-war social-democratic settlement, began to slip away to the point where these constituencies increasingly gave their electoral approval to the New Right with its Thatcherite economics and reactionary socio-political charter. The broad chronicle of what happened is well known. My focus, however, is on how the changes affected the conceptual disposition of parenting as culture, and the effect on parent–child relations. Since I regard child-rearing as being in part a political engagement, it will be helpful to see its post-1960s development within the context of the variety of realignments that have characterised British society. We may begin by noting that the Parliamentary move to the Right was not to the organic 'One Nation' ideal of older conservatives, with its commitment to paternalism and pragmatism. Instead it was to a determined neoliberalism that was not merely economic and corporate, but infected every tissue of the body politic, certainly as it evolved under Thatcherism, New Labour, and thereafter. In seeking to remoralise Britain, the New Right did so in its own image – that is, in terms of welfare, work, crime and punishment, and the promotion of choice, each expressed in terms of contractual obligations between the parties involved. But there was never much of a concerted effort to interfere with *personal* freedoms in relation to cohabitation, gender, sexuality, consumerism and what we think of as lifestyle. Under neoliberal regimes, these freedoms, however socially and emotionally harmful the consequences of certain features may be, simply coalesce alongside ruthless economic exploitation of labour, the marketisation of values, selective welfare services, and the privileging of the rich. Some groups, however, found that *their* lives were restricted – the socially excluded: the poor, the young and the dysfunctional – those who were largely outside the market and unable to compete in the global economy.

If we are to understand why or how the ideal of social-democratic child rearing gave way to narcissistic parenting, we need to keep these markers of social change in mind.

In accounting for the coming of parental narcissism in neoliberal times, the questions I set out to answer are as follows: what was the realm in which 'parenting' – as a verb – became so commonsensical in contrast to *being* – as a noun – a mother or father (preferably both) who raises their children? How far did the change in nomenclature reflect ideological objectives in the moulding of age relations? Through what means was the mission accomplished? And how successful were the facilitating strategies in reconfiguring the inherent parent–child intimacies? Being alert to the relevance of these questions will help us to recognise and understand not only what has transpired in the figuring of parenting as a cultural norm, but also the remaking of childhood in accordance with neoliberal precepts advanced by both the Right and the Left, albeit often for their different reasons. The links between each of the varying process hubs are complex and best summarised for the moment as intersectional interdependencies, moving at different speeds and assuming plural forms according to the broader political programmes in which they are always situated. Chapter Six offers a select overview of some of the alignments that have contributed to our culture of narcissism. Chapter Seven considers what I describe as the foundations for parental narcissism. It focuses on the emergence of the New Right, the early outlines of programmes to remoralise Britain, and coming of the new behaviourism as a means of socialising children (and their parents). In Chapter Eight, I provide a survey discussion of the New Labour era, when narcissism came of age. I argue that in the course of introducing a disciplinary state, the administrations presided over a cascade of government sponsored 'parent education' programmes, epitomised by the phenomenally successful reality television 'show', *Supernanny*, which popularised the behavioural approach in childcare. I conclude with the claim that in emphasising 'control' and 'contractual' attitudes, the authoritative parenting style, as promoted through parent education, oppresses children while serving the interests of neoliberalism and other sectional interests, such as those associated with identity politics, thereby impairing the nurturing of parental love as a social good.

SIX

Aspects of neoliberalism: political, economic and social realignments

It is a world where...the market forces which transformed the spheres of production and consumption relentlessly challenged our notions of material certainty and uncontested values, replacing them with a world of risk and uncertainty, of individual choice and pluralism and of a deep-seated precariousness both economic and ontological...it is a world where the steady increment of justice unfolding began to falter: the march of progress seemed to halt. But it is a society propelled by rising uncertainty but also by rising demand. For the same market forces which have made precarious our identity and unsure our future have generated a constant rise in our expectations of citizenship and...have engendered a widespread sense of demands frustrated and desires unmet.[1]

From the 'golden age' to modern times

In folk memory, the post-war period until the early 1970s is widely known as a time of reasonable certainty and security: high levels of employment, a rising standard of living, credit-based consumerism, better housing, the expansion of numerous personal and sexual freedoms, a new era of female emancipation, and a self-conscious and confident youth culture.[2] The decades were marked by a consensus of sorts, despite there being deep regional, religious, generational, gender and class divisions on various aspects of the reforming agenda. With respect to welfare, the economy, limited redistribution of resources, penal welfarism, and a measure of social justice there was broad public

---

[1] J. Young (1999) *The Exclusive Society: Social Exclusion, Crime and Difference in Late Modernity*, London: Sage, p 1.

[2] A. Marwick (2003) *British Society Since 1945*, London: Penguin Books; also his (1998) *The Sixties: Cultural Revolution in Britain, France, Italy, and the United States c. 1958–1974*, Oxford: Oxford University Press; D. Sandbrook (2007) *White Heat: A History of Britain in the Swinging Sixties*, London: Abacus.

acceptance of the post-war settlement. Such 'anti-social' behaviour as might occur was attributed to maladjusted personalities, poverty, and problem families.[3] In response, the deviant individual was to be reformed by a growing army of psychologically informed social workers. Of course, all this changed with the post-1960s transition to what is sometimes called Late Modernity, as it witnessed the shift from 'a world whose accent was on assimilation and incorporation to one which separates and excludes'.[4]

In the twenty years after 1973, says Eric Hobsbawm, society 'lost its bearings and slid into instability and crisis; and yet, until the 1980s it was not clear how irretrievably the foundations of the Golden Age had crumbled'.[5] Central to the crisis, he notes, was the Cultural Revolution with the rise of individualism, and the economic depression, which brought with it a restructuring of labour markets. In terms of individualism, by the 1970s it was clear that the early post-war model of the patriarchal nuclear family was much less stable than had been supposed, particularly as a growing number of married women entered paid employment, divorce rates spiralled, the number of lone parents increased, more births occurred outside marriage, cohabitation became popular and, helped by the expansion in university education, second-wave feminism established itself as an influential new social movement. Although the growth in affluence from the mid-1950s onwards was real enough, as we have seen, during the course of the following 20 years poverty was rediscovered, industrial relations were increasingly strained, social services encountered a growing volume of criticism, the fear of juvenile delinquency was a recurring theme, a public sense of economic insecurity grew and, from the late 1960s, a violent and intolerant politics seemed to emerge as the radical norm. Perhaps more serious in the long run, there was a growing dissatisfaction with the implementation of post-war democracy (it excluded so many people on grounds of ethnicity, gender and sexuality), and also with its apparent inability to understand and control a globalising capitalism. The ensuing bitterness (and disappointment) culminated in the political, industrial and economic crises of the 1970s as the economic boom

---

[3]   D. Garland (2001) *The Culture of Control: Crime and Social Order in Contemporary Society*, Oxford: Oxford University Press.

[4]   Young (1999), p 1.

[5]   E. J. Hobsbawm (1994) *The Age of Extremes*, London: Michael Joseph, p 403.

petered out and the mainly right-wing media declared Britain to be 'ungovernable'.[6]

The starting point for any discussion of social, political, economic and cultural realignments is to remind ourselves that within two interrelated contexts the Keynesian welfare state and its underlying values became increasingly unpopular. First, generally speaking, post-1960s political parties were shifting their ideological positions to the Right under the influence of neoliberal economics. Second, as social classes were being structurally reformed, so they constituted a different kind of electorate which, as traditional employments declined and trades union membership collapsed, became less interested in universal welfarism and social cohesion.[7] Seven new groupings have been identified arising from the fragmented class structures of globalisation as it has developed over the years: an 'elite'; the 'salariat' (higher paid large corporation employees and those in government agencies and public administrations); the 'proficians' (professional/technical); and the old working-class manual employees. Below these, comes the growing 'precariat' (characterised by their economic insecurity, moving in and out of employment with little sense of satisfaction or meaning), alongside the unemployed and the 'socially ill misfits'.[8] And adding to the debilitating uncertainty of class and identity has been the 'decline in comparability' of reward for skill and performance; the loss of a life narrative as permanent jobs have evaporated to be replaced by short-term contracts; and the rise of 'arbitrary reward' that pervades modern capitalist production and employment, and brings with it feelings of precariousness, of nervousness.[9] It is not hard to see how in such a climate many of the socio-economic assumptions of Keynesianism that had encouraged a liberal outlook came to be seen as antiquated.

Among the political class (elite groups within politics, the civil service, the professions, and the media), however, it was agreed that the liberalisation of British society should not (and could not) be

---

6   See, for example: A. Beckett (2010) *When the Lights Went Out: Britain in the Seventies*, London: Faber and Faber; A. W. Turner (2013) *Crisis? What Crisis? Britain in the 1970s*, London: Aurom Press; D. Sandbrook (2012) *Seasons in the Sun: The Battle for Britain, 1974–1979*, London: Allen Lane.

7   Garland (2001), pp 75–102; also D. Harvey (1990) *The Condition of Postmodernity: An Enquiry into the Origins of Cultural Change*, Oxford: Blackwell, part II.

8   G. Standing (2011) *The Precariat*, London: Bloomsbury, pp 8–9. On the concept of 'precarity', see I. Lorey (2015) *State of Insecurity. Government of the Precarious*, London: Verso.

9   J. Young (2007) *The Vertigo of Late Modernity*, London: Sage, p 63.

overturned. At the same time, the problem for those who worried about what were widely regarded as the social and malignant consequences of the liberalising process was how to manage this complex in accordance with party political objectives, while maintaining maximum electoral support.[10] The election of the Conservative government in 1979 was meant to 'stop the rot' – not competitive 'individualism', which neoliberalism saw as a moral virtue, but the layers of social indiscipline seen by many traditionalists as having accompanied 1960s' permissiveness into the crisis-ridden 1970s. This was the time when increasingly confident neoliberal constituencies became determined that never again would they risk the reins of social democracy slipping into the hands of a fractured and lacklustre older and class-bound establishment, too many of whom seemed willing to acquiesce in what the New Right saw as Britain's apparent economic, political and moral decline. In answer to the muddle of liberal ethics and the disassembling of the post-war settlement, and in the face of the failure of the self-indulgent Left to see beyond its own many (and often contradictory) limited interests, Thatcherism, invigorated by the intellectual dynamism of neoliberal think tanks, began to thrust ahead. It did so through record levels of unemployment, urban riots, Greenham Common peace protests, the bitterly fought miners' strike, the subsequent decline of effective trades unionism, the jingoism of the Falklands war, and the deregulation of the City, while successfully promoting economic and social egotism as a desirable ethic. The anvil of collective consumerism, on which 1980s Britain was forged, owed more to the belief that there was no such thing as society (Thatcher's famous remark) than one might think. What occurred was that the relationship between 'I' (the ego) and 'Me' (a socialised being), ideally working together as a coherent 'self', had already been disturbed by the tensions and ambiguities of the 1960s, and became even more seriously impaired through the heady mix of later materialism and sensualism, as well as frustration and alienation. Consequently, 'I' was left to strut its stuff, irrespective of the effect on 'Me'.[11] People were deprived of

---

[10] L. Black (2003) *The Political Culture of the Left in Affluent Britain, 1951–64*, London: Palgrave Macmillan; M. Jarvis (2005) *Conservative Governments, Morality and Social Change in Affluent Britain, 1957–1964*, Manchester: Manchester University Press.

[11] On 'I' and 'Me', see G. H. Mead (1934), *Mind, Self and Society: From the Standpoint of a Social Behaviorist*, Chicago, IL: Chicago University Press; A. Elliott (2005) *The Concept of the Self*, Cambridge: Polity, pp 24–31; N. Crossley (2005), *Key Concepts in Critical Social Theory*, London: Sage, pp 131–36.

those communes of knowledge of the sort that act as ballast to keep society afloat and sensible of its own fragility.[12]

The tribulations of 'post democracy': the rise of 'political disenchantment'

> The trouble with our politics is not too much moral argument but too little. Our politics is overheated because it is mostly vacant, empty of moral and spiritual content. [13]

According to the common view, late modern society exhibits fragile identities, economic precariousness, and 'liquid' relationships. No less important as a 'postmodern crisis' is our increasingly dysfunctional political system, on the one hand distorted in part as it is by global corporate power and, on the other, by a cynical electorate that appears to be gradually withdrawing from the democratic process. Colin Crouch claims that by the late 1990s a form of 'post-democracy' was clearly discernible:

> [I]t was becoming clear in most of the industrialized world that, whatever the party identity of the government, there was steady, consistent pressure for state policy to favour the interests of the wealthy – those who benefited from the unrestricted operation of the capitalist economy rather than those who needed some protection from it.[14]

Crouch remarks on the influence of particular structural forces, since by then there was no political interest comparable to the old organised working class in a position to withstand the challenge of the wealthy – being advanced through the corporate policies of neoliberalism – and the new political elite coming into their own around New Labour:

---

[12] E. Illouz (2008) *Saving the Modern Soul: Therapy, Emotions, and the Culture of Self-help*, Berkeley, CA: University of California Press, p 88. 'Knowledge' is more than 'ideas'; it refers to 'the vast assemblage of persons, theories, projects, experiments and techniques': P. Miller and N. Rose (2008), *Governing the Present*, Cambridge: Polity, p 57.

[13] Sandel (2013), p 13.

[14] C. Crouch (2004) *Post-Democracy*, Cambridge: Polity, p vii.

advisers, lobbyists, consultants and media propagandists.[15] Politics was returning to what it had been prior to the development of mass democracy, morphing into a means of serving the demands of the privileged and, therefore, reducing the spread of egalitarianism.[16] Democratic politics has dissolved into a mix of pressure groups and causes: the environment, the Third World, human rights, the homeless, animal welfare, etc., many of which, laudable though they are in principle, seem to reject the messy complexity of 'political' engagement, preferring to look to sterile visions of 'the community' – as in the fascination of political parties with focus groups.[17]

The emergence of 'political disenchantment' has been regularly noted by political scientists in terms of the 'rise of anti-politics' and 'the decline of Britain's civic culture'.[18] Colin Hay has argued that politics has become synonymous with 'notions of duplicity, corruption, dogmatism, inefficiency, undue interference in essentially private matters, and a lack of transparency in decision making'.[19] Although Hay disputes the apparent rise of political apathy, seeing a healthy trend in the move away from formal politics towards the more informal variety, he nevertheless acknowledges that the political process has been seriously undermined by neoliberalism's claims of political inefficiency and its inherent suspicion of state intervention, and by globalisation, both of which have reduced the electorate's faith in the efficacy of politicians to manage national affairs.[20] This feeling of helplessness has been similarly observed by Andrew Gamble who writes that modern era politics promised human beings 'control over their fate'. As the twentieth century progressed, however, events have 'dented this optimism, and spread scepticism about the ability of human beings any longer to control anything very much, least of all through politics'.[21]

---

[15] On the new political class, see P. Oborne (2014) *The Triumph of the Political Class*, London: Simon & Schuster; on the 'restoration of class power' after Keynesianism, see G. Dunenil and D. Levy (2004) *Capital Resurgent: Roots of the Neoliberal Revolution*, New Haven, CT: Harvard University Press; D. Harvey (2005) *A Brief History of Neoliberalism*, Oxford: Oxford University Press, pp. 5–38.

[16] Crouch (2004), pp vii–viii; A. Gamble and T. Wright (1999) *The New Democracy*, London: Wiley.

[17] Crouch (2004).

[18] G. Stoker (2010) 'The Rise of Political Disenchantment' in C. Hay (ed) *New Directions in Political Science*, Basingstoke: Palgrave Macmillan, pp 43–63.

[19] C. Hay (2007) *Why We Hate Politics*, Cambridge: Polity, pp 4–5.

[20] Hay (2007), p 5.

[21] A. Gamble (2000) *Politics and Fate*, Cambridge: Polity.

A historical perspective emphasises the decline in civic culture, and interestingly it shows that the major difference between the 1950s and the early 2000s was not the public's lack of trust in politicians (that had been lost since the 1970s), but 'in their sense that they can influence decisions and that the political system is responsive to them and well-functioning'.[22] The decline in electorate turnouts at all levels of elections is well known, as is the reduced membership of all parties, particularly among lower-status socio-economic groups; although participation in single issue organisations has risen. As to why the disenchantment has occurred, three reasons have been advanced. First, politics has become less partisan with the focus shifting to how politics achieves the desired ends, rather than the nature of the ends themselves; second, political organisations are no longer mass membership based but increasingly focused around professional activists; and, third, politics has become more 'economic', shaped by neoliberal theorising regarding the limitations and past failings of the state.[23] All this contributes toward a feeling of impotence, which is a potent influence on all manner of personal, relational and social insecurities, including those affecting parent–child relations.

A critique of institutional power, however disparate, is a necessary first step in securing a healthy egalitarian democracy, but progress depends on it being turned into an analysis of change and a programme of reform rather than wallowing in feelings of mournful inadequacy.[24] In prioritising the ambitions of the rich, while souring the spirit of democracy by undermining its institutions, particularly the idea that collectivism involves a communal responsibility for, and tolerance of, fellow citizens, 'post-democracy' weakens the fabric of civil society.[25] 'Post-democracy', however, evolves not only through manipulation by privileged economic and political alliances and their serving meritocracies, but also from the worship of 'difference': meaning lifestyles and identities empowered, pluralised, fragmented and subject to the dazzling array of possibilities and ambivalences inherent

---

[22] D. Kavanagh (1990) *Thatcherism and British Politics: The End of Consensus?*, Oxford: Oxford University Press, pp 145–7; Stoker (2010), pp 51–2.

[23] Stoker (2010), pp 53–57; Hay (2007), p, 5.

[24] Martin Kettle (2011) *Guardian*, 25 August; Young (1999), p 194.

[25] R. Sennett (1998) *The Corrosion of Character: The Personal Consequences of Work in the New Capitalism*, New York: Norton; Z. Bauman (2001) *The Individualized Society*, Cambridge: Polity; Young (1999) ; J. Ball and T. Clark (2013) 'Generation Self: What Do Young People Really Care About?' *Guardian*, 11 March; and 'Generation Boris' and the growth of neoliberal libertarian sentiments, *Economist*, 1 June 2013.

in 'liquid modernity'.[26] More specifically, as the feminist political philosopher Nancy Fraser has observed, with the rise of the search for, and fascination with, identity politics, class has to a large extent been decentred as we have moved away from problems of justice and the pursuit of post-1945 social democratic 'redistribution' to what she calls a 'postsocialist' politics 'in which the central problem is recognition'.[27] The consequences of this shift toward recognition, individualisation, identity, and therapeutics have been extensively discussed over the years. For the moment, I refer to 'tribulations about democracy' because the advance of neoliberal authoritative parenting cannot be accounted for as a solitary tributary of social change. It only makes sense when it is considered with reference to the decline of, or at best the frustration with, modern democracy, which is indicative of the loss of much of the social democratic attachment to progress that hitherto has encouraged us, admittedly in a confused and puzzling manner, in times of woe. No wonder Hobsbawm began his last book (*Fractured Times*) with the closing lines of Matthew Arnold's despairing 'Dover Beach':

> And we are here as on a darkling plain
>> Swept with confused alarms of struggle and flight,
>> Where ignorant armies clash by night!

Neoliberalism

A proper examination of the relationship of parenting to the changed political culture of the post-1970s era requires some consideration of the influence of neoliberalism, not simply its familiar economic and political features, but as a moral and cultural experience. We tend to overlook the fact that as parenting is part of culture, and as neoliberalism is so culturally decisive in determining our sense of 'the way things are done', then it and parenting are by no means strangers to each other. But we have to be cautious in our assessments. Neoliberalism is amorphous; it has no ruling centre; it works through 'suturing together contradictory

---

[26] Z. Bauman (2000) *Liquid Times: Living in an Age of Uncertainty*, Cambridge: Polity; Young (2007).

[27] N. Fraser (1995) 'From Redistribution to Recognition? Dilemmas of Justice in a Postsociaslist Age', *New Left Review*, 1, 212; N. Fraser and Axel Honneth (2003) *Redistribution or Recognition: A Political–Philosophical Exchange*, London: Verso; for critiques, see B. Barry (2001), *Culture and Equality: An Egalitarian Critique of Multiculturalism*, Cambridge: Polity; L. McNay (2008) *Against Recognition*, Cambridge: Polity, pp 126–61.

lines of argument and emotional investments' to find what has been termed 'systems of equivalence'.[28] Neoliberalism proceeds by finding 'space' for a multitude of interests, many of which are in competition with one another, while others are even in competition with *it*. By virtue of its continual quest for the 'equivalence relation', however, it is continually reconciling all disparities and, therefore, somewhat paradoxically, is able to embrace the world. In this way, child rearing (conceptually redefined as 'parenting'), as a cultural practice, has been absorbed into neoliberalism's disparate universe, where it remains snugly wedded to narcissism in its manifold disguises.

Gramsci's notion of cultural hegemony is helpful in identifying how it is that since the late 1970s popular consent for neoliberalism, originally little more than a set of ideas promoted by an economic and political sect, has been gradually constructed as 'common sense'. Over the years, neoliberalism has normalised 'a whole bundle of beliefs' as assumptions that are so taken for granted that their basis is hardly ever questioned. By the end of the 1980s these ideas, and what followed from them in terms of attitudes, behaviours, values, priorities, were well on their way to being established as a natural, normal and inevitable state of affairs, the fundamentals of which stipulated that human wellbeing was best served within an institutional framework characterised by the market, competitive individuals, private property and the superiority of private enterprise over public ownership.[29] Moreover, in so far as neoliberalism values market exchange "'as an ethic in itself, capable of acting as a guide to all human action, and substituting for all previously held ethical beliefs" , it emphasizes the significance of contractual relations in the marketplace'.[30] But the importance of the market alone needs to be kept in proportion. Colin Crouch has argued that in practice, as opposed to theory, neoliberalism is less attached to free markets than it is to the influence of the supra-national corporation in public life, which has had an impact on a variety of government policies. Speaking of the state, the market and the corporation, Crouch refers to 'a series of comfortable accommodations among all three'.[31] The supra-national corporation works to legitimise the claim

[28] S. Hall (2011) 'The Neoliberal Revolution', *Soundings*, 48, September, p 9–27.

[29] S. Hall, D. Massey and M. Rustin (2013), 'After Neoliberalism: Analysing the Present', *Soundings*, 52, Spring, p 13; Harvey (2005), pp 2–3.

[30] Quoted in Harvey (2005), p 3.

[31] C. Crouch (2011) *The Strange Non-Death of Neo-Liberalism*, Cambridge: Polity, pp viii–ix; Seamus Milne (2013) 'Corporate power has turned Britain into a corrupt state', *Guardian*, 4 June; also the special issue of *Critical Social Policy*, 2010, 30, 4.

that effective economic growth and development depend on market competitiveness, requiring increased labour market flexibility, which entails the transference of risks and insecurities from employers and the state to workers and their families.[32]

In establishing itself in this way, neoliberalism engaged in the comprehensive 'creative destruction' of 'divisions of labour, social relations, welfare provisions, technological mixes, ways of life and thought, reproductive activities, attachments to the land and habits of the heart'.[33] Thus, in its pluralities, it is inevitably incorporated into accounts of late modern social change. It both defines an economic and political system, *and* explicitly tutors ethical practices which, in having achieved cultural embeddedness (though never completely dominant), continue to have a profound impact on our lives – 'formally, practically, culturally and imaginatively'.[34] We should appreciate that this embeddedness (achieved in part through restricting the social-democratic stream of welfare protection), which sustains itself via contributory feeders, has affected parenting culture through promoting neoliberal values, including skill, routine, self-reliance, responsibility, empowerment, meritocracy, competition, contractualism, managerialism and individualisation – but *not* democracy. All of these move adroitly to secure what the Foucauldians refer to as 'the conduct of conduct'.[35] This has been the context in which social-democratic child rearing was creatively corroded.

The founding statement of the Mont Pelerin Society, credited with creating neoliberalism after the war, opened with the words 'the central values of civilization are in danger', and went on to claim that in many parts of the world 'the essential conditions of human dignity and freedom have already disappeared'.[36] The danger, according to the Society, lay not only in communism, fascism and dictatorships, but in all forms of state intervention in which the collective was

---

[32] Standing (2011), p 1; M. Sandel (2013) *What Money Can't Buy: The Moral Limit of Markets*, London, Penguin Books; for 'voice' in opposition to the market, N. Couldry (2010) *Why Voice Matters: Culture and Politics After Neoliberalism*, London: Sage.

[33] Harvey (2005), p 3.

[34] P. Mirowski (2009) 'Postface: Defining Neoliberalism', in P. Mirowski and D. Plehwe (eds) *The Road from Mont Pelerin: The Making of the Neoliberal Thought Collective*, New Haven, CT: Harvard University Press, pp 418–19, 428–9; Couldry (2010), p 2; B. Amable (2011) 'Morals and Politics in the Ideology of Neo-liberalism', *Socio-Economic Review*, 9, pp 11–15.

[35] Harvey (2005), p 11; Crouch (2011), p 12; Amable (2011), pp 15–21.

[36] *Statement of Aims*, 1947, online.

privileged over the individual. The political ideals of human dignity and freedom were wisely chosen for they speak to us intuitively and express images that we all find 'compelling and seductive'. But as David Harvey shrewdly observes, the 'values of individual freedom and social justice are not...necessarily compatible...[and, therefore,] any political movement that holds individual freedoms to be sacrosanct is vulnerable to incorporation into the neoliberal fold', especially, one might add, where the participants adopt a postmodern outlook emphasising relativism, diversity and difference.[37] As to why individual freedom and social justice are not necessarily compatible, Harvey writes that the pursuit of the latter:

> presupposes social solidarities and a willingness to submerge individual wants, needs, and desires in the cause of some more general struggle for, say, social equality or environmental justice...Neoliberal rhetoric, with its foundational emphasis upon individual freedoms, has the power to split off libertarianism, identity politics, multiculturalism, and eventually narcissistic consumerism from the social forces ranged in pursuit of social justice.[38]

Consequently, it has proved difficult, he says, to forge the required political action without offending those groups for whom individual freedom and recognition and expression of particular identities are paramount.[39] In fact, it has been much easier for neoliberalism, in common with postmodernism's love of the diverse, the relative, and the mystique of choice, to shape its own hegemonic status through the religiosity of materialism via mass consumerism, the pyrotechnics of celebrity worship, and across the narcissistic landscapes of libertarian individualism.

The neoliberal focus on the 'free, possessive individual', manifested through its economic practices and in collaboration with social movements devoted to their own exclusive interests, involving the ethos of social investment and the worship of recognition politics, has succeeded in bringing about the 'commercialization of intimate

---

[37] Harvey (2005), pp 5, 14; also Harvey (1990); F. Jameson (1984a) 'The Politics of Theory: Ideological Positions in the Postmodernism Debate', *New German Critique*, 33, pp 53–65; and his (1984b) 'Postmodernism, or Cultural Logic of Late Capitalism', *New Left Review*, 146, pp 53–92.

[38] Harvey (2005), p 41.

[39] Harvey (2005), p 42.

life' through manipulating what has been termed the 'cold intimacies' of 'emotional capitalism'.[40] It is hard to deny that this has resulted in the debasement of sensibility and the erosion of social–democratic character. Moreover, it has produced a form of individualisation which, in emphasising what many see as a minimal, risk–averse and freedom-seeking self, has malevolently affected parenting with regard to trust and security, love and obligation, duty and patience, and the rule of justice and fairness. It has been particularly damaging with regard to the ethic of self-sacrifice, which in the spirit of personal altruism used to require that we surrendered part of ourselves for the benefit of others. Where child rearing was involved, while this acknowledged our conceiving the child for our own (and fulfilling) purposes, one of the core strengths of the ethic was that as normally a primordial parental quality it was part of the greater universal good. This was in respect of the Kantian belief that all human beings are intrinsically valuable and, therefore, none should be treated in an arbitrary manner, rather they are ends in themselves.[41] Neoliberalism has done much to defile this view.

Narcissism in the nursery: feminism, neoliberalism and the social liberationist agenda

> The family is not here to stay. Nor should we wish it were. On the contrary I believe that all democratic people, whatever their kinship preferences, should work to hasten its demise…the 'family' distorts and devalues a rich variety of kinship stories.[42]

---

[40] Hall (2011), p 10; A. R. Hochschild (2003) *The Commercialization of Intimate Life: Notes from Home and Work*, Berkeley, CA: University of California Press; E. Illouz (2007) *Cold Intimacies: The Making of Emotional Capitalism*, Cambridge: Polity.

[41] L. Thomas (2006) *The Family and the Political Self*, New York: Cambridge University Press, pp 1–16; M. Sandel (2009) *Justice: What's The Right Thing To Do?*, London: Allen Lane, pp 120–3.

[42] J. Stacey ([1990]1998) *Brave New Families: Stories of Domestic Upheaval in Late Twentieth Century America*, Berkeley, CA: University of California Press, p 269. For the standard feminist view on the modern family, see P. Thane (2010) *Happy Families?*, London: British Academy, and the excoriating response by R. Norbert and S. Callan (2011) *History and the Family: Setting the Record Straight*, London: Centre for Social Justice.

The affinity with neoliberalism

Feminism has never just been about political campaigning. It has always sought to produce knowledge – 'feminist knowledge', which has meant connecting political activity and academic work.[43] This has been a very successful strategy for establishing a feminist 'frame' of reference in the evolution of social relations since the 1970s, which in turn has been a major influence in conditioning public perceptions of children and mothering.[44] It is important to recognise that feminism has achieved such a dominant presence by virtue of its association with various manifestations of neoliberalism, since the latter finds so much of the former conducive to its broader social cultural system in which it embeds its economic volition. The largely unspoken feminist/ neoliberal alliance has served to popularise the myth of the 'rise and fall' of marriage and the family, played its part in encouraging divorce and cohabitation, exaggerated lifestyle 'identity' as a social value, helped to make wage labour the *sine qua non* of women's 'equality', and promoted the concept of 'choice' as if it were *the* democratic feature of desire. Of course, neither feminism nor neoliberalism alone account for these social changes. They have been determined by combinations of complex and interdependent processes, not least the social, cultural, economic and political transformations that constitute the 'great disruption' of the post-1960s period: the dynamics of capitalist development; the restructuring of family and household; demographic and ecological crises; and the apparent democratising tendencies in social life.[45] However, with respect to mothering and children, feminism has sought to separate mothers from their young children, especially through exalting the virtues of the labour market and propagandising the claimed (and much disputed) 'benefits' of

---

[43] P. Abbott and C. Wallace (1997) *An Introduction to Sociology: Feminist Perspectives*, London: Routledge, pp 227–42.

[44] This follows George Lakoff's use of 'framing'. We know frames not only through our *common sense* – a 'cognitive unconscious' (a collection of metaphors used unthinkingly) – but also through language: 'All words are defined relative to conceptual frames', and because 'language activates frames', new frames require new language: 'Thinking differently requires speaking differently', G. Lakoff (2004) *Don't Think of an Elephant: Know Your Values and Frame the Debate*, Whilte River Junction, VT: Chelsea Green Publishing, p xv.

[45] F. Fukuyama (1999) *The Great Disruption*, London: Profile Books; Garland (2001), pp 77–89.

institutionalised childcare.[46] It has consistently undervalued and often denigrated mothering and motherhood, purveying the essentially childist view that the needs of children are socially constructed and should not be given priority, and that children themselves are an emotional, physical, and financial nuisance and burden. It is not that feminism consciously sought out the company of neoliberalism in advancing its social ideal, but the promise of the latter's 'free, possessive individual' was too tempting to resist.[47]

Some feminists have acknowledged the ambivalent relationship between their politics and the tentacles of late modern capitalism. Eva Illouz, the cultural sociologist, has written incisively about capitalism, the place of emotions, and the shaping of modern identity, paying particular attention to the role of psychology in providing the most influential narrative of self-development, one that has been especially fruitful for feminism in its critique of marriage and in articulating and privileging mothers' experiences.[48] The therapy culture, in drawing so extensively on the 'emotive ethic' for its legitimacy, connects feminism to 'emotional capitalism' as it subscribes to 'the logic of economic relations and exchange'.[49] Arlie Russell Hochschild is equally sensitive to feminism's relationship to 'the commercial spirit', although she refers to it as 'the abduction of feminism'.[50] Besides recognising the links between neoliberalism and feminism's ambivalence towards the family and motherhood, she observes that as Protestantism escaped from Weber's 'cage' of the church to become the 'spirit of capitalism' that drove men to become money makers, 'so feminism may be "escaping from the cage" of a social movement to buttress a commercial spirit of intimate life that was originally separate from and indeed alien to it'. The current cultural shift involving the family, love, marriage, and

---

46 There are many studies documenting the drawbacks of nursery care for young children, which are usually ignored in feminist and social policy literature. See, for example, S. Biddulph (2006), *Raising Babies*, London: Harper Thorsons; S. Gerhardt, *Why Love Matters: How Affection Shapes a Baby's Brain* (2004), London: Brunner Routledge; T. B. Brazelton and S. Greenspan (2001) *The Irreducible Needs of Children*, New York: Da Capo Press; P. Leach (1994) *Children First. What Our Society Must Do – And Is Not Doing – For Our Children Today*, London: Penguin Books.

47 Hall (2011), p 10.

48 Illouz (2007), pp 26–9; (2008), pp 114–15, 120–5.

49 Illouz (2007), p 4–5.

50 Hochschild (2003), p 13.

women (not men), she says, is more marginal than that of Protestantism and Capitalism, 'but the parallel is there'.[51]

Other feminist theorists, such as Hester Eisenstein and Nancy Fraser, have also come belatedly to concede the movement's affiliation with neoliberalism.[52] Although neither fully accepts feminism's responsibility for its collusion in the economic exploitation of women, Eisenstein's radical feminist position allows her to suggest that it was her 'liberal' sisters who were, as she puts it, 'seduced'. She acknowledges that feminism ensured that paid work for women has come to be equated with 'liberation' in a neoliberal competitive market place, which has resulted in an enormous class divide among women workers, favouring those who are educated, middle-class and white. Fraser refers to 'the cunning of history' as being responsible for feminism's botched Faustian pact. She knows full well what occurred, namely 'the disturbing convergence of some of its [feminism's] ideals with the demands of an emerging new form of capitalism – post-Fordist, 'disorganised', transnational...[which perhaps] unwittingly supplied a key ingredient..."the new spirit of capitalism "'.[53] Feminism, she writes, 'a perspective that once valorised "care" and interdependence now encourages individual advancement and meritocracy' and finds itself trapped in its own ambivalences brought about mainly through its three fundamental critiques of social democracy: the 'family wage'; a one-sided focus on 'gender identity' to the exclusion of others; and its dismissal of welfare state paternalism.[54] She wisely rejects the myth that second-wave feminism changed *mentalities* but not structural form, observing the absurdity of supposing that 'one could change while the other did not', and notes the critical occurrence, which is:

---

[51] Hochschild (2003), p 13; also (1983) *The Managed Heart: Commercialization of Human Feeling*, Berkeley, CA: University of California Press; (2012) *The Second Shift: Working Families and the Revolution at Home*, New York: Penguin Books; and B. Ehrenreich and A. R. Hoschild (eds) (2003) *Global Woman: Nannies, Maids and Sex Workers in the New Economy*, London: Granta.

[52] H. Eisenstein (2010) *Feminism Seduced: How Global Elites Use Women's Labor and Ideas to Exploit the World*, Boulder, CO: Paradigm Publishers; N. Fraser (2009) 'Feminism, Capitalism and the Cunning of History', in *New Left Review*, 56; (2013) *Fortunes of Feminism: From Women's Liberation to Identity Politics to Anticapitalism*, London: Verso.

[53] Fraser (2009), p 1.

[54] N. Fraser (2013) 'How Feminism Became Capitalism's Handmaiden – and How to Reclaim it', *Guardian*, 14 Oct.

that the diffusion of cultural attitudes born out of the
second wave has been part and parcel of another social
transformation…a transformation in the social organization
of post-war capitalism…the cultural changes jump-started
by the second wave…have served to legitimate a structural
transformation of capitalist society that runs counter to
feminist visions of a just society[55]

'Family studies'

One of feminism's most successful projects (accomplished with the help
of gay/lesbian academic activists and some 'postmodern' theorists) has
been to question the authenticity of 'the family', primary through the
establishment within sociology of the politically generated category
of 'family studies'. The reluctance to speak of 'the family', which is
dismissed as an 'abstract ideologically bounded system', together with
constantly querying its meaning, has been a key tactic in the academic
advocacy politics of feminism and gay/lesbian social theory.[56] From
its earliest days, as it pursued a social liberationist agenda, feminism
adopted a social constructionist standpoint in order to reject the
heterosexual family norm, with particular reference to mothering,
as natural. The favoured term now is 'family studies' since using the
signifier '*the* family' apparently draws on 'stereotypes that fail to take

---

[55] Fraser (2009), pp 1–2.

[56] R. Edwards and V. Gillies (2012) 'Farewell to the Family? A Reply', *Families, Relationships
and Societies*, 1, 3, p 431. For the feminist/gay/lesbian debate on the value of 'family'
as a concept, and its influence on family researchers, see the special issue of *Families,
Relationships and Societies* (2012), 1. For a sample of the feminist/gay/lesbian literature,
see S. Budgeon and S. Roseneil (eds) (2004) 'Beyond the Conventional Family: Intimacy,
Care, and Community in the 21st Century', special issue of *Current Sociology*, 52, 2,
March; J. Weeks, C. Donovan and B. Heaphy (2001) *Same Sex Intimacies: Families of
Choice and Other Life Experiments*, London: Routledge; V. Gillies (2003) '*Family and
Intimate Relationships: A Review of the Sociological Research*', London: South Bank
University; C. Smart (2007) *Personal Life: New Directions in Sociological Thinking*,
Cambridge: Polity. For a popular statement of the currently fashionable view of families,
see S. Golombok (2000) *Parenting. What Really Counts?*, London: Routledge, which
promotes the comforting half-truth that 'What matters most for children's psychological
well-being is not family type – it is quality of family life', p 104. 'Half-truth' because it
conceals the dependent and, therefore, consequential interplay between 'family type' and
'quality of family life'.

account of, and marginalize, the realities of diverse family lives'.[57] For these critics, 'the family' is too much of the Enlightenment's bourgeois grand narrative; it has been recast as kind of 'a moveable feast', not in time but as an ideological convenience, as in 'family practices', 'family connections', 'family lives', 'families of choice', or simply as a verb as 'doing family'.[58] Some academic activists prefer to shun 'family' altogether, referring instead to concepts of 'intimacy' or 'personal life', so as to transform 'the family' from the singular, always portrayed as oppressive from which women need 'liberating', to other forms of subjectivity.[59] This has established a veritable bazaar offering alternative ways of *doing* family which, as it claims to be non-discriminatory, reflects neoliberal moral relativism, with all of its accompanying risks for public grace.[60] The extent of the transformation, which is clearly visible in government publications, the media's lexicon, and throughout much of social policy, has been so successful that feminists now boast of their progress in 'the ongoing transition from feminism *and* family studies *to* feminist family studies, whereby we cannot imagine a family studies not shaped by feminist contributions'.[61] The turbulent nature of these developments and their social consequences for traditional heterosexual marriage, families and parenthood – and for children – was signalled in Elizabeth Beck-Gernsheim's study of 'family diversity', revealingly titled *Reinventing the Family: In Search of New Lifestyles*, and by the description of the 'post-familial family' as involving the transfer from a 'Community of Need to Elective Affinities'.[62] Children, however, not usually being in a position where they can effectively participate in such 'elections', have found themselves parcelled into the 'decline' of the nuclear family, the precariousness of cohabitation,

57 J. Ribbens McCarthy and R. Edwards (2011) *Key Concepts in Family Studies*, London: Sage, p 1; also J. Ribbens McCarthy, M. Doolittle, S. D. Sclater (2012) *Understanding family meanings*, Bristol: Policy Press.

58 D. J. Morgan (2013) *Rethinking Family Practices*, London: Palgrave Macmillan.

59 L. Jamieson (1998) *Intimacy: Personal Relationships in Modern Societies*, Cambridge: Polity; Smart (2007).

60 Sandel (2013).

61 Quoted in McCarthy Ribbens and Edwards (2011), p 3; see also the 'Cultural Turn in the Sociology of Family Life', in Smart (2007), pp 32–52.

62 E. Beck-Gernsheim (2002) *Reinventing the Family: In Search of New Lifestyles*, Polity/Blackwell: Cambridge and Oxford; U. Beck and E. Beck Gersheim (2002) *Individualization: Institutionalized Individualism and its Social and Political Consequences, London: Sage*, pp 85–100; also Z. Bauman (2003) *Liquid Love: On the Frailty of Human Bonds*, Cambridge: Polity.

the consequences of divorce and the emotional and time chaos that is the dual-income family.

Where feminism's chosen 'family practices' are concerned, its proponents have promoted what may be termed a 'good enough morality' that has been presented as the antithesis of individualist selfishness and social disarray of the kind said by its critics to accompany the decline of marriage.[63] Feminists and others are keen to distinguish their preference for 'intimate relations' in a diversity of 'partnerships', which they claim are just as committed, responsible and caring as those normally found in marriage.[64] This morality has been deployed to counter public worries about the consequences of divorce, certainly for children, as one of the partners (a parent), makes a 'unilateral withdrawal' and retreats from the marriage commitment.[65] There is little or no recognition that the coming of no-fault divorce in the 1970s benefited adults who may leave unhappy relationships and move on to further relationship opportunities, nor that:

> in withdrawing from promises to each other, in pursuing their own individual destinies, the partners also withdrew from an implicit contract with their children, whose stake in the partnership had not been a voluntary choice. The partners' quest for self-fulfilment was purchased by discounting the longer-term interests of their kids: by withdrawing some investment from their children, in order to invest in themselves. [66]

In much of the strategy for the 're-invention' of the family, feminists and others have been encouraged by social theorists such as Anthony Giddens who, through his promotion of 'intimacy', 'pure relationships', and 'life politics', and his admiration for same-sex couples as pioneering the way to new structures of personal life, has been a prominent advocate for new family forms. The unravelling of traditional

---

[63] C. Smart, B. Neale and A. Wade (2001) *The Changing Experience of Childhood: Families and Divorce*, Cambridge: Polity; Smart (2007); E. B. Silva and C. Smart (2004) *The New Family?*, London: Sage; C. Smart and B. Neale (1999) *Family Fragments?*, Cambridge: Polity; J. Finch and J. Mason (1993) *Negotiating Family Responsibilities*, London: Routledge.

[64] J. Lewis (2001) *The End of Marriage?: Individualism and Intimate Relations*, Cheltenham: Elgar.

[65] A. Offer (2006) *The Challenge of Affluence: Self-Control and Well-Being in the United States and Britain since 1950*, Oxford: Oxford University Press, pp 333–56, 316–17.

[66] Offer (2006), p 340, also pp 339–47.

marriage patterns, he says, involves 'essentially a massive process of institutional reconstruction, led by those concerned'.[67] Giddens claims that through '"Recombinant families"...divorce is being mobilised as a resource to create networks drawing together new partners and former ones, biological children and stepchildren, friends and other relatives...individuals appear not as withdrawing from the outer world but engaging boldly with it'.[68] Exactly how young children might participate in creating such networks is not explained. In practice, the 'recombinant' family looks very much like an exercise in egotism, or at best self-indulgent wishful thinking: with a bit of effort, we (adults) can have it all.[69]

One of the most cynical attempts to undermine parental responsibility towards children has been the campaign to question the extent to which so many children suffer adverse emotional and social reactions during and after their parents' divorce. The advocates of 'new family forms' reject what they call the 'harmism' inherent in

---

[67] A. Giddens (1991) *Modernity and Self-identity: Self and Society in the Late Modern Age*, Cambridge: Polity, p 177, and his (1992) *The Transformation of Intimacy*, Cambridge: Polity; also Weeks et al (2001).

[68] Giddens (1991), pp 176–7. See also Lewis (2001); F. Williams (2004) *Rethinking Families*, London: Calouste Gulbenkian Foundation. For these sentiments and the individualization thesis, see A. Elliott (2001) *Concepts of the Self*, Cambridge: Polity.

[69] See, for example, the rationale for individualism in Lewis (2001).

the dark view of divorce.[70] Instead, feminists speak of the 'supposed' effects on children, or the *temporary* nature of the upset the child experiences, and focus on what they claim is children's 'resilience' and their participatory role in 'changes in moral practices' as they learn to engage in the 'negotiation of new moral terrains'.[71] They argue that the 'genuine desire to improve the lives of children is quite a separate phenomenon to the powerfully symbolic and politically useful rhetoric of harm, suffering and innocence'. Thus feminism presents 'harmism' misleadingly as nothing more than 'a form of sentimental rhetoric that can be harnessed to political agendas'.[72] The implication here being, on the one hand, that to speak of the harm done to children through divorce is an innately conservative response motivated by a desire to preserve the patriarchal family structure and, on the other,

---

[70] There has been a campaign to change popular perceptions of the adverse consequences of divorce for children, using 'new' conceptual approaches that are said to reveal more nuanced outcomes for them. The campaign focuses on substituting children's so-called 'resilience' for 'harmism': see, for example, 'New Perspectives on Divorce', special number of *Childhood*, 10, 2 (2003), especially C. Smart, 'Introduction', pp 123–9; also C. Smart, B. Neale and A. Wade (2001) *The Changing Experience of Childhood: Families and Divorce*, Cambridge: Polity; A. E. Wade and C. Smart (2002) *Facing Family Change: Children's Circumstances, Strategies and Resources*, York: Joseph Rowntree Trust; C. Smart, A. Wade and B. Neale (1999) 'Objects of concern?: Children and Divorce', *Child and Family Law Quarterly*, 11, 4, pp 365–76. For a variety of views on the 'harm' (or not) done to children through divorce, see Offer (2006), pp 339–47; K. E. Keirnan (1997) 'The Legacy of Parental Divorce', *CASE Papers* 1, London: LSE; B. Rogers and J. Pryor (1998) *Divorce and Separation: The Outcomes for Children*, York: Joseph Rowntree Foundation; R. O'Neill (ed) (2004) *Does Divorce Matter?*, London: CIVITAS; P. R. Amato and A. A. Booth (1997) *A Generation at Risk: Growing up in an Era of Family Upheaval*, Cambridge, MA: Harvard University Press; M. Bhrolchain (2000), 'Parental Divorce and Outcomes for Children', *European Sociological Review*, 16, 1, pp 67–91; A. E. Goldberg and K. R. Allen (2013) *LGBT–Parent Families: Innovations in Research and Implications for Practice*, New York: Spring; P. Morgan (2000) *Marriage-lite: The Rise of Cohabitation and its Consequences*, London: Institute for the Study of Civil Society; P. Leach (2014) *Family Breakdown: Helping Children Hang on to Both Their Parents*, London: Unbound. See also A. James and A. L. James (2004) *Constructing Childhood, Theory, Policy and Social Practice*, Basingstoke: Palgrave Macmillan, pp 196-201.

[71] S. Sevenhuijsen (2002), 'A Third Way? Moralities, Ethics and Families', in A. Carling, S. Duncan and R. Edwards, *Analysing Families*, London: Routledge, p 137. The word 'supposed' is used in castigating Giddens' proposals for 'new family politics', 136–7; also Smart et al (1999), p 366; Smart et al (2001).

[72] Wade and Smart (2001), p 22; Smart et al (2001).

that feminists, unlike 'conservatives', do not have political agendas. By way of countering 'harmism', another feminist tactic has been to draw on the sociology of childhood to enlist 'agency' in order to position children as actors able to 'make decisions and choices within the context' of the circumstances of divorce.[73] What is ignored is any consideration of the complex place of 'structure' (and of 'power') in the working out of 'agency'. Agency, in practice, has two components. First, children as social actors: they clearly make a difference by being *in* society – for example, in family relationships. Second, being an actor, however, is not the same as being an agent. A social actor works from a subjective wish, but an agent *negotiates* with others in order to make a *difference*. The fact is that 'childhood agency has to be understood within the parameter of childhood's minority status'.[74] This is what makes children's standpoint so important in analysing culture.

Feminism, motherhood and mothering

Feminism's troubled, if not disturbing, attitude towards motherhood and mothering is understandable since both are so fundamental to the organisation and functioning of human society that attempting to reconstruct their meaning in terms that will satisfy the very particular interests of gender identity, as Nancy Fraser admits, is bound to produce a myriad of contradictions, duplicities and ambivalences. A critical problem for feminism has been how to deal with the 'certain tension between...not appearing to be against motherhood and children and...articulating the problems women face as mothers', whilst campaigning 'to try and change the conditions of motherhood which limit women's experiences and choices'.[75] The self-regard towards women is unconsciously displayed here with the implication being that the limitation felt by *some* women is a *universal* condition. But, as

---

[73] C. Smart (2000) 'Divorce and Changing Family Practices in a Post-industrial Society', *Family Matters*, 56 , pp 10–19.

[74] B. Mayall (2002) *Towards a Sociology for Childhood,* Buckingham: Open University Press, p 21; also A. James, C. Jenks and A. Prout (1998) *Theorizing Childhood,* Cambridge: Polity; M. Wyness (2015) *Childhood,* Cambridge: Polity; and D. Oswell (2013), *The Agency of Children: From Family to Global Human Rights,* Cambridge: Cambridge University Press.

[75] Richardson (1993), p 120; C. Everingham (1994) *Motherhood and Modernity: An investigation into the Rational Dimensions of Mothering,* St. Leonards, NSW: Allen and Unwin; A. Reilly(2008) *Feminist Mothering,* New York: State University of New York Press.

is shown by other research and social commentary, this is not true.[76] Historically speaking, in defining motherhood as a social construction, feminism has portrayed it through a continuous and repetitive literature as burdensome, a source of 'oppression', entailing a 'loss identity', as 'inherently unfulfilling and degrading', and as 'misery'.[77] In the 1980s a more cautionary approach developed with some feminists looking to 'womanly values' and attempting to reconcile motherhood within a gender-conscious family practice; others, however, ridiculed this move as 'maternal revivalism', claiming that it ignored 'the frustration, aggression and intense ambivalence also present in women's mothering experience'.[78] Since then the critique of anything resembling self-sacrificial motherhood has been ongoing as committed mothers find themselves denigrated through the rubric of the 'culture of total motherhood' and 'intensive mothering' – it has even been claimed that 'good' mothering is grounded in 'the interests of male dominance, capitalism, religious power, homophobia, and racism'.[79] Over the years, continuous feminist rhetoric has led to the privileging of a type of

---

[76] K. Hakim (2000) *Work–Lifestyle Choices in the 21st Century: Preference Theory*, Oxford: Oxford University Press; (2003) 'Public morality versus personal choice: the failure of social attitude surveys', *British Journal of Sociology*, 54, September; pp 339–45; A. Hagget (2012) *Desperate Housewives, Neuroses and the Domestic Environment, 1945–70*, London: Pickering and Chatto; J. Giles (2004) *The Parlour and the Suburb: domestic identities, class, femininity and modernity*, London: Bloomsbury Academic; S. Gerhardt (2010) *The Selfish Society*, London: Simon & Schuster.

[77] Aside from the feminist classics, see almost anything of Ann Oakley's early work; also D. Richardson (1993) *Introducing Women's Studies*, London: Palgrave Macmillan; R. Cusk (2001) *A Life's Work on Becoming a Mother*, London: Fourth Estate; R. Asher (2011) *Modern Motherhood and the Illusion of Equality*, London: Vintage; F. R. Elliott (1996), *Gender, Family and Society*, London: Macmillan.

[78] L. Segal (1999) *Why Feminism?*, Cambridge: Polity, p 45; also V. Byson (2003) *Feminist Political Theory*, London: Macmillan, 179–81, 185–6; S. M. Dornbusch and M. H. Strober (eds) (1988) *Feminism, Children, and the New Families*, New York: Guilford Press; S. E. Chase and M. F. Rogers (2001) *Mothers and Children*, New Brunswick, NJ: Rutgers University Press; S. Ruddick (1990) *Maternal Thinking*, London: Women's Press; P. DiQuinzio (1999) *The Impossibility of Motherhood*, London: Routledge; R. Parker (2011) *Torn in Two: Maternal Ambivalence*, Berkeley, CA: University of California Press.

[79] A. E. Kinser (2010) *Motherhood and Feminism*, Berkeley, CA: Seal Press, pp 1–2; also J. Warner (2005) *Perfect Madness: Motherhood in the Age of Anxiety*, London: Penguin Books; S. Hays (1996) *The Cultural Contradictions of Motherhood*, London: Yale University Press; J. Valenti (2012), *Why Have Kids?*, Boston, MA: New Harvest.

mothering that is characterised by a resentful attitude towards children, and the promotion of narcissistic 'ME-time'.[80]

Not all feminists, however, subscribe entirely to this agenda. Arlie Hochschild refers to 'the postmodern solution', which is 'to rid ourselves of the mother–child image, replace it with nothing, and claim that everyone is happy anyway'. She notes that the 'traditional' view as to what a child '"really needs" to thrive' is replaced by the terms '"succeed", "cope" and "survive"'. Popular psychology and advice books 'glamorize a life for women that is relatively free of the burden of this kind of care'. Fearful of returning women to the home, seen as the site of oppressive patriarchy, many feminists, she says, argue 'Stop feeling the loss. Don't feel nostalgic for the intact homes of the 1950s. You'll never get them back, and they weren't better anyway.'[81] Another feminist tactic used to devalue the 'mother–child image' is to deploy what Hochschild calls an 'Orwellian "superkid" language' to normalise what in the past would have been called 'neglect': for example, 'children in self-care'. She quotes from a manual on training children to be 'home alone', which advises them: 'The end of the workday can be a difficult time for adults. It is natural for them to sometimes be tired and irritable...Before your parents arrive at the Center, begin to get ready, and be prepared to say good-bye to your friends so that pick-up time is easier for everybody.' Other examples of this language include the currently popular euphemisms 'self soothe' and 'controlled crying' for leaving babies to cry themselves to sleep. This image of the 'happy child', concludes Hochschild, is that of 'postmodern stoicism', which is true provided we remember that it is an *imposed* stoicism.[82]

What is perhaps the principal feminist objection to committed mothering, which has done so much to foster the egotistical aspects of parental narcissism, and its latent childism, is clearly evident in some

---

[80] For 'unwitting testimony' of MEism in feminism, see I. Tyler (2005) 'Who Put the "Me" in Feminism? The Sexual Politics of Narcissism', *Feminist Theory*, 6, 1, pp 25–44; and her (2007) 'From "The Me Decade" to "The Me Millenium". The Cultural History of Narcissism', *International Journal of Cultural Studies*, 10, 3, pp 343–63; also Kinser (2010), pp xii–xi. MEism is promoted in the feminist accounts of French-style child rearing: Pamela Druckerman (2012) *Why Don't French Children Throw Food?*, London: Doubleday UK, and her (2013) *French Parents Don't Give In*, London: Black Swan; and Catherine Crawford (2013), *Why French Children Don't Talk Back*, London: John Murray.

[81] Hochschild (2003), pp 219–21; also A. Neustatter (2012) *A Home for the Heart. Home as the Key to Happiness*, London: Gibson Square Books.

[82] Hochschild (1995) 'The Culture of Warm Politics: Traditional, Post-Modern, Old Modern and Warm Modern Ideals of Care', *Social Politics*, 2 (3), p 339.

recent criticisms of Winnicott's portrayal of the 'good enough mother' where, it is claimed, the mother appears primarily as the child's object. She is said not to exist as someone 'who has her own desires'; the objection being that 'the child gets attention, the mother does not':

> The mother does not simply get less: she gives up the very thing care and education are about instilling the child with. The mother's time is taken by the tasks of care. Her desire and autonomy are subjected to the changing and often arbitrary needs of the infant. She is expected not to respond to attack, so that the child would be convinced she survives them. Human satisfaction resides in interpersonal exchange but, to make it possible, the parent has to be shut in with someone who cannot reciprocate and does even exist as a whole person: the infant she holds and contains is not yet an integrated person who is capable of relating... The engagement with the world that the child would later be capable of enjoying follows directly upon the parent's being barred from the same activity...[The mother] endures the monotony so that the child may have the richness. [83]

One has to ponder this interpretation for a few moments in order to behold the chasm between it and 'love', and to digest the full extent of its narcissism. The feminist psychoanalyst Jessica Benjamin, however, defended Winnicott when she argued that mothering is an 'activity', since the mother participates in the process whereby the child forms a personality through her 'mental work of representation or thinking'.

---

[83] G. Gerson (2004) 'Winnicott, Participation and Gender', *Feminism and Psychology*, 14, 4, p. 575; for similar feminist objections to the baby being 'prioritized', see M. Shapira (2013) *The War Inside: Psychoanalysis, Total War, and the Making of the Democratic Self in Postwar Britain*, New York: Cambridge University Press, pp 131–2; also the critique of Bowlby in M. Vicedo (2013) *The Nature and Nurture of Love: From Imprinting to Attachment in Cold War America*, Chicago, IL: University of Chicago Press. An alternative way of viewing this relational majesty is to see 'love' as 'the wish to care, and to preserve the object of the care ... An impulse to expand, to go beyond, to stretch to what is "out there". To ingest, absorb and assimilate the subject in the object ... Love is about adding to the world – each addition being the living trace of the loving self; in love, the self is, bit by bit, transplanted onto te world. *The loving self expands through giving itself away to the love object* ... love means an urge to protect, to feed, to shelter, also to caress, cosset and pamper ...', Z. Bauman (2003) *Liquid Love. On the Frailty of Human Bonds*, Cambridge: Polity, pp 9-10. Emphasis original.

In this sense, 'mothering' consists of 'two active subjects [who] may exchange, may alternate in expressing and receiving, co-creating a mutuality that allows for and presumes separateness'.[84] But critics found the idea of parental agency problematic arguing that while Benjamin looks at 'the ways in which holding changes the child, she does not do so on how it changes the parent. The child develops. The mother is there to facilitate this development'.[85] These comments point to the feminist refusal to accept that a mother may *continue* with her personhood (she is already a person) *through* prioritising her baby's needs. As Winnicott suggested, it is through the sensitivity of the mother that the baby overcomes his or her internal asocial needs and 'civilization would start again inside a new human being', which would be achieved through 'mutual understanding'.[86] Here are two contrasting views of a mother's personhood: the feminist yearning for an independent identity – the social liberationist's 'authentic personal life', and Winnicott's socially integrationist image of the mother giving her baby the means to become a fully human person. From the closing decades of the last century, as the remaining chapters will show, in large measure, the latter view has been compelled to give way to the former.

---

[84]   J. Benjamin (1988) *The Bonds of Love: Psychoanalysis, Feminism and the Problems of Domination*, New York: Pantheon Books, p 29.

[85]   Gerson (2004), p 578.

[86]   Quoted in Shapira (2013), p 132.

SEVEN

Laying the foundations for parental narcissism

'From "The Me Decade" to "The Me Millenium"'[1]

With the ending of the 'golden age', and the beginning of 'new times', c.1973–74, it soon became clear that nothing would ever be the same again. The major texts of 'golden age' reformism – Anthony Crosland's *The Future of Socialism*; J. K. Galbraith's *The Affluent Society*; Gunnar Myrdal's *Beyond the Welfare State*; and Daniel Bell's *The End of Ideology* – were all written between 1956 and 1960, and presumed the continuation of a society that was at ease with itself.[2] The 1960s put paid to that. From the late 1960s onwards, with their experiences of the perceived failures of the post-war settlement in mind, a number of interests, of all political persuasions, began to aggressively promote their grievances and their claims in a variety of arenas, becoming ever more vociferous and gathering political momentum. It was a resurgent conservativism, the New Right, increasingly confident of its ability to change the course of Keynesian economics and welfare, while simultaneously shaping the ongoing social revolution to its own ends, that came to dominate the political discourse. The Labour Party, having abandoned socialist principles, was exposed to the vicissitudes of its own sectarian politics and the multiple desires of the aggrieved, which together evoked from it a spectacle of confusion, incompetence and not a little tragedy. As the New Right progressed, it began to implement not only a neoliberal economic programme, but also, and critical for the success of the programme, an agenda for the restructuring of what was still thought of as social-democratic culture. A vital element in this process was the reconfiguration of the family's emotional economy, critically with reference to notions of parental responsibility and parent–child relations. The task was undertaken with the help not so much of

---

[1] I. Tyler (2007) 'From the "Me Decade" to the "Me Millenium"', *International Journal of Cultural Studies*, 10, 3, pp 343–63; (2005) 'Who put the "Me" in feminism?: The sexual politics of narcissism', *Feminist Theory*, 6, 25, pp 25–44.

[2] E. J. Hobsbawm (1994) The *Age of Extremes: The Short History of the Twentieth Century*, London: Michael Joseph, p 286.

a 'policy transfer' from the USA, as a social–scientific tool, deployed through the expertise of health, education and welfare professionals, with the intention of changing people's behaviour, namely the 'new behaviourism' and the associated 'learning theory'.[3] In time, as Chapter Eight will show, the behavioural approach (along with neuroscience and 'infant determinism') became integral to New Labour's policy process, being presented as normal and natural, just another feature of 'common sense'. This chapter, whose guiding theme is the process of 'remoralisation', examines some of the reasons why this came to be, and its impact on the ethos of parenting.

The New Right emerges: Sir Keith Joseph and the 'cycle of deprivation'

The 'cycle of deprivation'

In the early 1970s Sir Keith Joseph, Secretary of State for Social Services in the Conservative government and one of the principal theoreticians of the New Right, made three critical speeches setting forth what came to be known as the cycle of deprivation hypothesis, which sought to explain the persistence of socio-economic disadvantage through generations.[4] The emphasis was placed on 'family pathology' as a transmission mechanism of intergenerational social deprivation: inadequate, deprived parents pass on to their children habits and behaviours that were said to have either caused or exacerbated their disadvantaged condition, leading the children to reproduce the cycle of deprivation throughout their own lives. If the cycle were to be broken, a number of government 'interventions' would be necessary, including social services casework, playgroups, nursery education, and instruction in parent preparation for existing parents and older children. The first and best known speech (1972) was given to a conference of local authorities organised by the Pre-School Playgroups Association; the second, to a seminar of the Association of Directors of Social Services; and the third, stressing links between the hypothesis and a Department of Health and Social Security (DHSS) sponsored initiative, 'Preparation

---

[3]   D. P. Dolowitz with R. Hulme, M. Nellis and F. O'Neill (2000) *Policy Transfer and British Social Policy: Learning from the USA?*, Buckingham: Open University Press; K. Baistow (2001) 'Behavioural Approaches and the Cultivation of Competence', in G. C. Bunn, A. D. Lovie and G. D. Richards (eds) *Psychology in Britain*, Leicester: BPS Books, pp 309–29.

[4]   Andrew Denham and Mark Garnett (2001), *Keith Joseph*, Chesham: Acumen, and for the 'cycle of deprivation', pp 219–25.

for Parenthood', at the annual conference of the Pre-School Playgroups Association.[5] The speeches generally divided opinion. For the Right, it seemed obvious that in thinking in terms of 'intergenerational continuities', Joseph was identifying a non-controversial social reality – clearly, among the principal causes of deprivation was an absence of individual responsibility, which included neglectful parenting. Many on the Left, however, critical of what they saw an ideological leaning toward 'blaming the victim' in focusing on 'lifestyle' and personal choice, argued that Joseph denied the importance of structural factors and distribution issues in accounting for poverty and other social ills. Where poverty was the issue, however, by emphasising 'structures' as causal factors the Fabian socialist tradition denied the poor any agency in deciding how to live their lives. For many commentators, this would come to be seen as a political mistake since it left open the way for the much more punitive analyses under Thatcherism.[6]

In his review of British social life post the permissive age, Joseph claimed that the family environment with loving, responsible parents was central to healthy child development, recording that children 'who do not get any guidance on how to behave from their parents suffer from emotional starvation'.[7] He noted recent advances in child psychology and argued strongly that children's 'early years' were significant influences on their later behaviour. He was particularly concerned that the intellectual and emotional neglect of young children should be tackled (this was one reason why he supported the work of the Pre-School Playgroup Association), and while he did not deny the importance of economic and social influences, he was always anxious to advocate more thought and effort being put into parent education. If families were to function normally, breaking the cycle of deprivation was deemed to be imperative and, therefore, Joseph set his social services department the task of achieving this end, initially through formulating a research programme involving a number of academics and social services personnel, which he hoped would be followed by legislation.[8] Although by the end of the 1970s, the 'cycle' theme had lost its political cachet, it served to promote the concept of individual responsibility and was important in familiarising a number of different audiences – professional, educational, governmental, NGOs and the

---

5   For background detail, see J. Welshman (2012) *From Transmitted Deprivation to Social Exclusion: Policy, Poverty and Parenting*, Bristol: Policy Press.

6   On the 'revival' of agency, see Welshman (2012), pp 11–15.

7   K. Joseph (1974) *The Times*, 21 Oct.

8   Welshman (2012), pp 2–31, 38.

public – with the idea that parenting was not something that just happened, certainly not among those who were soon to be designated as the 'socially excluded'.

The sources of the hypothesis

My concern here is not so much with the speeches themselves as the thinking behind them, and the extent to which they pointed the way to the behavioural approach to child rearing that began to characterise Thatcherism and went on to be widely used under New Labour and subsequent governments. The immediate origins of the speeches go back to the 1960s and the debates surrounding the problem family and the rediscovery of poverty, which had aroused Joseph's interest. In common with many others, he worried about the apparent link between the family environment and juvenile delinquency, arguing that it was not merely a matter of deprivation that led to criminal behaviour, since many children survived such circumstances. By the end of the decade it was evident that Britain was culturally and economically unsettled. In 1970 Enoch Powell made his infamous 'rivers of blood' speech to highlight the 'race question' as part of his challenge for the Conservative leadership. Against the background of demonstrations, industrial militancy, vandalism and growing concerns about crime, the Conservative Shadow Cabinet held a secret meeting in preparation for the forthcoming general election, out of which came a commitment to re-establish a respect for the law through rigorous new legislation.[9] In this context, Joseph's interest in the 'cycle' viewed deprivation not solely as a problem of inequality or inadequate resources, but as a feature of a more widespread social malaise, characterised by what he regarded as the declining subservience to the exercise of power and authority necessary for political order. In other words, he saw parenting as a matter of government.

The evidence on which Joseph drew for his ideas was fivefold. First, there was a fairly extensive problem family literature stretching back to the late nineteenth century. The cycle hypothesis, however, looked to redesign the problem family concept for a new historical context, and with it to elaborate on the importance of parenting as a focus for treating dysfunctional social relations. The second source was a body of criminological research into the generational influence of family and parental behaviour in creating juvenile delinquency;

---

[9] S Hall, C. Critcher, T. Jefferson, J. Clarke, B. Roberts (2013, 2nd edn) *Policing the Crisis*, Basingstoke: Palgrave Macmillan, pp 268–9.

third, were a number of local psychiatric studies on child abuse, which also emphasised generational factors. The fourth body of evidence derived in part from the Plowden Report's recommendation for the establishment of educational priority areas designed to counter the effects of poverty, and also from the work of the influential US psychologist Urie Bronfenbrenner. Bronfenbrenner was interested in generational responsibilities and socialisation (claiming that there was an extremely low level of parental involvement in British children's lives), and emphasised the value of 'early intervention' in the form of pre-school education, lauding the value of the US Head Start programme in encouraging poor parents to make good the deficit in their child-rearing responsibilities.[10] The fifth source was the 'rediscovery' of child abuse that by the early 1970s was being publicised by the NSPCC's Battered Child Research Unit and, from 1973, the Tunbridge Wells Study Group (TWSG – self-appointed and ad hoc). Joseph, together with members of his department, attended the founding conference of the TWSG in May 1973, and there is little doubt that the growing concern about the matter and subsequent public enquiries into child deaths influenced discussion on how to deal with families caught in the 'cycle'. Within a few days of the conference, Joseph decided to establish a public inquiry into the killing earlier in the year of seven-year-old Maria Colwell by her step-father. The report (1974), which unleashed something of a 'moral panic' with the child's death being seen as symbolic of what was 'wrong' with Britain, was read as confirmation of the need to tackle the issues surrounding the deprivation/depravation conundrum, and much else besides.[11]

All these influences were evident in a major address given by Joseph in 1974, and designed to open his bid for the leadership of the party. The speech, significantly entitled 'The Family and Civilised Values', is important not so much for what it tells us about Joseph's primary

---

[10] H. Silver and P. Silver (1991) *An Educational War on Poverty: American and British policy-making, 1960–1980*, Cambridge: Cambridge University Press, pp 187–209; Welshman (2012), pp 39–44, 58–62; for Bronfenbrenner's role in Head Start, see M. A. Vinovskis (2005) *The Birth of Head Start*, Chicago, IL: University of Chicago Press, and J. Welshman (2010) 'From Head Start to Sure Start: Reflections on Policy Transfer', *Children & Society*, 24, pp 89–99.

[11] N. Parton (1985) *The Politics of Child Abuse*, Basingstoke: Macmillan, pp 72–77. Other influences on Joseph's thinking included the debates following the 1967 legislation on abortion and family planning, particularly with reference to what was described as 'casual breeding and unwanted pregnancies' among social classes IV and V: see Welshman (2012), p 60.

concerns to move the party to the right, but for the degree to which it voiced many of the anxieties, not only of the Conservative Party, but also of a cross-section of public opinion.[12] This is a telling consideration because these anxieties were to be influential on Thatcherism, and did much to create the authoritarian landscape in which parents and children were slowly being reconstituted throughout the period. Joseph lamented what he saw as a general undermining of governance that was diverting parents away from their duties to ensure the education, health and welfare of their children, as well giving them appropriate values, advice and guidance. The decline in educational standards which, he said, echoing the *Black Papers*, was all too obvious, he connected to rising rates of delinquency, hooliganism, and illiteracy, while 'the bully boys of the left' were destroying universities and giving a foretaste of a 'left-wing dictatorship'. The same people, led by intellectuals, denigrated patriotism and national pride under the banner of 'internationalism', and sowed 'a hatred of their own country'. Such 'well-orchestrated sneers', he continued, coming from elites within education and the media, 'have weakened the national will to transmit to future generations those values, standards and aspirations which have made England admired the world over'. The left, he claimed, always want the state to do more for the poor, whereas the right thing to do was to help the poor to help themselves. In a world where 'permissiveness' was leading to anarchy and disorder, 'We must fight the battle of ideas in every school, university, publication, committee, TV studio, even if we have to struggle for a toehold there…We have the truth.' Joseph, against advice, then lapsed into eugenic rhetoric, saying 'the balance of our population, our human stock, is threatened' and warning that lower-class teenage mothers were breeding future problem children.[13] These latter remarks were hugely controversial and Joseph found himself ridiculed throughout the media and attacked by social and medical opinion across the political spectrum; as he became an embarrassment to the party so he withdrew his bid, leaving Margaret Thatcher later to successfully challenge Ted Heath for the leadership.

---

[12] On Joseph's desire to shift the Conservative Party to the Right see K. Joseph (1976) *Stranded on the Middle Ground: Reflections on Circumstances and Policies*, London: Crown Prosecution Service.

[13] K. Joseph (1974) *Sunday Times*, 20 October; Denham and Garnett (2001), pp 265–72.

Preparation for, and dimensions of, parenthood

When he first promoted the cycle hypothesis, Joseph's immediate task was to encourage research on whether preparation for parenthood, which was now seen as 'the key to the intergenerational processes at work within the family', in addition to other economic and social welfare measures, had a role in breaking the cycle, and also in alleviating problems of 'personal and emotional deprivation' that were 'not confined to poor or large families or families in bad housing'.[14] In late 1972 to early 1973, along with Mrs Thatcher, as Secretary of State for Education and Science, he had a series of 14 consultations with 30 professional, voluntary and other organisations in order to discuss child development and the role of parenting, specifically its emotional and psychological dimensions. Although the consultants felt that there was 'extensive ignorance about the developmental needs of children and the role of parents in meeting them', it soon became clear that parenting was a complex governmental matter involving a number of relationships between parents, local authorities, and professional agencies. The main topic of the meeting proved to be not preparation for parenthood in any narrow sense, but 'the importance of parenthood in our society and the need for it to be supported in every possible way' so as to promote not 'a frightening picture of the "ideal" parent but rather that of an ordinary "good enough" parent'.[15] In terms of a parent education movement, there was evidently little that could be examined since the single example of an ad hoc parent education movement was the Halifax Association for Parents, established in 1968 and linked to the Paris-based international Federation for Parent Education. The Association worked with a range of groups, often in conjunction with the LEA and through discussions with relevant BBC TV producers. The Health Education Council was particularly keen to see the work of the Association extended. Other forms of potential parent education included further education services, community activities, playgroups and nursery schools, and home visiting by health and educational visitors.[16]

In April, 1973, a two and a half day seminar on 'dimensions of parenthood' was held at All Souls College, Oxford, with Michael

---

[14] DHSS (1974a) *The Family in Society: Preparation for Parenthood. An Account of Consultations with Professional and Voluntary and Other Organizations*, October 1972 to February 1973, Foreword (London), pp 5–7. For the research programmes undertaken by the SSRC, see Welshman (2012).

[15] DHSS (1974a), Foreword, p 8, also pp 11–13.

[16] DHSS (1974a), pp 24–5.

Rutter and Uri Bronfenbrenner being two among a number of prestigious speakers coming from several involved disciplines. Chairing the proceedings, Joan Cooper, Director of Social Work Service at the DHSS, remarked that a question mark hung over 'the viability of traditional family patterns in a world being dominated by science and technology'. The family, she said, 'may have reached a crisis point. Changes may be the precursor of a decaying family system or of developments...which cannot yet be analysed.' After outlining a number of the changes – in the role of women, of fathers, the growth of affluence, and the extension of personal freedom – she asked 'how traditional parental and social roles are to be redefined, reorganised or supplanted'.[17] Bronfenbrenner confirmed Cooper's concern, quoting from the White House Conference on Children (1971) to melodramatic effect that 'America's families and their children are in trouble, trouble so deep and pervasive as to threaten the nation. The source of the trouble is nothing less than a national neglect of children and those primarily engaged in their care – America's parents.' He continued with multiple examples of what he presented as the deteriorating situation of families, parents, and children, noting in particular the separation of children from adults and the omnipresence of television.[18] But despite these forebodings, the conference rapporteur detected anxiety in the proceedings as to what constituted 'good' or 'bad' family life, and how to refine and analyse 'problems'. She advised that perhaps 'malfunctioning' was a more appropriate word than 'deprivation', and warned of the danger of inserting 'value assumptions' into the discussions. The seminar concluded that in considering 'preparation for parenthood', the parents themselves should be asked what they wanted.[19]

There are two reasons why these meetings were important in the evolution of parent education. First, they tell us that in the context of the end of the post-war consensus and the economic difficulties of 1971–74, the New Right saw parenting as a means of re-evaluating the issues focusing around poverty, problem families, economic redistribution, the concept of equality and, more broadly, the contested (by the Right) prestige of working-class culture, much of which still held to the values of community, solidarity and a sense of 'class' identity. Since 1945 mainly left-wing sociologists, economists,

---

[17] DHSS (1974b), *The Family in Society: Dimensions of Parenthood. A Report of a Seminar held at All Souls College*, Oxford 10–13 April 1973 (London), pp 10–11.

[18] DHSS (1974b), pp 91–100.

[19] DHSS (1974b), pp 105–13.

social administrators, and social critics, such as Richard Hoggart and Raymond Williams, had set the agenda on these matters within the academy, education, social services, and parts of the media.[20] In initiating a research programme, Joseph was establishing a new framework for the analysis not merely of the 'transmission of deprivation', but for the long-term remoralisation of British values which, according to critics, had become impregnated with moral turpitude, as exemplified by the neglect of meritocratic ideals and the undermining of personal responsibility in favour of egalitarianism and social environmentalism. Although Joseph was irritated by the sceptical academic response to his hypothesis, the more important point was that as his overall analysis gained political ascendency, so the energies of the left was confined to answering his critique of the welfare state, rather than to presenting its own programme of economic and social revival.

Second, with respect to the converting perception of parenting, what it was and what it should be, the significant conclusion was that it required 'preparation' and that, as behavioural learning theory claimed, it could be 'learned'. This was a critical recognition given the apparent social and personal disorder in the post–1968 climate of rising unemployment, increasing trades union militancy, the rapidly changing structure of families through divorce, cohabitation and single motherhood, and the influence of sexual permissiveness and libertarianism. Where the Left for the most part tended to welcome social liberation, the New Right was perspicacious in selecting from among the changes those that fitted into its developing neoliberal project in a manner so as not to alienate those sections of the electorate gaining from them. In such a world, where personal relationships were being unsettled, subject as they were to a complex of new and little understood economic and political forces, and the family was being restructured, child rearing could not be left to chance. If modernity had assumed untrammelled continuation of patriarchal norms, post modernity was wrought with disarray and, for conservatives (and others) disarray in the family was but a step away from unbridled licence.

---

20 Silver and Silver (1991); B. Simon (1991) *Education and the Social Order. British Education since 1944*, London: Lawrence and Wishart; A. Wooldridge (1994) *Measuring the Mind: Education and Psychology in England c. 1860–1990*, Cambridge: Cambridge University Press.

The New Right, the Labour Party and the remoralising of Britain

The Labour Party's role in ending progressive education

In Chapter Four, by way of accounting for the decline of the social-democratic spirit at the end of the long sixties, I briefly discussed the campaign against progressive education in relation to the short-lived Children's Rights movement. Here I focus on the role of the Labour government as it accelerated the demise of the progressive temper by competing for popular support with the New Right, which seemed to have captured so much of the public mood – a programme that continued under Thatcherism before being elaborately restructured in the social disciplinary philosophy of New Labour's 'Third Way' By the mid-1970s, the curtailing of educational progressivism was under way through the rise of the conservative doctrine of 'accountability and control' which, as it attracted parental support, served the purposes of the New Right in spreading and popularising its doctrine. Leading employers, echoing the claims of the *Black Papers*, and supported by the right-wing press, regularly complained about the bias against business to be found among many teachers, the 'declining' levels of numeracy and literacy, and the allegedly poor work ethic of school-leavers. The behaviour of adolescents, it was reported, had deteriorated; they were now 'more questioning...less likely to respect authority...[and] more likely to resent guidance about their general appearance'. One large employer warned against a teaching profession that 'has more than its fair share of people who are actively politically committed to the overthrow of liberal institutions, democratic will or no democratic will'.[21] In terms of how issues were being linked into what is now called 'a narrative', *The Times* equated 'the wild men of the classroom' with trade union 'disrupters' and 'wreckers'.[22] For these critics, the problems had been sown in the primary schools which, encouraged by the Plowden Report's progressivism, focused on children's 'experiences' and engaged in innovative and liberal teaching methods. The fact that in practice the vast majority of the schools were anything but progressive did not deter the conservative charges. In essence, Conservatives were equally determined to undermine the comprehensive schools, since

---

[21] Quotations, C. Chitty (2014) *Education Policy in Britain*, Basingstoke: Palgrave Macmillan, pp 34–5.

[22] Quoted in Simon (1991), p 7; also CCCS (Centre for Contemporary Cultural Studies) (1981) *Unpopular Education*, London: Hutchinson, p 212.

they were seen as being more concerned with fostering egalitarianism than basic skills, and with failing to train pupils in the values necessary for 'a cohesive society with an effective and cultured leadership'.[23]

The situation was exacerbated by the crisis at the William Tyndale school in Islington where a group of radical teachers, in attempting to democratise teacher–pupil relations, and to create a curriculum for severely disadvantaged children, found themselves alienated from the parents and the Labour controlled local education authority before being dismissed in 1976. The 'scandal' became the beacon for demands for the accountability of teachers to government and parents, a campaign which, as it gathered momentum, helped to silence liberal ideals.[24] Those teachers who looked to Labour for support were disappointed. Indeed, Labour had a history of opposition to progressivism, student radicalism, and often also to teacher trade unionism. In many respects, even its commitment to comprehensive schools was as much about 'individual destinies' as about 'collective advance'.[25] Unsurprisingly, then, the Party was sympathetic to populist criticism. By the 1970s, the Labour leadership, and the majority of its local authorities, had no enthusiasm for child-centred schooling. Against an increasingly coordinated campaign by the Conservative party, its supporters in academia and the press, and a number of affiliated pressure groups, Labour politicians prepared to control the curriculum and teaching styles according conservative views on the needs of the economy and the values of utilitarianism.[26]

The official turning point came in 1976 when the Prime Minister James Callaghan, in a major speech that opened the 'Great Debate' on education, attempted to seize the electoral initiative by abandoning the Party's support for educational reform, saying that he would 'slam the lid and screw it securely down'. Child-centredness was to be replaced by a commitment to the 'world of work', as the Party turned resolutely against those teachers and pupils opposed to classroom authoritarianism,

---

23 Simon (1991), pp 379–82; K. Jones (1983) *Beyond Progressive Education*, London: Macmillan, pp 77.

24 Simon (1991), pp 444–6.

25 Jones (1983), pp 64–7.

26 Chitty (2014), pp 46–7. Groups included the Centre for Policy Studies, Friends of the Education Voucher Experiment in Representative Regions, and the Conservative Philosophy Group which, in conjunction with the much older Institute of Economic Affairs (IEA), provided the Conservative Party with an intellectual base from which social-democratic Labour was successfully challenged and routed.

school uniforms and corporal punishment (not abolished until 1986).[27] In rejecting the progressive trend, Labour also implicitly rejected the 1960s' liberalising of age relations. By the 1970s, national and local politicians were promoting the view that children 'needed' discipline at home and at school; that they should be taught the value of hard work; that in place of 'democratic' discussion, obedience was the necessary requirement of them; and that neither the school nor the home should be places of 'free expression', rather their role was to instil in children a respect for authority, hierarchy, and for 'normal' moral values. In advancing this message, Labour no doubt reflected public opinion for increasingly working-class parents had grown impatient with progressive social-democratic influences and looked on school as primarily an avenue for occupational and, therefore, social class mobility. As it was popularly presented against the background of the 'exhaustion of consent', the Tyndale affair symbolised for these parents the danger of allowing left-wing middle-class ideas of progressive child rearing and schooling to override the 'common sense' of the 'real' world.[28]

The child as metaphor: from Colwell to Bulger

Besides the controversies surrounding the cycle hypothesis and progressive and egalitarian education, there were two further crises that contributed to, and in part also reflected, the rightward drift in British culture. Although both have been written about at great length, they are discussed here in order to relate them to the decline of the social-democratic family as a humane and optimistic environment for children and their parents. One involved the rediscovery of child abuse, as was dramatically illustrated by the case of Maria Colwell, beaten to death in 1973 by her stepfather shortly after having been unwillingly returned from foster care to the home of her natural mother at the behest of social workers. The other concerned the abduction by two truanting ten-year-old boys (Jon Venables and Robert Thompson) of two-year-old James Bulger from a Liverpool shopping mall, after which they abused the toddler, before killing him with a brick and leaving his body on a railway line to be run over by a train. Each of these episodes, as we know well, served as a metaphor for a variety of confused and

---

[27] On the reassertion of 'rationality' over 'Romanticism', see R. Skidelsky (1969) *English Progressive Schools*, London: Penguin Books, pp 243–57; also Chitty (2014), p 45; Simon (1991), pp 444–51; Jones (1983), pp 68–94.

[28] Hall et al (2013), pp xv–xvii, 215, 243.

often contradictory anxieties expressing a sense of bewilderment and disorientation, and played a significant role in sculpting a pervasive image of a violent and unstable society.

The inquiry into the death of Maria Colwell proved crucial in establishing child abuse as a social problem. After the child's death, there began a long and emotional public discussion involving problem families and related controversial issues: how to identify such families, and what to do about them; the allegedly distorting influence of left-wing and feminist ideas among social services staff; the nature and responsibilities of parenting in a 'risk' culture; and the broader matter of the welfare state in a society marked by degrees of fundamental economic and social change.[29] In 1976, a House of Commons Committee, which had been taking evidence on 'violence in marriage', had its remit broadened to include violence in the family. Its report, *Violence to Children* (1977), acknowledged that 'violence against children is only part of the much larger problem of child abuse and neglect' adding significantly, but without comment, 'and how children *should* be brought up', as it recognised that children had to contend with various forms of physical and emotional pain.[30] The causes of abuse were listed as mainly social and psycho-medical, including the cycle of deprivation, stress, isolation, poor mother–child bonding, and unwanted pregnancies. The report urged the community to have a heightened sense of its duty towards *families* with young children – not to the children themselves – and recommended the government to give local authorities greater financial aid for prevention, with additional grants to agencies such as the NSPCC. The government responded with circulars and consultative documents, but little in the way of new resources. In a different historical context this parliamentary concern to safeguard children might have sustained social-democratic aspirations; indeed, these might have given the inquiry more focus. By the late 1970s, however, frustration, disaffection, cynicism and suspicion were suppressing the kindness necessary for the continuation of the liberal approach to child rearing. Instead, the focus began to move towards 'protection' of children 'at risk', which in time became a major social services industry, involving social workers, teachers, lawyers, the police, academics, NGOs and numerous private agencies.[31]

---

[29] Parton (1985), pp 69–99.

[30] House of Commons (1977) 'Violence in the Family: Violence to Children', *1st Select Committee Report, House of Commons Papers*. Emphasis added.

[31] N. Parton (2006) *Safeguarding Childhood: Early Intervention and Surveillance in a Late Modern Society*, Basingstoke: Palgrave Macmillan.

One of the most influential themes of the 1979 general election campaign, set against the background of economic difficulties, bitter industrial disputes, uncertainty as to the pace and direction of social change, and the right-wing claim that the country was becoming ungovernable, was that, in Mrs Thatcher's words, Britain needed 'less tax and more law and order', as it remained under the destructive influence of 1960s' liberalism, which glamorised political violence, ridiculed traditional morality, incited civil disobedience, and purveyed pornography. These, said the Conservative election manifesto, were 'not matters for the police alone' – teachers and parents also had a role to play, as did the community. By the late 1970s it was *de rigueur* to refer to 'the British crisis' – of capitalism, class struggle, and political legitimacy in connection with consent and coercion.[32] At the emotional centre of this crisis, immediate and gut-wrenching, was the figure of a horribly abused dead little girl, seemingly failed by everyone who was responsible for her health and safety.[33] Among large sections of the general public, regardless of their politics, in some intangible but deeply felt personal sense (shaped and manipulated in part by the media), the killing of Maria Colwell seemed to be evidence of what happens when society loses its moral sense.[34]

But it was 'the Jamie Bulger affair' (February–December, 1993), with media coverage 'nothing less than phenomenal', that proved to be a significant cultural turning point, albeit complicated and ambiguous, in age relations, as it seemingly gave final proof of the 'breakdown of the family', the rise of a dysfunctional 'underclass', and 'childhood in crisis'.[35] The case had a number of interrelated features that served to accelerate the fading optimism regarding adult–child relations. First, and clearly one of the most disturbing features, was that a child had been killed by other children (an extremely rare occurrence), which unsettled conventional notions of childhood innocence: how could 'innocent' children have killed an 'innocent' child? In normal discourse:

---

[32] Hall et al (2013), pp 310–13.

[33] Parton (1985), pp 89–97.

[34] Other high profile inquiries into child deaths included Jasmine Beckford (1985), Kimberly Carlisle (1987) and Tyra Henry (1987).

[35] H. Davis and M. Bourhill (1997) '"Crisis": The Demonization of Children and Young People', in P. Scraton (ed) *'Childhood' in 'Crisis'?*, London: UCL Press, pp 28–57; B. Franklin and J. Petley (1996) 'Killing the Age of Innocence: Newspaper Reporting of the Death of James Bulger', in J. Pilcher and Stephen Wagg (eds) *Thatcher's Children: Politics, Childhood and Society in the 1980s and 1990s*, London: Falmer Press.

Ten-year-old children tend to feature in mediated crime reporting as idealised innocent victims in relation to which the deviancy of the 'other' is defined. Here such conventional assumptions became challenged and this gives the Bulger case a much greater societal purchase, as we (the viewer, the reader) are effectively confronted by the implications of the realisation that those *formerly* conceived of as innocent victims might pose a profound threat to themselves.[36]

More than anything else, the theme of 'the killing of innocence' conditioned the moral outrage aimed at the two boys, as it developed between the time of the child's death and the outcome of the trial. Second, it was a 'stranger' killing – a 'street crime', the initial abduction being caught on a security camera, which provided the iconic image (which chimed with the sensationalist media accounts surrounding the so-called child 'crime wave' from 1991 onwards).[37] The murder, however, seemed to expose all children to risk (and, by implication, as parents, 'us', too), thereby adding to uncertainty.[38] At the same time, the risk was confusing: it seemed to come from *other* children, but also by implication, *our* children. The third feature was the projection of 'evil' onto 'childhood' (regularly endorsed by reference to William Golding's *Lord of the Flies*). This grew out of the trial judge's description of the killing 'as an act of unparalleled evil and barbarity', which encouraged the media to portray the two boys as 'Freaks of Nature'; 'they had hearts of unparalleled evil'; the 'Devil Himself Couldn't Have Made a Better Job of Two Fiends'; and, only slightly less apocalyptic, 'We have a world where children are growing up virtually as savages.'[39] A *Times* editorial solemnly warned:

---

[36] C. Hay (1995) 'Mobilization Through Interpellation: James Bulger, Juvenile Crime and the Construction of a Moral Panic', *Social & Legal Studies*, June, 4, 2 , pp 198–20.

[37] T. Newburn (1996) 'Back to the Future? Youth Crime, Youth Justice and the Rediscovery of "Authoritarian Populism"', in Pilcher and Wagg (1996), pp 68–70. The killing of a child by a stranger was most unusual. In 1991, for example, all of the 74 under-fives who died illegally did so at the hands of either a family member or a family friend: N. Cohen, *Independent on Sunday*, 21 February, 1993.

[38] Hay (1995), p 201.

[39] Quotations in Davis and Bourhill (1997) pp 47, 50; also Franklin and Petley (1996), pp 138–39.

> Children should not be presumed to be innately good. In the lexicon of crime there is metaphysical evil, the imperfection of all mankind; there is physical evil, the suffering that humans cause each other; and there is moral evil, the choice of vice over virtue. Children are separated by necessity of age from none of these. (25 November 1993)

Elsewhere, *The Sunday Times* (28 November 1993) opined its conservative message of despair: 'We will never be able to look at our children in the same way again...Parents everywhere are asking themselves...if the Mark of the Beast might not also be imprinted on their offspring.'

But there was a fourth aspect that was ultimately more damaging for age relations than any other, namely the unleashing of an extraordinary level of adult malevolence towards the boys, 'unprecedented in recent times'. The trial judge confirmed the retributive atmosphere in declaring that they should be 'locked away for very, very, many years'.[40] On the day the guilty verdicts were announced the *Daily Star* featured front-page photographs of 'killer' Venables and 'killer' Thompson above the headline 'How do you feel now you little bastards?'. Several newspapers campaigned to have the original sentences extended, and published lurid accounts of the expense to taxpayers of providing a 'soft' life for the boys in the secure units to which they were sentenced.[41] The most intellectualised justification for retribution came from the BBC's urban affairs correspondent David Walker, who wrote approvingly that 'punishment exists to satisfy society's sense of just deserts. This is a nerve ending which material civilisation has not yet anaesthetised. To pooh-pooh that yearning to see perpetrators of crime, young no less than older, are punished is to put social cohesion at risk.'[42]

The public anxieties surrounding the 'violent society' of the 1970s, themes of which continued through to the 1990s, can be seen as having been socially constructed by statistics, the judiciary, and the media. The latter being involved in the social production of news and, therefore, a sense of the world as we think we know it: 'they provide the base-line interpretations, influence "lay" attitudes, mould the ideological climate and are instrumental in the orchestration of political and public responses'. However, just as the public do not approach making sense

---

[40] Quoted in Franklin and Petley (1996), pp 140.

[41] With few exceptions, little thought given to the deeply troubled circumstances in which the boys lived – see Franklin and Petley (1996), pp 142–7.

[42] Walker (1993) *The Times*, 26 November.

of crime *tabula rasa*, but instead bring 'to bear interpretative schema, uninspected assumptions, common sense, tacit knowledge and forms of reasoning', so parents were approaching parenting in a similar manner, though perhaps one embedded in a more psychologically bounded subjectivity.[43] And as the public mood, propelled by a combination of anxiety, envy, misunderstanding, and not a little disappointment at the way life in the welfare state had turned out, adopted conservative and increasingly vengeful views on crime and punishment, so the culture of parenting gradually shed its liberal sympathies and reverted to more authoritatively secure patterns of child rearing. Children had put upon them an 'essentialism', under which they were crudely identified as 'Other' – distant from us and, by implication, not only 'different' but also inferior (the child as unfinished implies the *desirability* of being the complete adult). The outcome of essentialism has been described as 'demonization and the creation of monstrosity'.[44] The 'monster' serves the purpose of being the figure against whom we can all unite. After Bulger, wrote Marina Warner, 'the child has never been seen as such a menacing enemy as today. Never before have children been so saturated with all the power of projected monstrousness to excite repulsion – and even terror.'[45] The revengeful mood had been lurking around for some time, always ready to spring on the poor, the young and the marginalised. Bulger catapulted it into a new and audacious prominence that was to find an amenable burrow under New Labour.

The 'punitive turn' and the emergence of 'vindictiveness'.

An influential feature of the processes of political and social realignment that occurred in the last quarter of the twentieth century was the increasing importance of crime and the 'culture of control' as a means

---

43 Hall et al (2013), p xiii.

44 J. Young (1999) *The Exclusive Society: Social Exclusion, Crime and Difference in Late Modernity*, London: Sage, pp 96–120; also J. Petley (1997) 'The Monstrous Child', in M. Aaron (ed) *The Body's Perilous Pleasures: Dangerous Desires and Contemporary Culture*, Edinburgh: Edinburgh University Press; B. Goldson (1997) 'Children in trouble: state responses to juvenile crime', in Scraton (ed), pp 133–6. Demonisation is 'a process through which individuals, groups or communities are ascribed a public, negative reputation associated with pathological malevolence often popularly represented as "evil"', P. Scraton (2008) 'Demonization' in B. Goldson (ed) *Dictionary of Youth Justice*, Cullompton: Willan Publishing, p 132.

45 M. Warner (1994), *Managing Monsters: Six Myths of Our Time* (Reith Lectures), London: Vintage Books, pp 34–4.

of neoliberal governance.[46] This focus on crime, criminality and criminals has had important consequences for adult–child relations and, therefore, also on parenting. Quite simply, children, especially those of the poor, were demonised through 'nuisance' being conceptualised as criminal behaviour.[47] By virtue of the intense media frenzy around child 'crime waves' in the 1980s, the widespread hysteria following the Bulger murder and its social and political consequences, and the creation by New Labour of 'anti-social behaviour' as a 'zero tolerance' crime, the juvenile delinquent was positioned as a principal figure in the articulation of risk – alongside the so-called underclass – as expressed indiscriminately through anxiety and uncertainty.[48] In this despairing medley, 'the community' was portrayed as being in need of protection from troubled and troublesome children who were deemed to be a threat *to*, rather than a part *of*, its literal and figurative existence. Unsurprisingly, and not unusually, within the context of 'precarity' (a spectrum of insecurities), voices soon came forward to 'reassert one's values as moral absolutes, to declare other groups as lacking in value, to draw distinct lines of virtue and vice, to be rigid rather than flexible in one's judgements, to be punitive and excluding rather than permeable and assimilative'.[49] In trying to understand what was happening from the 1980s onwards, we should see the threat of risk as part of the more general relocation 'as modernist conceptions of crime and control are progressively replaced…by a new crime complex'.[50] In this complex, young people felt the full impact of the criminological 'punitive turn': namely a redirection away from social democratic welfarism, emphasising reform and rehabilitation, towards 'punitiveness': punishment that relies 'on an emotive and vindictive

---

[46] D. Garland (2001) *The Culture of Control: Crime and Social Order in Contemporary Society*, Oxford: Oxford University Press.

[47] B. Goldson (2001), 'The Demonisation of Children', in P. Foley, J. Roche and S. Tucker (eds) *Children in Society*, Basingstoke: Palgrave; P. Squires (2008) *ASBO Nation: The Criminalisation of Nuisance*, Bristol: Policy Press; Hendrick (2003) *Child Welfare. Historical dimensions, contemporary debate*, Bristol: Policy Press, pp 224–34.

[48] Scraton ed (1997); F. Furedi (2006) *Culture of Fear: Revisited*, London: Continuum; Z. Bauman (2006) *Liquid Times: Living in an Age of Uncertainty*, Cambridge: Polity.

[49] Young (1999), p 15. On 'precarity', see I. Lorey (2015) *State of Insecurity. Government of the Precarious*, London: Verso.

[50] T. Newburn (2007) *Criminology*, Cullompton: Willan Publishing, p 330.

infliction of pain and harm in order to humiliate and dehumanize offenders'.[51]

Where the sociology of vindictiveness is concerned, there are similarities between, on the one hand, its analytic referencing of the underclass, criminals and juvenile delinquents and, on the other, the frequently 'vindictive' (and fearful) behaviour of adults towards children (their own and others).[52] This is not to use the word just in the sense of 'revenge'; but as referring to spitefulness, grudge, ill-will. Nor is it to claim that there is an inevitable fit between vindictiveness and public perceptions of children and child rearing. But it is to insist that facets of resentment and punitiveness could be found instructing the mood of contemporary child rearing as it manifested shades of parental narcissism. And the importance of the character of the prevailing *mood* should not be underestimated: a dour mood can unhinge a kind act. Thus we should look a little more closely at the concept of vindictiveness in order to clarify its sociological perspective for age relations. The force of the distinctions made between adults and children needs to be appreciated, because so often the latter, as 'becomings', inhabit an ambivalent position regarding ontological security, vis-à-vis adults, as in the exclusion/inclusion binary.[53] In all such binaries, informed as they are by the sense of indeterminancy, the threat of exclusion (as felt by adults) is always present, and this produces an essentialism whereby the (high) values of those feeling threatened are prioritised above the (low) values of those perceived as threatening.[54] Consequently, via both the sense of economic injustice and the prevailing vulnerability, the process of 'othering' involves 'resentment' and 'dehumanisation', and this facilitates violence, both symbolic and literal. In order to create Jock Young's 'good enemy', we have to identify them as being responsible for our difficulties, to portray them as not like us, as 'inherently evil, intrinsically wicked'. This process, dehumanising others, not only

---

51 J. Muncie (2008) 'Punitiveness', in Goldson (ed), pp 278–9; also J. Muncie (2008a) 'The "Punitive" Turn in Juvenile Justice', *Youth Justice*, 8, 2, pp 107–21.

52 J. Young (2007) *The Vertigo of Late Modernity*, London: Sage.

53 A. James, C. Jenks and A. Prout (1998) *Theorizing Childhood*, Cambridge: Polity; N. Lee (2001) *Childhood and Society: Growing Up in an Age of Uncertainty*, Buckingham: Open University Press; M. Wyness (2006) *Childhood and Society*, Basingstoke: Palgrave Macmillan; R. Smith (2010) *A Universal Child*, Basingstoke: Palgrave Macmillan.

54 J. Young (1999).

creates the gulf between 'us' and 'them', but provides us with the justification for being unmerciful in our actions.[55]

The same sort of thinking is an important feature of adult–child relations, particularly in behavioural aspects of parent education and certainly in much of the child-rearing literature, as well as in feminist accounts of motherhood where children, apparently so naturally *different* from us, are regularly portrayed as liabilities of one sort or another. Moreover, in the broader context, concepts of evil and wicked are frequently used by politicians and the media to describe children's behaviour, criminal and otherwise. Thus (adapting Young's 'good enemy') in separating ourselves off from children, we are free to 'act temporally outside of our human instincts because we are dealing with those who act inhumanely', namely children as disrupters and spoilers. In some senses, children resemble the so-called underclass since it, too, may be seen as heterogeneous and ill-defined in its nature. As they are unsettlingly characterised – essentialised – in the media, and by developmental psychology, the parent education business, and teaching unions (the latter forever tiresomely complaining about troublesome pupils), so children become a 'ready target for resentment' and an 'easy focus of hostility'.[56] Moreover, even when the critique is couched as an altruistic concern for what is said to be happening to 'childhood', children continue to be perceived as a social problem.[57] Vindictiveness, says Young, is often caused by 'relative deprivation downwards', which is experienced by those who feel that the poor, the unemployed and other welfare recipients are getting 'an easy ride' at the expense of 'hard working families', and as a result there is much popular support for welfare cuts. A similar feeling of resentment may be said to exist among many parents, succoured by populist (mainly feminist) rhetoric, which is forever telling them that they are at the beck and call of their children, that they are continually being lectured at by experts, that they are subject to the vagaries of state interference and that, as mothers, their identities are repressed by the misery and frustration of childcare. As with perceptions of the poor and the dysfunctional, these feelings

---

[55] J. Young (2003) 'Merton with Energy, Katz with Structure: The Sociology of Vindictiveness and the Criminology of Transgression', *Theoretical Criminology*, 7, 3, p 400.

[56] Young (2003), p 401. They become 'liminal figures', representations of the 'limit of the human', D. Kennedy (2006) *The Well of Being: Childhood, Subjectivity, and Education*, New York: State University of New York Press, p 7.

[57] Wyness (2006), pp 73–113; also C. Piper (2008) *Investing in Children: Policy, Law and Practice in Context*, Cullomton: Willan Publishing; Smith (2010).

can easily breed a subtext among parents that encourages them 'to punish, demean and humiliate' their children.

To survive in late modernity requires the acceptance of at best frustration and at worst unhappiness, with constant disappointment somewhere in between. Employment very often involves a level of precariousness that is unsettling; it is also often unsatisfying, poorly paid, demands long and unsociable hours and, where children are to be cared for, '"quality time" as a euphemism for "little"'.[58] The struggle of dual-job and increasingly multi-form families to manage schedules – financial, temporal, emotional – requires 'restraint and sacrifice that turns simple displeasure (a sense of unfairness) into vindictiveness'.[59] Just as in this climate the socially excluded are vulnerable to hurtful discrimination, so, too, are children – they may be victims of a kind of adult indignation, envy and bitterness at their apparent freedom from adult responsibilities and their irrepressible need for care and protection.[60] This is a dangerous cocktail of discontent that can infect parent–child relations, one that culturally writes a sullen script that in its more extreme form encompasses a barely disguised child hatred, which is embraced in what Chris Jenks has called 'the Dionysian child' buttressed by 'Adamic original sin' and confirmed by a vulgar notion of Freud's 'id'.[61] Moreover, it may be added, also by a series of often mutually contradictory images used to allocate children to convenient adult-centric narratives involving innocence, nostalgia, vulnerability, abuse and sentimentality – each playing on the theme of victim and threat. Such a cocktail not only severely limits the opportunities for children's participation in the struggle for *their* recognition, but also in the long run has malign consequences for all manner of humanist social relations as they become alien to empathetic and convivial optimism.

The 'new behaviourism' and problematising children's behaviour

The long-term historical roots of our responses to the evolution of neoliberalism since the collapse of Keynesianism are not the

---

[58] Young (2003), p 405. Emphasis original. On disputed claims to working parents' time spent on child care, see N. Gilbert (2006) *A Mother's Work*, New Haven: Yale University Press.

[59] Young (2003), p 405.

[60] For these concepts, see Young (2003), p 404, and his source, Svend Ranulf (1938) *Moral Indignation and Middle Class Psychology*, Copenhagen: Levin and Munksgaard.

[61] Scraton (ed) (1997), pp 166–8; C. Jenks (1996) *Childhood*, London: Routledge, pp 70–3.

main concern here. All the same, as has been argued, the culture of neoliberalism has considerable relevance for parenting, not least its incorporation of the 'psy complex' into its strategies, namely that network of theories and practices that transform psychological knowledge into something useful in 'making up people'. Where children are involved, this refers to the ways in which the psy sciences contribute to our way of *seeing* children, and influencing (perhaps determining) the nature of our relations with them. With behaviourism in mind, the power of these disciplines to gain social credibility lies 'in their claimed technical capacities to administer persons rationally, in light of a knowledge of what made them tick'.[62] Thus in identifying both the place and the meaning of 'parenting' in a neoliberal 'therapeutic' culture, the role of the 'new behaviourism' in problematising children's behaviour, particularly that of pre-school children, has to be carefully examined.

To begin, it is worth reiterating Karen Baistow's judicious enquiries:

> under what conditions it became possible to construe parenthood in terms of a group of 'skills' called 'parenting', or to see the solution to various social problems lying in the 'empowerment' of parents through 'parent training'… and how it has become possible for different 'authorities', for example social workers, community nurses and health visitors (as well as psychologists), to consider it desirable legitimate, and feasible to conduct behavioural interventions with parents and their children.[63]

My focus is not so much on the techniques of the parenting programmes, but on the socio-cultural aspects of two aspects of behaviourism's political and social significance. First, the way in which the 'therapeutic culture of the self' has become so pervasive, and, second, how this cultural shift connects with contemporary age relations between adults and children, and with what consequences. Drawing initially on Baistow, we see how and why this particular adaptation of a much criticised psychological tradition (behaviourism) was able to re-establish itself as an ethically legitimate scientific 'knowledge system', not only for the specifics of parent education but also for the philosophical basis of child rearing, with its implications for understandings of children and

---

[62] P. Miller and N. Rose (2008) *Governing the Present*, Cambridge: Polity, p 9.

[63] K. Baistow (1998) 'Behavioural Psychology as a Social Project: From Social Engineering to the Cultivation of Competence', PhD, University of London, pp 37–8.

childhood. It will become clear that in facilitating 'parental narcissism', and despite providing a number of benefits to disadvantaged children, behavioural approaches have also exacerbated the more repressive features of childism, while serving several of neoliberalism's imperatives, such as managerialism, responsibilisation, contractualism, economic rationality and forms of individualisation.

Discursive changes

As was shown in Chapter Five, in the United States earlier critiques of behaviourism dismissed it as 'punishment in the guise of treatment which involved changing people's behaviour against their will'.[64] But, despite its reported demise in the 1970s and continuing pessimism regarding behavioural psychology's moral and intellectual viability, by the 1980s in Britain it was drawing less critical attention and, notwithstanding the 'cognitive revolution', continued to prosper.[65] In social work, for example, there were determined efforts made to promote behaviourism in opposition to the 'fads' of the 1960s and 1970s, which were described as 'optimistic, outgoing, and soft-hearted'.[66] Similarly, and significantly for our purposes, in addition to its growing popularity among clinical psychologists treating anxiety disorders, behaviourism in Britain underwent a significant expansion beyond the clinic into the 'well' community in health, welfare and education. The concerns involved mainly individual and family problems as

---

[64] Baistow (2001), p 310; for 'the problem of behaviourism', see (1998), pp 27–31; also D. Ingleby (1970) 'Ideology and the Human Sciences', in T. Pateman (ed) *Counter Course*, Harmondsworth: Penguin; and his (1981 edn) *Critical Psychiatry: The Problems of Mental Health*, London: Penguin Books.

[65] Baistow (1998), p 31; S. Marks (2012), 'Cognitive Behaviour Therapies in Britain: The Historical Context and Present Situation', in W. Dryden (ed) (2012), *Cognitive Behaviour Therapies*, London: Sage, pp 6–10. For the pioneering role of Eysenck in Britain in promoting behavioural therapy, see M. Derksen (2001) 'Science in the Clinic: Clinical Psychology at the Maudsley', in Bunn, Lovie and Richards (eds), pp 267–9, and H. Eysenck and S. Rachman (1965) *The Causes and Cures of Neurosis: An Introduction to Modern Behaviour Therapy Based on Learning Theory and the Principles of Conditioning*, London: Routledge.

[66] B. Sheldon (1982) *Behaviour Modification*, London: Tavistock, p 1. Apparently, the demand for training courses was proving 'hard to satisfy', p 3. Sheldon was an evangelical exponent of behaviourism in social work. For the coming together of cognitive approaches with the behavioural, see his (1995) *Cognitive-Behaviour Therapy: Research, Practice and Philosophy*, London: Routledge.

health visitors, nursery personnel and family support workers began to regularly use behavioural techniques in their work with mothers of infants and young children. Teachers were also encouraged to use behaviourist techniques in managing pupil behaviour.[67]

The question is how was it possible for behavioural approaches to permeate everyday life, given the initial unpopularity of behaviourism? The answer is similar to what Baistow has shown for the United States: it lies in the 'discursive changes' within post-war behaviourism, which saw a move away from affecting the behaviour of others to the emergence of the 'autonomous, self-managing behavioural subject', in line with a new emphasis on 'changing conceptualisations of personal power and control'. Three critical influences coming from the USA were at work here.[68] First, the transfer to Britain of 'social learning theory' whereby the individual was no longer seen as the passive subject of 'environmental determinism' but rather as an 'interactional and transactional' individual who both affected and was affected by the social environment.[69] The social contribution of psychology was to enable people to produce and regulate events in their lives: 'Mastery of the self became the object of concern in psychological discourses', not only for purposes of self regulation, but also because 'self-management' laid the possibility of personal determinism.[70] Second, with a 'socially sensitive behavioural psychology', the key evangelising theme of which was that psychology should be 'given away' to 'everyone': psychologists would adopt a 'learner-centred teaching role', helping ordinary people to 'change concepts of themselves and what they could do'. The new emphasis was on expanding 'freedom' by 'cultivating competencies'.[71] Thus, theoretically, the older concentration in 'behaviour modification' on eliminating 'undesirable' behaviour through aversive techniques was rejected in favour of emphasising 'positive reinforcement' through a 'constructional approach', which heeded the idea of human rights. British advocates saw in this approach not only the opportunity to

---

[67] Baistow (2001), p 309. On the popularisation of behavioural therapy and CBT in practice, see Marks (2012), pp 6–10.

[68] For details and full references, see above, pp 182–91.

[69] A. Bandura (1977), *Social Learning Theory*, Englewood Cliffs, NJ: Prentice-Hall. Briefly, the theory postulates that people learn within a social context by 'observing', 'imitating' or 'modelling' others. The focus is on 'rewards' and 'reinforcements', or punishments that we receive for our behaviours. See above, p 187, n 76; also see Sheldon (1982), pp 38–91.

[70] Baistow (2001), p 312.

[71] A. Bandura (1974) 'Behavior theory and the models of man', *American Psychologist*, 29, p 865.

'increase social competence' in clients but also to give them 'insight into their own behaviour by organising therapy in a concrete, achievable way'.[72] The third influence grew from the displacement of the traditional dyadic model of doctor–patient/psychologist–client by a triadic model of consultant–mediator–target whereby the psychological professionals became 'supervisors' rather than therapists. Behaviourists reasoned against over-reliance on 'experts', and for working within the individual's 'natural environment' with 'those people to whom he is naturally related'; these were to be the 'reinforcers' to whom psychology was to be given away. These were the people best placed to do the reinforcing, and their role as 'contingency managers' was to 'rearrange environmental rewards and punishments, which strengthened or weakened specified behaviours' with 'a smile or a candy, a bicycle or a slap' and thereby 'modify the behavior of the individual by strengthening or weakening it'.[73] Where children were concerned, clearly the aversive 'slap' was not deemed to be out of place.

Unsurprisingly, these influences needed a context in which to prosper, and as with so much else in understanding post-1970s late modernity, the coming of the New Right changed not only the economic and political landscape, but also, much more imperceptibly, cultural attitudes and behaviours. In this respect, it is important to see the rise of behaviourism as helping the ideologues to transform British society. We have only to think of Keith Joseph's keen interest in what were in effect schemes of behaviour modification, to see how the economic, moral and, indeed, philosophical strands of so much of New Right social thought found the promise of behaviourism in homes, schools, prisons and health services, immensely attractive. But behaviourism also brought economic advantages that linked it to neoliberalism. In introducing market principles into health, welfare and education, Mrs Thatcher made 'the cult of the audit' critically important and, therefore, behaviourist practices in the hands of cheap paraprofessionals became politically popular, as did the concept of

---

[72] I. Goldiamond (1974) 'Toward a constructional approach to social problems. Ethical and constitutional issues raised by applied behavior analysis', *Behaviourism*, 2, p 14; also C. Hattersley (1979) 'A Constructional Approach to Social Problems', *Social Work Today*, 10, 40, pp 10–12. Behaviour modification proved to be popular in Britain in the movement led by Hans Eysenck.

[73] R. G. Tharp and R. J. Wetzel (1969) *Behavior Modification in the Natural Environment*, New York: Academic Press, p 3.

'measurability', making it conducive to managerial objectives.[74] Much to the delight of those involved, this was the environment in which behaviourism could flourish, witnessing a proliferation of behavioural change techniques, together with their application to an ever-widening range of human problems. As far as 'techniques' were concerned, as we saw in the discussion of American influences, from the 1970s there was increasing emphasis on both sides of the Atlantic on 'behaviour modification as pure technique'. Notwithstanding some professional doubts, understanding *why* the 'technique' worked was not considered to be a prerequisite for using it, since if all practitioners were to be trained in the theory, this would hinder its deployment among non-specialists, such as health visitors, teachers and parents, and this in turn would restrict the spread of behavioural approaches throughout the community.[75] In Britain, as in the United States, the emphasis on technique was important because it implied that behavioural problems were themselves technical rather than pathological. To this extent, these problems were normalised, just as the normal was problematised throughout the community, thereby providing a place for the behavioural approach in a variety of social policies.

Reaching into the community

From the 1970s, the psychologising of everyday problems became widespread as a growing number of new child candidates were identified

---

[74] K. Asmussen (2011) *The Evidence-Based Parenting Practitioner's Handbook*, London: Routledge, pp 46–55; P. Moran and D. Ghate (2005) 'The Effectiveness of Parenting Support', *Children & Society*, 194, pp 329–36; M. S. Zeedyl, I. Werritty and C. Riarch (2008) 'One Year On: Perceptions of the Lasting Benefits of Involvement in a Parenting Support Programme', *Children & Society*, 22, 2, pp 107–8. For the quotation, see S. Jenkins (2006) *Thatcher and Sons*, London: Allen Lane, chapter 13. My thanks to Paul Smith for this reference.

[75] W. Yule (1975) 'Teaching Psychological Principles to Non-Psychologists', *Journal of Association of Educational Psychologists*, 10, 3, pp 5–16; M. Herbert (1981) *Behavioural Treatment of Problem Children: A Practice Manual*, London: Academic Press; K. Hewitt (1981) 'Overactvity in Children: How Health Visitors Can Help', in *Health Visitor*, 54, pp 276–8; ; N. Hastings and J. Schwieso (1981) 'Social Technik: Reconstructing the Relationship between Psychological Theory and Professional Practice', *Oxford Review of Education*, 7, 223–9; D. Milne (1986) *Training Behaviour Therapists*, Beckenham: Croom Helm; J. Carr (1986) 'Giving Away the Behavioural Approach', *Behavioural Psychotherapy*, 16, pp 78–84; P. Appleton, J. Douglas, T. Fundudis, K. Hewitt, and J. Stevenson(1989) 'A Trouble Shared is a Happy Budget', *The Health Service Journal*, June, pp 760–1.

involving a much wider range of childhood behaviours and with the age range extending backwards to infancy.[76] Originally, the target groups were homogeneous categories such as the psychiatric, those with specific behaviours, or constellations of disordered behaviour. Increasingly, however, behaviourists were listing more typical, even normative, behaviours as in need of systematic attention, particularly those of infants and preschoolers, whose behaviour was charted in a newly developed 'behavioural checklist' for assessment purposes. This led to the conclusion that relatively minor untreated problems could develop into ones that were more serious. Simultaneously, claims were made that existing service providers were unable to cope with the apparently growing demand. Consequently, from the 1980s, partly with an eye on budgetary constraints, but also with ever expanding target groups in mind, health visitors, social workers and, to a lesser extent, teachers and parents, were designated as the 'new behaviourists', and routinely began to deal with common 'problems' associated with preschool children, using behavioural techniques, usually the

---

[76] For references to this paragraph, see N. Richman (1975) 'Prevalence of Behaviour Problems in Three Yeaer Old Children', *Journal of Child Psychology and Psychiatry*, 16: 277-87; N. Richman, J. Stevenson and P. J. Graham (1982) *Pre-School to School: A Behavioural Study*, London: Academic Press; M. Chazan, A. F. Laing, J. Jones, G. C. Harper and J. Bolton (1983) *Helping Young Children with Behaviour Difficulties*, Beckenham: Croom Helm; J. Douglas and N. Richman (1984) *My Child Won't Sleep: A Handbook of Sleep Management of Preschool School Children*, Harmondsworth: Penguin; J. Douglas (1989) *Behaviour Problems in Young Children*, London: Tavistock/Routledge; N. Richman and R. Lansdown (eds) (1988) *Problems of Preschool Children*, Chichester: John Wiley; Herbert (1981) and his (1989) *Discipline: A Positive Guide for Parents*, Oxford: Blackwell, and (1984) *Working with Children and Their Families*, Leicester and London: BPS and Routledge; J. Douglas (ed) (1988a) *Emotional and Behavioural Problems in Young Children: A Multidisciplinary Approach to Identification and Management*, Windsor: NFER-Nelson; Sheldon (1982); C. Webster-Stratton and M. Herbert (1994) *Troubled Families – Problem Children*, Chichester: John Wiley.

constructional approach, in group sessions and parent training clinics.[77] The problem areas for resolution or management included crying, sleeping, eating, 'overactivity', enuresis, 'tantrums', inattention and disobedience. Significantly, however, these childhood difficulties were presented as the result of 'deficit' parenting. Behaviourism, as mentioned, did not see children's problem behaviour as emanating primarily from psychoanalytic or family–psychodynamic causes; instead, it was said to arise from 'maladaptive adjustment' between parent and child (regardless of the deeper causative factors), which had been reinforced through inappropriate parental management. Thus, children, parents and usually paraprofessionals were brought together in behaviour modification programmes in which changing parental behaviour became as much the objective as modifying that of the child.

The degree to which all practitioners, especially those looking to meet financial targets and in search of a 'quick-fix', followed the humanistic guidelines, or would even make effective assessments, is unknown. In recommending a 'management plan', however, some textbook authors admitted that looking for a cause of the 'problem behaviour' 'can be a fruitless and pointless one' and, therefore, it was better 'to focus on the "here and now"'; others stressed the presence of multiple causal factors at work.[78] However, without knowing the nature of individual assessment plans used in treatment, it is impossible to know how they were implemented and with what results for individual children. How many practitioners, one wonders, heeded the advice of Milton Senn, the eminent American psychiatrist:

> The problem child is invariably trying to solve a problem rather than be one. His methods are crude and his

---

[77] Health visitors were promoted as being most suitable for the new community based behavioural treatments since they had ready access to the under-fives and their parents: Hewitt (1981); K. Hewitt, P. Appleton, J. Douglas, T. Fundudis, and J. Stevenson (1990) 'Health Visitor Based Services for Pre-school Children with Behaviour Problems', *Health Visitor*, 63, pp 160–2; K. Hewitt and W. Crawford (1988) 'Resolving Behaviour Problems in Pre-School Children: Evaluation of a Workshop for Health Visitors', *Child: Care, Health and Development*, 14, pp 1–7; Stevenson(1989); K. Hewitt, A. Hobday, and W. Crawford (1989) 'What do Health Visitors Gain from Behavioural Workshops', *Child: Care, Health and Development*, 15, p 265–75; K. Hewitt, L. Mason, W. Snelson, and W. Crawford (1991) 'Parent Education in Preventing Behaviour Problems', *Health Visitor*, 64, pp 415–17. For health visitors as new behaviourists, see Baistow (1998), 116–37.

[78] J. Douglas (1988b) 'Behaviour Disorders: Principles of Management', in Richman and Landsdown, pp 132, 131–50; Chazan et al (1983); Richman et al (1982).

conception of his problem may be found faulty, but until the physician has patiently sought, and in a sympathetic way found, what the child was trying to do…he is in no position to offer advice.[79]

For behaviourists, however, advice plus treatment was irresistible. One of the main attractions of their procedures, echoing the psychology of neoliberalism in privileging activism and personal responsibility, was that they offered the promise that 'something can be done'.[80] This has long been a critical feature of all parenting education, both in respect of combating social exclusion and of 'supporting' certain groups of disadvantaged families. From the perspective of the uncertain self, surrounded by dissolution and liquidity, doing 'something' (to someone) and successfully changing their behaviour, particularly within the family, is 'empowering'. Thus in modifying the behaviour of one's children, through the hard work of learning new parenting skills and applying them as routines, parents are made to feel enabled as autonomous selves, becoming well positioned to continue life-long learning, ever ready to change according to circumstances – they are ideal neoliberal citizens.

Adherents to the behavioural approach have always claimed that it enhances parent–child relationships, lessens parental anxiety and insecurity, stimulates the capacities and self-confidence of mothers, extends their parenting skills and teaches them a set of rules to use throughout their parenting lives. Clearly, the emphasis is adult-centric in focusing on the importance of 'understanding the needs and values of parents', to continually provide 'a sympathetic understanding of the feelings of those adults who are working with the child', and to be mindful that many parents in experiencing 'stress and strain' require 'understanding and support rather than criticism or blame'.[81] The techniques taught are ideologically supportive of parents, and attractive to them (and to government agencies), because they 'leave the parents always where they should be, in charge'.[82] 'Children who need their hands holding as they nod off demand time that busy parents may not

---

[79] Quoted in Preface to Herbert (1981). Herbert was keen to present behaviour modification as ethical, pp 4–5; see also Sheldon (1982) on ethics, pp 222–45. For an explicit instruction to practitioners to treat children with sympathy and to respect their 'dignity', see M. Chazan et al (1983), pp 3, 9.

[80] Baistow (2001), p 326. Emphasis added.

[81] Asmussen (2011), pp 146–50; Douglas (1988b), p 132; Chazan et al (1983), p 29.

[82] P. Randall (1987) 'In Charge', *Community Care*, 19 November, pp 24–6. Emphasis added.

always be able to spare...a child who is unable to go to bed whilst still awake and fall asleep naturally without parents being present... constitutes a residual problem.'[83] The successful solution to sleeping problems is seen 'to lie not in the feelings or subjective involvement of the parent, an essential psychodynamic theme, rather, it is suggested, that this subjective involvement is part of the problem'.[84] Thus, in solving the 'problem' parents were advised: 'step one' is 'to discard all subjective information'. The solution, lies 'in the "objective", "rational", "detached" assessment, treatment and evaluation by parents of their own and their children's behaviour'.[85] Consequently, as Baistow says:

> In the process of becoming amenable to the calculation and order of this behavioural knowledge, the child is transformed from the psychodynamic host of oedipal conflicts and ego defences into a troublesome but rectifiable product of bad management practices. In the same way the insecure pathogenic mother of psychoanalysis becomes the incompetent 'parent', who with the assistance of a detached, but concerned science may be transformed into an 'effective manager'.[86]

These children are objectified since, in being unable to sleep without parental comfort, they are transformed into a problem for 'busy' parents who must *train* the child in order that *they* may remain 'busy'.[87] The management accent is also evident in an approving account of a schoolboy exhibiting 'disturbed behaviour' who, after the failure of various disciplinary procedures, was subjected to a 'contingency management programme' after which he was seen by his teachers as "'a bit of a challenge to disciplinary skills", rather than as a "seriously disturbed boy" in need of "psychiatric investigations" and "special

---

[83] P. Randall (1990) 'Children with Sleep Disturbance', *Midwife, Health Visitor and Community Nurse*, 26, 9, pp 328–32.

[84] Baistow (1998), pp 131–2.

[85] P. Randall and C. Gibb (1988) 'Behaviour Problems: Everyone's Concern', *Midwife, Health Visitor and Community Nurse*, 26 (9), pp 310-12, pp 310–12.

[86] Baistow (1998), p 132. For assessment recommendations re 'contingency management', see Herbert (1989); Douglas (1984, 1988b, 1989); Sheldon (1982), pp 142–221. For his ethical considerations, see pp 222–45.

[87] Randall (1990), p 328.

care"'.[88] In the author's view, the latter diagnosis was to be avoided as it would have required the input of scarce professional resources, been time-consuming and very expensive, whereas the former was relatively quick and produced an apparently successful outcome.

Unsurprisingly, by the end of 1980s, there was increasing support for Eysenck's view that 'there is no neurosis underlying the symptom but merely the symptom itself. Get rid of the symptom and you have eliminated the neurosis.'[89] No wonder behaviour modification – the off-shoot of a marriage between an anti-humanist philosophy, associated with B. F. Skinner, and a technique derived from laboratory experiments with animals and humans – was described by a critic as 'frankly materialistic, positivistic, causal–reductive' whereby 'The self – or sense of self – is merely a product of our sociocultural environment generating self-knowledge and self-control. Freedom and dignity are illusions and autonomous man is a mythical animal.'[90] It was this 'science' of treatment that health visitors and social workers in particular were being urged to adopt in their practice. The optimism of the 1960s had long gone. As one influential behaviourist explained, 'In these days of economic recession, people tend to favour hard-headed notions, such as accountability, efficiency, and effectiveness… behavioural methods…capture the spirit of the times'.[91] There could hardly be a clearer statement of neoliberalism's rejection of the social-democratic impulse to help people to be better than they are. But more was to come. As the next chapter argues, New Labour determined to redesign British (certainly English) society in ways that while indebted to Thatcherism, went far beyond its parameters to envisage a far more complex disciplinary state, in which parental narcissism played a significant role.

By way of conclusion here, a word of caution is necessary. Social change rarely proceeds in an orderly manner. This chapter has been concerned to argue for the influence of the New Right in remoralising British social relations and for its early use of the behavioural approach to child rearing. But it is important to recognise that throughout the 1970s and 1980s behaviourism was by no means universally accepted since just as it was being propagated so one of the most influential guides to liberal child rearing was being published: Penelope Leach, *Baby and Child Care* (1977), which became the best-selling manual

---

[88]   Sheldon (1982), p 153.

[89]   Quoted in Marks (2012), p 3.

[90]   J. Ehrenwald (ed) (1991) *The History of Psychotherapy*, Lanham, MD: Jason Aronson, p 445.

[91]   Sheldon (1982), pp xiii, 223.

during the next 30 years.[92] Leach's popularity, and that of other liberal guides, suggests that the social-democratic parenting ethos, while under pressure, continued to be present – certainly with reference to discipline, and especially among the middle class who the Newsons, in their comprehensive child-rearing study, found to be '*on principle*' more democratically inclined.[93] In other words, parenting cannot easily be compartmentalised; there are always class-based differences, and in any period, new and old styles usually co-exist with one another – at least for a time. Nonetheless, the fact that social-democratic parenting continued to be practised does not mean that the ideals it embodied remained steadfast in the face of neoliberal and social liberationist family values – they did not; it was the latter that came to be seen as the cultural norm.

---

[92] The manual sold over 2 million copies worldwide by 2010. See also her (1994) *Children First*, London: Penguin Books. However, she has been constantly sniped at by feminists and others for being too child centred. See C. Hardyment (1995) *Perfect Parents*, Oxford: Oxford University Press; S. Mesure (2011) 'Let's Face it, Babies Change Your Life', *Independent*, 22 October; B. Morrison (2011) 'She Who Must Be Obeyed', *Independent*, 22 October.

[93] J. Newson and H. Newson (1978) *Seven Years Old in the Home Environment*, Harmondsworth: Pelican, p 445. Emphasis original.

EIGHT

The New Labour era, and beyond: narcissism comes of age

> [N]orms of conduct for the civilised are now disseminated by independent experts...They operate a regime of the self where...one is encouraged to understand one's life, actually or potentially, not in terms of fate or social status but in terms of one's success or failure acquiring skills and making the choice to actualise oneself.[1]

In the last chapter we saw how the foundations for parental narcissism were laid through the emergence of the New Right with policies and attitudes that were intended to erode social-democratic assumptions and remoralise British social relations. I showed that the new behaviourism, in facilitating less kindly ways of problematising and responding to young children's 'problem' behaviour, was the principal contributor to the restructuring of child rearing in favour of parental convenience. I also claimed that in changing the broader context in which child rearing occurs, so the meaning and understanding of parenting was altered. This chapter, in focusing on New Labour's innovatory ideal of disciplinary governance, encoded in neoliberal practice, explains how it was that with reference to parent education, the behavioural approach grew in influence in being deployed as normal and natural, becoming just another feature of common sense.[2] In order to relate parenting to the broader culture, and to illustrate aspects of New Labour's conception of children, the chapter opens with brief accounts of how they were used as 'human capital' in social investment schemes, and how the well-known ASBO policy positioned them primarily as threats to social order. This is followed by a sustained discussion of the

---

[1] N. Rose (1999) *Powers of Freedom: Reframing of Political Thought*, Cambridge: Cambridge University Press, p 87.

[2] For an overview of New Labour's attitude to children, especially the 'remaking' of childhood, see H. Hendrick (2003) *Child Welfare: Historical Dimensions, Contemporary Debate*, Bristol: Policy Press; for the 'new behaviourist' strategy, see M. Harrison and T. Sanders (eds) (2014) *Social Policies and Social Control: New Perspectives on the 'Not-So-Big-Society'*, Bristol: Policy Press.

manner whereby the concept of parenting was revised and packaged through parent education programmes whose ethics, promoted in reality television parenting 'shows', were absorbed as normal and desirable. My concern is to identify some of the ways in which these developments, within the context of neoliberal politics, encouraged a parenting style that, in emphasising authority, control, discipline and contractual relations, is now so different from that expressed in the social-democratic ideal of the post-war settlement.

Neoliberal children: the 'iconic' child as human capital

'You call us the future, but we are also the present.'
(Children's Forum statement to UN General Assembly[3])

The emergence of the child as an iconic figure in social investment programmes was the result of the stresses and strains in the European social model which, in facing the new social risks that followed from the demise of Keynesianism, embraced the view that change and innovation were essential for the continuance of European prosperity in a global age. European political elites agreed that in place of old-style 'negative welfare', which transferred 'risk' from the individual to the state, a *positive* welfare society should be encouraged in which the state remains important but is not dominant: it would be 'primarily a *social investment* and *regulatory* agency'.[4] Such a state would privilege 'interventionism and activism' – the former seeking to deal with problems at source, while the latter referred to 'people helping themselves' and to local communities being involved in the delivery of their own welfare services.[5] It soon became clear that the success of welfare reform required the creation of a new type of citizen, in what was to be a reconstituted civil society, one prepared to shed the mindset of social-democratic welfare in favour of the requirements of 'the transition to a post-industrial society'.[6] It was as part of this transition process, particularly the moulding of neoliberal citizens, that New Labour determined to remake both the family and childhood through the reworking of age relations in the broadest sense of what

---

[3]   Cited in D. Stasiulis (2002) 'The Active Child Citizen: Lessons from Canadian Policy and the Children's Movement', *Citizenship Studies*, 6, 4, pp 507–38.

[4]   A. Giddens (2007) *Europe in a Global Age*, Cambridge: Polity, pp 30–3, 97.

[5]   Giddens (2007), p 102.

[6]   P. Taylor-Gooby (2004) *New Risks, New Welfare*, Oxford: Oxford University Press, p 3.

we might think of as the 'social imagination': the place where the sense of self is settled in respect of others.[7]

The term 'social investment state' (SIS) was originally coined as a way of encouraging 'investment in *human capital* wherever possible rather than direct provision of economic maintenance'.[8] This state had four overriding objectives, to: i) generate economic dynamism and contribute to flexible labour markets; ii) ensure that childhood experiences do not lead to disadvantages in adulthood; iii) prevent exclusion from the labour market and society; and iv) certify a sustainable level of support for the elderly.[9] In pursuit of these ends, three main reasons were identified as to why a 'child-centred social investment strategy' was vital for the future: i) social skills and strong cognitive abilities were essential in order to be a 'post-industrial winner'; ii) a child-focus was a *sine qua non* 'for sustainable, efficient, and competitive knowledge-based production system'; and iii) 'All... evidence indicates that (early) childhood is the critical point at which people's life courses are shaped' and, therefore, 'A social investment strategy aimed at children must be a centrepiece in any policy for social inclusion'.[10] Thus the child took on an 'iconic status'.[11]

During New Labour's administrations (1997–2010) social policy expenditures were processed as investments, on the assumption that current spending would reap future dividends and prepare national economies for the global marketplace – social policy could be a 'productive factor'.[12] There are numerous examples of New Labour's

---

[7] Hendrick (2003), pp 234–53.

[8] A. Giddens (1998) *The Third Way: The Renewal of Social Democracy*, Cambridge: Polity, pp 9–101, 117.

[9] J. Jenson (2006) 'The LEGO (TM) Paradigm and New Social Risks: Consequences for Children', in J. Lewis (ed) *Children, Changing Families and Welfare States*, Cheltenham: Edward Elgar, p 27.

[10] G. Esping-Andersen and S. Sara (2002) 'The Generational Conflict Reconsidered', *Journal of European Social Policy*, 12, 1, pp 5–21; also Giddens (2007), pp 91–6, who links social investment in children to policies for gender equality – an adult-centric socio-political end, as does OECD (2006) *Starting Strong* (ii), Summaries, p 1.

[11] R. Lister (2003) 'Investing in the Citizen–Workers of the Future', *Social Policy and Administration*, 37, 5, October, pp 427–43; A. Dobrowolsky (2002) 'Rhetoric Versus Reality: The Figure of the Child and New Labour's Strategic "Social Investment State"', in *Studies in Political Economy*, Autumn, pp 43–73.

[12] A. C. Hemerijck (2011) 'Social Investment in Jeopardy', in M. McTernan (ed) *Social Progress in the 21st Century*, London: Policy Network, Wiardi Beckman Stichting, Foundation for Progressive European Studies (FEPS), p 25.

human capital approach to children, one of the clearest being the *Every Child Matters* (ECM) agenda, culminating in the Children Act 2004. It did not go unnoticed among commentators that although making valuable recommendations for the improvement of children's lives, the focus of the agenda was on training the 'citizen-worker', confirming children as 'becomings' rather than 'beings' in their own right in the here and now.[13] As the sociologist Alan Prout observed with reference to the reduction in child poverty programme, the focus 'is on the better adult lives that will, it is predicted, emerge from reducing child poverty. It is not on the better lives that children will lead as children.'[14] The objectifying tendency was evident in the ECM's projected 'outcomes': 'being healthy, being safe, enjoying and achieving, making a positive contribution, and economic well-being'. In addition to emphasising 'early intervention and effective protection', the focus was on a particular choice of values: achievement rather than enjoyment; education rather than play; while the words 'making a positive contribution' recalls the stereotypical image of the child as a potential threat: the implication being that if not 'a positive contribution', then something negative. Equally, 'being healthy, being safe', in pointing to 'protection', also involves control and surveillance.[15] Nor, thinking of their futurity was there any mention of helping children to develop fulfilled adult lives beyond the realm of being responsible citizens and conscientious employees. The major omission concerned children's rights, as the document failed to acknowledge the child's *right* to particular goods, services or treatments. Yet it is in being able to claim a 'right' rather than having to rely on the goodwill of others that gives one the status not only of a citizen, but also of a moral agent. Rights are important because they 'enable us to stand with dignity, if necessary to demand what is our due without having to grovel, plead or beg or to express gratitude, and to express indignation

---

[13]   F. Williams (2004) 'What Matters is Who Works: Why Every Child Matters to New Labour. Commentary on the DfES Green Paper *Every Child Matters*', *Critical Social Policy*, 24, 3, p 408.

[14]   A. Prout (2000) 'Children's Participation: Control and Self-realisation in British Late Modernity', *Children & Society*, 14, 4, p 305; also A. James and A. L. James (2008) 'Changing Childhood in the UK: Reconstructing Discourses of "Risk" and Protection', in James and James (eds) *European Childhoods*, Basingstoke: Palgrave, p 111.

[15]   For the victim/threat dualism, see Hendrick (2003), pp 1–17; C. Piper (2008) *Investing in Children, Policy, Law and Practice in Context*, Cullompton: Willan Publishing, pp 20, 67–72; N. Parton (2006) *Safeguarding Children: Early Intervention and Surveillance in a Late Modern Society*, Basingstoke: Palgrave Macmillan, pp 139–63.

when what is our due is not forthcoming'.[16] Nowhere, however, was the disregard of rights more clearly displayed than in the government's approach to the criminalising of children as a 'nuisance'.

The discipline of ASBO (anti-social behaviour order) culture: breeding childism

> Britain has never been at a more insecure moment...Anti-social behaviour is actually at the foundation and root of instability.[17]

Britons, according to *Time* magazine, 'have never been very comfortable with the idea of childhood'; indeed, it seems that we 'just don't like children much'.[18] A *YouGov* poll (2008) appeared to confirm this impression. Of those adults questioned just under half (49 per cent) saw children as increasingly a danger to each other and to adults; 43 per cent felt that something should be done to protect us from children; more than a third (35 per cent) reported feeling the streets are infested with children; and nearly half (49 per cent) disagreed with the statement that children who get into trouble are often misunderstood and in need of professional help.[19] But public opinion is not formed in a void. The *Observer* columnist Henry Porter noted that popular 'intolerance and hatred of young people...is matched by the Labour government'. You have to go back to Dickens' time, he wrote, 'to find a period when children were viewed with such suspicion and impatience'.[20] The childist climate led the four Children's Commissioners for the UK to compile a report for the UN which, among a welter of criticisms,

---

[16] Quoted in M. D. A. Freeman (1983) *The Rights and Wrongs of Children*, London: Frances Pinter, pp 32, 35. The rights referred to are 'moral rights, usually in the sense of ideal rights, but sometimes also conscientious rights'; also his (2007) 'Why It Remains Important to Take Children's Rights Seriously', *International Journal of Children's Rights*, 15, 1, pp 5–23, and P. Alderson and M. John (2008, 2nd edn) *Young Children's Rights: Exploring Beliefs, Principles and Practice*, London: Jessica Kingsley.

[17] David Blunkett, Home Secretary (2003) quoted in G. Hughes (2007) *The Politics of Crime and Community*, Basingstoke: Palgrave Macmillan, p 110.

[18] *Time*, (2008), C. Mayer, '*Unappy, Unloved and Out of Control*', 26 March. For the current low position of GB in the league table of children's happiness, see G. Rees, A. Andresen and J. Bradsaw (eds) (2016) *Children's views on their lives and well being in 16 countries. A report on the Children's Worlds survey of children aged eight years old, 2013-15*. York.

[19] For similar prejudices, see ICM poll for Barnardo's, *BBC News* (2011) 3 November.

[20] Porter's blog, 22 November 2008.

accused the government of maintaining a punitive youth justice system, breaching the human rights of children through ASBO orders, demonising adolescents as 'yobs', and criminalising young people for 'hanging around'.[21]

On coming to power, New Labour looked to the Bulger tragedy as a symptom of 'family breakdown' and, within the context of combating social exclusion, made tackling youth crime a priority. Under the rubric of 'no more excuses', the government legislated a major piece of neoliberal legislation: the Crime and Disorder Act 1998 (followed by the Anti-Social Behaviour Act 2003), which introduced the 'anti-social behaviour order', augmented in further legislation by the 'anti-social behaviour contract'.[22] Among the more significant criticisms of ASBO policy was that anti-social behaviour was defined in *perceptual* terms as 'behaviour which causes or is likely to cause harassment, alarm or distress to one or more people who are not in the same household as the perpetrator'. The policy also ran counter to the British 'common law tradition', under which an individual may act as he or she chooses, so long as it is legal. With the ASBO, however, if individual actions are seen as 'threatening', 'distressing' or 'frightening' by others, then those others may apply to a magistrates' court for an order banning the individual's behaviour, which exposes marginal groups, such as young people, to the discretion of local officials. One of the most controversial sections of the Act was the abolition of *doli incapax:* the presumption that children between ten and 13 did not know the difference between right and wrong in the sense of being liable for conviction of a *criminal* offence. Other stigmatising sections included the introduction of child curfews for children under the age of ten, and Child Safety Orders for the same age group, ostensibly designed to prevent young children from becoming involved in either delinquent or anti-social behaviour. In being a reaction against both 1960s' welfarism and 1980s' 'progressive minimalism', the Statute gave the youth justice system an overarching mission: 'to prevent offending by children and young persons'.[23] Where previously the aim of youth justice had been

---

[21] UK Children's Commissions Report to the UN Committee on the Rights of the Child, 2008.

[22] For the influence of the behavioural approach, see M. Harrison and T. Sanders (eds) (2014) *Social Policies and Social Control: New Perspectives on the 'Not-So-Big-Society'*, Bristol: Policy Press.

[23] Quoted in T. Newburn (2007) *Criminology*, Cullompton, Willian Publishing, p 731. For some of criminological/psychological thinking behind the Act, see P. Squires and D. Stephen (2005) *Rougher Justice: Anti-social Behaviour and Young People*, Cullompton: Willan Publishing, pp 42–67.

to minimise stigma and divert the young person away from being criminalised, the 1998 legislation brought both first-time offenders and troublesome youngsters below the age of criminal responsibility into the ambit of the criminal justice system.[24] In this respect, in being central to the promotion of 'law and order' politics, the Act signalled the full politicisation of youth crime through a new agenda that was fixated around notions of punishment and retribution as features of re-moralisation.[25] Not the least of its intentions, in privileging judicial alacrity, the Act sought to replicate 'authoritative' parenting through following the precepts of behavioural psychology in stipulating that punishment should quickly follow the proscribed act in order to be most effective.[26]

It seems clear, then, that New Labour's ASBO project was an important example of the disciplinary impulse, as it contributed to the making of the mood of intolerance, suspicion, fear and resentfulness toward young people. But it was more than this. In terms of being a behaviourist policy tool, the ASBO was also a means whereby the government dealt with a problem that had beset Thatcherism, namely controlling the public behaviour of individual family members through intervention strategies, without appearing to interfere with the principle of neoliberal individualism.[27] This is clear if the government's disciplinary proclivities are seen against its broader objective, which was to penalise 'offensive' behaviour through its 'civil renewal agenda', emphasising 'respect' and 'responsibility' (important New Labour themes) rather than tolerance and liberty.[28] Under the influence of behaviourally-inclined control theories of crime (which minimised the relevance of deprivation as a causal factor), this was a further development in 'the decline of the rehabilitative ideal' that occurred from the 1980s onwards as punishment, in expressing public sentiment,

---

[24] T. Bateman and J. Pitts (2005) *Youth Justice*, Lyme Regis: Russell House Publishing.

[25] J. Pitts (2003) *The New Politics of Youth Crime: Discipline or Solidarity?*, Lyme Regis: Russell House, pp 1–31.

[26] Pitts (2003), pp 35–6.

[27] The ASBO was not confined to young people. By 2005, however, over 40 per cent were issued against under 18 year olds. For background to the 'ASBO culture', see Squires and Stephen (2005), pp 1–13, 42–67.

[28] A. Von Hirsch and A. P. Simister (2006) 'Penalising Offensive Behaviour: Constitutive and Mediating Principles', in Von Hirsch and Simister (eds) *Incivilities: Regulating Offensive Behaviour*, Oxford: Hart Publishing, pp 115–32; Hughes (2007), p 74.

became a respectable penal objective.[29] Michael Freeden, the political theorist, has argued that New Labour had a 'muted' approach to liberty. Self-development and growth were replaced by talk of 'equality of opportunity, life chances', while emancipatory politics receded from view. In Blair's hands, free-will became a quasi-religious notion of individuals' responsibility not 'growth of personhood'. Individual liberty and individuality had little place in the lexicon of New Labour where the emphasis was on the group: the British people, the community, the family. Only one individual activity was singled out for approval: 'successful entrepreneurs'. Individual liberty was connected to employability rather than to autonomy.[30]

Generally, ASBO policy can be seen in the context of responding to the economic and social effects of globalisation, but more specifically the legislation, which came with a strong emphasis on parental responsibility, was designed as a multi-faceted contribution to eliminating nuisances, regenerating local economies, enhancing personal morality and legitimising new forms of governance.[31] Furthermore, the ASBO climate concealed a perceptual sleight of hand, whereby individual agency was successfully portrayed as one of the principal causes of community malaise, rather than the cause being the anti-social consequences of structural social and economic changes produced by neoliberalism.[32] In this respect, the ASBO, as policy and as a cultural peg, needs to be understood in the realm of New Labour's acceptance of the cycle of deprivation thesis, expressed in terms of a concern about the social pathology of the socially excluded underclass. The policies through which social inclusion was to be wrought were sourced not only from social investment, but also from the spread of behavioural approaches among professionals in mental health, social work, education, welfare, and childcare, and from the equally

---

[29] D. Garland (2001) The *Culture of Control: Crime and Social Order in Contemporary Society*, Oxford: Oxford University Press, pp 8–9, 15.

[30] Michael Freeden (2005) *Liberal Languages*, Princeton, NJ: Princeton University Press.

[31] J. Young (2007) *Vertigo of Late Modernity*, London: Sage, p 38; also J. Jacobson, A. Millie and M. Hough (2008) 'Why Tackle Anti-social Behaviour', in P. Squires (ed) (2008) *ASBO Nation: The Criminalisation of Nuisance*, Bristol: Policy Press, pp 37–56, also p 11.

[32] Hughes (2007), pp 118–19, 125; E. Burney (2005) *Making People Behave: Anti-social Behaviour, Politics and Policy*, Cullompton: Willan Publishing, pp 16–44.

'behaviourist' disciplinary practices of retributive crime control.[33] It was from within this complex that parenting education was developed and prioritised as a policy strategy designed to 'behaviouralise' children (and parents) while empowering parents, especially mothers, in the organisation of their lives. New Labour was much more determined than previous governments in drawing together research findings from multiple disciplines, including the increasingly favoured neuroscience of early intervention, and moulding them into strategies for the creation of a new civic order, which repudiated those features of permissiveness that were deemed to stand in the way of making Britain a disciplined, 'modern' (a favourite New Labour concept) neoliberal state.

Parenting in New Labour's neoliberal universe

There is clearly a problem in today's world in making the individual do what he or she as to do, and it is a much more complex problem than in the past. Changes in the family are both the product of that more complex world and a contribution to its complexity. The implication of this complexity is that society cannot afford simply to leave this responsibility to the family. It has to explore new patterns and methods of support for the family and the action required effectively to socialize the next generation.[34]

Since the late 1940s, as citizenship grew in complexity, the relationship between the family and government became increasingly intimate. Following concerns with the problem family during the early post-war years, the 'rediscovery' of poverty in the 1960s, the recurring anxieties about juvenile delinquency, and the cycle of deprivation thesis in the early 1970s, a number of government and charitable agencies began to interest themselves in the idea of preparation for parenthood. Although several half-hearted attempts were made to develop parent education/support programmes, and a number of practical initiatives emanated from the Open University, the National Children's Bureau, and the Study Commission on the Family, and the Conservative government

---

[33] A. Deacon (2000) 'Learning from the US? The Influence of American Ideas Upon "New Labour" Thinking on Welfare Reform', *Policy& Politics*, 28, 1, pp 5–18. On the behavioural influence, see Squires and Stephen (2005), pp 62–67, and Harrison and Sanders (eds) (2014).

[34] V. George and P. Wilding (1999) *British Social and Social Welfare*, Basingstoke: Macmillan, p 76.

established a Cabinet Committee on the Family in 1983, little happened where organised parenting programmes were concerned, perhaps reflecting Thatcher's view that, aside from financial considerations, the state should have a minimal role in family affairs.[35] By the early 1990s, however, a more coherent policy for parent education was emerging. Several government departments (the Home Office, Health and Education, the Lord Chancellor's Office) were starting to relate their specific jurisdictions to the quality of parenting; for example, in relation to juvenile offenders, the care of young children, classroom behaviour and school exclusion (where the behavioural approach was already well established), and the effects on children of family breakdown.[36] Consequently, funding became available for a number of government sponsored parenting programmes. By 1994, the Parent Education and Support Forum had been established, and a number of voluntary agencies were involved in delivering services through health visitors, play workers and family social workers.[37] On the eve of New Labour's election victory, various groups of professionals were humming with praise for parenting programmes, overwhelmingly targeted at 'disadvantaged' groups, and supported by the 'growing body of research which shows that "it works"'. The bulk of the research came from US studies (directed by the imperatives of US social science), many deriving from Head Start and other War on Poverty programmes, and all claiming to show that the programmes improved not only parents' morale, but also children's health and educational attainments, while reducing the likelihood of their law-breaking, and generally raising their prospects.[38]

---

[35]   G. Pugh and E. De'Ath (1984) *The Needs of Parents: Practice and Policy in Parent Education*, London: NCB/Macmillan; R. Smith (1997) 'Parent Education: Empowerment or Control?', *Children & Society*, 11, pp 108–16; C. Smith (1996) *Developing Parenting Programmes*, London: NCB.

[36]   Smith (1997), p 110. For behaviourism's advance in schools from the late 1980s, see K. Baistow (2001) 'Behavioural Approaches and the Cultivation of Competence', in G. C. Bunn, A. D. Lovie and G. D. Richards (eds) *Psychology in Britain*, Leicester: BOPS Books, pp 323–4.

[37]   Smith (1997); C. Smith and G. Pugh (1996) *Learning to be a Parent*, London: Family Policy Studies Centre.

[38]   For US social science, see Chapter Five.

New Labour's turn to 'parenting'[39]

Prior to New Labour, parental narcissism had been encouraged by the growing therapeutic culture – we may think of it as an emotive discourse – associated with risk, individualisation and consumer life style.[40] More particularly, it was promoted indirectly through certain features of Thatcherism, including neoliberal morality in relation to markets, the idea of the 'free, possessive individual', wage labour activism, and notions of self-reliance and responsibility. But it was during New Labour administrations that this narcissism reached its modern apotheosis in popular culture, which it has continued to retain under succeeding governments. What happened was that as the social democratic ethic declined, and neoliberalism gained ascendency through 'political rationalities' and 'technologies' of government, the New Labour era heralded the development of a disciplinary state, albeit

---

[39] M. Daly (2013) 'Parenting Support Policies in Europe', *Families, Relationships and Societies*, 2, 2, pp 153–74. The parenting programmes were set within 'family policy', which included a range of sub-policies designed in conjunction with the 'social investment state'to counter 'social exclusion'. For family policies, see S. Gewirtz (2012) 'Cloning the Blairs: New Labour's Programme for the Re-socialization of Working-class Parents', *Journal of Education Policy*, 16, 4, pp 365–78. On policies and programmes: K. Asmussen (2011) *The Evidence-Based Parenting Practitioner's Handbook*, London: Routledge; H. Churchill (2011) *Parental Rights and Responsibilities*, Bristol: Policy Press; J. Lewis (2011) 'Parenting Programmes in England: Policy Developments and Implementation Issues, 2005–2010', *Journal of Social Welfare and Family Law*, 33, 2, pp 107–21; D. Hartas (2014) *Parenting, Family Policy and Children's Well-Being in an Unequal Society*, Basingstoke: Palgrave Macmillan. On parenting and social exclusion: R. Levitas (1998) The Inclusive Society?, *Social Exclusion and New Labour*, London: Macmillan; J. Welshman, *From Transmitted Deprivation to Social Exclusion: Policy, Poverty and Parenting*, Bristol: Policy Press; V. Gillies (2005) 'Meeeting parents' needs? Discourses of 'support' and 'inclusion' in family policy', *Critical Social Policy*, 25 (1), pp 70-90.

[40] For the influences coming from the United states, see E. Herman (1995) *The Romance of American Psychology*, Berkeley, CA: University of California Press; and E. Illouz (2008) *Saving the Modern Soul: Therapy, Emotions, and the Culture of Self-Help*, Berkeley, CA: University of California Press.

one characterised by a number of ambiguities and ambivalences.[41] In so doing, in effect it democratised parental narcissism through its policy programmes sponsoring behavioural child-rearing techniques and emphasising the authoritative parenting style, with its prioritisation of control as a parenting objective.

New Labour was always intensely conscious of the past: among the leadership, the obsession with modernising and its commitment to the future (Blair's 'a new dawn has broken') were both premised on an impatience with, and a distaste for, many of the social values of twentieth-century liberal democracy. Despite all the talk of being 'new' and 'modern', New Labour brought with it the aura of a conservative morality fuelled by its historical memory of the social issues that haunted post-1960s' politics, which it saw as being critically restrictive if Britain were to become a primary centre of global capitalism. The more serious of these issues included generational deprivation, child poverty, the fragmentation of communities, juvenile crime, the emergence of an underclass, declining educational standards, the lack of parental responsibility, and the break-up of the family. On the other hand, the political forces favouring social change in family structure and personal relationships were too electorally significant and too well entrenched within the new middle-class elite and their allies to allow for legislative protection of the 'traditional' family and its children, or for any significant reconsideration of the social and financial policies that were said to have encouraged divorce, cohabitation, sexual permissiveness and unbounded individualism.

The party's Third Way solution to the difficult and controversial problems was to accept the structural consequences of social change, but to combat 'moral decline' (often used as code for the 'welfare dependency culture') through a comprehensive programme of social investment, together with an intricately conceived project for the renewal of civil society emphasising individual and communal duties and obligations.[42] The focus of attention was on poorer working-

---

[41] These are not different domains, but represent 'intrinsic links' between rationalities as 'styles of thinking, ways of rendering reality thinkable in such a way that it is amenable to calculation and programming', and technologies, which help rationalities to become operable, as 'assemblages of persons, techniques, institutions, instruments for the conducting of conduct'. P. Miller and N. Rose (2008) *Governing the Present*, Cambridge: Polity, pp 15–16. For the disciplinary state, see R. Smith (2003) *Youth Justice: Ideas, Policy, Practice*, Cullompton: Willan Publishing; and J. Pitts (2003) *The New Politics of Youth Crime: Discipline or Solidarity?*, Lyme Regis: Russell House.

[42] For the behaviourism of the policies, see Harrison and Sanders (eds) (2014).

class families, since middle-class lives were largely ring-fenced by their economic and social solvency. A critical constituent of the government's strategy was to make parents, particularly mothers, not only more responsible for the running of their increasingly dual-income households, but also to position them as crucial agents in the reconfiguring of childhood as a status condition bounded by control and children as future worker-citizens. Drawing on earlier parent education schemes, parenting was to assume a new significance and to be conceptually rethought. Unlike 'childrearing', it now referred to a normative distinction between positive and negative parental behaviours; it emphasised 'activation' in the 'doing' of parenting; and it suggested the need for behaviourally taught 'skills' that are learned in order to be an effective parent.[43] In all senses, the objective was to produce confident, knowledgeable and empowered parents, and children who were disciplined, compliant and self-reliant.

One of most important influences on New Labour's social thought, and certainly on parenting, as we have seen, was the popular trauma unleashed by the Bulger affair, hyperbolised by the *Guardian* as 'Tragic proof that a society has lost its soul' (a headline, incidentally, reflecting middle-class anxiety about what it saw as social deterioration).[44] The killing, and the hysterical aftermath, served to contextualise recurring public concerns from across the political spectrum about some of the consequences of the 'liberal society'. New Labour, however, even before it had the name and was elected to government, was selective about which criticisms it endorsed. Bulger provided an opportunity for the disciplining of certain categories of disordered and dysfunctional social relations, without offending important economic and electoral interests, such as lightly regulated commerce and finance and, as mentioned, those sections of the electorate enthralled with consumerism, the politics of identity and sexuality, and the associated social liberationist ways of 'doing' family. Bulger also facilitated the development of two interrelated policy strands: an instrumental investment in children as human capital to combat social exclusion, and the connected remaking of working-class childhood in terms of the broader objective to transform local communities (usually working class and poor) through personal dependability, social cohesion and

---

[43] Daly (2013).

[44] On the critical retreat of the middle class from supporting welfarism, see Garland (2001), pp 148–56.

civic order.[45] This was the context in which, given that poor parenting was a risk factor, the concept of parent education came to be formally adopted, expanded, managed and theorised. It also explains why, as it developed, New Labour's parenting policy framed itself within two distinct but coordinating sets of problematics, commonplace in social and penal welfare theory, and historically core attributes of the adult–child relationship: the child (and family) *at* risk, and the child (and family) as *a* risk.[46]

The ethics of the parenting programmes[47]

In seeking legitimacy for its programmes, New Labour always called upon the 'evidence-based' nature of its early intervention strategies, buttressed by theories of infant determinism and neuroscience. In labelling programmes and policies in this way, the intention was to present them as scientific and, therefore, true. In so doing, the government concealed the fact that as with all child rearing practices, they were, 'always evaluative, and laden with moral choices'.[48] This is inevitable when everything involved in the parent–child relationship is 'ethical all the way down'.[49] In avoiding the ethics of child rearing, however, the relational aspects were minimised, or even denied. Instead, the principle of instrumentality – children as a 'productive factor' – was

[45] Home Office (1998) *Supporting Families: A Consultation Document*, London: HMSO; Hendrick (2003), pp 205–54; N. Parton (2006) *Safeguarding Childhood: Early Intervention and Surveillance in Late Modern Society*, Basingstoke: Palgrave Macmilllan, pp 84–99; M. Daly (2010) 'Shifts in Family Policy in the UK Under New Labour', *Journal of European Social Policy*, 20, 5, pp 433–43.

[46] Hendrick (2003), pp 7–11; on risk and intervention, see Piper (2008). The two themes were conflated through the *Every Child Matters* documentation (2003/4), the *Respect Action Plan* (2006), and *Reaching Out* (2006).

[47] For the programmes, see note 39; also H. Churchill and K. Clarke (2010) 'Investing in Parenting Education: AA Critical Review of Policy and Perovision in England', *Social Policy and Society*, 9, 1,.pp 39-53.

[48] However, it should be noted that much of the criticism of neuroscience and infant determinism derives from a hostility to Bowlby's attachment theory. See J. Kagan (1998), *Three Seductive Ideas,* New Haven, CT: Harvard University Press; E. Lee, J. Bristow, C. Fairclough, J. Macvarish (2014) *Parenting Culture Studies*, Basingstoke: Palgrave Macmillan. For a counterview, see S. Gerhardt (2004) *Why Love Matters: How Affection Shapes a Baby's Brain*, London: Brunner Routledge.

[49] S. Ramaekers and J. Suissa (2011) *The Claims of Parenting: Reasons, Responsibility and Society*, London: Springer, pp 79, 94, ix.

emphasised. This was clear from New Labour's initial family strategy document on coming to power, *Supporting Families*, which included among its priorities provision for parental services, with guidance being seen as an urgent requirement for all responsible parents, not merely the disadvantaged.[50] Similarly with the foundational and behaviourally focused Sure Start Programme (1998), aimed at poor families with pre-school children, and introduced as a cost-effective lynchpin in policies to reduce social exclusion, where the objectives were:

> [T]o work…[with] parents and children to promote the physical, intellectual and social development of babies and young children – particularly those who are disadvantaged – so that they can flourish at home and when they get to school, and thereby break the cycle of disadvantage for the current generation of young children.[51]

As part of the strategy, the NFPI was established, Parentline received additional funding, and Family Nurse Partnership health visiting programmes were introduced, as were home–school contracts. We have seen that the punitively orientated Crime and Disorder Act 1998 extended intervention in family life through ASBOs, just as Parenting Orders and Child Curfews were made to compel parents to be more proactive in preventing juvenile crime and anti-social behaviour; and new legislation was passed in 2000 to enhance parental responsibility for children to attend school, with fines or imprisonment for parents who failed to comply. Numerous similar policies followed throughout the New Labour era (*Every Child Matters*, 2004; *Guidance for Local Authorities in England*, DfES, Oct 2006; and *Every Parent Matters*, 2007), which were intended to confirm government thinking on 'how to support and engage parents'.[52]

The parenting programmes were presented in terms of 'style', the proper practice of which was seen as the basis for the success of all interventionist family policies. Of the three main styles – authoritarian, authoritative, permissive (a fourth – neglectful – was later added) –

---

50 Home Office (1998) *Supporting Families: A Consultation Document*. London: The Stationery Office.

51 Quoted in K. Clarke (2006) 'Childhood, parenting and early intervention: A critical examination of the Sure Start national programme', *Critical Social Policy*, 89, 26 (4), p 704. The four objectives of Sure Start were improving health, social and emotional development, the child's capacity to learn, and strengthening families and communities.

52 For a helpful survey of policies during the period, see Churchill (2011), chapter 7.

which, as we saw (Chapter Five), derived from American developmental child psychology and were assessed through the degree to which each one deployed 'control' ('demandingness') and 'warmth'/'sensitivity' (responsiveness), the officially favoured mode was the authoritative. The programmes claimed to encourage parents to exhibit towards their children: 'High levels of parental acceptance…High parent warmth… An open style of communication…Democratic decision making… Mutual respect…Mutual trust…Personal agency and responsibility… Independence and autonomy', so as to produce a panacea of ideal child behaviour: 'a secure identity…higher self-esteem…greater autonomy…higher levels of morality, social responsibility and pro-social behaviour…higher achievement and school competence…greater resistance to peer pressure…less risk of mental health problems…later onset of sexual behaviour…resistance to substance use and abuse'. Over the years, apparently hundreds of studies have proven that this approach delivers children well-suited to the demands of the evolving social and economic order, and as adolescents they are 'high in competence, individuation, maturity, achievement motivation, and self-regulation': in other words, perfect neoliberal citizens.[53]

Authoritative parenting techniques are taught to parents through the behavioural 'social learning' support programmes, such as the Webster-Stratton Incredible Years and the Triple P – just two of many that can be accessed in numerous formats. The strategy identifies parenting as both a private, domestic, discipline-driven process of socialisation serving a number of ends and, more specifically, a decidedly future-oriented behavioural process integral to government policy objectives. What is significant is that parents tend to be positioned in terms of

---

[53] Asmussen (2011), pp 83–6. S. Greenspan (2006) 'Rethinking "Harmonious Parenting" Using a Tree-Factor Discipline Model' refers to the idea that the empirical evidence supports a two-factor model of discipline ('warmth' and 'control') as a 'myth', p 8. On adolescence, see D. Baumrind (1991) 'The Influence of Parenting Style on Adolescent Competence and Substance Use', *Journal of Early Adolescence*, 11, pp 56–95. Some of the research on authoritative parenting is done through observation, but more often questionnaires are used which, like observation, are open to all sorts of errors and inconsistencies. Moreover, there is no one universally approved questionnaire. Much depends on the criteria for allocating parents to the different parenting styles. See G. Dwer (2010) 'The Authoritative Parenting Style: Warmth, Rationality, and High Standards', http//www.parenting science.com. For a critical view of the research, see A. Kohn (2014) *The Myth of the Spoiled Child*, Boston, MA: Da Capo Press, pp 35–51, and his (2005a) *Unconditional Parenting*, London: Atria; also P. Moran and D. Ghate (2005) 'The Effectiveness of Parenting Support', *Children & Society*, 19, pp 329-336.

their technique. This means that they are 'largely abstracted from the web of relationships in which they live' and, therefore, the programmes downplay the importance of understanding the contextual meaning of situations, ignoring the significance attributed to the relational circumstances.[54] This leaves managerial skills to determine the confines of the relationship, and evaluate its meaning, rather than the other way around. What is rarely examined is the long-term effect of behavioural intervention, such as leaving sleepless babies to cry themselves to sleep (so-called 'delayed responding').[55] The problem of infant sleeping patterns is portrayed operationally (see Chapter Five), so that the baby's difficulties are interpreted as causing more problems for parents than for the child. The psychoanalytic perspective is completely ignored. The advised solution is 'rational, detached management…not parental soul-searching regarding either their infant's behaviour or their own motives.'[56] Parents appear to be happy with this approach, since what they liked about the 'skills' segments of the programmes was the specificity of taught techniques for a particular situation and the 'take-home' tips.[57] However, in an example of the mixed messages regarding 'mothering' that are often given out by the programmes, maternal care for young children, while seen as important in the practice of Sure Start, is simultaneously thrown into doubt with mothers of 'disadvantaged children' also being told that non-maternal care (that is, nurseries) is better than arriving at school with 'no school experience'. Hence wage labour becomes a *duty* for parents, not least in giving their children the 'benefit' of nursery care, thereby prioritising 'school experience' over other forms of social wisdom and the worker-citizen over the carer-citizen.[58] Unsurprisingly, then, as a review commissioned by the coalition government proclaimed, the overall purpose of parenting was to ensure that children had the necessary skills and attitudes to make them 'school ready' and 'life ready' with the emphasis on positive and compliant behaviour, appreciating the importance of paid work,

---

[54] Clarke (2006) p 708; Ramaekers and Suissa (2011), pp 80, 84; Greenspan (2006), pp 5–12.

[55] P. Moran, D. Ghate and A. van der Merwe (2004) *What Works in Parenting Support? A Review of International Evidence*, London: Department for Education and Skills, p 47.

[56] K. Baistow (1998) 'Behavioural Psychology as a Social Project: From Social Engineering to the Cultivation of Competence', PhD, Goldsmith's College, University of London, pp 134–5.

[57] P. Moran et al (2004), p 61.

[58] Clarke (2006), p 714. Emphasis added.

avoiding drug and alcohol abuse and rejecting criminal and violent behaviour.[59]

In general, the overriding purpose of parent education seems to be that of raising parental self-confidence. This is seen as the prerequisite for changing specific parental behaviours with regard to giving children more praise, shouting less often and reducing the amount of violent punishment. Evaluations of Sure Start Centres emphasise their contribution to 'parental empowerment'.[60] The programmes intend to make parents feel 'good' about themselves, and 'feel themselves... supported', which means promoting parental strengths and 'steering away from a purely deficit model that focuses on problems, weaknesses and risk factors'.[61] The approach always seeks to be 'non-stigmatising, sensitive to different cultures and ways of bringing up children'. A recent guide to delivering 'evidence-based parenting support', in focusing on 'Understanding the needs and values of parents' and asking 'why do parents need help?', advised practitioners to be 'respectful and non-judgemental', and treat parents 'in a manner that is genuine and empathic and values them as a person'. The therapies were to provide parents 'with a warm and supportive therapeutic environment', with improved 'psychological outcomes', a reduction in 'anxiety and depression', and an increase in their 'self-esteem'.[62] The evaluations of different programmes regularly boast of their 'successes' with 'all of the adult participants' having 'gained confidence in themselves as parents...modified their perceptions of their children's problem behaviour...learned useful behavioural management techniques', and been '*empowered...as adults*'.[63] The organisers were keen to show that the programmes were likely to have had an impact on other areas of parents' lives, such as giving them greater self confidence, facilitating more friendships, taking up courses, developing support networks,

---

[59] G. Allen (2011) *Early Intervention: The Next Steps*, An Independent Report to Her Majesty's Government. Submitted, January, pp 2–5.

[60] Churchill (2011), p 138.

[61] Moran et al (2004), pp 19–20.

[62] HM Treasury and DfES (2005), *Support for parents: The best start for children*, London: Crown copywright, p 11; also Asmusssen (2011), pp 141–2, 146–69.

[63] M. Manby (2005) 'Evaluation of the Impact of the Webster-Stratton Parent–Child Videotapes Series on Participants in a Midlands Town in 2001–2002', *Children and Society*, 19, p 327; M. S. Zeedyk, I. Werritty and C. Riach (2008) 'One Year On: Perceptions of the Lasting Benefits of Involvement in a Parenting Support Programme', *Children & Society*, 22, 2, p 99. Emphasis added.

and having the skills to cope with day to day stress.[64] Nor were the budgetary aspects of the programmes overlooked as the individual programme's relatively short duration and low cost were cast as critical in assessing its value. The organisers of one scheme were pleased that a six-week short course could produce positive lasting outcomes for '£200 per client or less', which was deemed to be 'a good use of public funds, given that health economists analyses indicate that investment in the early years can yield benefits at a ration as high as 13:1'. There was a further saving in that where previously parents had looked to professional or paraprofessional support when in need, now they looked to informal networks of family and friends. One can almost hear the relieved tone of the comment: 'This finding points, again, to the economic benefits of support programmes, for statutory services will clearly be less stretched if parents feel less need to call on them.'[65] But making accurate evaluations are much more difficult than this up-beat reporting suggests, in part owing to the imperfect state of knowledge regarding surface achievements, and also to the problematic nature of the concept of evidence based.[66]

While much of the concern for parental well-being is desirable for the welfare and happiness of both parent and child, in reporting on the programmes almost no thought has been given to the views of the children involved. Among a few researchers, however, there is some disquiet regarding these children, if only in recognising that parental satisfaction is not the same as improved outcomes for children. A serious weakness in the programmes, reflecting the absence of psychoanalytic interest, is that there tends to be an emphasis on dealing with so-called anti-social behaviour, rather than 'internalising disorders' such as child depression and anxiety. Similarly, and significantly in terms of the programmes' innate childism, in a literature that was 'very "un-child-centred"', desirable outcomes for children were 'nearly always defined by how adults want children to be rather than by how children are inherently', and little attention was given to how children want their

---

64 Zeedyk et al (2008), pp 101–7.

65 Zeedyk et al (2008). pp 107–8. For insight into the economics of purchasing and delivering the programmes, see Lewis (2011), pp 113–14, 116.

66 On the neglected issue of imperfect knowledge regarding lack of data collection and reluctance of journals to accept, and authors to submit, negative results, see Moran et al (2004), p 94; Moran and Ghate (2005), pp 329–3. For the concept of 'evidence based', see Piper (2008), chapters 5 and 7. On the ways that research studies are open to different interpretations, see Kohn (2005a), *inter alia*. In entering the public domain, this 'research' is always subject to control for political, personal and professional reasons.

parents to be; there was no interest in the child's perspective on good parenting. No wonder that children are much less positive about the interventions.[67] All too often the fact that children live very much 'in the moment', and not the future, is overlooked. While left-wing critics are sceptical of aspects of parent education, they tend to ignore the children's rights position, preferring to focus on state surveillance of the family, and of mothers in particular. They present the adult-centric view, namely that parents should be allowed to 'experience parenthood within *their own* moral framework without being subjected to moralising', and that the approach to parenting should be 'family-centric' rather than a 'child-centric'.[68] The role of the state in being 'overly concerned' about what the poor do to their children is described as 'morally dubious and politically exploitative'.[69]

Childism unveiled: *Supernanny* – the dominatrix in the nursery

The genre of reality TV

In an age where so many individuals are desperate to be other than they are, it is not surprising that reality television, sometimes referred to as 'transformational' or 'lifestyle', and meaning the presence of ordinary people in 'unscripted' situations, claims to 'change lives'; it is about a willingness to put the self into a public frame where one will be scrutinised, judged, applauded, condemned, admired and envied.[70] This emphasis on the 'self' helps to conceal the politics of the genre in so far as the political is ostensibly eschewed, except for oblique references to cultural politics, which is always implicit rather than explicit. Culture is normally presented via social difference rather than social class, as being about the politics of identity rather than that

---

[67] Moran et al (2004), pp 21–3, 38, 61; D. Ghate and M. Ramella (2002), *Positive Parenting: The National Evaluation of the Youth Justice Board Parenting Programme*, London: Youth Justice Board.

[68] Hartas (2014), p 90; E. Lee et al (2014).

[69] Hartas (2014), p 90; on parent's rights as opposed to those of children, see pp 109–12; also H. Reece (2013) 'The Pitfalls of Positive Parenting', *Ethics and Education*, 8, 1, pp 42–54.

[70] A. Biressi and H. Nunn (2005) *Reality TV: Realism and Revelation*, London: Wallflower, p 2; G. Palmer (2008), 'Introduction: The Habit of Scrutiny', in *Exposing Lifestyle TV*, Farnham: Ashgate, p 1.

of any kind of group or collective action.[71] This is hardly surprising since such determinism derives from neoliberalism's intrinsic desire for 'governance at a distance'. In effect, the 'shows' (therein lies their theatricality), in promoting the ethics of 'ways to live', work to reinforce 'the neoliberal faith in the transformative power of personal growth and responsibility' thereby obscuring economic and political structures and government policies.[72]

One of reality television's most important deceptions is that it *appears* to displace old forms of authority, political and otherwise, and substitute them with a disingenuous advocacy of the empowered self, as the author of personal integrity.[73] Being on, and speaking to, the camera seems to authenticate the self, although in reality there is no certainty involved for what the camera 'sees' is always provisional: it is but a momentary understanding. As Christopher Lasch wrote, 'the emergence of a therapeutic ideology that upholds a normative schedule of psychosocial development…gives further encouragement to anxious self-scrutiny'.[74] In other words:

> To understand narcissism, as a contemporary malaise rather than pathology, is to understand the desire to consolidate a sense of one's self in a culture seemingly devoid of meaning and of objects and relations providing self-affirmation. Consequently, identity is affirmed through the luxury of a consolatory mirror image afforded by the ubiquitous presence of the media in our lives.[75]

The ubiquity of the media has created a space for ethics to become entertainment as the programmes involve examining relations between the self and the social and the choices we make: information about the care and management of the self, explanations of the tensions between collective versus self-interest, and audience participation

---

[71] Biressi and Nunn (2005), p 3.

[72] G. Hawkins (2001) 'The Ethics of Television', *International Journal of Cultural Studies*, 4, 4, pp 412–26; R. Becker (2006) 'Help is on the Way: Supernanny, Nanny 911, and the Neoliberal Politics of the Family', in D. A. Heller, *Help is on the Way. The Great American Makeover: Television, History, and the Nation*, Basingstoke: Palgrave Macmillan, p 176.

[73] In many respects this is similar to what happens in the chatrooms of parenting websites. The internet has facilitated both a new authoritative voice and an opportunity to focus on the self. I owe this point to Allison James.

[74] C. Lasch (1979) *The Culture of Narcissism*, New York: Norton, p 48.

[75] Biretti and Nunn (2005), p 100.

in quests for the truth of the self – 'who do you think you are?'[76] Clearly, our postmodern 'ways of living' are always structured by risks and uncertainty, and it is these that the genre of lifestyle television placate by offering its advice in a light-hearted and always optimistic tone in order to dispel nagging anxieties. The ideological pull of the reality format is that in its paradoxical indifference to 'reality', it is an aspect of contemporary apprehension, one that encourages the self to limit the possibility of complex analysis, since complexity suggests contradiction, partiality and ambivalence which, in so far as they destabilise complacency, are incompatible with narcissism's quest for security. If the programmes are to succeed, the viewer has to 'see' and bear witness to change and resolution through an unfolding drama around 'our' lives, thereby confirming the action as 'real' and 'true'. But more than mere entertainment is at issue. The marketing jargon of the shows presents them as 'edutainment', that is 'a social marketing "place" strategy', involving the 'deliberate insertion of socially desirable information into entertainment vehicles with the purpose of changing an audience's knowledge, attitudes and behaviour'. As a format, in presenting the productions as 'shows', never as documentaries, this allows for the airing of potentially threatening or sensitive topics in a reassuring manner, while simultaneously reaching an audience that might otherwise be elusive and, therefore, masks their intention to affect social change.[77]

Supernanny

Supernanny is only one of a number of child-training 'reality' television shows to have been broadcast in Britain since the early 2000s, some of which continue to run as repeats (here and around the world), including *Supernanny USA, Nanny 911, Brat Camp, Honey, We're Killing the Kids, Demons to Darlings, House of Tiny Tearaways, Little Angels, The World's Strictest Parents, Blame the Parents, Driving Mum and Dad Mad, Bringing Up Baby Wife Swap, Extreme Parental Guidance* and *Three Day Nanny*. Although there are differences between these programmes, they all share a similar premise, namely that unless authoritatively disciplined, children, especially young children, pose problems for, and threats to, their parents and, by extension, either presently or in the future, to the wider community. Integral to this deceit is that parents (usually

---

[76] Hawkins (2001), p 412. Emphasis original.

[77] R. Ganeshasundaram and N. Henley (2009) 'Reality Television (Supernanny): A Social Marketing 'Place' Strategy, *Journal of Consumer Marketing*, 26, 5, pp 311–19.

mothers), are responsible for their children's 'bad' behaviour by virtue of 'deficits' in their parenting styles. The implication is that mothers who lack the requisite 'skills' necessary for 'good' parenting, also lack those required for responsible citizenship. In this way, the public and the private are conjoined to produce a certain kind of social and apparently natural commonality that is itself disciplinary.

Since first screened in 2004, *Supernanny* has been an international hit in more than 48 countries. Jo Frost secured the role by answering a magazine advertisement in 2003, after having worked as a nanny for 15 years. She was promoted as a 'no-nonsense' professional nanny, who teaches parents how to stop 'unruly bad behaviour'; she has a 'frank and up-front style' and a 'recipe of strict discipline and tried-and-tested techniques'; she compels parents to 'confront the real issues behind' their children's behaviour, teaching them 'how to turn the kids around'.[78] On the *Supernanny* website, in addition to Frost's books and DVDs, there are blogs, 'naughty steps', 'rewards charts', and various other items for sale, accompanied by the promise that 'with Supernanny techniques you can transform a chaotic family life into a haven of peace and tranquillity'. Viewers are encouraged to send in videos of their own children, with the enticement that 'we may even ask you to be on the show!' Although the programmes are ostensibly concerned with 'positive parenting', many of the techniques used might be better described as punitive, based as they are on assumptions derived from behaviour modification. In practice, we see the 'problem' children being publicly (and without their consent) subjected to a regime of more or less non-negotiable discipline, whereby unquestioning obedience is rigidly inculcated, and is reinforced through systematised rewards and punishments. In the format, the child is deliberately subjected to humiliating conflict situations – bedtimes, meals, sibling aggression, washing and dressing – which usually result in repeated periods of tearful distress before the child *learns* to accept the new disciplinary routine. We rarely either see or hear the child's standpoint, nor do we know the history of her/his relational experiences, or those of the family. Instead, the parent–child relationships tend to be presented as fixed and confined (and framed in the present by the camera), as in a photograph. The programme format conceals the child's silence through the dramatic structure of the visual narrative as it purports to *show* the true context and pattern of the child's behaviour. Consequently, each child portrayed becomes emblematic of an adult-centric construction

---

[78] F. Green (2007) 'Supernanny: Disciplining Mothers through a Narrative of Domesticity', *Storytelling: A Critical Journal of Popular Narrative*, 6, 2, pp 99–107.

of 'the naughty child', to which there is no court of appeal. A critical feature of the show is the positioning of the audience to disregard the child's tears (aside from their dramatic value in creating tension and atmosphere); they appear as merely consequential of a failure to obey, of wilfulness and, therefore, are not *our* responsibility. So we ignore the child's misery and, in as much as the child is 'suffering', thereby violate a cardinal moral virtue: empathy for the anguish of others, one of the primary means by which we assert our humanness – what the philosopher Charles Taylor calls the giving of respect.[79]

The dominatrix image

The image of Frost as a dominatrix, and its implications, is rarely mentioned (although she is not unaware of it herself), no doubt for fear of what it might say about aspects of parental power in particular and, more generally, the spectre of sexuality in adult–child relations. Nonetheless, the figure of the dominatrix as a cultural presence (with all the accompanying feminine paraphernalia), pervades the script, explicating a psychology of 'pain' and 'pleasure', mediated through 'submission' (control) – a recurring theme in all child-training shows as they exemplify the virtues of authoritative parenting. This image, however, does more than colour the 'tone' of the drama. It often instructs its practice, foregrounding, as it does, the significance of 'punishment' (in behaviourist language: 'sanctions' or 'penalties') as integral to parenting as a 'skill' in applying a managerially 'rational' disciplinary routine. In the early publicity photographs for *Supernanny*, we see Frost looking stern in a purple suit jacket with her slightly tilted head, hair in a tightly secured bun, and with full red lips. She looks over her dark framed heavy black spectacles as she rests her left hand on her hip and raises her right hand, index finger pointing at us, the viewers. The *Evening Standard* asked, 'Is this dominatrix the new Dr Spock?'[80] In his interview with Frost in the *Independent*, Nick Duerden wrote: 'she'll *whip* your children into shape with a spell on the naughty step and some dominatrix-style finger wagging'.[81] Frost says the dominatrix image was not her idea but the production company's: 'They thought the power dressing would distinguish me immediately, and it did.' In a revealing admission that shows her confidence in the public's

---

[79] C. Taylor (1989) *The Sources of the Modern Self*, London: Harvard University Press, pp 12–13.

[80] M. MacDonald (2004), 'Is this the new Dr. Spock?', *Evening Standard*, 23 July.

[81] N. Duerden (2007) *Independent*, 'Jo Frost: Nanny State' September. Emphasis added.

acceptance of the dominatrix-style frame of discipline for children, she says, 'It did bring me a certain fan base, yes. I got letters…let's face it, there are men out there who are attracted to suits and heels, right?' Elsewhere, she tells a story about answering the phone for a Prince's Trust fundraiser, when the male caller offered an extra £50 if she would say 'You've been very, very naughty.'[82] When asked about marriage, she replies that her friends tease her that it will be 'an older man and that he'll live in Soho and be wanting a lot of discipline'.[83] Duerden reminds her that critics say she appears to have a 'fetish for punishment', personified by the Naughty Step (which was available for purchase via her website), and that it was a popular feature in the show's magazine, with readers encouraged to send in pictures of their own children on them. He suggests that this amounts to 'public ridicule'. To which Frost replies: 'All I can say is this: what I'm doing with children is good, solid common sense.' When asked by another journalist how the 'naughty step' 'apology' can be sincere (the child must apologise 'sincerely' before being allowed off the step), she replies: 'I'm telling the parent, have more respect for *yourself*, don't allow the child to treat *you* like that.'[84] This idea of respect for the self is critical to the behaviourist approach to empowerment being the gateway to subjective gratification and personal responsibility.

The opening segment of the show, where we see and hear the parents' enunciation of the destruction allegedly perpetuated by the child upon the household, serves to establish the child as bad/evil.[85] In response, Frost emphasises the application of consistently applied discipline, structured around a loosely applied version of the behaviourist notion of 'positive enforcement'. *Supernanny*, however, is characterised by varying degrees of physical restraint of one sort or another (a common feature in parenting shows): the submission element is attained, for example, by physically forcing the child to stay on the naughty step (or in the 'naughty room') until the 'sincere' apology has been offered; by repeatedly carrying a distressed and struggling child with sleep 'problems' back to bed (in silence); and by holding small children firmly by the arms and, in a threatening voice, with a wagging finger, telling them that they have been 'very, very naughty'. Furthermore, by way of adding to the implicitly violent atmosphere, parental accounts of

---

82 D. Aitkenhead (2006) 'You've been very, very naughty', *Guardian*, 22 July.

83 MacDonald (2004).

84 Aitkenhead (2006). Emphasis added.

85 C. Fowler and R. Kambuta (2011) 'Extreme Human Makeovers: *Supernanny*, the Unruly Child, and Adulthood in Crisis', *Literature Interpretation Theory*, 22, 3, pp 268–9.

their children's behaviour often draw on war-like references: a seven-year-old is compared to 'a bomb waiting to explode'; dressing a four-year-old 'takes up to two hours to win the battle'; mealtime is 'like a war'; parents regularly report having 'lost the battle' for control; and in a notice for the programme, Frost enticed the audience with the promise that 'we've got some real tyrants in the next series'.[86]

Inadequate mothers and evil/bad children

A characteristic of *Supernanny*, and similar parenting shows, is that the mother is shown to be in need of help – she is always 'at her wits' end'. Mothers are often 'inadequate', but not normally because they are neglectful, punitive or insensitive. Usually, they are too lax or inconsistent or disorganised, and though there may be a certain amount of viewer tut-tutting at their apparent incompetence, this is always presented as understandable and our sympathy for the plight of the mother (and ourselves in her shoes) is integral to the show's success. We, the viewer, are judge and jury; but we are guided by Frost's tone and facial expressions, and instructed by the syntax of the programme to be rehabilitative in our verdict, rather than retributive. While the mother is the beleaguered figure around whom the drama unfolds, leading to a satisfactory and reassuring solution, she needs the presence of the bad/evil child without which the concepts of a 'parenting deficit' and 'empowerment' would be irrelevant: only this child can *initiate* the narrative that through Frost's counsel, and the mother's 'skill' acquisition, will lead to the 'happy' family conclusion. This child is also the central *visual* motif around whom the drama fixes its points of reference, emotionally and, critically, as 'edutainment'. This is why the most dramatic footage, edited without any concern for the children's obvious distress must be of them 'at their most tormented': crying, struggling, screaming, fighting, running about wildly; with their behaviour always described as 'unacceptable' (one of Frost's favourite words) – never as 'a legitimate protest' at what empathetic observers

---

[86] Fowler and Kambuta (2011), p 268.

might describe as unreasonable parental demands.[87] Although the mother's deficit parenting is portrayed as a contributing factor to, or indeed the source of, the disruption, she always redeems herself since, as the programme proceeds, through expert tutoring she will come to recognise her own deficiencies and become a better parent. She will be absolved, heroically. Children, however, can never be trusted in and for themselves; it is only through being continuously subject to consistent parental control – conditional parenting – that they can be *in* the family. In effect, the child is in a contractual situation, on permanent probation, forever potentially disruptive – an archetypal permanently marginalised other. This is why permissive parents, who foster friendship with their children, are frowned upon by the purveyors of the authoritative approach: they blur the boundary on which the 'otherness' of age relations depends.[88]

Perhaps surprisingly, one of the most pertinent critiques of the show came from Gina Ford, the best-selling 'Queen of the Routine'.[89] Ford, however, noted that the programmes used 'very disturbed families'

---

[87] Aitenhead (2006). Other feminists, however, ignore both the distress and the exploitation of the children, preferring to focus on the 'upset, and anxiety and humiliation of the mother', and on the degree of surveillance and regulation to which mothers are subjected. The content of the shows is accepted as true, since they are said to provide 'helpful tips for parenting', and help to 'bridge the gap between expectation and experience': Green (2007); R. Feasey (2011) 'Mothers on the Naughty Step: Supernanny and Reality Parenting Television' posted by author, Bath Spa University. See also T. Jensen (2010) '"What Kind of Mum are you at the Moment?" Supernanny and the Psychology of Classed Embodiment', *Subjectivity*, 3, pp 170–92; (2011) '"Watching with My Hands Over My Eyes": Shame and Irritation in Ambivalent Encounters with "Bad Mothers"', *Radical Psychology*, 9, 2, radicalpsychology.org/vol9-2/; and J. Bristow (ed) (2009) *Standing Up to Supernanny*, Exeter: Societas, Academic Imprint.

[88] On not becoming friends, see Tanya Byron a clinical psychologist reported in Liz Hull (2012) 'Why, as a parent, you should never be tempted to treat your child as a friend', *Mailonline*, 20 July; see also behavioural psychologist Aric Sigman, quoted in Hull (2012), *Mailonline*, 20 July, and his (2009) *The Spoilt Generation*, London: Piatkus.

[89] G. Ford, (2008) 'How TV's nasty nannies wreck children's lives', *Mailonline*, 16 October. Ford relates how she withdrew from making a reality series because 'instead of being helpful and informative', the programme was going to be 'sensationalised'. The series later appeared as BBC's 'House of Tiny Tearaways', fronted by Tanya Byron. Among the first critics of reality parenting TV were O. James (2005) *Observer*, 1 May and in the USA, A. Kohn (2005b) 'Supernanny State', *The Nation*, 23 May. In 2006 the UN Committee on the Rights of the Child criticised the invasion of children's privacy and the regular portrayal of children 'in a terrible light'.

where the apparent misbehaviour of the children was 'extreme', requiring prolonged psychological help rather than being 'subjected to public humiliation' of the kind directed at them after each show as found in TV chatrooms. The programmes, she said, encouraged the idea that children 'are a different breed who need to be tamed' with normal toddler behaviour being 'demonised'; they delighted in humiliating children and advocating 'shame-and-shame' methods, such as the 'naughty step' (endorsed by celebrities). She noted that there was even a market in portable 'naughty steps', promoted as 'so you never need leave home without one'. In calling for the government to intervene to protect children, Ford wondered if 'Instead of branding our children as bad, it's time we took a long, hard look at ourselves and why we, as a Nation, are prepared to watch innocent children being exploited for our entertainment.' A journalist commenting on another parenting show, Tanya Byron's *Little Angels*, provided part of the answer: 'The sheer awfulness of the children's behaviour made for compelling television.'[90] Compelling (and reassuring), of course, because it helps to legitimise childist attitudes: it is visual proof – and what could be more compelling – of what we all know about children, which is that they need discipline.

The narcissistic self

If the disturbing figure of the dominatrix *Supernanny* has been ignored or glossed over, the equally pervasive presence of emotional narcissism in contemporary parenting also remains similarly unacknowledged. The danger of parental narcissism is that as it exploits the frailty of altruism and self-sacrifice as humanist virtues, so it waylays faith, hope and optimism, thereby ultimately corrupting our ethics and our moral character. Throughout reality parenting television, undue concern with the self surfaces obliquely in references to self-scrutiny, or reflexivity, usually as a means of contextualising the exercise of parental authority in order to be in control.[91] Indeed, the behavioural instinct of the shows instruct parents that if they are not keeping children and, implicitly, also themselves, in their 'proper' place by dominating them, then they are at fault; they are (like the owners of disruptive and dangerous dogs) personally responsible for violating a 'natural' order of adult/child domination which, in the broader sense, resembles human domination

---

[90] J. Brown (2007), 'Tyranny of the child gurus: You don't have to be a paranoid parent', *Independent*, 22 May.

[91] Kohn (2014), pp 60–5.

of the natural world. This is important because the dislodging of place – in social relations, as in Nature – threatens to undermine order itself.

This instruction is framed within the narcissistic format that is reality television as it encourages the latent desire to be seen and known so that the 'minimal self' may be validated.[92] The successful imposition of order upon the child becomes testimony to one's being as a fully authenticated self. More subtly, however, the narcissism is fuelled by homage to a false sense of empowerment, which, unbeknown to the parents, links individualisation to neoliberal polity. The ME-ism is innocently acknowledged in *Supernanny*'s famous slogan (which could just as easily be applicable to any consumer durable): 'How to get the best from your children.' In reply to the suggestion that this is a curious inversion of what might be expected, namely that perhaps parents should worry about 'giving', rather than 'getting', reportedly 'Frost just looks mildly surprised at this thought'.[93] Oliver James captured the slogan's essence when he remarked: 'It's all about you.' No wonder, then, that the blurb for the book *Ask Supernanny* (2006) succinctly lauds the narcissistic appeal of behavioural child training: 'Want your life back? You need Supernanny!' The message being that prior to having children, you had a 'life', which you have since lost; only through having control over your children can you get 'it' back. This enticement to egotistical possession of the self at the expense of a child, implicitly confirms the neoliberal notion of ownership and the mainly feminist view of the child as in effect a robber who burgles the mother's identity and, therefore, must be marginalised so as not to deny the female 'me'.[94]

No doubt there is a reluctance to admit that we watch these shows because they tell us that 'the problem with "out of control" children is not *their* unhappiness', rather it is 'the fuss and bother they cause to grown-ups…What Supernanny ultimately offers, and what people evidently want, is a regime for making children less inconvenient.'[95] This is true, as far as it goes. But it needs to go further. The clue lies in the appeal to an apparent 'transformation' (the road to enablement) which, inevitably less than complete, fuses the knowing eye of surveillance with the uncontent ego, thereby producing identities that

---

[92] Biressi and Nunn (2005), p 102.

[93] Aitkenhead (2006).

[94] As we have seen, this is a familiar feminist theme – see Chapters 4 and 6, notes 106 and 83 respectively.

[95] Aitkenhead (2006). Emphasis added.

are inherently dispersed, doubtful and precarious.[96] The illusory but comforting message is that through control of our children, *we* can overcome *our* difficulties and, once again (as in a mythical past), we can be a happy family and, therefore, be *happy* – the promise to recapture a lost harmony, in an unharmonious age, represents the political use of nostalgia. So the show usually ends with parents and children together, thanking Supernanny for 'making us a family again' – as if *it* were the solution. In fact, through its assumed 'technologies of citizenship', and the accompanying rhetoric of empowerment, which omits politics, reality television parenting is better seen as a strategy for the governing of parents and children in order to remoralise their relationship on behalf of neoliberalism and its narcissistic henchmen.[97]

Children and dogs: what's in a name?

We are, it seems, involved in a relatively new relationship between postmodernity and non-human animals: particularly with respect to pet-keeping, ecologically friendly zoos, animal parks, and wild-life sanctuaries.[98] Surveys suggest that we increasingly treat pets as family members, giving them human names, diligently attending to their welfare, and experiencing mental distress at their demise. We spend millions of pounds on satisfying pet 'needs': food, clothes, housing, toys, photographs, medical care and cemeteries. What may well be happening, although the evidence is still sketchy, is that pets, especially dogs, are being given equal status to children. Many pet owners now refer to themselves as 'pet parents' and, in the USA at least, as 'Mommy' and 'Daddy', with some research suggesting that 81 per cent of those surveyed regarded their dog as equal to their children. Not only are disciplinary procedures for dogs and children similar, so, it seems, is our language and its rhythms.[99] During the last decade or so, the domestication of dogs has gathered momentum with the expanding dog-training market being dominated by Victorian Stilwell's reality tv show *It's Me or the Dog* (shown in more than 40 countries), and Cesar Millan's hugely successful award winning USA spectacle, *The Dog*

---

[96] Palmer (2008), p 8.

[97] B. Cruikshank (2009) *The Will to Empower Democratic Citizens and Other Subjects*, London: Cornell University Press, pp 1–18.

[98] A. Franklin (1999) *Animals and Modern Cultures*, London: Sage; E. Cudworth (2011) *Social Lives with Other Animals*, Basingstoke: Palgrave Macmillan.

[99] S. Coren (2011) 'Do We Treat Dogs the Same Way as Children in our Modern Families?', *Psychology Today*, 2 May.

Whisperer (shown in more than 85 countries). Sewell advocates the 'positive approach' to training, based on the principle of cooperation, while Millan specialises in rehabilitation, rather than simply dog training, although his methods are widely used for training by owners. Millan is famous (infamous) for treating dogs as pack animals which, he says, requires that owners exert strong leadership and total control. Owners should give 'exercise, discipline and affection' – they usually, he says, give too much of the last of these and not enough of the first and second.

So it was not without significance that in an episode of the American cartoon *South Park*, in an attempt to control her son, Eric, the mother first summons both *Nanny 911* and *Supernanny* to no avail, before turning to Millan who succeeds in successfully disciplining poor Eric. Obviously, in terms of popular culture this episode links dogs to children in two respects: as problems, and as being amenable to the similar disciplinary procedures. But it also evinces a disturbing childism that surreptitiously belittles democratic virtue. The similarity is usually voiced in a light-hearted manner. Under the line, 'Should you treat your children like dogs?', *Guardian* columnist, Lucy Atkins regales us with tales to this effect: 'the notion that dogs and children share a need for calm, assertive "pack leaders" and that both need exercise, discipline and love seems reasonable. No wonder such theories are challenging the trend for indulgent "helicopter" parenting.' She continues by confirming that 'On parenting websites, blogs, websites and Twitter, the guilty admissions are all the same: the training techniques of…"The Dog Whisperer", work on kids too', and she quotes 'tough love' psychologist Aric Sigman who, claiming 'universals in "behaviour modification techniques"', reports that 'parents are finally realising that the tail is wagging the dog. Authority is a good thing.'[100] Similarly, 'parenting coach', Judy Reith, who used dog whisperer techniques on her terrier, and now also applies them 'every day' to her three daughters: 'You need to be unpopular sometimes and lay down the law.' The deputy head of Battersea Dogs' Home concurred, advising, 'If your kids are behaving badly treat them like a dog', using 'positive reinforcement'. Sue Atkins (founder of Positive Parenting) endorsed this recommendation: 'I have laughed at times about the similarities between puppies and children.'[101] Likewise, an 'adviser' to Gina Ford, in answer to the charge that Ford's methods were like those of a 'dog

---

[100] L. Atkins, 2009, 'Should you treat your children like dogs?' *Guardian*, 7 December.

[101] Quotes from Rebecca English, 2006, 'If your kids are behaving badly treat them like a dog', *Mailonline*, 29 August.

trainer', replied 'But I think well-trained dogs are lovely, happy dogs and well-trained babies are lovely, happy babies.'[102]

The sociology of media studies has long been aware that 'Parenting and dog training formats organized their ethical dilemmas along similar trajectories, with comparable terminology and techniques': both refer to 'tough love', calm regular routine is emphasised, while corporal punishment and bribery, are frowned upon.[103] Generally the programmes share a managerial rational approach through the use of impassive and consistent discipline, which is 'learned'. The parenting of the child/dog 'is conceptualized as an ongoing process of learning, reflection and importantly self-appraisal; a domesticated model of the self-actualising and enterprising subject of contemporary capitalism', and since parenting is seen as a lifestyle option, it is a reflexive practice. Thus, the ethical dilemmas of parenting/dog ownership articulate the contemporary plotting of parental responsibility, with dogs symbolically representing semi-literate, anti-social, truanting and obese children who figure so prominently in the moral panic rhetoric surrounding the socially excluded. Furthermore, the shows promote dog–owner relationships, like those of parenting children, that involve us in 'a fantasy of reciprocity', meaning that what we put into the training routines affects the degree of satisfaction obtained, thereby exemplifying the important neoliberal contractual ethic of hard work bringing just rewards. The objective is to produce the ideal dog (child): devoted, loyal, subservient, easily pleased, protective, good looking, publicly admired and a credit to its owner.

With companion animals (pets), the fundamental relationship is between human beings and the natural world where the former, through varieties of anthropomorphism, dominate the latter.[104] With children, the relationship is between adult selves, as *beings* (civilised and complete) and children as *becomings* (uncivilised and incomplete) – not quite 'beings'; perhaps as 'bodies' less than humanly whole.[105] The 'less than completeness' loop has historically sustained the rhetoric of child rearing through socialisation (think of Elias's 'the tempering of

---

[102] Quoted in A. Asthana, 2007, 'Baby guru's method "like dog training"', *The Observer*, March.

[103] For this paragraph, I draw on M. Andrews and F. Carter (2008) '"Who Let the Dogs Out?" Pets, Parenting and the Ethics of Lifestyle Programming', in Palmer (ed), pp 39–48.

[104] Yi-Fun Yuan (1984) *Dominance and Affection*, London: Yale University Press.

[105] A. Giubilini and F. Minerva (2013) 'After-birth Abortion: Why Should the Baby Live?', *Journal of Medical Ethics*, 39 (5), pp 261-63. See also E. Uprichard (2008) 'Children as "Being and Becomings": Children, Childhood and Temporality', *Children & Society*, 22, 4, pp 303–13.

drives and affects'), a feature of 'civilisation', achieved through adult inducement, displeasure and punishment of children in pursuit of 'the constant restraint and foresight' that they are said to need for adult life.[106] But as we yearn to persuade Nature to our own narcissistic Lacanian 'mirror image' so, also, our relationship to children can be similarly regarded.[107] We desire them, and yet we are reluctant to see them for who they wish to be (as with Nature, for what it is).

The effect of the parenting industry on parent–child relations

A long time ago Bob Dylan warned that the times were 'a changin'', and that those standing in the way should step aside if they could not 'lend a hand'. He was right – up to a point. We are sometimes caught in historical pincer movements of one sort or another. But whether or not we choose to lend a hand is always a matter of *choice*, the nature of which depends upon our moral sagacity. In reflecting on parenting in the New Labour era and beyond, it might be useful to begin by looking back to the mood in which behaviourism was being popularised in the early 1980s, and remind ourselves that by then post-war optimism had long seeped away before neoliberal tenets of rational management, accountability and efficiency, and the promise that in tackling personal problems, 'something can be done'. It is a foreboding thought: in times of gloom and angst, when the 'skeleton is at the feast', people (including parents) are harder hearted, more instrumental, and ultimately pessimistic in outlook. In such a climate, it is easy *not* to see that from the child's standpoint, parent–child relations are always 'intimate…unchosen…and…between unequals', making them difficult for children to negotiate.[108] In the shift from being a mother or father who rears children to becoming 'a parent' who does 'parenting', the parent–child relationship has been covertly redesigned. It has become a kind of postmodern querying of the 'traditional' family, the implication being that 'bringing up children is, in principle, a task or a job conceptually distinct from biological relationships between adults and children, and is something that any gender or sexuality,

---

[106] S. Mennell and J. Goudsblom (eds) (1998) *Norbert Elias on Civilization, Power and Knowledge*, Chicago, IL: Chicago University Press, p 59.

[107] J. Mason (2009) *An Unnatural Order: The Roots of our Destruction of Nature*, New York: Lantern.

[108] Ramaekers and Suissa (2011), p 115.

in any kind of relationship, can do'; it has become little more than a versatile functional relationship.[109]

What began in the 1960s as a feminist campaign to de-legitimise 'traditional' mothering (and all the psychic and cultural valuables in attendance) in favour of gender equality was easily absorbed by neoliberal governments from the 1980s onward as they strove to advance low-wage labour market flexibility and submit social-democratic welfare rights to the conditionality of behavioural economics.[110] The feminist critique of women as full-time mothers, led to campaigns for greater provision of so-called 'high quality' nursery care, and provided governments with the excuse to despatch increasing numbers of young children to a patchwork of public and commercial childcare facilities (in large part staffed by many of the very same mothers who previously had been caring for their own children at home, and who now worked for minimum wages). The government's intention, and that of feminists, was to separate pregnancy, the birth process, breast feeding, and 'bonding' (universal features of motherhood) from child-rearing practice, thereby making mothers 'free' to contribute to the growth of dual-income households, while ignoring how this influences the restructuring (and destabilising) of the family as a social institution. These parties (aside from some conservative defenders of traditional family-values), each seeking their own version of the 'transformation of intimacy', have been pleased with subsequent economic, social and cultural developments as the 'new family forms' accorded with their overlapping economic, social and political objectives. The social-democratic family was seen by neoliberal governments and the feminist/gay–lesbian alliance as a block on the pluralities of individualisation deemed necessary for the 'post-welfare' advanced capitalist economy, and for 'recognition' politics. The free-ranging individual, with limited commitments, ostensibly freely chosen, was the desired end. But since Thatcherism, government also has had a primary interest in cultivating a civic ethic – largely focused around the idea of personal responsibilisation – through encouraging the revival of agency, not least because it wished to hasten if not the 'death of the social', then a substantial reshaping of it. Feminism, and sections of the Left, however, became uneasy with aspects of this

---

[109] Ramaekers and Suissa (2011), pp 127–8.

[110] N. Gilbert (2008) *A Mother's Work: How Feminism, the Market, and Policy Shape Family Life*, London: Yale University Press; Taylor-Gooby (2004); G. Standing (2011) 'Behavioural Conditionality: Why the Nudges Must be Stopped – an Opinion Piece', *Journal of Poverty and Social Justice*, 19, 1, pp 27–38; Harrison and Sanders (eds) (2014).

project. The attraction of New Labour and subsequent governments to behaviourally-focused neuroscientific-based infant determinism, coupled with a dedicated policy objective of early-years intervention, in making families, particularly mothers, more subject to surveillance, has proved to be particularly contentious, as have policies designed to turn all single parents into paid employees.[111] This tells us that the market of desire is full of contradiction.

The emphasis on behaviour control in parent education, as one of (if not *the*) cardinal feature of conditional child rearing, reflects far more than simply a facet of behavioural psychology: it expresses a politically ominous and defeatist conclusion that certainty – and the protection of the self it is assumed to bring in an age of precariousness – can only be found through the application of contractual managerialism, be it in the home, the classroom, the nursery or the detention centre. Albert Bandura, one of the forerunners of the 'giving away' of psychology, in buttoning down his imagination, dismissed civil libertarian concerns regarding the controlling impulse innate in the new behaviourism: 'All behaviour is inevitably controlled, and the operation of psychological laws cannot be suspended by romantic conceptions of human behaviour, any more than indignant rejection of the law of gravity as anti-humanistic can stop people from falling.'[112] So it was that Diana Baumrind came to the rescue of her liberal colleagues, many of whom were being attacked by the Right for allegedly encouraging radicalism through their supposed attachment to anti-authoritarianism, and by feminists for contributing to the 'imprisonment' of mothers in child-centred domesticity. Baumrind's invention of a Third Way parenting style allowed her to make its centre-piece just what the Right had claimed was lacking in American liberalism, namely the discipline of 'firm control'. Feminists also liked Baumrind because the style promised less work for mothers; it was a counter to 'intensive mothering' – being 'intensive' about one's life, one's work, one's hobby, one's diet was ok, but not one's children.[113]

This chapter has argued that what is central to parent education with its emphasis on control (and the authoritative style) are notions

---

[111] Hartas (2014); V. Gillies (2007) *Marginalised Mothers: Exploring Working-Class Experiences of Parenting*, Abingdon: Routledge; Churchill (2011); Harrison and Sanders (2014).

[112] Quoted in B. Sheldon (1982) *Behaviour Modification*, London: Routledge, p 224.

[113] S. Hays (1996) *The Cultural Contradictions of Motherhood*, London: Yale University Press.

of conditionality (in effect contractualism).[114] What is omitted in the promotion of this ideal, is any consideration of the connection between 'control' as technique and 'conditional' as a moral choice.[115] Why this is so, is easily explained. While 'authoritative', when positioned between authoritarian and permissive, looks intuitively reasonable, it is also egotistically appealing in saying that as a parent you can have it both ways: you can be in charge, but also assume the mantle of a democrat. Within this reasonableness, however, is concealed the conditional: I give you something and you do something for me. Of course, the public rhetoric of child rearing disavows the idea of the contract, since the 'love' of parents for their children is supposed to be unlimited. As a sentimental abstraction, this may be true. But as practice, as action-oriented parental behaviour, as recommended by the 'tough love' parenting gurus, this is not the case. No matter how much behaviourists may try to conceal it, the principle of conditionality is always undermining of its opposite. In Alfie Kohn's words, it presupposes 'an awfully sour view of children – and, by extension, of human nature'.[116] This is evident if we remind ourselves of Baumrind's dogma: 'the rule of reciprocity, of paying for value received, is a law of life that applies to us all... The parent who expresses love unconditionally is encouraging the child to be selfish and demanding.' This is a classic theme of both behaviourism and neoliberalism: nothing is for nothing – 'no rights without responsibilities'. In such a world, self-sacrifice is a lonely orphan.

The truth seems to be that in a narcissistic culture, in which to criticise the concept of punishment is described as 'utopian', the principle of conditionality is popular because it lends itself to the mystique of the taught technique as it presumes a definable set of 'conditions' that can be learned by parents and children in their respective contexts as skills used to induce required patterns of behaviour, and in so doing confirms a sense of security. This kind of child rearing is essentially an economic view of consanguinity that obliges us to be cautious in our relationships

---

[114] For just a few examples of 'control' in 'authoritative' style literature, in addition to the numerous books of Frost, Ford and Byron, see C. Green (2006) *The New Toddler Taming*, London: Vermillion; N. Joffe and J. Roberts (2011) *The Mumsnet Rules*, London: Bloomsbury; H. Murkoff (2012) *What to Expect: The Second Year*, London: Simon & Schuster; and Sigman (2009).

[115] Authoritative parenting has also been criticised for lacking parental flexibility and the 'tolerance' that would give it the ability to be situationally flexible within context, Greenspan (2006), pp 5–12.

[116] Kohn (2005a), pp 12–19.

in order to shield ourselves against the risk of 'anarchic' children who by their nature seem to make the human-affairs marketplace even more parlous than it already is. In its inherent narcissism (the weary, brittle psyche), such mothering and fathering repudiates the 'parental love' that, as we have seen the philosopher Laurence Thomas claim, in generating in the child a sense of *'cherished uniqueness'* surpasses even 'morality' as the 'first among intrinsic goods'.[117] And, therefore, it rejects the social-democratic ideal, preferring instead to embrace the mock certainty of what Nikolas Rose famously described as 'governing the soul'. Our children, however, are left unconsoled.

---

[117] L. Thomas (2006) *The Family and the Political Self*, New York: Cambridge University Press, pp 19–20. Emphasis original. For earlier reference, see p 15, n 46.

PART FIVE

Therapeutic reflections

What shall we do now and how shall we live? (Tolstoy)[1]

Introduction

In this book I have argued that the manner of child rearing that developed from c. 1920s until c. 1970s, especially under the influence of post-1945 social democracy, was very different from that which followed during what is often called late modernity. Whereas the first period had as its ideal a psychoanalytically informed parental desire to help and understand children, and to treat them with tolerance and empathy, in the latter years, through the tutelage of neoliberalism, new social movements, notably second-wave feminism, striving for identity and recognition, and the psychology of the new behaviourism, we have witnessed the emergence of parental narcissism – impatient, anxious, managerial, controlling, disciplinary – as an expression of the minimal self. To an extent, this may be something of a caricature. But it is not, I think, untrue. Our world is profoundly troubled in all sorts of ways, and whether we like it or not, we are all involved. Probably the majority of us would like it to be different, and bookshops are filled with well-intentioned analyses suggesting how to escape the mire. Where parent–child relations are concerned, as a first step, I suggest that we need to recognise the extent to which children suffer from childism, and be clear about how we got to be where we are. This book has attempted to do that: to show how and why we have reached the present position characterised as it is by the narcissistic impulse. While it has not been possible to consider *all* the reasons that explain the omnipresence of egotistical mean-spiritedness, I conclude with an overview of some thoughts about what has been a major historical feature of our contemporary malaise, namely the well documented interest in, some would say obsession with, the Self – not only to the detriment of others, but also to that of our potential to fulfil our better natures. While the Victorians, under the sway of the momentous changes wrought by the industrial revolution, urbanisation,

---

[1]   L. Tolstoy (1886, 1935) *What is to be Done*, Oxford: OUP.

class conflict, and the rupture between science and religion, struggled to reconcile the self to the social (if not to God), our secularised predicament is that having abandoned the social, seemingly we have nowhere to go. We are adrift.

The themes connecting individualisation and therapeutics, as they impinge themselves on the intimacies of our personal relationships, are so central to our modern preoccupations that it is impossible to understand how parenting came to be narcissistic, and what that involves, and with what malign consequences, without appreciating the significance (cultural, social and political) of these dynamic influences on current (adult) subjectivities. Unfortunately, those who cast doubt on the wisdom of the direction of social change are often dismissed out of hand by postmodernists and other disciples of social liberation, as 'elitist and anachronistic' or as being uncritically supportive of 'the sociological triptych of patriarchal pessimists' whose work is said to exude 'implicit nostalgia for a lost era of secure male employment... and for a time of stable families and communities'.[2] However, the debates surrounding the politics of the self, not least the disputed relations between it and narcissism, indicate both the intensity of the emotions aroused by these topics and their continuing relevance to social thought in the abstract and to the daily comings and goings of our lives. In this respect, I argue that post 1970s parenting has been shaped by narcissism and its ideologically derived affiliates. My comments are intended to illuminate the reciprocity between this narcissism and our current absorptions, and its impact on parent–child relations. I identify the consequences for children and parents, and implicitly speculate on the promise of a future steered by a socialist politics that consciously chooses 'moral clarity' and is guided by the belief that human beings have within them something more than just a therapeutic pocket-book.[3]

Before proceeding to the relationship between the narcissistic personality (individual and collective) on the one hand and, on the other, 'reflexive individualisation' (not as 'reflection', but as 'self-confrontation with the effects of risk') and 'therapy', it is worth noting

---

[2] A. Elliott and C. Lemert (2009) *The New Individualism: The Emotional Costs of Globalization*, London: Routledge, p 65; S. Roseneil (2007) 'Sutured Selves, Queer Connections: Personal Lives at the Cutting Edge of Individualization', in C. Howard (ed) *Contested Individualization: Debates about Contemporary Personhood*, Basingstoke: Palgrave Macmillan, p 128. The triptych refers to Z. Bauman, L. D. Putman and R. Sennett.

[3] S. Neiman (2009) *Moral Clarity: A Guide for Grown-Up Idealists*, London: Bodley Head, p 105.

as a point of historical concreteness Hobsbawm's apt summation of what occurred following the collapse of the Golden Age (1945–70s), the environment in which parental narcissism first began to slip into culture:

> The old moral vocabulary of rights and duties, mutual obligations, sin and virtue, sacrifice, conscience, rewards and penalties, could no longer be translated into the new language of desired gratification. Once such practices and institutions were no longer accepted as part of a way of ordering society that linked people to each other and ensured social cooperation and reproduction, most of their capacity to structure human social life vanished. They were simply reduced to expressions of individuals' preferences, and claims that the law should recognize the supremacy of these preferences. Uncertainty and unpredictability impended. Compass needles no longer had a North, maps became useless…It found ideological expression in a variety of theories, from extreme free-market liberalism to 'postmodernism' and its like, *which tried to sidestep the problem of judgment and values altogether, or rather to reduce them to the single denominator of the unrestricted freedom of the individual.*[4]

It is true that until the 1960s, this 'moral vocabulary' had its own gender, sexuality, ethnic and age exclusions, which created much unhappiness and injustice, and was by no means always democratic. Nonetheless, Hobsbawm's tone and what it hints at, provides a helpful guide, not only to the decline of social-democracy, but also the accompanying deterioration of the socialist Left as a force of resistance to the dissipation of select Enlightenment values, including happiness, reason, reverence and hope (however muddled and contradictory the articulation of some of these undoubtedly were).[5]

---

4   E. Hobsbawm (1994) *Age of Extremes: The Short Twentieth Century 1914–1991*, London: Michael Joseph, pp 338–9. Emphasis added.

5   Neiman (2009), part 2.

NINE

Narcissism and the 'politics of recognition': concepts of the late-modern self

I take my desires for reality, for I believe in the reality of my desires. (May 1968 graffiti)

A late-modern point of departure: the 'postsocialist' condition and the politics of redistribution/recognition

The work of the eminent feminist political philosopher Nancy Fraser regarding the 'postsocialist' condition and the politics of 'redistribution or recognition' is fairly well known, referring as it does to social and economic equality as a political goal and to claims for group differences, the rise of identity politics, and the decentring of class. Fraser worries that a revision has occurred in the way 'in which justice is imagined... away from a socialist political imaginary, in which the central problem is redistribution' to a position 'where the central problem of justice is recognition'. The political imaginary is no longer that of 'classes' seeking to defend their 'interests', end 'exploitation', and win 'redistribution'. Instead, 'there are culturally defined "groups" or "communities of value" who are struggling to defend their "identities", end "cultural domination", and win "recognition"'. She reminds us of the critically important reality in which this shift has happened, namely 'a resurgent economic liberalism' that has become even more omnipresent since the 1980s.[6] Redistribution was a term central in the political discourse of post-1945 'egalitarian liberalism', as it strove to provide economic, social and political security for a social democracy. Issues relating to 'questions of difference', however, were sidelined, which was a mistake.

---

[6] N. Fraser (1997) *Justice Interruptus: Critical Reflections on the 'Postsocialist' Condition*, New York: Routledge, pp 2–3; and N. Fraser and A. Honneth (2003) *Redistribution or Recognition? A Politico-philosophical Exchange*, London: Verso. See also K. Olson (ed) (2008) *Adding Insult to Injury: Nancy Fraser Debates her Critics*, London: Verso Books, and L. McNay (2008) *Against Recognition*, Cambridge: Cambridge University Press, pp 126–61.

In their political–philosophical exchange, Fraser and Axel Honneth (a German philosopher who champions 'recognition' politics), agree that 'Today the relation cries out for interrogation' as 'struggles over religion, nationality, and gender are now inter-imbricated in ways that make the question of recognition impossible to ignore'[7] At the same time, however, economic inequalities are growing under the impact of neoliberal forces promoting corporate globalisation and weakening the structures that previously enabled some degree of country-wide redistribution. Fraser and Honneth also agree that any valuable concept of justice must encompass both redistribution and recognition and that the latter cannot be seen as 'a mere epiphenomenon' of the former. Fraser proposes a 'two-dimensional' conception of justice that encompasses both objectives without reducing either one to the other, while also arguing for a distinction between the economic and the cultural. This seems to be a fruitful approach given that under contemporary neoliberalism, the market (along with corporations) has become increasingly autonomous from government control. But it does not entirely overcome the tension that arises where contests over identity occur 'in the context of an economic order that stresses the building of lifestyle and identity but in which the building blocks are less and less substantial' (and, one might add, unequally distributed among age groups).[8] Although Honneth acknowledges that an adequate understanding of justice should encompass redistribution *and* recognition, he nevertheless proposes a 'normative monism' of recognition, maintaining that the latter must be 'the fundamental, overarching moral category, while treating distribution as a derivative'. For Honneth, then, socialism's 'ideal of redistribution' is merely 'a sub-variety of the struggle for recognition'.[9]

But 'recognition' is not a homogeneous category. Charles Taylor, the Canadian philosopher, whose work in some respects pioneered the debate, distinguishes between two forms of recognition, each occupying a different sphere: a public, which has become increasingly influential, and an 'intimate' where we witness 'the formation of identity and the self taking place in a continuing dialogue and struggle with significant others'.[10] In Taylor's Hegelian influenced view, human identity is constituted through dialogue, what he calls

---

[7]   Fraser and Honneth (2003); for a guide to the debate, S. Thompson (2006) *Political Theory of Recognition: A Critical Introduction*, Cambridge: Polity.

[8]   J. Young (2007) *The Vertigo of Late Modernity*, London: Sage, p 69.

[9]   Fraser and Honneth (2003), pp 2–3.

[10]   C. Taylor (1995) *Philosophical Arguments*, London: Harvard University Press, p 232.

the 'dialogical character'. In other words, I cannot become my own identity without recognition – 'dialogue' – of others who help to shape and nourish my understanding of who I am. These relations are both overt and internal, and the 'others' are always 'significant': 'My own identity crucially depends on my dialogical relations with others.'[11] For Taylor, identity and recognition are inseparable from each other and, therefore, either misrecogniton or non-recognition 'can inflict harm, can be a form of oppression, imprisoning someone in a false, distorted, and reduced mode of being', which affects their ability to realise themselves.[12] Thus, the projection of 'an inferior or demeaning image on another can actually distort and oppress, to the extent that the image is internalized'.[13] As might be expected, where the focus is on feminism, the gay/lesbian community, and multiculturalism, as it is in these writings, children are ignored. But children are central figures in the intimate (family) sphere; it is where parent–child relations (the first human relationships, especially those between mother and infant) are most influential and life-forming. After all, it is 'On the intimate level…[that]…we can see how much an original identity needs and is vulnerable to the recognition given or withheld by significant others.'[14] This raises the question: if adult identity is so dialogical and interdependent on 'significant' others for formation and nurturing, what happens to children's identity? Under the reign of narcissism, the value of adult identity – a kind of 'authentic' self – blots out the presence of the children, leaving them as little more than insubstantial shadows. The Fraser–Honneth exchange is helpful in contextualising the significance and the consequences of the adult-centric cultural struggle to try to achieve certitude and contentment through both the construction and the recognition of an empowered and reassuring 'self' as, for example, through parent education. This, however, illustrates the exclusion of children from an exchange that rhetorically claims to be focused on a *just* distribution of the value of human worth. The omission of children makes the procedure suspect because they are denied participation in 'the dialogic nature of subjectivity, identity and agency'. The problem with recognition politics, however 'socialist' its sponsors try to make it, is that in its enthusiasm to counter the alleged asocial individualism of liberal thought, there is, as Lois McNay has argued, a relative absence of a 'sociological understanding

---

11 Taylor (1995), p 231.

12 Traylor (1995), p 225.

13 Taylor (1995), p 232.

14 Taylor (1995), p 232.

of power relations'. Where McNay worries about 'the most limited understanding of identity and agency in the context of the reproduction of inequalities of gender', I worry about the reproduction of *unjust* inequalities of age, and the damage they implicitly inflict on a vision of universal humanism.[15]

My view follows that of the philosopher Richard Rorty, who asks whether 'cultural recognition' is a useful concept for leftist politics, and concludes that the idea that cultures have 'positive value' simply 'by virtue of being cultures seems absurd'.[16] Rorty dismisses the idea that we should show 'respect for differences', preferring to emphasise an older leftist position that 'we all share a common humanity' and should fight together to 'overcome prejudice against stigmatised groups' rather than 'grant recognition to the cultures of these groups'. It was only with the coming of second-wave feminism and other new social movements that 'the need to eliminate prejudice' was pushed aside in favour of 'the need for recognition'. Rorty wants to see prejudice and discrimination tackled through enlightening prejudiced people as regards the 'common humanity' (which, we should remember, includes children) they share with the stigmatised, rather than arguing for the differences through 'cultural recognition'. A critical consequence of this transition has been that little was done to ensure better allocation of resources for *all* social groups suffering discrimination and injustice; economic equality got left behind. This book shares Rorty's doubts that 'in order to eliminate prejudice' we need a 'transformative recognition politics of deconstruction'.[17] It also agrees that such a politics prefers 'not to talk about money' since it mistakenly thinks that 'the principal enemy is a mind-set rather than a set of economic arrangements'.[18] This is not to deny the importance of mind-set, but everything in its place.

The self and identity politics

To Be That Self Which One Truly Is. (Carl Rogers)[19]

---

[15] McNay (2008), p 3.

[16] R. Rorty (2000) 'Is "Cultural Recognition" a Useful Concept for Leftist Politics?', *Critical Horizons*, 1, 1, February, pp 7–20.

[17] Rorty (2000), p 16, quoting N. Fraser (1995), 'From Redistribution to Recognition? Dilemmas of Justice in a "Postsocialist Age"', *New Left Review*, 212, p 88.

[18] Rorty (2000), p 18; also Rorty quoted in Z. Bauman (2004) *Identity*, Cambridge: Polity, pp 35–6.

[19] C. Rogers (1961) *On Becoming a Person*, Boston: Houghton Mifflin.

One of the recurring anxieties surrounding the late modern focus on dilemmas of exclusion and inclusion arises in the search for ontological security, free of neoliberal economic uncertainty and sustained by recognition. This has proved to be elusive. Clearly, ontological *insecurity* is intimately bound up with a set of dilemmas relating to self, identity and individualisation which, for parents, involves their conception of parenting in the abstract as much as lived reality. In order to examine these dilemmas further, especially in the light of what modern therapeutics privileges as the 'new individualism', we need to appreciate not only narcissism (as popularly understood and as a psychological condition), but also its erstwhile companion, namely the *imagined* self, and the ways in which it is bolstered. In looking to the practice of selfhood, we can begin linking it to some well defined features of our era: role playing, gender, choice, alienation, risk and, not least, consumption.[20] Throughout much of the social sciences and humanities, selfhood is seen as 'flexible, fractured, fragmented, decentred and brittle', and this and other descriptions of the self can influence the way in which we understand the subjective experience of identity. Central to our notion of who we are (though this is never a stable perception), is how we view our agency, that is the degree of active participation we have in determining our personal experience through being free to draw upon a variety of resources. This 'self-constitution' is not entirely in our hands, since it 'happens to us, through the design of other people, the impact of cultural conventions and social practices, and the force of social processes and political institutions'. It is, then, uncertain as to whether social forces or individuals themselves are foremost in the manner in which the self is constituted. In the parenting environment, however, the neoliberal emphasis is on self-interpretation as the means of 'knowing':

> We are selves only in that certain issues matter for us. What I am as a self, my identity, is essentially defined by the way things have significance for me, and the issue of my identity is worked out, only through a language of interpretation which I have come to accept as a valid articulation of these issues.[21]

It has been the making of the (neoliberal) 'language of interpretation' that has been so effective in stultifying the public good generally,

---

[20] A. Elliott (2001) *Concepts of the Self*, Cambridge: Polity, pp 1–17.

[21] Taylor, cited in Elliott (2001), pp 4–5.

notably in frustrating the nurturing good that exemplifies the bond between parents and their children.

No new social movement in Britain has been more effective in claiming 'recognition' than feminism, if only through its tactical slogan, 'the personal is political', which helped it to become influential in debates and political actions surrounding 'personal experimentation, self-transformation, lifestyle and identity politics'– modes of operation, as it were, that have become popularly reflexive in how we conceive and do our daily lives.[22] Women's liberation, says Eli Zarnetsky, was the 'successor to psychoanalysis as a theory and practice of personal life'.[23] In developing its initial authority, feminism, together with other social liberationist ideologies, through 'advocacy research' from within universities, successfully evolved into a self-perpetuating creative system of (cultural) knowledge, eulogising concepts of diversity, recognition and introspection.[24] Inspired by the cult of authenticity, these continue to have a privileged role in therapeutic culture – what the cultural sociologist Eva Illouz refers to as 'the glamour of misery' and 'suffering and self-help as global forms of identity'.[25] In working in this manner, feminism has been assisted by the rhetoric of a postmodern relativistic notion of social liberation that in privileging difference assails universal categories – 'mothering', for example, becomes merely a 'social construction' – and focuses instead on 'the creation of the self, the articulation of cultural style, and the production of fluid alliances for specific political interventions in concrete social processes'.[26] The new concepts of the self and identity, as attached to social liberationist movements, are presented as reflecting 'not a turning away from public life', but as expressing a 'genuine global reach in inspiring progressive and transformative politics', leading to the 'retracing the constitution

---

[22] Elliott (2001), pp 12–15.

[23] E. Zaretsky (2005) *Secrets of the Soul: A Social and Cultural History of Psychoanalysis*, New York: Vintage Books, p 329.

[24] Rorty (2000), pp 11–12 on cultural studies and knowledge. For 'advocacy research', see main 'Introduction', note 5.

[25] C. Taylor (1994) *The Ethics of Authenticity*, London: Harvard University Press, pp 25–74; E. Illouz (2003) *Oprah Winfrey and the Glamour of Misery: An Essay on Popular Culture*, New York: Columbia University Press; (2008) *Saving the Modern Soul: Therapy, Emotions, and the Culture of Self-Help*, Berkeley, CA: University of California Press.

[26] Elliott (2001), p 14.

of the self, selfhood, and individual subjectivity'.[27] But even if this portrayal was accurate (and it is not), the danger remains that children are left isolated in the squelch of adult authenticity.

Individualisation, identity and the self: 'a fate, not a choice'

> To be modern is to find ourselves in an environment that promises us adventure, power, joy, growth, transformation of ourselves and our world – and at the same time threatens to destroy everything we have, everything we know, everything we are.[28]

There is one consideration of individualisation that is of special interest to parental narcissism: the shaping of it as a social process by the neoliberal schema, and the extent subsequently to which individuals are being liberated to become free agents. The idea of personal freedom is naturally an alluring enticement. Ideally, our enthusiasm needs to be restrained, for, as with the silence of children regarding their recognition and identity, so here, too. As the consequences of divorce, single motherhood, cohabitation, gay/lesbian parenthood and reproductive technologies all make clear, children are vulnerable to the foibles of other people's freedom, whether malign or benign. They are caught up in the repercussions of what is perhaps the most vexed feature of late modernity, as elaborated by Elizabeth Beck-Gernseim who, as mentioned in the Introduction to this book, speaks of 'individualization' as 'a two-fold tendency':

> On the one hand, the traditional social relationships, bonds and belief systems that used to determine people's lives in the narrowest detail have been losing more and more of their meaning...Now men and women can and should, may and must, decide for themselves how to shape their lives – within certain limits at least...On the other hand... people are linked into the institutions of the labour market and welfare state, educational system, legal system, state

---

27 Elliott (2001), pp 15–16, 135; also C. Lemert (1997) *Postmodernism is not what you think*, Oxford: Blackwell, p 128; J. Lewis (2002) *The End of Marriage? Individualism and Intimate Relations*, Cheltenham: Edward Elgar.

28 M. Berman (1983) *All That is Solid Melts into Air: The Experience of Modernity*, London: Penguin Books.

bureaucracy, and so on...These institutions produce various
regulations – demands, instructions, entitlement – that are
typically addressed to individuals rather than the family as
a whole. And the crucial feature of these new regulations
is that they enjoin the individual to lead a life of his or her
own beyond any ties to the family or other groups – or
sometimes to shake off such ties and to act without referring
to them.[29]

No wonder Bauman says that 'individualization', in which relationships
are 'a mixed blessing', is 'a fate, not a choice'.[30] The individualisation
thesis, so important in studies of family, intimacy and identity, has
proved to be contentious, in part because it points to a fairly radical
transformation in relationships, including the claim that it may
democratise family life and the accompanying ethical choices, and
also because it relates to postmodernism's clichés: social and personal
ambivalence, fragmentation and diversity.[31] Selfhood, however,
preoccupies our contemporary experience because it goes a long way
toward defining us as *individuals*. Moreover, through the historical
acceleration of instability and incoherence, nowadays individuals,
in order to adapt to changing personal, social and institutional
circumstances, reflexively build and modify their biographies.[32] But the
place of children in this paradigm is ignored; they are forever tagging
along behind us.

According to Bauman, contemporary culture entails two sets of
strategies – involving oppositions – in the making of identity: *modern*
and *postmodern*.[33] In the former the emphasis was on mastering the self
through control and rationality, with too much of the latter ignoring the

---

[29] E. Beck-Gernsheim (2002) *Reinventing the Family: In Search of New Lifestyle*, Cambridge:
      Polity, p ix.

[30] Z. Bauman, *Liquid Love. On the Fraility of Human Bonds*, Cambridge: Polity, p vii, and his
      Foreword, in U. Beck and E. Beck-Gernsheim (2002) *Individualization*, London: Sage, p xvi.

[31] Z. Bauman (2001) *The Individualized Society*, Cambridge: Polity; also R. Fevre (2000) *The
      Demoralization of Western Culture: Social Theory and the Dilemmas of Modern Living*,
      London: Continuum; J. Brodie (2007) 'The New Social "isms": Individualization and Social
      Policy Reform in Canada', in Howard (ed), pp 153–70.

[32] Howard (2007) 'Three Models of Individualized Biography', in Howard (ed) (2007), pp
      25–6.

[33] Z. Bauman (1990) *Modernity and Ammbivalence*; Z. Bauman (1993) *Postmodern Ethics*,
      Oxford: Blackwell; Z. Bauman (1995) *Life in Fragments*; see also Elliott (2001), pp 144–7.

importance of 'sentiment'.[34] The self was a carefully designed project, emphasising stability, reliability, consistency and predictability. In their desire for the perfect self, men and women believed 'that things can always be better, that identities can be more solid and ordered, that life can function more smoothly'.[35] Unfortunately, however, the search for control is illusory, and with disappointment – for example, in the post-1945 settlement – came anger and frustration and suspicion and withdrawal. In late modernity, on the other hand, everything is fluid, not fixed; long-term commitment is avoided; things are unmoored:

> To keep the game short means to beware long-term commitments...Not to get tied to one place...Not to wed one's life to one vocation only. Not to swear consistency and loyalty to anything or anybody ... to take care that the consequences of the game do not outlive the game itself, and to renounce responsibility for such consequences as do.[36]

So we become creatures of ambivalence as 'I' come and go – transient and superficial, available for purchase at any one of a number of personality kiosks. We are, however, also moral in the sense that individualisation makes us choose. Our ethical codes become wedged between the modern and the postmodern, forever struggling to find peace of mind, in part through the public display of therapeutics; and usually with children in tow.

The 'modern' world tried to erase all ambivalence through legislating for morality but, when confronted with momentous social change, it ultimately lost the struggle to resolve the dialectic of freedom and control. Consequently, we now feel compelled to face not only all the uncertainties, but also the probabilities, leaving us to fashion some sort of reconcilability between the two. In as much as modern times have fragmented the certainty of the 'old' morality, we are all relative beings, forever engaged in permanent (de) construction. Yet there is also that part of us that yearns for the 'solid' days of yesteryear - as if precarity never existed until now. Thus, in the postmodern marketplace, we feverishly purchase expert opinion on how we (the 'reflexive' 'I') should prevail. Bauman refers to this as the privatisation of the self. Once this process is under way:

---

[34] Fevre (2000).

[35] Elliott (2001), p 145; P. Heelas (1996) *The New Age Movement*, Oxford: Blackwell.

[36] Z. Bauman (1997) *Postmodernity and its Discontents*, Cambridge: Polity, p 89.

moral reasoning and evaluation becomes little more than responding to the task at hand, with technical forms of rationality dominant; we attempt to clear the mess of yesterday's action, but only in order to get on with tomorrow. And we act without giving ourselves enough time to think of the long-term effect of our doings – upon the self, other people, or society at large.[37]

But there is no going back to the 'modern'. Individualisation, constantly changing its form, has transformed identity from a given into a task one cannot refuse.[38] This individualisation is the abstract system in which neoliberalism is concealed as it works to fetishise both the idea of (enforced) choice *and* personal responsibility as virtue:

> If (individuals) fall ill, it is because they were not resolute or industrious enough in following a health regime. If they stay unemployed, it is because they failed to learn the skills of winning an interview or because they did not try hard enough to find a job. If they…agonize about their future, it is because they are not good enough at winning friends and influencing people…This is…what they are told and what they have come to believe.[39]

In arriving at this view, and living with 'the danger of personal disintegration', which is a result of modern–postmodern tensions and contradictions, people come to possess a 'minimal' self, pummelled by narcissism as they can no longer distinguish between self (often confused with 'personality) and 'non-self"; consequently, they seek refuge in fragile egoism, clumsy selfishness and the illusionary (and always temporary) banishment of insecurity.[40]

As to the environment in which parental narcissism has emerged and grown, however much 'life politics' may have opened up opportunities for certain groups, it is by no means as universal as Giddens (and the Becks) suggest, if only because too much emphasis is put upon human agency and too little on the interplay between agency and the constraints imposed by social structure. To suggest that the 'destiny of

---

[37]   Elliott (2001), p146, summarising Bauman.

[38]   Bauman, Foreword, Beck and Beck-Gernsheim (2002), pp xiv–xvi.

[39]   Bauman, Foreword, Beck and Beck-Gernsheim (2002), pxvi.

[40]   C. Lasch (1984) *The Minimal Self: Psychic Survival in Troubled Times*, New York: Norton, p 16.

individuals' is 'in their own hands' merely evades the graphic complexity of all that lies behind the glibness of defining 'identity' as forming a 'trajectory'.[41] Social structural constraints have particular relevance for children, since they are so beholden to their own developing capabilities regarding their claim to distributive justice.[42] Giddens admits that parent–child relations are 'something of a special case, because of the radical imbalance of power involved, and because of their centrality for socialisation processes'. It is only as the child moves towards 'adulthood and autonomy' that 'more elements of the pure relationship tend to come into play'. He also recognises that children require 'moral courage' under the impact of divorce as they 'often suffer profoundly from the dissolution of the family household.[43] Consequently, younger children in particular are excluded from pure relationships and the opportunity for reflexivity with the inevitable consequence that their interest becomes subservient to those of their individualised parents. This helps to explain the absence of any discussion of children in the individualisation literature, either as subjects with their own moral claims separate from those of their parents, or as citizens. Children are treated as little more than closet figures: passive objects of parental 'love' – an 'anchor for one's life'.[44] Under such conditions, there can be little or no 'democracy of the emotions' where children are involved. Contrary to the claims surrounding individualisation as democratic, the reality is that 'life politics' (and the popular therapeutic 'self help' culture it promotes) has contributed to a state of collective precariousness in which 'moral blindness' is widely experienced.[45] Moreover, in contrast to the uncertainties inherent in composing a mature self that can cope with frustration while recognising the obligation to engage in relational virtue, the promise of this politics turns out to be false.

Given the stresses and strains inherent in parenting, and taking into account the use of children as human capital, emotional investments

---

[41]   Quoted in Howard (ed) (2007), p 30.

[42]   J. Qvortrup (2009) 'Childhood as a Structural Form', in J. Qvortrup, W. A. Corsaro and M.-S. Honig (eds) *The Palgrave Handbook of Childhood Studies*, Basingstoke: Palgrave Macmillan, pp 21–33; also D. Oldman (1994) 'Childhood as a Mode of Production', in B. Mayall (ed) *Children's Childhoods: Observed and Experienced*, London: Falmer Press, pp 153–66.

[43]   A: Giddens (1991) *Modernity and Self-Modernity: Self and Society in the Late Modern Age*, Cambridge: Polity, pp 48, 11.

[44]   U. Beck and E. Beck-Gernsheim (1995) *The Normal Chaos of Love*, Cambridge: Polity, p 73.

[45]   Z. Bauman and L. Donskis (2013) *Moral Blindness: The Loss of Sensitivity in Liquid Modernity*, Cambridge: Polity.

for shoring up the parental self, Beck and Beck-Gernsheim's apprehension in respect of individualisation and particularly 'the nature of love', catches a critical feature of parental narcissism, since with the 'crumbling away' of the old industrial society:

> [A] modern form of anarchy is breaking out, with love on its banner, and a thousand delights and obstacles in its path. It is this quest for personal freedom and satisfaction here and now, which can so quickly revert into hatred, desperation and loneliness, that is leaving its mark on the divorce and remarriage figures, on overlapping and serial families, as millions of people go in search of happiness.[46]

Accordingly, Giddens' claim that in late modernity individuals have the opportunity to put together a personalised character as they work through their own 'elective' biography with the assistance of 'experts', needs to be critically evaluated on behalf of children. Similarly with the view that our era has seen a transformation in the nature of 'intimacy' towards what are sometimes referred to as 'negotiated relationships', unlike those of the past in 'simple modernity'.[47] In bringing new freedoms, individualisation also brings destabilising factors. The world is a 'runaway world' and as a result people feel 'bereft and alone', lacking psychological supports and a sense of security provided by the more traditional settings. Our contemporary struggle to reconcile the unsocialised 'I' with the socialised 'Me' (itself a rarity these days) is overwhelmed by a frenzied neoliberal narcissism, such that we cannot cope with the rapidity, the variety and the globalised nature of inputs that constitute being a modern person. In practice, this has meant a radical revision of the experience of responsibility for the 'Other'. All too often the postmodern approach to morality is 'the celebration of the "demise of the ethical"', as:

> Ethics itself is denigrated…as one of the typically modern constraints now broken and destined for the dustbin of history…In our times the idea of self-sacrifice has been delegitimized; people are not goaded or willing to stretch themselves to attain moral ideals and guard moral values;

---

[46] Beck and Beck-Gernsheim (1995), p 170.

[47] L. Jamieson (1998) *Intimacy: Personal Relationships in Modern Societies*, Cambridge: Polity; (1999) 'Intimacy Transformed? A Critical Look at the "Pure Relationship"', *Sociology*, 33, 3, pp 477–94.

politicians have put paid to utopias; and yesterday's idealists
have become pragmatic.[48]

But we can't blame politicians entirely; we must share the responsibility.
Too often the tendency is to shrug off personal moral culpability,
claiming that we are all victims of either a smothering amoral miasma,
or one defined by unsettling ambivalence. Ambivalent we may be, but
the onus is on us to work it out and bear the consequences.[49] Giddens
wisely observes that in order to be ontologically secure, we have to
answer a number of 'existential questions', one of which concerns
'the existence of other persons', in which respect, 'Intersubjectivity
does not derive from subjectivity, but the other way around.'[50] The
unavoidable truth, a very *human* truth, is that:

> Intersubjective relation is a non-symmetrical relation. In this
> sense, I am responsible for the Other without waiting for
> reciprocity, were I to die for it. Reciprocity is *his* affair...I
> am responsible for a total responsibility, which answers
> for all the others and for all in the others, even for their
> responsibility. The I always has one responsibility *more* than
> all the others.[51]

The 'Other' (the child), then, *is* unavoidable.

The therapeutic culture

> The calm existence that is mine when I
>   Am worthy of myself. (Wordsworth, *The Prelude*)

or:

> Don't knock masturbation, it's sex with someone I love.
> (Woody Allen)

However much the origins of the therapeutic may lie in either the
mid-nineteenth century or the inter-war period, it is only relatively
recently, since c. 1960s, that society's lust for this cultural goody has

---

[48] Z. Bauman (1993), p 2.

[49] Bauman (1993), pp 10–15.

[50] Giddens (1991), pp 47–52.

[51] Bauman (1993), p 85, quoting Emmanuel Levinas. Emphasis original.

become so much part of the fabric of ideologies of individualism, choice, self-awareness, emotional well-being and style. The exponential rise of the therapeutic has made it difficult to study since it is both 'omnipresent and ephemeral', expressing itself in a multiplicity of ways and circumstances, while encompassing the spectrum of discourses, social practices and cultural artefacts that characterise our lives.[52] The therapy ambience includes the voluminous self-help literature and related personal attendance courses, lifestyle journalism, confessional and transformative reality TV, human-resource management practices, counselling for relationships, trauma and victimhood, and varieties of personal psychotherapy, much of which is 'quick-fix' and rooted in CBT. For parents, as we have seen, there are the ever popular behaviourist-oriented parenting courses, offered by a multitude of providers, each one claiming to facilitate the 'happy family' life through maternal 'empowerment', skill acquisition and child training schedules. In addition, there are countless childcare websites and chat rooms, supplemented by acres of mainly feminist journalism, all of which in emoting the maternal perspective, leave children's voices unheard.

Unsurprisingly, the scale of therapeutics has given rise to many controversial debates, polarised between those who regard therapy as regressive, narcissistic, inimical to political change and encouraging privatism, and those who see it as providing innovative opportunities for 'life politics' and hitherto marginalised groups. Obviously, the range of sociological and cultural interpretations to date and the multiple varieties of therapy and their meanings, make the task of sociologically capturing it as culture extraordinarily complex, if not elusive. To penetrate the therapeutic, it is necessary to confront the contradictions of our lives, which are 'ever inseparable from consumer capitalism, mass media, bureaucratic rationality, and professional self-interest'.[53] It is a difficult task, but since 'the future is not inevitable', we should make the effort.[54]

Let me start by suggesting that in many respects the contemporary psyche suffers from a form of 'hypocognition' – the absence of an idea with which to understand particular phenomena. Given this lacuna, human beings are bereft of reliable personhood markings and are left to seek salvation of a kind through therapeutics, which we hope will

---

[52] K. Wright (2010) *The Rise of the Therapeutic Society*, Washington, DC: New Academia Publishing, p 1.

[53] Wright (2010), p 5.

[54] D. Garland (2001) *The Culture of Control: Crime and Social Control in Contemporary Society*, Oxford: Oxford University Press, p 201.

provide us with the necessary frame. The concept of the frame comes from the social linguist George Lakoff, who defines framing politically with reference to the failure of US progressives to cope effectively with the arguments of the political Right. Lakoff's basic contention is that the Right has *ideas*, developed in think-tanks inside and outside academia, and promoted systematically through publishing and the predominantly conservative media. The Left, on the other hand, has few ideas. It suffers from 'conceptual gaps' and, therefore finds itself always having to respond with 'facts' to the ideas of the Right, and within *its* linguistic 'frames'.[55] By way of explicating his thesis, Lakoff cites the work of Robert Levy, the anthropologist and psychiatrist, who developed the theme of 'hypocognition' through his research into why there were so many suicides among Tahitians. He discovered that although Tahitians *experienced* grief and *felt* it, they did not see it as a 'normal emotion' and, what is most important, had no concept for it. Being unable to explain grief and seek help, they resorted to suicide. So it is with modern social life where, as reflexivity demands self-confrontation in the face of risk, we are without an *idea*, a reliable, comprehensive, problem-solving frame. In desperately looking to alleviate the disparate woes of our lives, we turn to therapeutics, which holds out the promise of facilitating us to manage our selves and thereby find, if not absolution, then solace.

But what was it about therapeutic culture that helped to undermine the social-democratic ideal in child rearing (and continues to do so in relation to 'unconditional' parenting), turning it into little more than a long-running television/social media spectacle, hosted by personalities espousing varieties of behaviourism? We can get an idea of what was involved through briefly surveying some critiques of the therapeutic – conservative, neo-Marxist, and radical feminist – each distinguished by a disapproval of 'the cultural shift towards interiority', which is seen as counterproductive to meaningful and rewarding social life.[56] The 'moral collapse' interpretation is usually associated with Philip Reiff's culturally conservative *The Triumph of the Therapeutic*, where he equated the therapeutic with 'interiority', whereby with the decline of the older Christian era, the therapeutic gave rise to a society in which to be 'self improved, is the ultimate concern of modern culture'.[57]

---

[55] G. Lakoff (2004) *Moral Politics*, Chicago, IL: University of Chicago Press, p 24.

[56] Wright (2010), pp 3, 14. All, however, have been age-blind in their analyses. The following paragraphs are adapted from Wright (2010), pp 13–48.

[57] P. Rieff (1966) *The Triumph of the Therapeutic: Uses of Faith after Freud*, Chicago, IL: University of Chicago Press, p 62.

Following Nietzsche, Durkheim and Freud, and writing in the middle of the 1960s' social and sexual revolutions, Rieff saw cultural and personal decline as the demise of 'the Western Spirit'; it was an era that produced 'the liberation of the id and consequently the dominance of unruly and disruptive forces of the self'.[58] Rieff (together with Lasch and others associated with the Frankfurt School, fearing the decline of the Enlightenment ideal of autonomy), claimed that therapy 'seeks to create a confident and prosperous individual without a sense of higher moralities; it dispenses with the great riddles of life in exchange for a modest and durable sense of well-being'; thus what is important, says Rieff, 'is to keep going'.[59]

A neo-Marxist view, though not unconcerned with the moral implications of emotivism, sees the therapeutic culture as one of the key means whereby the state, via 'the emotivist ethic', has displaced traditional morality in order to secure legitimacy. This has been an enterprise staffed largely by psychologists, who redefined behaviour as pathological in association with the coming of victimhood; and, as traditional authority has declined, portrayed guilt as a matter of the personal psyche, thereby constituting 'the great escape from responsibility'.[60] And as therapy 'talked' away unpleasant feelings, so it enhanced self-sufficiency in the preoccupation with the self; although, of course, the escape is never complete.[61] This kind of analysis, in focusing on government justifying itself, views therapy as a form of social control that proceeds through privatism and the cultivation of 'My Life' to actualise depoliticisation. The therapeutic, it has been said, encourages citizens 'to perceive political issues, conflicts, and inequalities as personal failures subject to personal amelioration'; it substitutes individual adaption for social change, and offers a politics that has little to do with either issues of redistribution or collective action.[62] Similarly, in considering the realm of the psy sciences, Nikolas Rose points to 'the systems of power in which human subjects have been caught up', and how they have 'provided the means whereby human subjectivity and inter-subjectivity could enter the calculations

---

[58] Wright (2010), p 16.

[59] Rieff (1966), p 35; see also Zaretsky (2005), p 4.

[60] J. Nolan (1998) *The Therapeutic State: Justifying Government at Century's End*, New York: New York University Press, p 7; Wright (2010), pp 17, 1.

[61] Wright (2010), p 18.

[62] Quoted in Wright (2010), p 25.

of the authorities'.[63] In disseminating psychological knowledge through the services of the helping professions, the rationalities of business managers, and also the 'psychotherapies of normality (how we relate to ourselves and to others), a new universe of the self has been produced with life becoming subject to 'clinical reason'.[64]

Feminism has long had an ambivalent relationship with the therapeutic. For radical feminists there is nothing to be gained from the therapy, which simply works to propagate 'the myth of women's empowerment'.[65] The notion of enablement through therapy for mothers, however, is closely linked to the importance that all feminisms have always attached to the subject-self in terms of reflexivity, identity and lifestyle (*choosing* the ingredients for the way one lives). In relation to motherhood and mothering, the view is that the 'talking' emphasis on the personal probably hindered progress towards women's liberation since '"The personal is political" may not be a revolutionary challenge to the status quo but rather an unwitting collaboration with the forces of stability in contemporary capitalist culture.'[66] Understandably, this raises once again the issue of the extent to which feminism has collaborated with neoliberalism as culture in pursuit of its goals in relation to shifting mothers out of the home (the 'patriarchal prison') into wage labour, advancing institutionalised childcare under the rubric of educational progress, and culturally legitimising mothers' emotions *per se* in child rearing. The irony is that radical feminists do not see their own complaints as a feature of the role of the emotive in therapeutic culture, torn as they are between the alternative visions of Giddens and Beck vis-à-vis 'reflexivity' being with or against such 'expert-systems' as psychology and psychoanalysis.[67]

Clearly, many feminists have long bemoaned psychotherapeutic counselling practices, often through analogies comparing psychiatry to a marriage that allegedly controls women through dependency

---

[63] N. Rose (1990), *Governing the Soul. The Shaping of the Private Self*, London: Routledge, p 7.

[64] N. Rose (1999) *Powers of Freedom: Reframing Political Thought*, Cambridge: Cambridge University Press, pp 90–1.

[65] D. Becker (2005) *The Myth of Empowerment: Women and the Therapeutic Culture in America*, New York: New York University Press; Wright (2010), pp 33–7.

[66] D. Cloud (1998) *Control and Consolation in American Culture*, London: Sage, pp 129–30.

[67] S. Lasch (1994) 'Reflexivity and its Doubles: Structures, Aesthetics, Community', in U. Beck, A Giddens and S. Lash (eds) *Reflexive Modernization: Politics, Tradition and Aesthetics in the Modern Social Order*, Cambridge: Polity, p 116.

and false ideals of feminisation.[68] The therapeutic is criticised for 'the repackaging of the psychological as power', which is said to reproduce 'what has long been the cultural norm for women: the colonisation of both the interior world of the psyche and the small world of intimate relationships'.[69] But this fails to appreciate 'the myriad ways in which women not only embrace the therapeutic, but also resist it and use it for their own ends'; whether psychology has served women well or ill, 'it was neither and it was both'.[70] The coincidence of interests between psychology and feminism is best appreciated by Eva Illouz, who, with reference to what she terms the corrosion of the traditional structure of marriage, comments: 'Despite the patriarchal and misogynist views of psychologists...from the start the categories of psychological discourse entertained affinities with feminist thought...Psychology and feminism, both popularized, would ultimately merge to form a single powerful cultural and cognitive matrix.'[71]

So it is that as therapeutics privileges mothers' experiences, via feminism's exploitation of psychology, so it obscures the importance of children's emotions. It is almost as if childhood suffering was discounted because it is only 'a passing phase', an oppression that you, literally, 'out grow'.[72] Where parents are involved, the psychological and cultural emphasis is on the dictum of emotivism, which is that 'truth is grasped through sentiment or feeling, rather than through rational judgment or abstract reasoning': 'I think, therefore I am' becomes the subjective 'I feel, therefore I am.'[73] While children do figure therapeutically in certain clinically accepted circumstances, there is little or no *normalising* of *their* ordinary emotional lives in the therapeutic

---

[68] Wright (2010), pp 33–5.

[69] Becker (2005), pp 1, 10.

[70] E. Herman (1995) *The Romance of Psychology: Political Culture in the Age of Experts*, Berkeley, CA: University of California Press, p 313.

[71] Illouz (2008), pp 114–15, 120–5; also (2007) *Cold Intimacies: The making of emotional capitalism*, Cambridge: Polity, pp 26–9; Herman (1995), pp 276–304. For a sympathetic account toward feminism, see M. Thomson (2006) *Psychological Subjects: Identity, Culture and Health in Twentieth-Century Britain*. Oxford: Oxford University Press, pp 278-87. But he finds it hard to shake off Nikolas Rose's well known verdict that for all its protestations, feminist therapeutics remained individualist: 'we should not be misled by the rhetoric of sharing and communality which we find in these tales', quoted p. 285.

[72] S. Kitzinger (1997) 'Who are you Kidding? Children, Power and the Struggle against Sexual Abuse', in A. James and A. Prout (eds) *Constructing and Reconstructing Childhood: Contemporary Issues in the Sociological Study of Childhood*, London: Falmer Press, p 186.

[73] Quoted in Nolan (1998), p 6.

literature; their 'voice' is silenced by the volume of 'mother talk', as I term it, which, through feminism and its media outlets, has achieved an iconic status. In pathologising (demonising) their (mis) behaviour – from 'tantrums', bedtime fears, 'fussy' eating and 'naughtiness' to the extremes of 'oppositional and defiant disorder' (ODD and ADHD) and the 'pathological demand avoidance syndrome' (all 'feelingly' presented by mothers and then therapeutically ennobled) – children are culturally *moulded* into being a cause, often *the* cause, of maternal 'triumphant suffering', expounded through the prism of theatrically staged 'victimhood'.[74] In most respects, Illouz's 'saving of the modern soul' has been on behalf of adults.

Despite its ambivalences, many social theorists look favourably on the therapeutic, especially as it connects with 'life politics', arguing that it offers liberating opportunities rather than only emotional constraints or narcissism and emotional self indulgence. For Giddens, therapy is to be understood as part of the process of the democratisation of the family and social relations; it is essentially 'a methodology of life-planning'. He refers to the 'capable individual' being able to:

> harmonise present concerns and future projects with a psychological inheritance from the past. Therapy is not just an adjustment device. As an expression of generalised reflexivity it exhibits in full the dislocation and uncertainties to which modernity gives rise...It can promote dependence and passivity; yet it can also permit engagement and reappropriation.

He admits, however, that therapies confirm 'the separation of the lifespan from extrinsic moral considerations'.[75] Thus, aside from the moral loneliness of the (adult) therapeutic subject (who is essentially self-referential), which has a significant effect on parent–child relations, it is clear that children, by virtue of their age and status position, have been prevented from participating in 'life politics' and do not qualify as 'capable individual(s)' and, therefore, have suffered from injustice and sustained injury to *their* subjectivity.

The therapeutic culture is a helpful frame through which to consider the development of 'parenting' as 'family practice', and 'parent education' as a therapeutically oriented business, because it makes visible a number of the presuppositions regarding how adults perceive

---

[74] Illouz (2008), pp 152–96.

[75] Giddens (1991), p 80.

themselves in their world and their attitudes toward relationships beyond the self. It also reveals both the scale and the manner in which the public and the private arenas, and the economic and the emotional fields, through force of circumstance, have embraced one another since the 1970s. Thus, in being an example of 'emotional capitalism', too often it leads to an emotional life that follows the logic of the market and, therefore, subscribes to a sense of frustration stitched with alienation.[76] And yet, for the advocates of various forms of 'life politics', the adult self is essentially one that is emancipated. The idea of 'my' emancipation runs through the therapeutic discourse from at least the 1960s in new social movements as it reflects one of modernity's most pervasive obsessions. In the words of Daniel Bell, the self became 'the touchstone of cultural judgment'; or, as Alasdair MacIntyre expressed it: 'I cannot genuinely appeal to impersonal criteria, for there is no impersonal criteria'.[77]

The therapy culture, then, illustrates the significance of the quest for 'pure relationships' (in the belief that they are also secure) embraced by the emotive will.[78] And this in turn connects to contemporary life as it departs from 'the bleak coldness of the public sphere'.[79] But while the therapeutic helps to provide a release from the tense precariousness that engulfs us, in lacking a critical perspective, it is always working *within* the cultural constraints of neoliberalism. The rituals of parent education, for example, promote the illusion of empowerment to be achieved through the technology of behavioural child training. In reality, though, the technology encodes parents in the micro systems of global consumerism *and* its underlying individualist ethics. But more than this, through the narcissism of our own muddled intimacies, despite our belief to the contrary, we are made less free than ever before. Intimacy, ideally a source of wonder and comfort and happiness, has become a jailer as it structures feelings in accordance with shoring up a minimal sense of self, which parades its emotional wares in a vulgar, charmless and grasping emporium. Where late modern parenting is concerned, under the guidance of neoliberal therapeutics, it seems that we prefer the apparent control of the authoritative style to participating in what would be an enlivening albeit unpredictable struggle, namely to reason and feel ourselves beyond the search for so-called authenticity

---

[76] Illouz (2007), pp 4–5; also Nolan (1998), pp 20–1.

[77] Both also quoted in Nolan (1998), p 3.

[78] A. Macintyre (1984) *After Virtue: A Study in Moral Theory*, London: Bloomsbury; see also Illouz (2007) for the 'new emotional style', pp 16–18.

[79] Nolan (1998), p 5.

into the fraternity of true altruism – the sort that characterises child rearing at its best. Of course, these are bleak and depressing times. We can, however, begin to resist their lurid invitation to acquiescence by reminding ourselves of Tolstoy's achingly moral question: 'What shall we do and how shall we live?' In order to eschew being 'without bonds', and to assert their human value, it is necessary to accept the ineluctability of fragility, structured as it is by insecurity; only then can we become cognisant of our potential.[80] Contrary to what we have been taught over the last few decades by selfish interests determined to shape the world to their own craven desires, as parents, the wisest – and the bravest – path forward is to jettison the contract (it has never been much of a guarantee anyway) and open-heartedly engage in helping and understanding our children as *they* work at growing up. The self-sacrifice involved will imperil contemporary narcissism; but that will be wholly to our credit and ultimately to our benefit.

---

[80] For a discussion of 'bonds' and the human relationship, see Bauman (2003), pp vii-xiii.

Index